Regarding Politics

Regarding Politics

Essays on Political Theory, Stability, and Change

Harry Eckstein

UNIVERSITY OF CALIFORNIA PRESS
Berkeley   Los Angeles   Oxford

University of California Press
Berkeley and Los Angeles, California

University of California Press, Ltd.
Oxford, England

Copyright © 1992 by
The Regents of the University of California

Library of Congress Cataloging-in-Publication Data

Eckstein, Harry.
    Regarding politics: essays on political theory, stability, and
change / Harry Eckstein.
        p.   cm.
    Includes bibliographical references and index.
    ISBN 0-520-07167-0 (cloth). — ISBN 0-520-07722-9 (paper)
    1. Political science. 2. Political stability. 3. Political
development. I. Title.
JA38.E24   1992   91-18245
320—dc20   CIP

Printed in the United States of America

1 2 3 4 5 6 7 8 9

For Silvia
with love and gratitude

CONTENTS

PART I · INTRODUCTION

1. Background   /   *3*

PART II · POLITICAL SCIENCE

2. Political Science and Public Policy   /   *19*

3. A Perspective on Comparative Politics, Past and Present   /   *59*

4. Case Study and Theory in Political Science   /   *117*

PART III · POLITICAL STABILITY

5. A Theory of Stable Democracy   /   *179*

PART IV · CHANGE, DEVELOPMENT, REVOLUTION

6. The Idea of Political Development: From Dignity to Efficiency   /   *229*

7. A Culturalist Theory of Political Change   /   *265*

8. "Observing" Political Culture   /   *286*

9. Explaining Collective Political Violence   /   *304*

PART V · CIVIC INCLUSION

10. Civic Inclusion and Its Discontents   /   *343*

11. Rationality and Frustration   /   *378*

INDEX   /   *397*

PART I

Introduction

ONE

Background

The essays in this book were written over a period of thirty years. They might have spanned six years more, my first article having appeared in 1955.[1] Political science was very different then, and not just because of its operative "paradigm." The journal in which my first article appeared still *paid* its contributors. One of its coeditors was William Robson, a professor of public administration at the London School of Economics and a luminary in the Labor party and the Fabian Society. The other was Leonard Woolf, who, of course, was not a professional political scientist at all. Evidently, Max Weber's soul-searchings were not yet common. We did not yet worry about the relation of science to political action. Nor did we fuss about value-neutrality. And the dividing line between "scientific" and "literary" writing had not yet fully hardened.

The next three decades were a heady period of transition in the field, not least in my subfield, comparative politics. The changes that occurred in the field after 1960 (a short period, as academic time is measured) surely produced an instance of scientific "revolution." The first cause of that revolution can as usual be found in uncomfortable facts that accustomed modes of thinking in the field left puzzling. My generation in political science lived under the shadows of the Nazis and the holocaust; of Stalin; of the use of nuclear weapons; of the large-scale appearance of new nations; of the disappointment of democratic expectations in these nations; of the appearance of issues of political development; and much more. Old, familiar methods of study in political science left all these events and processes mystifying.

The "revolution" in political science was profound. It even involved questioning so basic a matter as the way political scientists defined their subject of study. David Easton was the leading figure in raising that issue.

(A few people, no longer read in the 1950s, had raised the issue during the 1920s—for instance, George Catlin in *The Principles of Politics*.) I also raised it in an article not republished here.[2] The article went far beyond Easton's reformulation of the way political scientists conceived their subjects, politics and political systems; although what I argued remains a basis of much of my work, its impact on others was close to zero.

The overriding purpose of the revolution in political science was to make the field more scientific, in the manner of the "harder" and more successful fields of inquiry. That revolution, it seems to me, took a wrong turn from the start. A reaction against its objective has by now occurred, and political science and comparative politics have as a consequence become fields divided against themselves—fields in which more or less radical extremes are engaged in an unfortunate *Methodenstreit* that can bear no fruit but, until we outgrow it, can do much harm. In brief, the field, while I have worked in it, has traveled from its 1789 to its Thermidor, but not yet to anything analogous to Empire, Restoration, or what Lyford Edwards considered the last stage in the "natural history" of revolutions: a return to normality. Sad and in many ways ironic; but this course has not been dull; at least we took little, or nothing, for granted.

I discuss these points in some detail in this chapter. I also try to clarify the admittedly almost invisible thread that ties together the disparate essays that follow and explain why they are in fact disparate.

Consider first the general attempts to transform comparative politics (to which chapter 3 provides an introduction, at an early stage).

Our Estates-General, as it were, was an interuniversity seminar, funded by the Social Research Council; it met in the summer of 1952 at Northwestern University. The council, at that time, provided resources to bring together, for substantial periods (six weeks, in our case) and for intensive collaboration, groups of scholars in the same field but from different universities. Such scholars would otherwise have had only superficial contact through publications, private correspondences, or in the turmoil of the brief meetings of professional societies. (It seems unfortunate that the council long since discontinued providing the petty funds needed for such meetings of minds, but that is not to the point here.)

In our case the initiative to bring together a seminar in comparative politics was taken by Roy Macridis, who then taught at Northwestern. Macridis gathered a group of mostly youngish Turks—most of whom have gone on to superlative careers—who agreed that comparative politics needed a thorough overhaul. My own role in the seminar was peripheral in most ways and central in others. Macridis, a former teacher of mine at Harvard, brought me into the group as a graduate student *rapporteur*. The official function of rapporteurs is, of course, to take and distribute notes on the discussions among the full-fledged participants. But it is hardly a secret that, by obvious devices, rapporteurs can, and perhaps must, influence and slant the notes. Besides, Macridis had asked me to write a general paper on the state of comparative politics and possible directions for radical change in it, as an initial platform for the group's discussions, and I wrote a final report on what the seminar seemed to agree upon. Thus my role in the field's 1789 hardly was that of a mere note-taker.[3]

As usual the "revolutionaries," including myself, knew much better what they wanted to tear down than either the nature of their hoped-for academic millennium or how to bring it about. One of our grievances was that comparative politics was not really comparative: the study of governments was divided into American government, on one hand, and all non-American governments, on the other. As for the other countries, comparative politics seemed to us parochially oriented to the major powers of Europe (although, by then, area studies—Europe, rather incongruously, was not considered an "area"[4]—had been well launched, offsetting the long Eurocentered bias in the field). The field, because of its emphasis on formal-legal (constitutional) rules, also seemed "vertically" truncated, neglecting the consequences for politics of its social setting. It seemed atheoretical as well—essentially descriptive, with some offhand interpretations sometimes thrown in. A particular shortcoming arose from the static nature of almost all comparative political studies: the lack of theories of change. Even though it was common to begin the description of a polity with a brief chapter on its history, that is not at all the same thing.[5]

All this we wanted to change, as did a later conference on the subject at Princeton (1953), and a Social Science Research Council committee on comparative politics was established after the Princeton conference.

It was only natural for embryonic scientific revolutionaries to flounder during the first years when most scholars in the field continued to work in familiar ways, as should have been expected. It was also expected that the revolutionaries would want quick and great results. The effect, unfortunately, was a growing fixation on what is usually now called "grand theory"—theories that, rightly applied, potentially can either explain everything or provide a "framework" (whatever that is) for doing so. There was a tendency to try to leap directly from start to finish: in Evelyn Waugh's sarcastic characterization of the United States, to proceed "from barbarism to decadence, skipping the intermediate stage of civilization." What seemed most wanted was a sort of equivalent of unified field theory, which left the narrower theories to be worked out later. Robert Merton has described this approach as "all-inclusive speculations comprising a master conceptual scheme from which . . . to derive a very large number of empirically observed uniformities of social behavior."[6]

All-inclusive theoretical system building had a distinguished past in modern times, chiefly in German thought, for example, that of Hegel and Marx. But certain contemporary American influences seem to me much more responsible for the tendency to construct grand theory in comparative politics. A major influence was Thomas Kuhn (probably to his dismay). In 1962 Kuhn published his splendid, provocative book on "scientific revolutions."[7] The book challenged the common view that progress in the "hard" sciences has been steadily cumulative. Kuhn argued, instead, that progress has occurred fitfully, through convulsive ("revolutionary") changes in virtually all aspects of a field: that is, through the collapse of a consensual "paradigm" of inquiry and of the "normal science" based on it and the rise of a fundamentally different paradigm. Just exactly what the idea of a scientific paradigm, and a shift in paradigms, meant to Kuhn was never entirely clear to me, except through example—the term referred to something like the change in astronomy from the Ptolemaic to the Copernican system (about which Kuhn had written earlier) or, in physics, from the Aristotelian to the Galilean concepts of motion. Beyond that, what mattered was consensus on how scientific work gets done and how progress is achieved.

At any rate one soon heard that comparative politics, being in process of revolution, needed a new paradigm. But this was generally taken to mean all-inclusive theory, in Merton's sense and in the German sense of a *Weltauffassung*, a full-fledged theoretical system, not a mere *Weltanschauung*, a perspective for viewing experiences.

This meaning, it seems now, resulted from a confusion of Kuhn with Talcott Parsons. Parsons, who had studied in Germany, devoted his academic life to the related tasks of constructing a "general theory of action," beginning with his mammoth first book and culminating in the multiauthored *Toward A General Theory of Action* of 1951.[8] In the process Parsons developed a highly general (and rather idiosyncratic) "systems" theory, elaborated in a set of "pattern-variables" held to be "functional prerequisites" for the existence and persistence of any social system. Parsons generally referred to his "theory" as a "frame of reference," which leaves cloudy whether he meant it to be merely a potentially useful basis for coherent theory building (an unusually large, detailed *Anschauung*) or a theory that already contained less grandiose theories, as special cases. I think the second view is correct; consider that in later work, with Neil Smelser, Parsons tried to swallow economics into his framework,[9] before beginning the process of absorbing political science.[10] (I was asked to coauthor a book on the subject, but it was never begun.)

If Parsons and Kuhn are put together, grand theory—all-inclusive theory presented as a ready-to-wear scientific paradigm—results. In the 1960s and 1970s political science was in fact inundated with such "theories," which waxed and waned. That is not to say that less grandiose work, on special problems, was not also going on. But grand theory was the prevalent aspiration and tended to carry off the prizes. In rough order we were offered, as would-be paradigms, group theory, a political version of functionalism (the most conspicuous "framework" at the time I wrote chapter 3 below), a revived version of power-elite theory, two kinds of political systems theory (Almond's and Easton's), political-culture theory, and political rational-choice theory, not to mention a number of more ephemeral schemes. A small industry of books attempting to explain the would-be paradigms also developed during this period.

My attitude toward this activity was mixed. I taught seminars in comparative politics during the period, and in these I expounded and criticized the grand theories. After all, they played the central role in the field. Some of them also certainly were clever, based on erudition, and made for good discussion. But the whole enterprise seemed to me barren because it seemed to have things upside down. One does not, godlike, create a "normal science" out of chaos. Where such a thing exists it grows from the bottom up, through the results of narrower inquiries; broad theories are developed to subsume narrower theories rather than the narrower theories simply being elaborations of a priori broader theories. Still broader theories are developed in the same way. Grand theories I regarded, and still regard, as ultimate and probably unattainable ends. In other words I opted to work on what Merton called theories of the middle range, perhaps by taste (or ability) but also under the influence of philosophers of science like Karl Popper and Gustav Hempel.

Granted that some perspective on one's subject always underlies inquiries into it. It may also be true that it is better to be explicit about one's perspective than to leave it implicit—though I am not at all convinced of this. But if perspectives are regarded as finished theories or frameworks merely to be filled in by such theories, awful things tend to happen. Perspectives become dogmas, and dogmas radically split scholars. They create sectarian conflicts instead of mutual support and sensible divisions of labor. They prevent precisely the cumulation of knowledge that the frames of reference are supposed to facilitate. Intellectual sins result as well. Theories often are little more than translations into the jargon of a would-be paradigm; devious means are used to save (grand) theory; and results that seem clearly to refute such theory tend to be presented as supporting it (with the addition of an epicycle or two or more): Rikerian coalition-theory, a branch of political rational-choice theory, is a good case in point.[11]

Moreover, when fields are in such a conflict-ridden, utterly unintegrated condition, wholly unwanted reactions to the mainstream are almost bound to occur, making bad worse. In comparative politics, two such reactions to the "revolution" that started in the 1950s now seem to be in full swing. One creates a danger of pedestrianism (not a major problem before the

1950s). This reaction is giving priority to techniques over substance—not least, nowadays, aggregate statistical techniques. Such techniques are useful tools of inquiry, but when they become primary over substance, grotesque results emerge.[12] The other reaction threatens to produce high-flown obscurantism. It involves the renunciation of rigorous, theoretical problem solving in favor of the shadowy worlds of hermeneutics (of purely interpretative social science, in which "meanings" are already regarded as explanations), or one or another "critical" dogma (usually neo-Marxist or quasi-Marxist), often on the assumption that the task of social scientists is not so much to understand the world as to criticize and change it. Both reactions are only too alluring. This is true not only because we seem to have "progressed" only from disrepute to disarray, but also because the reactions free one, in different ways, from the burdens of hard thought. Both permit one, essentially, to be "idea-free": either the techniques, applied to data, churn out results; or ideas are supplied by presumed empathy or by prefabricated systems of ideas.

To return to the earlier point: Inquiry cannot proceed without some perspective on one's subject, wherever that might come from: for example, "normal" science, personal values, class position, gender. Whether or not it might be better to leave such perspectives as silent major premises, one simply cannot do so in a period of open ferment at that level of inquiry. For reasons too complex to go into here, I concluded some years ago that only two of the grand theories of comparative politics were legitimate contenders for the status of points of departure in the field: political-culture theory and rational-choice theory. (I have discussed the reasons in an essay not republished here.)[13] At one time, I contemplated doing research to determine, via predictive "strong inference" procedure, which of the two was the more promising tack to take, but I regret that the research project was never done. Still, faced by the choice, I opted for the culturalist perspective (for reasons also too complex to discuss here) without being a "true believer." However, chapters 7 and 8 in this volume may be read as a defense of my choice, in that there I try to disarm the most common criticism of culturalist theory in political science.

To avoid possible misunderstanding, it should probably be added that what I have written about comparative politics (politics at the macrolevel) does not apply to the study of political "behavior" (politics at the micro-level, in which I include political psychology, participation, most studies of interest groups and parties, and, especially, studies of voting behavior and public "opinions"). That part of political science, in which ferment started much earlier—as far back as the 1920s—was never encumbered by grand theory. It was rooted in, and remained in, the middle range—a fact that might well have been taken as a lesson by inquirers concerned with the political macrolevel. If microlevel study in political science has had a demon, it has been mindlessly technical work—relying too much on statistical techniques to convert data automatically into theory. More recently, one grand theory of macropolitics, rational-choice theory, has also invaded micropolitics, for dubious reasons and with dubious results (see chapter 11). But that is not apropos here.

My own ineffectual attempt to set political science on a new course did not involve grand theory. It grew out of a theory of the middle range. In 1961 I wrote a monograph on the conditions of political stability and instability, especially in democracies, published five years later as an appendix to a book (see part III of this volume). The core argument of the monograph was that political stability results from "congruence" (similarity, defined in special ways) between the authority patterns of governments and those of specified nongovernmental institutions and organizations. The theory was only tenuously based on empirical observation, and because rigorous testing was bound to be a costly matter, I conducted, to help determine whether testing was worthwhile, a probe into the plausibility of the theory in a country that it absolutely had to fit and about which I had only minimal prior knowledge.[14] Convinced by that inquiry that testing was in fact worthwhile, I undertook additional testing through a group project (with Ted R. Gurr as codirector) that produced much print but no definitive test.[15]

Such undertakings often have quite unexpected results. In this case the most important unanticipated consequence was that the subject matter of political study came to seem ill conceived to me: there was no reason why it should not, and every reason why it should, encompass any and all authority patterns of social units, both large and small. The focus solely on the state, and matters that are state oriented (political parties, interest groups, and so on), struck me as both logically specious and stultifyingly limited in scope, space, and time.[16]

So I set out on a lonely journey intended to transform political science at its most basic level: the way it conceives its subject. The initial result was an article published in 1973.[17] In a book (coauthored with Ted R. Gurr) I pursued the matter on a much larger scale, discussing in great detail the dimensions and subdimensions of the complex phenomena that are authority patterns and the problems of operationalizing them and suggestions for doing so—for the accurate description of particular cases and for potential, systematic comparisons. Gurr and I also added rather lengthy speculations on the causes and consequences of variety in authority patterns.[18]

All these ideas fell on deaf ears. Although nothing in what was argued precluded concerns with governmental phenomena, the field was too state oriented to pay attention to so radical a proposal. I have in fact been told that the book written with Gurr was the major mistake of my academic life. I agree that the book was the greatest failure of my career, judging by its impact (nonimpact?), but I do not think of it as a mistake. It strikes me now as rather overdone, but still fundamentally right in its central argument and useful in its elaborations. Perhaps others will also come to regard it as such, though I doubt it.

In my own work, nongovernmental patterns of authority crept back in, as an independent variable, through work since 1985 on "civic inclusion"—the tendency over time to include in politics, in workplace decision making, in education, and in other institutional realms, people previously excluded from them. I came to this interest via Tocqueville's argument (to which I assent) that social "development" involves irresistibly increasing equality in "the condition of men," and via the large literature on the disappointing results of growing political equality: the literature on nonparticipation, new oligarchies, "crowd" and "mass" behavior, and political machines. That interest led to inquiries into authority relations in lower-class families, in supposedly participatory workplaces, and in lower-class schools (these matters are discussed in part V of this book). And so the old interest in nongovernmental authority remains alive, after some odd twists and turns and in the context of a very different concern.

I would not be distressed if the essays in this book were simply regarded as disparate, the products of an incorrigible fox. I do not dislike hedgehogs, although I do not particularly admire them either. Still, we are told that all products of the mind contain some elements of autobiography, even if deeply buried. And I have long been conscious of a unifying thread in what I have done. To be sure, the work involved led to some efforts in which autobiography played no discernible part: usually conceptual or methodological efforts; but even these grew out of personal concerns. When I review the whole, it looks to me like pieces of a jigsaw puzzle, where most fragments are missing, as is the whole picture.

Growing up in Germany just before and after the Nazis came to power hardly is a forgettable experience, and it hardly leaves one with a sense of intact understanding. The experience certainly left me in a state of mystification, a sense of the world as an enigma. (I recall reading the beginning of Kafka's *Amerika* as an uncannily *naturalistic* rendering of my own experiences as a child immigrant to the United States.)

The collapse of the Weimar Republic and the rise of the Nazis coincided exactly with the waking of my political awareness. I remember it now only in the disconnected pieces expected of early memories.

At the beginning, strange men appeared in brown uniforms, wearing an odd symbol on armbands; they were given to singing and marching in torchlight parades. No one seemed to take them seriously in the discussions

I was allowed to listen to in my talkative family, and childhood and school on the whole took benign and cheerful courses. The men in brown seemed like figures in a prolonged masquerade. I do recall an early false note, when talk dwelled on depression and unemployment; but this supposedly dramatic event seemed to affect my family only through a sudden shortage of salad oil. Soon, though, much greater dissonances occurred. I remember vividly the fateful January 30, 1933. A man of no great note, whose rantings I had sometimes heard on the radio, had become chancellor, succeeding a number of other inconsequential, and transient, men; the town in which we lived (near Frankfurt) was decked out in flags bearing swastikas; and when I came home from school an air of calamity seemed not only to possess our house but also to take possession of me. Then things appeared to settle down for a while—but only for a while. The later experiences that I recall in bits and pieces have no firm chronological order.

One of the first memories of later events was being forbidden to visit or play with my best friend, the son of a government official. It soon became apparent that the reason was an ineradicable blemish, the fact that I was a Jew; and I became convinced myself that being a Jew was, somehow, shameful. (Perhaps that helps explain the later assumption, which takes the shape of "positive theory" in my academic work, that our realms of self-determination are severely constricted by forces somehow thrust upon us.) I remember also the boycotts and the boarding up of Jewish shops. There were three especially icy peaks in that range of experiences. One night some men came knocking on our front door and asked for my father. I heard the knocking and demand and then went back to sleep. The next day I was told that the men had ordered my father to dress and my mother to bid him farewell because she would not see him again. But the next morning he was back; he had worn his Iron Cross, earned in the First World War, to the ordeal, and the local fat man and bully had made plain that harm would be done to a decorated German soldier only over his considerable body. That added dread to earlier feelings of shame and the vague sense of disaster. During that time, too, going to school usually involved passing through a gauntlet of insults, threats, and frequent barrages of stones. So I took to avoiding the streets, and instead walked in lonely alleys and fields, in the safety of an unpeopled world. In 1934, my parents released me from that ordeal by sending me to a Jewish secondary school in Frankfurt. That was of course a much more anonymous place, though also lonely and, in its own way, enigmatic to a ten-year-old boarder in a house of strangers. In December 1936 that interlude also came to an end when my parents managed to send me to America: a rescue that felt like an expulsion into exile.

All this occurred before the much more atrocious events to come, from the *Kristallnacht* to the final solution. And I have omitted the more mundane experiences of that period: incessant paramilitary marches by brown-shirts and blackshirts; waves of anti-Semitic propaganda; emigrations; friends becoming strangers; random mayhem; growing despair. For each Jew (and others), Nazism had its special abysses of experience, but Nazism was not simply a set of disjointed personal memories. It was a whole world out of joint, which touched and polluted every aspect of social life. Of course, viewed a half century later, the peaks of personal and collective experience overshadow all else. When I recollect them, I still feel deep revulsion (coupled, no doubt, with sublimation).

What I have written should suffice to make the point that my academic work is rooted in autobiography that, despite appearances, gives it co-herence. I have no doubt that the very choice of political science as a "major," as soon as I discovered its existence at the university, grew from a deep wish to understand the forces mysteriously governing politics that also seemed to govern my life. But I soon became a disenchanted, though not yet openly rebellious, student of politics; I already had experience of the consequences of being "different." Although the time was postwar and postholocaust, my professors seemed still to live in a well-ordered world of textual elucidations, of constitutional descriptions and interpre-tations—in short, of polite and genteel scholarship. In that world the Wei-mar Republic, for example, still incongruously loomed larger than the Nazi period. Nazism, of course, was mentioned, but without noticeable grasp beyond the perception of villainy (inspired, one professor told us, by Hobbes). In general, it seemed to be regarded as a deviant episode, a singular upheaval, its horrors traceable either to a misguided electoral system or to too-easy legal dismissals of chancellors or else to demonic flaws in the German "character." Certain "political theorists"—for ex-ample, the theorists of mass society and power-elite from Robert Michels to Joseph Schumpeter—were dismissed as antidemocratic "irrationalists" who were therefore wrong, as were Graham Wallas and Walter Lippmann writing about instincts and stereotypes in early political psychology. I could not see that being congenial to democratic myths might be a cri-terion of validity. And the irrationalists spoke to my inner world much more comprehensibly than the others. I kept my own counsel about this, for fear of being myself consigned to the world of misanthropic, thus mistaken, political scientists. But by 1952 I was certainly ripe and eager for "revolution" in comparative politics; in the condition in which I began study in the field it seemed incapable of explaining anything significant.

The problems on which I have always concentrated—political stability and instability, political violence, and the politics of "inclusive" (mass) societies—are sufficiently accounted for by these personal experiences. But some other points, personal and otherwise, should be added.

First, my interests came to encompass a much wider scope than the German experience. This occurred in two ways. Simply through the normal processes of education, it became evident that Nazi Germany was hardly unique, even in its most egregious aspects—as in fact I had always surmised; the holocaust, for instance, was only one case of the "killing fields," from the slaughter of the Anabaptists to Stalin's purges and beyond. Probably more important than this realization was that, while studying and living in England, I became aware of both a fundamentally decent and fair society and undisrupted history as a counterpoint to earlier experiences. Thus, added to my American experience, political "stability" became a real phenomenon, not just an abstract opposite of instability (and of the dark side of mass behavior). This is the personal background to the essay that is chapter 5 of this book, an essay that played a pivotal role in my academic life.[19] Still, even in that essay the earlier experience is central, not only in the problem tackled in the essay but, much more, in its argument that stable democracy is the less frequent case, perhaps even a rare exception, contrary to all I had been taught.

Second, I was never so much intrigued by the egregious in Nazism (and in politics generally)—either the demons or saints it mobilized—as by the general tenor of life in the Nazi world: the minutiae of life in that frenzied society. Hannah Arendt found evil "banal" even in Eichmann; to me the banality of evil and essence of Nazism existed much more in day-to-day relations, which after all are by far the greater part of social life.

No doubt that is why what gripped me most in Crane Brinton's *Decade of Revolution* was not the guillotine but his discussion of "the little things" of the Terror: its "revolutionary" clothes, its bric-a-brac, its toys (miniature guillotines, etc.), its penchant for renaming, even its revolutionary beds.[20] Brinton writes:

> The guillotine, prison, Jacobin clubs, political elections, even political riots— these might all be avoided, especially by the obscure; but no one could altogether avoid clothes, theaters, furniture, cafes, games, newspapers, streets, public ceremonies, birth, death, and marriage. On all this, the Revolution . . . left its mark. It broke in rudely on the accepted ways of millions of humble people, turned their lives inside out, made them take part in a public life keyed to an amazing pitch of collective activity.[21]

So it was in Nazi Germany, and in my childhood.

The fact that I have avoided writing about the Nazis' worst excesses may well have psychological roots, but it is surely also true that some version of "normal" day-to-day life went on within the system. Moreover, I suspect that if one could make sense of some of the petty inanities of that life—like the edict issued to Walter Nolde to stop painting, the subject of Siegfried Lenz's brilliant novel *Deutschstunde*—much else might also fall into place. Lenz's novel in fact is the only work on Nazi Germany that managed to induce in me a feeling of illumination, but of course not of the social-scientific kind.

This brings me to a final point. I am not at all sure that the understanding I have wanted is attainable through social science. At bottom it involves passions that may simply defy dispassionate understanding. They may well be material fit only, or more, for artistic empathy and visions. But social science is the way I have chosen to grasp what I can of the world. And having chosen that way, I have tried to live up to its vocational demands. In regard to these I have long tried to follow Max Weber's strictures, which I find wholly convincing (as described in chapter 2): to keep passions out of the classroom and academic publications, and to cultivate a certain coldness and distance from the phenomena—*especially* where personal emotions are most involved and the phenomena closest to personal experience. It is child's play to be *engagé* when one's deeper emotions are safely uninvolved; it is much more difficult to cultivate detachment from one's own wounded sensibilities.

NOTES FOR CHAPTER 1

1. Harry Eckstein, "The Politics of the British Medical Association," *Political Quarterly* 26 (1955): 345–359.

2. David Easton, *The Political System* (New York: Knopf, 1953); Harry Eckstein, "Authority Patterns: A Structural Basis for Political Study," *American Political Science Review* 67 (1973): 1142–1161, and (with Ted Robert Gurr) *Patterns of Authority* (New York: Wiley, 1975).

3. A good summary of the seminar's discontents and hopes may be found in Roy C. Macridis, *The Study of Comparative Government* (New York: Random House, 1955).

4. I discuss this matter in "A Critique of Area Studies from a West European Perspective," in *Political Science and Area Studies,* ed. Lucian W. Pye (Bloomington: Indiana University Press, 1975). This essay is not included here.

5. See Macridis, *Study of Comparative Government,* 7–13.

6. Robert K. Merton, *Social Theory and Social Structure* (Glencoe, Ill.: Free Press, 1939), 5.

7. Thomas S. Kuhn, *The Structure of Scientific Revolutions* (Chicago: University of Chicago Press, 1962).

8. Talcott Parsons, *The Structure of Social Action* (New York: McGraw-Hill, 1937).

9. Talcott Parsons and Neil J. Smelser, *Economy and Society* (Glencoe, Ill.: Free Press, 1956).

10. See especially "The Distribution of Power in American Society," *World Politics* 10 (October 1957): 123–143.

11. See William H. Riker, *The Theory of Political Coalitions* (New Haven: Yale University Press, 1962), and the summary and analysis of pertinent findings in

Eric R. Browne, *Coalition Theories: A Logical and Empirical Critique,* Sage Comparative Politics Series 01-043 (Beverly Hills: Sage, 1973).

12. The quintessential example, I suppose, is Arthur S. Banks and Robert Textor, *A Cross-Polity Survey* (Cambridge: MIT Press, 1963).

13. Harry Eckstein, *Support for Regimes: Theories and Tests,* Center of International Studies Research Monograph 44 (Princeton: Princeton University, 1979), esp. 40ff.

14. The inquiry led to a book, *Division and Cohesion in Democracy: A Study of Norway* (Princeton: Princeton University Press, 1966).

15. The nature of the project and speculations about why it fell short of its aims are discussed in Harry Eckstein, *The Natural History of Congruence Theory,* University of Denver, Monographs on World Affairs, 44 (Denver, 1979).

16. See my article, "On the 'Science' of the State," *Daedalus* 104 (1979): 1–20 (not republished here).

17. Eckstein, "Authority Patterns."

18. Eckstein, *Patterns of Authority.*

19. The Norway depicted in my book of 1966 (see n. 14) provided a later, even less qualified example of a decent and durable democratic polity and society.

20. Crane Brinton, *A Decade of Revolution: 1789–1799* (New York: Harper, 1934), 142–150.

21. Ibid., 142.

PART II

Political Science

TWO

Political Science and Public Policy

Author's Note: In the introductory chapter, I wrote about the influence on me of Max Weber's views on the imperatives of the academic vocation. These views are spelled out and elaborated here. The occasion for the essay was a request to address a plenary session of the American Political Science Association on the relations of political science to public policy— probably because I was at that time a political consultant in Washington. The editor of the book in which the essay appeared, being himself active in political consulting, no doubt expected a much different argument. At any rate, he wrote an introductory note dissociating himself from my views. But experience in Washington had convinced me that Weber's views on the essential separation, though intersection, of the policy maker's and social scientist's vocations were, if anything, understated.

I place the essay first in this section because it augments points made in the chapter on background and because most (certainly many) political scientists probably are drawn to the field because they want somehow to affect the political world. But they rarely achieve clarity about the natures of the scholarly and activist vocations. This essay clarified the matter for me. I hope it will for others.

As pointed out in chapter 1, I omit from this section on political science what are (for me, but not others) my most important articles on the field of political science: "Authority Patterns: A Structural Basis for Political Study," *American Political Science Review* 67 (December 1973): 1142–1161,

This essay was published in *Contemporary Political Science: Toward Empirical Theory*, ed. Ithiel de Sola Pool (New York: McGraw Hill, 1967), 121–165. For the context in which it appeared, and additional reflections, see the endnote I have appended to it. Reprinted by permission of the publisher. Copyright © 1967 by the McGraw Hill Publishing Company.

THE TENSION BETWEEN "SCIENCE"
AND "POLITICS" IN MAX WEBER

How then can the affinities and tensions between political science and political activity be defined? What boundaries separate and what areas of overlap join them? Although, as stated, this question has been more often avoided than confronted, we are not without guidance in regard to it. A handful of social scientists (and their critics) have explicitly dealt with it and worked out positions that may serve as reference points—among them Max Weber, to an examination of whose position on the subject the rest of this chapter is devoted.

There are reasons for this emphasis on Weber, quite apart from the fact that concentrating on his position is one way to limit discussion of so widely ramified a problem and to proceed critically or with approbation from what has been said about it. Most important is the unrivaled intensity, extensiveness, and clarity of Weber's confrontation of the issue. Whether one agrees with his views or not, one must at least recognize that they are devoid of platitudes, laziness, wishfulness, ambiguity, mere exhortation, or vainglorious pretense. In many essays, letters, and speeches, spanning his life from student days to the twilight of his university career,[2] his "powerful mind . . . strove restlessly for clarity [about this issue] at levels where his contemporaries were satisfied with ambiguities and clichés,"[3] fully living up to his demanding conception of maturity as "trained relentlessness in viewing the realities of life and the ability . . . to measure up to them inwardly."[4] These qualities of his reflections have given them great influence, to the extent that some of his views, fresh and challenging when first stated, may now indeed seem commonplace—an influence evident most of all in the more thoughtful positions differing from his that have been stated since his time, for in the main these have been worked out with Weber's arguments as a frame of reference and constant counterpoint.[5]

To deal as intensively and influentially as did Weber with the relations between social science and public affairs required more than intellectual force. Two other factors above all contributed to that intensity and influence, both of which may make Weber especially relevant to us: his personal orientation to the scientific calling and his temporal location in the development of social science and its social and political context.

In regard to Weber's orientation to science as a career, the most essential point is that his attitudes are typical, even if in an enlarged form, of those of political scientists for whom the topic of this chapter appears as a problem: those who know a tension between the politics of the study and those of the hustings and corridors of power. Weber, even if not a political scientist in the narrow departmental sense, was preeminently what Gerth and Mills call a "political professor." Like many of us, he engaged in scholarly work, "not in order to seek . . . a quietistic refuge . . . but rather to snatch from [it] a set of rules which would serve him in his search for political orientation in the contemporary world."[6] Like many of us, too, he soon experienced that science and scholarship were not so easily turned to a mere instrumental purpose, so readily made subservient to political activity. They imposed imperatives of their own, as does any special calling, made special demands on personal resources and moral conscience, and like other specialized vocations, had both peculiar capabilities and peculiar limitations. Being political scientist and politician appeared to him, first as identical, then separable but complementary, then separate and in certain senses even antithetical roles. Yet as his closer friends (Troeltsch, Jaspers, Michels) invariably stress in their remembrances, the desire to join the two in some manner never left him, even as the sense of their separateness deepened and the academic vocation, through its own demands, came to consume his time and energies.[7] Aron puts it precisely in saying that in his life and work he "both separated and united politics and science,"[8] a phrase that would surely serve well also as a general characterization of political science and its practitioners.

Some biographic details will clarify these points. The larger setting in which Weber was formed was a new nation, in which life, especially for educated men and precocious youngsters, had many characteristics familiar in the more recently new polities, not least a pervasive political cast. A political event, unification, was the decisive experience of his generation, coloring all other experiences. A powerful leader who had unified the country was devoting himself to the task of endowing it with international status and power and was using political means to help Germany rapidly catch up economically and socially with more advanced countries. Highly organized structures of political competition existed, and previously inactive groups were becoming mobilized in politics; the political system was, however, greatly skewed in favor of executive domination, both formally and as a result of a lack of political skills, ideological and parochial dissensions, and sterile romantic aspirations in the movements and parties. Under such conditions, it is natural that "all ultimate questions without exception" should seem, as they did to Weber, "touched by political events."[9]

Later he was to develop an elaborate intellectual basis for his perception of life as political in every aspect, hence for the primacy of politics, which anticipated totalitarianism with the prevision of a Tocqueville. I refer to his argument that political "development" is a process of continuous public expropriation of private spheres, beginning with the gradual expropriation by the "state" of means of violence, proceeding to the expropriation by the power monopolists of economic means, and culminating in the public expropriation of education and artistic creativity, the whole becoming subject to the caprices of unfettered charismatic leaders and the routines of servile bureaucrats. That vision was based on historical sociology, but even more fundamentally on the tenor of life in the national macrocosm of his youth.

To this add the intensely political atmosphere of his domestic microcosm. Weber's father was simultaneously a councillor of the city of Berlin and a member of both the Reichstag and the Prussian Diet. The Weber house throughout his childhood was full of politicians and political intellectuals, engaging in constant discussion of questions that Bismarck's domination raised for party politicians and intellectuals alike: questions of the relations between political power and ideals, between unlettered men of action and scholarly men of ideas, between vocal political philosophies and mute objective forces, between the growth of democracy and that of bureaucracy and plebiscitary leaders. But there was also in the home a splendid historical and philosophical library to which the young Weber had full access and that represented a quite different pole of life. At fourteen he was writing historical essays so precocious that he was (unjustly) accused of plagiarism—essays mainly concerned with the ruthless appraisal of political sacred cows, like Cicero. At seventeen he was trying to formulate laws of history and reflecting on the sociology of religion, but doing so in order to obtain dependable bearings in life, not out of any "mere objectivity" (his own phrase).[10] Objectivity for its own sake he considered then already an inadequate and truncated stance in life, just as he had already come to think of even the loftiest ideals as self-indulgence and self-corroding, when unrelated to realistic possibilities. Steeped in politics, immersed in books, youthfully cynical about the impotent ideologues, casuists, and political amateurs in the drawing room, his adolescent reflections were increasingly ruled by visions of the power obtainable through the scientific knowledge of life. At that point, politics and social science were certainly not seen as separate in any fundamental sense.

Only after finishing his legal and historical studies at the university did a note of conflict appear, and then only for the most mundane of reasons: Should he accept an academic job or make an extramural career? The latter deeply attracted him ("I have an extraordinary longing for a practical job"); becoming a scholar he found at least "congenial," although financially hazardous; and he began to see that the latter course, which relatives and mentors alike urged on him, might not satisfy his longing for practical activity. "Temporarily," he writes, "purely scientific work has lost all its excitement, because I live under the impression that practical interests . . . pose combinations not to be grasped by science."[11] Nevertheless—because of an unsuccessful application for a legal job?—he continued abstruse scholarly research (on the legal implications of Roman agrarian history) and joined a group dedicated precisely to the task of grasping practical combinations scientifically, the *Verein für Sozialpolitik*, a policy-oriented group of academics, civil servants, and businessmen, for whom he prepared a large study of agricultural labor in East Germany.

By 1892, at age twenty-eight, he was at work lecturing at the university in Berlin, and by 1893 appointed professor extraordinary and fully launched on an academic career. Yet he had made no final choice of science as against the active life, based on a sharp sense of any need for such a choice. If his work for the *Verein* was mainly a piece of research, then his inaugural professorial lecture was essentially a policy statement based on that research, and it has been published not in the volumes of his "scientific" writings but in a special volume of "political" essays.[12] It dealt primarily with the need for public policy to arrest the drift of peasants from the East German estates into urban areas in order to maintain Germany's power position vis-à-vis the Slavic peoples; a second theme was the need to provide "political education" to those still largely excluded from power but politically on the rise. About the same time, too, Weber became involved in Naumann's *Evangelisch-Soziale Verein*, a somewhat amorphous group of well-intentioned, politically oriented theologians, professors, artisans, and workers. Naumann had been converted by Weber himself to the view that the state should pursue a "social" policy (i.e., welfare and development policies within a liberal political framework) and that such a policy presupposed national security and power, and even more, a socialism of administrable policies, not merely of theories, antipathies, and utopian aspirations.[13]

Thus, at the very moment Weber was launching himself as a prodigy professor, politics and scholarship still seemed to him closely linked and the very fate of Germany to depend on political education and policies informed by relevant research. Nor had his mercurial rise as an academic allayed his doubts about whether he was "in the right place,"[14] not even after he had received, in 1896, the accolade of succeeding Knies in the chair of economics at Heidelberg and had there become immersed in the intense intellectual life of a circle that included Troeltsch, Jellinek, and Neumann.

In the same period, however, doubts and soul-searchings about politics and its relation to science—still mundane, but less humdrum than the mere question of choosing a job—appear. Mainly, they have to do with the world Weber had encountered in his attempts to play an active role in politics. That world seemed to him to consist largely of powerful, unscrupulous, and myopic *Realpolitiker*, lofty but impotent idealists, and servile, narrow-minded functionaries. Largely as a result of his involvement with Naumann's group, he came to realize that good intentions and objective knowledge were nothing politically without funds, organization, and special skills.

At the same time, no existing political machine attracted him. None stood for everything he considered essential: the national idea, democracy, liberalism, and a "social" policy;[15] and they were all themselves populated by self-seekers, bureaucrats, and futile ideologues. Moreover, these concrete disillusions were accompanied by the first signs of profound abstract questionings. Did not the laws of morality lie beyond human reason, in the realm of the passions? Were there any absolute imperatives, or did not every special realm of life impose unique, perhaps contradictory, demands? Did not politics, as such a special realm, also require special aptitudes and attitudes, a special *Sinn?*

There has been much sympathetic and malevolent speculation about Weber's prolonged physical breakdown at this point of his career, the three-and-a-half years of almost total incapacitation that were never to be fully overcome. Such afflictions no doubt have deeper causes, but it is reasonable to think that the tensions which had accumulated between his career orientations contributed a share. Having drifted into the demanding work of teaching and research—"If I don't work until one o'clock, I can't be a professor," he had told his wife—he remained, despite prodigious success, emotionally ambivalent toward that work, convinced of the truncation of human life involved in "mere objectivity," yet unable to find solid bridges from objective reason to practical and socially creative activity.

These career tensions reflected, or were reflected in, other tensions. As a good citizen in a new state, he was a fervent patriot and nationalist, but repelled by the state's authorities and policies, and more important, deeply aware that science and scholarship transcended all political boundaries. As part of his conception of academic integrity, he was detached and reserved in the classroom, despite great oratorical gifts and an impulse to demagoguery, even poetic prophecy, that made him feel at ease haranguing a political meeting and panic-stricken at the very thought of a lecture. He wanted to train his students for more than a bookish life, but felt obliged not to impose on them anything not readily recognized as appropriate to responsible teaching. Underlying all was an ethical tension. Morally exacting on himself and others in a personal sense, Weber was becoming increasingly convinced that what is dignity in a man might be the height of irresponsibility in politics and quite indifferent to scientific judgment. He could not then, or later, take the easy ways out of becoming either an ethical absolutist or relativist. He had gradually become, and remained, an ethical *pluralist,* that is to say, a believer in the government of different life-spheres by different imperatives, so that even the mere business of choosing a job involved, in his own words, a choice among warring gods.

Whether or not this explains his personal calamity, the fact is that he emerged from it by squarely confronting the two most fundamental questions the social scientist as would-be politician can ask: What can social science contribute to the shaping of our personal and social lives? And what is our position in historic process, what forces shape and have shaped that position, and how can these forces be controlled? Although he remained interested in the minutiae of policy and was occasionally active in the congresses of the *Verein für Sozialpolitik*, the period from 1903 to World War I was mainly devoted to these questions and led to a vast output of historical sociology, as well as to the philosophic writings that will concern us later.

With the war, the Bolshevik Revolution, and Germany's defeat in 1918, he turned again mainly to immediate political questions, especially the impending political reconstruction of Germany and the probable course of communism in power. He also again became absorbed in political activities, including publicist agitation against the Imperial regime, participation as an expert consultant in the Versailles peace negotiations, a major role on the constitutional advisory committee that fathered the Weimar Constitution, a short-lived membership in the Munich workers' soviet, and an abortive parliamentary candidacy for the Democratic party (he still had difficulties finding political machinery to which he could unreservedly attach himself or that would accept his uncompromising and idiosyncratic contributions).[16]

His intense return to immediate political affairs did not mean, however, that a new synthesis of the scientific and political vocations had been worked out during the long years of sociological study and philosophic reflection, and certainly not a regaining of his earlier innocent belief in the identity of politics and social science. On the contrary, he had only gained clarity (as it seemed to him) about their separate natures and requirements, their restricted areas of overlap and mutual relevance, and dignified acceptance, touched by pathos, of the boundaries of his own professional life-sphere. The position to which he had then come he elaborated in two gigantic lectures, "Politics as a Vocation" and "Science as a Vocation," delivered in 1918 before the students at the University of Munich—lectures requested (ironically?) by the students to obtain his guidance in their own choices of careers. They have since become two of his most celebrated essays and the best summaries of the views we shall sketch below.

WEBER'S CONTEXT

Weber's ambivalent career aspirations—familiar in a milder form to most political scientists—thus help explain the intensity and extensiveness of his thought about our topic and these in turn explain his influence on others. Neither, however, would have been so great had he not worked during a pivotal phase in the development of social science and its context which externally defined and heightened his inner tensions. This is important not only for understanding his questions and positions but also for judging their relevance to ourselves.

Most fundamental to Weber's outlook was an encompassing social prognosis based on a judgment of what was salient in his present and decisive for the future. Weber saw social life as in process of becoming characterized by an unimaginably complex "functionally specific" social differentiation, a rapid multiplication of specialized and bureaucratized compartments, with narrow expertise replacing wider-ranging knowledge and activity, special associational attachments in place of more diffuse identifications, and rationally devised routines encroaching widely on personal spontaneity. Creativity and broad self-realization in that specialized and bureaucratized world could only come genuinely, he thought, from extraordinary men in times of extraordinary stress and falsely to alienated individuals indulging sterile cravings for "personal experience," and even the works of the extraordinary men, the charismatic figures, could only punctuate the march of routinization. Politics and academic life themselves were instances in point. Politics in all its aspects was increasingly becoming administration, and administration bureaucratized; academic work, increasingly, a special professional role, subdivided into numerous still more special fields. Moreover, the relationships between politics and higher education were becoming governed by the requirements of the functionally specialized society. The university's *raison d'être* was less to cultivate broadly educated men than to train the higher functionaries. The scientist and scholar himself increasingly achieved access and influence in politics as a kind of occasional functionary, a "consultant," and less than formerly through spontaneous personal involvement in a prestigious social class that was also a ruling class in Mosca's sense. Weber thought that judgments about the relations between politics and social science, to be pertinent, must be predicated upon this general tendency—a tendency he considered farthest advanced in the United States, which, with Tocqueville, he regarded as an intimation of the future of all social life.

In other senses, too, Weber's work was done during a politically and academically pivotal time. He stood near the beginning of mass democracy and other forms of mass politics; in his lifetime, the politics of warring ideologies and doctrines was still fresh; the mass media were being developed, and he wrote presciently about popular journalists as a special political class, advertisers as hidden political influences, and sensationalism for the sake of sales as a source of political irresponsibility;[17] he witnessed also the early stages of that further expropriation of private spheres involved in revolutionary socialism and the growth of welfare states and planned societies. As for the academic setting, his career came not long after the emergence of a specifically methodological consciousness in social studies, attributable to the diffusion of natural science ideas to other spheres. When he began his work, an academic war was raging in Germany between those holding that the natural and social sciences were quite identical and those who utterly separated them (into *Naturwissenschaften* and *Geisteswissenschaften*);[18] at the same time there were embryonic conflicts over the nature of concept formation for purposes of social analysis, over basing social theory upon historical studies or logically deduced models, over the powers of statistical method, and over the question of the uniqueness or comparability of social phenomena. All this is familiar to us; the only differences are that the orthodoxies have changed and the revolutions have become routines. Just because of that, however, Weber is crucial for finding lines of continuity and points of change in the work and orientations, intramural and extramural, of social scientists.

Needless to say, however, these points do not imply that his ideas were not affected by peculiar aspects of his person and context which bear upon their cogency and pertinence. For example, numerous commentators on his work have pointed out, rightly, that, despite wide travels and even wider historical study, his vision could never quite transcend the Germany of Bismarck and William II: a new nation characterized by a rampant officialdom, by Machiavellian leadership succeeded by pathetic dilettantism at the top, by an impotent opposition of high-minded but impractical ideologues, by ingrained party bureaucracies (which we know best from Michels's work), and not least, by a certain political constraint upon professors who, after all, were paid functionaries of the state. But even more important to the shaping of his ideas, if only because less widely understood, was a personal factor: the profound effect of his Protestant background upon his outlook.

In his sociologies of religion and economics, Weber stresses the sublimation of religious forces and tensions in worldly activity. We have reason to think that this emphasis, central to his originality, grew out of inner experience. Weber's ambivalences and tensions probably stemmed, at bottom, from the influences of very different, and estranged, parents: a gpolitical, worldly, practical, temperamental, morally liberal but domestically authoritarian father; a deeply pious, warm, dutiful, emotionally contained, morally demanding mother, intensely active in typically Protestant religious-humanitarian work. Of these two, the pious mother's influence was much the greater at the deeper levels of personality, the worldly father's more discernible on the surface. Weber was never religious in the conventional sense. Condescendingly respectful toward the pious, he had a thoroughly disenchanted attitude toward church religion, despite contempt for the self-display of Promethean atheists like Nietzsche. His youthful letters, however, display deep religious longings, and in his own life he compulsively acted out much of what he discerned in the Protestant ethic. Those close friends who saw in his somber dignity of bearing and the biblical force and imagery of his speech a secularized evangelism were certainly discerning.[19]

The Protestant ethic ruled his life and colored his views on politics and science in several momentous ways. Most important perhaps were his distrust and fear of passion as against sober matter-of-factness and the rationally systematic organization of personal life—a distrust and fear all the deeper for not expressing an emotionally incapable person but one who recognized with dread the stultified life of rational automatons. Weber also derived from the Protestant outlook a tendency toward the absorption of his personality in a larger order: that of the "vocation." Choosing a career he saw as more than a superficial preference for a special line of work. He saw it as taking on a calling, and that meant, to the Protestant, the assumption of compelling duties. To have a *Beruf,* a profession, was to be a kind of cell in an ordained network of "mechanical solidarity," in which each segment, even the least spiritual, was regarded as a kind of priesthood, working with "worldly asceticism" *ad majorem gloriam Dei.* As is characteristic of the Protestant devotee, Weber felt a "need to be crushed under a load of work"[20] and "took pride in belonging to a fellowship of self-forgotten workers, who knew nothing better than devotion to the work at hand."[21] Even after his breakdown had softened him into greater tolerance for his own and others' weaknesses, he remained a worldly ascetic, oscillating between compulsively hard and scrupulous work and near-collapse, his energies incommensurate with his conception of duty. More important than the sheer effort demanded by the Protestant calling is, for us at any rate, its requirement of total commitment and the doctrine of separate ethical realms for different vocations, each equally ordained by transcendental authority and each attuned to a special function in the overall order of life. This especially made the choice of vocations momentous. At the same time, Protestantism greatly heightened the burdens of that choice, as of all choices, by enjoining total self-responsibility for it, as a good and a necessity. Neither ascription nor other authority could absolve one from such responsibility; and the vocation itself was not anything like the traditional corporation, a regulated community, but at most an abstract fellowship of atomic individuals who had heeded similar calls and were continuously responsible for themselves.

This is not said, however, to sociologize away at the outset what Weber said about the gulfs and bridges between the two vocations that attracted him. Although his thought on our topic was compounded simultaneously out of abstract intellectual factors that we readily recognize and considerations largely alien to us, it remains to be seen how much of it is, by virtue of special personal and contextual factors, dead intellectual history and how much still vital, by virtue of its abstractness or pertinence to our own context. Toward this end, we must now sketch his position in some detail and then return to its setting and our own to help in an appraisal.

WEBER ON POLITICS AND POLITICIANS

The role of political scientists in policy making is, of course, always affected by highly variable considerations: by what they currently know, by who happens to be in power, by the opportunities at various levels actually available to contribute to policy. Weber, however, wisely relegated (anyway, tried to relegate) such desiderata to a secondary role in his reflections, concentrating on more constant factors that affect positions on the matter largely irrespective of time and place. What, he asked in regard to practical politics, is its intrinsic nature? What manner of men does one encounter in it? What are the conditions of operating effectively in the policy-making process, and what makes for political impotence? What, if any, are the special imperatives of politics and the conditions and functions defining them? With regard to scientific work, his questions have a similar cast: What are its characteristic ends, techniques, capabilities, and vocational demands? Absolutely noncontextual thought about such questions is probably impossible, and Weber's reflections clearly were tied to modern social science and modern politics in a general sense; but by that very fact, he avoided being either too abstract to be informative in any context or too concrete to be pertinent in a setting different from his own.

Weber's conceptions of politics, political efficacy, and political imperatives rest upon five predicates: (1) politics is a realm of power and violence; (2) it is (especially in modern times) a matter of managing, and working in, complex organizations; (3) it is (again from the modern standpoint) a professional, not avocational, sphere, in which the crucial actors are political careerists and entrepreneurs; (4) it is a life of choice and commitment, hence for passionate men; and (5) since its choices are nothing if not systematically implemented, the passionate men must be not mere sentimentalists but "men of perspective" who harness ardor to judgment and calculation. These premises need elaboration.

Politics as Violence. "Politics as a Vocation" begins with a sober definition and ends in an impassioned sermon, but the beginning and ending form a unit because both concern the central role in politics of power, force, and violence. As for the definition: Politics, says Weber, obviously has ends and operates through institutions, but these are in no case distinctive to the political realm; what is distinctive to it is its instrumentality, the use of violent coercion, actual or potential, by political institutions in the service of political goals. In premodern societies, that instrumentality was dispersed among many structures and used competitively; in modern ones, it has been expropriated and become concentrated in territorial societies by "states."[22] Hence "all political formations are formations of violence," regardless of their purposes;[23] the modern state is a special formation claiming a monopoly over the legitimate use of force in a territory.[24] Coercive power, in that sense, is to politics what money or its equivalents are to economic life. Either may be used for good or ill; either may be accumulated with or without scruples; but purposes and restraints do not alter the nature of the currency. " 'All they that take the sword shall perish with the sword' and fighting is everywhere fighting."[25]

The definition becomes harangue when Weber reflects on what it implies for the relations between politics and ethics. Mainly it implies that certain ultimate ethical positions are simply incompatible with politics—above all those inspired by the Sermon on the Mount and, in a larger sense, all ethics of pure intention.[26] Political ethics must not be sentimental but "responsible," in the sense that they must take into account the intrinsic nature of politics and involve willingness to adjust means pragmatically to ends, even at the likely cost of adjusting the ends themselves to available means. This call to moral trimming as nothing less than an imperative hardly expressed Weber's own sentimental preferences, shaped as they were by the more tender and exacting influences of pious Protestantism. On the contrary, it leads him to a bitter warning:

> He who lets himself in for politics, that is, for force and power as means, contracts with diabolical powers, and for his action it is not true that good can follow only from good and evil only from evil. . . . Whosoever contracts with violent means for whatever ends . . . is exposed to its specific consequences. This holds especially for the crusader, religious and revolutionary alike. . . . The genius or demon of politics lives in inner tension with the god of love. . . . Everything striven for through political action operating with violent means and following an ethic of responsibility endangers the salvation of the soul. . . . [There] are inexorable consequences for [the politician's] action and his inner self, to which he must helplessly submit, unless he perceives them.[27]

Not to face up to this imperative is to be doomed to a noble futility, like that of Bismarck's unworldly opponents, or worse, to supplying a facade of sublimity to diabolical men. The lesson is, of course, intended for moralists, not social scientists, but for the latter there is an added message: To work in politics is not only to contract with coercion but to face up to a theodicy, for in politics one will always also encounter undeserved suffering and unpunished injustice inflicted by the power wielders, and most important of all to the professional academic, "hopeless stupidity" among the high and mighty. Social scientists who act in politics must not only dampen sentiments but learn to suffer fools and to work with them; they certainly ought not to expect that a scientific argument will be persuasive solely because of its scientific status. Power, justice, and sophistication are all too imperfectly correlated.

Access and Bureaucracy.   Stupidity and his own scruples are, however, by no means the most important barriers to the social scientist's political influence. More decisive are questions of access: whether one can obtain it at all, the means required to get it, and what one has access to when it has been obtained. Most crucial to this matter is Weber's conception of politics as extremely complex, routinized organization, punctuated in some cases by the short-lived paroxysms of charismatic rule.

To influence policy one must, of course, have the attention of those who make it or themselves have influence. But just identifying the decisive actors in modern bureaucratized systems of government may be almost insuperably difficult. The difficulty arises only in part from the sheer complexity of bureaucratic systems, with their intricate internal specialization, involved methods of coordination, many-layered hierarchies, and confusions of formal competence and real power—although complexity and polycentricity are important. It is also a result of the defenses bureaucracies develop against external influence. These include obfuscating locations of responsibility by using the "official secret," a specifically bureaucratic invention that may also be used to establish an unwarranted air of superior knowledge vis-à-vis outsiders.[28] Bureaucrats put outsiders at a disadvantage by overwhelming them with real and false mysteries and tend further to diminish their contributions by shunting them through, and often losing them in, the labyrinths of their routines. To these routines they are committed partly by habit and partly by vested interest, for narrow specialization chains them to their jobs. Weber thus clearly foresaw, indeed had some personal knowledge of, the not uncommon experience of government "consultants" whose uncertainties (about locations of power, about proper and feasible policy) grow with acquaintance.

Indeed, he felt that bureaucratic structures applied their defenses even to insiders—to other bureaucrats and, most of all, to their supposed political masters. Bureaucratic decision making he saw less as a process of imaginatively using pertinent information and expertise in the pursuit of clearly understood goals than as a more mechanical process of repetitively acting out routines and as an internally competitive process, the object of competition being to obtain for each segment a modicum of autonomous power. Overall, such structures were highly efficient, which is why they had everywhere replaced other modes of administration. They got things done (e.g., collected taxes well, applied regulations well, produced data and briefings efficiently, kept track of records, worked out sensible divisions of labor, engendered expertise), but their production, like that of other machines, was only quantitatively impressive, not qualitatively creative.

The obvious alternative to working through bureaucratic channels is to be active "politically" in the conventional sense. That too, however, raises problems. One is the very power of governmental bureaucracies; a second is that the organs of political competition, parties and pressure groups, are themselves in modern states complex bureaucratic structures, having structural intricacies, mysteries, routines, and specialized vested interests of their own. Yet such is the efficiency of these structures, whether administrative or "political," that circumventing them altogether—for example, by activity in well-intentioned but weakly organized civic groups like Naumann's or the *Verein für Sozialpolitik*—was, for Weber, tantamount to opting out of politics altogether. One could not wish away the central importance of complex organizations in all phases of political life and to be efficacious one had to accommodate activity to them.

Politicians. What manner of men worked and controlled the political machines? Weber's answer to that question rested on a distinction between men who live "for" politics and those who live "off" it. To live for politics was, most simply, to be devoted to politics but not materially dependent on it—in other words, to be a political "amateur," one who loves politics for its own sake, the model of that sort of politician being the landed notables and other men of substance who constituted the main political class in representative oligarchies. Living off politics, per contra, meant being a "professional," that is, engaging in politics for the purpose of acquiring values (money, goods, status), even if not only for that reason. Political professionals had, of course, always existed. The princes who had built feudalities into states, for example, had used such men systematically in their struggles against ecclesiastic and secular corporations. But with the progress of political expropriation, the professionals had greatly multiplied and become much more than instruments. Modern politicians, whether bureaucrats or not, were largely men tied to politics not just for ideal rewards but dependent on it as well for safety (i.e., security), income, and deference, hence oriented to political spoils and booty—political acquisition—for their own sakes.

This had obvious and important consequences, two above all. First, it meant that the rational definition of political goals and means would be distorted not only by complexity and routines but also by the need of political actors to do things that would further, or at least not imperil, their personal command over values. Thus bureaucratic timidity grew out of a need for personal security no less than the institutional routinization of bureaucratic roles. Politicians had to calculate the gains and losses in popularity and financial supporters entailed by stances in politics. They were impelled also to get out of political power what they could while power lasted and to ensure themselves against the possible loss of it by rendering services to those who could provide *pantouflage:* remunerative private positions when public careers had ended or been interrupted.

Closely related to this is the appearance and signal importance of new kinds of political entrepreneurs. The early entrepreneurs in politics had been robber barons literally speaking: expropriators and monopolists who, by ruining competitors, had built large kingdoms out of petty principalities. Their means had been military force and a surer justice and greater administrative efficiency. Rationalizing their staffs and armies, raising their outputs while lessening costs, giving the public what it wanted, they gradually drove out of the market less efficient or more scrupulous producers of political goods. Once power had been concentrated, however, political entrepreneurship took the form more of exploiting it systematically for other ends (e.g., economic ends) or establishing a kind of brokerage between political power and private aspirations. Its prototype, although not sole manifestation, Weber saw in the American "boss" who built up reservoirs of reliable voters, activists, and technicians and used them to place men in official jobs and to obtain through them politically allocated values for himself and his clients. Weber did not entirely frown upon that kind of entrepreneur or the systems of patronage and spoils in which he flourished, but indeed regarded him as a constructive counterweight to the petrified routines of bureaucracies. Truly innovative political entrepreneurship, however, he thought could come only through charismatic figures who, by mobilizing and channeling anxieties and fervors in troubled times, could thoroughly unsettle and perhaps reshape routinized political systems, even if their creations were themselves fated to fall into the hands of careerists and doomed to routinization.[29]

Effective Politics.   Coercive force, complex organization, careerists and entrepreneurs of power are, however, not all there is to politics. They are only instrumentalities and general aspects of its structural components. Each of the components may make a part of its business the attainment of autonomous power, the maintenance of routines, or the acquisition of material values, but the function of the whole is to make and realize a society's most consequential choices—to define the ends and means to ends in the service of which the awesome coercive powers and technical capabilities of states are to be mobilized. These choices are often cruelly difficult, partly because of the instrumentalities used to carry them out, partly because they are often compelled by circumstances rather than entirely voluntary, partly because they must often be taken hastily on insufficient information or reflection. What imperatives for political action, especially efficacious action, follow from this aspect of politics?

The most important requirement it imposes, in Weber's view, is that those who wish to work political effects have what he variously calls enthusiasm, *Glauben* (faith or belief), *ira et studium* (scorn and bias), and passion.[30] In the first place, this is because of the fact that pure power politics is futile and senseless. It may create transient disturbances and ephemerally satisfy base appetites, but Weber saw clearly the mere destructiveness and inner weakness of the cultists of power (like D'Annunzio) and of the "braggarts and parvenus" who use it mainly for "vain self-reflection" (like McCarthy).[31] Second, faithful enthusiasm is required also because defining goals entails, at some point, making moral commitments, and moral commitments, in Weber's view, cannot be worked out by technical calculations only. Third, it is required to reduce hesitation in the face of great pressures, responsibilities, and objective uncertainties. And it is needed because of the very instrumental and structural characteristics of politics. Willingly to use coercive power as means implies forceful convictions, not weak half-certainties, and attempting to move the complex, inscrutable machines of politics against the strong resistances of their routines calls for great energies that can come only from strong passions.

In these senses politics is most certainly a realm for sentiment. Indeed Weber, despite his somber passages on the generally petty routines and stakes of politicians, always regarded politics as the preeminent realm for human heroism and the highest area of human liberty, since it offered the greatest opportunities for making consequential choices and effecting them against powerful impediments.

Just as pure power is politically senseless, however, so also is pure sentiment—"sterile excitation," as Simmel called it. If choices are to be implemented by practical activity, including coercive power, choosing is not so light a matter as it is in print and talk. Passion may be requisite to it, but so is "responsibility," "judgment," "assessment"—dispassionate appreciation of relevant givens and genuine possibilities, rational calculation of the various benefits and costs of alternative ends and means, and pragmatic understanding of the real relations between ends and means, including understanding of, and willingness to accept, the "tragedy with which all . . . political action is interwoven," namely, that sublime purposes may be realized only if compromised and pursued by morally inconsistent means.[32] Weber's efficacious political actor is, in essence, what President Kennedy called himself, an "idealist without illusions," a man of "tamed passion," there being also two corruptions of the species, idealists with illusions (excited romantics) and illusionists without ideals (pure careerists and entrepreneurs of power); but since the latter always exist, a condition of efficacious political action is learning to work with and through them, to some extent at least on their own terms.

SCIENCE VERSUS POLITICS

Weber's reflections on the relations of social science to public policy were worked out with reference to this model of political instrumentalities, structures, actors, functions, and conditions of efficacy and a similarly general model of social science. From these reflections two villains emerge: arrogant social scientists who overstep their role and pusillanimous politicians who do not live up to theirs. The essential thrust of Weber's arguments is not only to affirm a substantial role for empirical social science in responsible political action, but also to deny its sufficiency (or anything even approaching it) for the conduct of political affairs. In social scientists Weber wished to awaken mainly a sense of limitation vis-à-vis politics, indeed all "practical" life, and a sense of the distinctive demands of their chosen vocation; for politicians he emphasized responsibilities of which neither social scientists nor anyone else could relieve them; for both he wanted to define the distinctive characteristics of their callings and the dangers of identifying them too closely or separating them too widely.

To clarify why and how he proceeded toward these ends, the following matters now need discussion: (1) how Weber viewed the nature, capabilities, and limitations of social science; (2) what contrasts and strains he deemed to exist between the political and scientific roles; (3) at what points he considered these contrasts small enough to warrant the close identification of the roles; and (4) what perils he thought might follow from failure to grasp the nature of their differences and compatibilities.

Weber's social science was in most respects consistent with modern "behavioralism" in political and social studies. Many proponents of the latter indeed respectfully confess his inspiration in regard to their formulation of problems, modes of conceptualization, theoretical approaches, types of model building and hypothesizing, and the use of certain techniques for gathering and processing data. Just for this reason Weber is widely thought of as a man who glorified the work and capabilities of scientists and affirmed a close identity between the natural and social sciences. In fact, the contrary is the case. All of his writings on science are pervaded with a sense of its limitations, to a pitch occasionally verging on despair, and many of these writings are specifically concerned with drawing large contrasts between the natural and social sciences and pointing out the specially great limitations of the latter. To be sure, he did not revile science as do the professional antipositivists, and he most certainly did not glorify some nebulous unscientific "wisdom," "prudence," or "experience" as they do. But he was at the very least a positivist without illusions.

Weber, of course, did not think of the natural and social sciences as absolutely different. In many respects they were certainly similar, having substantially the same purpose (to discover trustworthy empirical generalizations about phenomena), using largely similar techniques (those of systematic observation, logic, and quantification), and requiring rather narrow specialization (if only because their methods demand hard and devoted work with voluminous minutiae: "brooding at one's desk" over "thousands of trivial calculations").[33] To this extent they also have similar power—and similar limitations.

The power of science is that it alone can provide valid knowledge of relations among phenomena, social or "natural." If one wishes to know what effects interest rates have on employment or productivity, whether and to what extent political campaign techniques affect voting turnout and voting preferences, whether upward social mobility creates mainly satisfaction or heightens perceptions of deprivation, in what ways changes in electoral systems may affect party systems, or any similar matters, "nomological" knowledge is indispensable.[34] Men do have beliefs about such relations apart from scientific laws, based on individual common sense, folk wisdom, experience, intuition, or cosmological philosophies; but these beliefs are themselves nomological knowledge, in a cruder form and built on shakier foundations than those of science.

Weber summarizes the limitations of science in saying that it cannot, however much it may be perfected, discover "meaning" in life. Every epoch that tastes of the tree of knowledge is, in his view, fated to discover that the meaning of existence eludes it, except insofar as it creates such meaning for itself, in other ways;[35] indeed, to the extent that life becomes "scientized" meaning recedes and men become "estranged" from the world. What did Weber mean by this?

First and best known, he meant that science cannot provide any guides to personal conduct or any means of choosing among "ultimate" alternatives. Before Tolstoy's questions—"What shall we do and how shall we live?"—it remains silent.[36] Even when desirable ends have been chosen, it cannot solve or reduce such problems of conduct as whether such ends sufficiently sanction undesirable but unavoidable means, or whether in choosing and pursuing desirable ends the possibility of undesired repercussions should be taken into account, or how to deal with conflicts among conflicting desirable ends.[37] To the medical practitioner, for instance, it offers a highly developed technology for relieving suffering and extending life, but it cannot tell him whether to do so is good and in what cases it may be justifiable to end life as redemption from suffering. To the political scientist, it may offer technical knowledge of how to maintain a certain system of rule, but it cannot provide guides to whether that system is intrinsically valuable or more so than probable alternatives. In the most general sense, science may tell us much about what the world is like, but says nothing about whether its nature is sublime or diabolic and whether it is sensible to live in it at all.[38] Not only how to live but even whether to live are ineluctably questions for choice and compromise. And as science advances, the "meaning" of life, in the sense of a moral orientation toward it and moral understanding of it, may recede in several senses: as a result of an overestimation of the powers of science and the surrender of re-sponsibilities for creative choice to its technicians; as a result of the fact that science continuously discovers new facts and relationships to integrate into moral conceptions of the world; and most of all, because science offers ever greater and more fateful technical means for working effects, hence for defining choices of ends and means. Weber could not foresee specif-ically the concrete possibilities that exist for us—to destroy virtually all life, to prolong almost all suffering, to uproot, incarcerate, coercively police, or indoctrinate whole peoples—but he certainly saw the principle of the thing and realized that every new technical possibility imposes new bur-dens. He foresaw also the likelihood of technology being increasingly relied upon to define choices lying beyond it, for the sake of the semblance of choosing wisely.

In saying that science does not discover "meaning" in life, Weber had in mind, second, a characteristic of the very nomological knowledge it provides: the intrinsic transience and tentativity of that knowledge and the extent to which, as a result, it makes all individual contributions to science fragmentary and ephemeral. To be a scientist means to belong to a devoted company that proceeds gradually and with painstaking labors toward the objective of absolutely dependable empirical knowledge of the world, but never attains that objective. There are no ultimate and absolute tests for generalizations about observed data. New data constantly present them-selves as scientific technology itself makes possible wider and deeper ob-servation; in any case, there is no way to know when data have been exhausted. The generalizations of science themselves generate new gen-eralizations, themselves become new data and sources of new actions that constitute new data, and may always be made more general, simpler, or more powerful. Science, therefore, knows no rest, only continuous striving. The scientist's judgment must be always in abeyance, every new finding being doubtful or a source of new mysteries, and he, as individual, is merely a figure in an endless collective process which is itself only a fragment of the whole of mankind's intellectual activity.[39] "It is the fate of every sci-entist to see his work surpassed," says Aron, following Weber,[40] who him-self holds out to scientists the biblical injunction, "thousands of years must pass before you enter into life and thousands more wait in silence," as especially pertinent to them.[41]

The endless progressiveness of science seems to Weber to denude life of meaning because he agreed with Tolstoy that it makes death senseless. For men chained to an infinite progress, "life should never come to an end; for there is always a further step ahead for one who stands in the march of progress. And no man who comes to die stands upon the peak which lies in infinity."

Weber especially contrasted this transience of science with the permanence of art. Both are creative, but the creations of artists stand in the march of progress in a very different sense. Technical progress may offer new possibilities to artists, and, in a sense, "enrich" their work; many artistic innovations (e.g., the Gothic style, evolving orchestral composition) have in fact originated in technological advances as much as in aesthetic inspiration. But no work of art is ever surpassed, in the sense of being made aesthetically less valuable by new artistic techniques. All works of art are legacies, all accomplishments of science merely episodes.[42]

Science is estranged from life also because of its extreme specialization. Scientific progress carves up the world of phenomena into ever narrower fields in each of which progress itself makes work continuously more taxing and more life-absorbing. Hence the scientist must pay in growing ignorance of the whole for every increment of knowledge of its parts. Synthesis may be possible, but may only create new special fields carved out of the margins of old specialties (e.g., "political sociology") or be bought at the price of inadequate knowledge of what is synthesized.[43]

Finally, science cannot invest life with "meaning" because it is necessarily abstract and in that sense "unreal," even though its abstractions may be intended to capture the true blood and sap of life.[44] Weber's science is certainly not Plato's philosophic sun, the reality of which is poorly reflected in the shadows of concrete experience, but just the reverse. Its concepts, models, formulas, hypotheses, indices, and correlations are themselves shadows of reality through which men try to make experience intelligible, if not meaningful. The abstract "concept," argues Weber, appeared to the Greeks as the key to eternal truth as against transient opinion. Reformation scientists still believed in science as a way to God, hidden and remote from us but revealed in His creations (even "in the anatomy of a louse"). Now, however, science is recognized as consisting of no more than heuristic devices, helpful in interpreting life but separated from it by an insurmountable barrier between abstraction and concreteness. The specialization of scientists is relevant to this point, too, since all their laws and regularities, as well as being abstract, capture only aspects of the complexity of concrete configurations.

Reading through such passages, one may get the impression that Weber tried to glorify the scientist as a kind of antihero, willingly engaging in consuming labors that can come to no end, no fullness, no foreknowledge, and no moral guides to life. Up to a point this is probably so, and it corresponds to the Protestant's gloomy sense of vocation. But it is as well to reemphasize also the other side of his view of science: his belief that, whatever may give life "meaning," science is indispensable to any sort of technical mastery over it, so that the effective attainment of any creative aspiration depends to a large extent upon scientific knowledge. In stressing the limitations of science, Weber tried to affirm that human life retains large areas of genuine liberty and creativity regardless of scientific progress, while at the same time stressing the large extent to which free, creative choices may themselves be senseless without the technical knowledge that science alone provides.

All this pertains to every kind of science. Even with regard to that small slice of intellectual life constituted by the sciences, however, Weber was a pluralist. The social sciences particularly seemed to him to require distinction from the natural because of two characteristics, both of which make them less powerful in achieving nomological knowledge and the technical mastery it provides.

First is the fact that human acts, individual or in social aggregates, have "meanings" to the actors which vary among individuals and cultures. These meanings include intentions, that is, goals toward which actions are directed, normative expectations, and culturally peculiar attributions of significance. In that sense, "social facts" were not conceived by Weber à la Comte as mere objects, or even quite à la Durkheim as ways of acting imposed by external constraints,[45] but as behavior inextricable from subjective, internal meanings, despite the possibility of a purely objective observation of human action and the undeniable role of external forces in conditioning internal meanings.

How does this affect the nature and weaken the capabilities of the social sciences? In the first place, it makes them more complex than other sciences because it adds a distinctive variable—and "meaning" *is* a variable, since it is not deducible (not fully, anyway) from universal psychological traits. This variable is omitted only with the gravest consequences, since subjective orientations do not always closely reflect objective circumstances, may independently have causal effects, and always intervene as intermediary forces between objective conditions and their objective consequences. Such orientations must, therefore, always play a role also in attempts to use the social sciences technically, that is, in social engineering: the same "policies" in different cultures may have vastly different effects, not so much because objective conditions differ but because the meanings of the conditions and policies may be variously interpreted. At the same time, however, meanings are extremely difficult to get at and one's formulations of them difficult to test when one thinks that one has got at them. *Verstehen,* or empathy—the power of projecting oneself into the object of study—is important in social study, but adds to it a special problem not fully soluble by standardized techniques of inquiry and hence an added source of arbitrariness that widens the gulf between reality and scientific constructions.

The second distinctive characteristic of social science limiting its powers is that its subject, according to Weber, and again contrary to Comte, is not fixed and static but inherently "developmental."[46] This is not to say that it is "progressive"; Weber in fact attacked all "scientific" theories of progress as assuming value standards not determinable by science.[47] It means only that human history brings forth ever new social forms and patterns of action rather then merely repeating old ones. The processes of historic change, moreover, are hardly predictable by deterministic historicist cosmologies, precisely because men can, by means other than science, invest life with meaning and make, even if within limits, creative choices on the basis of their orientations. Weber wanted, according to Aron, to preserve the "drama" of history—its irregularities, accidents, and purposive strivings—against any thoroughgoing mechanical determinism.[48] Even more important, he wanted to stress that social science theories cannot be cumulative in the same sense that the theories of natural science are. In the social sciences all the possibilities for infinite process previously mentioned exist, but in addition to them old observations and the theories they support may become irrelevant (not just enlarged, improved, transcended) through historic processes of creative innovation. In that sense, the social sciences are sciences "to which eternal youth is given";[49] at any point in time, social scientists may find that history demands of them a virtually fresh start.

One may ask how it is possible to be a social scientist at all when one holds such views about meaning and creative development in human affairs. Weber could be a committed social scientist despite these views because he believed in the plain necessity of science for efficacious creative action and because the special characteristics of social behavior seemed to him only to restrict the capabilities of social science in certain senses, not to make it futile. To an extent, one can indeed avoid all cultural and historical peculiarities in social science by developing very abstract and general theories (like models of "rational" optimizing actions or theories of the universal functional imperatives of social life), but only at the unavoidable costs of widening the gulf between theory and reality and being uninformative in regard to less general, possibly more important questions. These costs Weber himself would not incur; hence his own broadest generalizations are always middle-range theories pertaining to concrete historic processes and cultural systems of meaning.[50] At the same time, he believed that a modicum of human experience could be grasped by universal scientific "laws" independent of history, such as those of psychology, and a larger portion by the study of proximate causality, even if still another portion was amenable only to "interpretative understanding"; and he believed also that systematic comparative historical study, aided by psychological theory as well as a more nebulous empathy, could make motives and meanings understandable by tracing them to their origins (as he himself traced the motives of modern capitalists to Protestant beliefs). Social science to Weber consisted, in essence, of an admixture of laws, hypotheses about proximate causes and trends, and empathetic understanding, corresponding to the combination of determinism, probability, and choice—of necessity, circumstance, and creativity—that constitutes social life.

On the basis of these sketches of what is involved in being a politician or social scientist, one can readily see huge contrasts between their roles. Let us list only the most general and important.

First, since choice is the essential business of politics—choices of ultimate goals that require moral commitments and of immediate means that cannot be purely technical since they may have to be selected upon inadequate technical knowledge and may pose moral problems of their own—politicians need, and generally develop, passionate convictions and a sense of certainty, even personal infallibility. The social scientist's vocation, per contra, is morally silent and implants a zealous uncertainty, dispassion, and tentativeness, and a deep sense of the fallibility of all personal beliefs and labors.

Second, political work must always be done with reference to concrete, extremely complex social wholes, whereas social scientists work with abstract and simplified conceptions that concern only fragments of social experience. Both may be highly specialized, but they are specialized in different senses. Political specialization involves the distribution and coordination of tasks that are themselves highly complex, whereas scientific specialization involves splitting concrete complexity into abstract fragments. Scarcely a single special political task does not involve psychological, economic, administrative, and sociological considerations in complicated combination, but these are just what scientific specialization disjoins.

Third, political work is always done in large, substantially routinized organizations that must be moved and jockeyed if anything is to be achieved. The organizations, moreover, are not merely instrumental facilities to be adapted at will to any purpose, but to an extent ends in themselves, in that the politicians' careers may be bound up entirely with maintaining their positions in them and preserving their routines. Consequently, adapting means to political ends is not just a matter of impersonal calculations but entails also a host of personal stakes and considerations, large and petty. In contrast, social scientists work mainly as individuals, have to endure only a minimum of routine, and see the relations of ends and means principally as abstractly logical problems—not least when pronouncing on political matters, with which their own incomes, safety, and deference are not bound up.

Fourth, political and scientific space and time have very different dimensions that make for contrary perspectives. Political space is parochial, tied to specific societies, whatever visions there may be to the contrary; scientific space is inherently ecumenical. The politician's time perspective is inherently constricted; the social scientist's is expansive and indeed, in a sense, infinite. Politicians must generally act expeditiously even if that entails making commitments upon little or no preparation; in any case, their work lies in the present moment or immediate future. Social scientists, on the other hand, may sit long and patiently making their myriads of trivial calculations, safely knowing that nothing will be impaired by the ticking away of time, except possibly self-esteem; and their work is free of temporal constriction also in that its end is always infinitely remote.

This list of contrasts could certainly be enlarged. For example, one could, and probably should, add to it contrasts between scientific and political communication, such as those entailed in teaching as against persuading and those between the religious openness and honesty of scientific communication and the compulsive mystifications and flimflam of politics. What has been said, however, should suffice to make the essential point, which is that the contrasts between the scientific and political callings are such that they will produce considerable strains when their practitioners encounter one another or cross vocational boundaries. Because they evolve different orientations—different *vocational* systems of meaning—professional politicians and social scientists are likely to be mutually unreceptive and antipathetic, as well as highly ineffective when engaging themselves outside of their accustomed spheres, although one should immediately add that this is so only insofar as they properly understand and practice their vocations. There certainly have been politicians who felt more at ease among scientists and scholars than in politics itself (Balfour, for example) and even more scientists and scholars who took readily to politics; but they have rarely been notable politicians or accomplished scientists.

Strain, however, does not imply irrelevance and the desirability of utter separation. Weber's thought about the relations of social science to policy making was certainly not intended to construct an elaborate rationalization for indulging that "craving of his soul for failure" which Leo Strauss has somehow detected in him.[51] His aim, as I understand it, was just the opposite: to promote the potency of both social scientists and politicians by clarifying for the one what he can do in public affairs and for the other what he must do; by identifying clearly areas of overlap and complementarity between the two roles and equally clearly corrupting dangers that may arise when they are joined; and of course, by stating explicitly factors that may make for strains in any case but all the more so when they are unrealized.

Certainly Weber's claims for the contributions social scientists can make to policy qua social scientists are far from inconsiderable. Although they cannot provide scientifically ultimate value standards, there is much they can do, at least potentially (i.e., to the extent that they actually possess scientific knowledge and can adjust themselves sufficiently to the ways of the political world). Given an explicitly stated goal, they can supply knowledge of technical means for its attainment. Even if they cannot measure the intrinsic ethical value of a goal, they can assess its "meaningfulness" in a given setting, that is, whether it makes sense to pursue the goal at all. They can help determine with precision the impact on other spheres of pursuing any special goal and hence the overall costs of a policy. Through logical analysis they can also make explicit the more general values implied by clusters of goals and judge the consistency of goals with one another.[52] They can elucidate what data and theoretical knowledge are ideally required to choose among alternative means to ends. And they can study values and goals as empirical givens—for example, expose the preconditions and consequences of their being held and thereby help men to decide whether to hold them at all.[53]

It is true that all this is only instrumental and that the political decision maker must take into account factors in no sense scientific, in ways not purely technical, in making even instrumental choices. But it is also true that social scientists can be especially useful in policy making precisely because their orientations are so different from, and complementary to, those of politicians. They can, for instance, serve to dampen passions where coolness may be essential, detect self-serving pettiness in political purposes and calculations, induce a sense of uncertainty where false conviction may be self-defeating, help politicians to see through comfortable but dysfunctional routines, provide a larger sense of space and time where narrowness and haste may have bad consequences—in short, help politicians to avoid the faults of their own virtues, always provided that they achieve rapport with them without assuming the politician's own distinctive orientations.

However, in stressing the *complementarity* of the scientific and political vocations, Weber was also necessarily insisting on their essential separateness. Most important, he saw two serious dangers in a too close identification of them, one pertaining to social science, the other to politics, but both expressed a single, more general fallacy, that of "scientism"—which means literally what it says, regarding science as an "ism."

The chief danger social scientists should avoid in regard to political activity is to play at being moral teachers, agitators, demagogues, and "prophets" in their professional capacities, most of all in the classroom (although by no means only there). The fundamental reason for this is, of course, Weber's conception of the limits of empirical science. Weber did not accept Comte's vision of a scientistic ethics: the belief that as there is no room for free judgment in physics so there will be none in social life once the sciences pertaining to it are perfected. That view seemed to him simultaneously to misunderstand science and morality and to endanger human dignity.[54] Nor did he subscribe to the attitude Jacques Ellul considers inherent in the technician's approach to decision making: the belief that all problems have unique solutions deriving from purely technical considerations, so that as technology advances the necessity for moral choice diminishes.[55] Even in regard to instrumental decisions, let alone commitments to ultimate ends, scientific calculations leave room for other considerations and creative choices because of the inherent uncertainties, abstractness, finitude, simplifications, and fragmentation of science. For "values," then, science is irrelevant, for "evaluations" insufficient, even though its adequacy for the latter grows with technological advance.

There is an additional reason for ruling moral preaching and policy recommendations especially out of the classroom. This is the inherent asymmetry of the teacher-student relationship. After all, the teacher's authoritative position can easily be used to stifle discussion and contradiction on controversial matters. Students and teachers in any case do not enjoy "equal time" if they disagree on matters eminently subject to disagreement. Teachers can permanently harm students who make themselves obnoxious to them through examination marks and other means. Students tend to be respectful and impressionable anyway and to crave leaders and guardians rather than teachers, as well as being unaware of the fallibility of the petty gods who reveal themselves on the lecture platforms. And on the other side, teachers may be tempted to court easy popularity by generating sentimental excitements rather than demanding exacting empirical work and ruthless analysis, of both themselves and their students. Should teachers nevertheless wish to preach, plenty of less asymmetric channels are available to them for doing so.

It was said in Weber's time, and still is today, that moral teaching and the closely related academic concern with policy questions are justified because the end of higher education is the whole cultivation of men rather than specialized training. Weber, however, was strongly for the latter, not just because the specialized society requires specially trained experts, but, more important, because for him cultivated men do not surrender or fail to realize their moral autonomy, the right and duty of resolving problems of conscience in their own way. Moral men may, after all, be cultivated in two ways. One may teach them a particular version of morality; or one may sternly refuse to interfere with and lessen their sense of a creative liberty of choice, which is the essence of moral personality. So strongly was Weber for the latter approach that he greatly preferred the heated moral histrionics of Treitschke and Schmoller to teachers who believed that it was permissible to parade values and policy judgments on the lecture platform provided they were presented with cool detachment; he preferred the outright demagogues because they were less likely to deceive anyone about what they were doing.[56]

Contrary to common belief, these views do not connote that Weber was an ethical "relativist." Partly they stem from his ethical pluralism, that is, his belief that different realms of activity impose varying imperatives, the scientific vocation demanding a certain ascetic self-control in sentimental matters. Mainly, however, they reflect his fear of encroachment upon men's moral autonomy, without which no ethical life exists at all and which he considered the creative motor of human development. He saw the complete life as combining knowledge (science), conscience (morality), and will (passion), much as did Freud, and wished to keep each integral and intact.[57]

His own reaction to the reception of Freudian theory by friends who used it to justify sexual promiscuity in the name of "healthy living" illustrates his position. Weber greatly admired Freud's scientific work but considered it potentially dangerous to moral life: (1) because there is no reason to consider healthy nerves a moral absolute as against other values, like self-constraint and heroic suffering; (2) because he foresaw, with rare prescience, the possibility that psychoanalytic clinicians would encroach on personal responsibilities by becoming a new species of *directeurs d'âme;* and (3) because he considered Freudian theory to be as transient and inadequate as any other scientific theory. He also feared that transforming it into a moral code would rigidify it in a still highly inadequate form, preventing the realization of its scientific promise and thus threatening *both* morality and science.[58]

"Scientism" might also take a second form. If the need for choice is especially pressing and decisions are especially difficult to make, politicians, including bureaucrats, may become not too resistant to social scientists but just the opposite, too susceptible, abdicating to scientists their own responsibilities. They may themselves come to regard scientific knowledge and techniques as a surrogate "ism," a kind of revelation that obviates fateful choices. Weber loathed the surrender of moral responsibility in all men, but most of all in those who had chosen a vocation the very essence of which is decision making. He foresaw, however, that with the advance of political expropriation, with the growing complexity and momentousness of rule, a powerful tendency toward the "scientification" of politics and administration might arise, especially since scientific advance would occur simultaneously with "political development." This possible tendency he regarded simply as yet another kind of routinization of spheres in which liberty and creativity had prevailed. He also regarded science as another potent weapon of mystification with which bureaucrats might overwhelm their supposed masters, especially if successfully joined to the already highly developed weapon of the "state secret."

SYMBIOSIS AND SEPARATION

All the essentials of Weber's ideas on relating social science to political activity have now been sketched. As is often the case with his thought, however, summary is difficult. The alternate bursts of energy and inactivity that went into his work left much of it fragmentary, episodic, and in the end, inconclusive—all the more so since he died before his time, while almost all his major work was still in progress. By the time he gave his last lectures on politics and science, he had isolated and analyzed the chief elements of the problem of relating them, but although the lectures state with unparalleled clarity and vigor the nature of these elements, they do not present any final, clear-cut position on the problem. Perhaps this was because Weber had not come to any such position. But perhaps he simply would not state it because he felt that choices of career, and of ways to relate them to other choices, had in the last analysis to be his students' own moral burden—that he could only help them to be "responsible" by clarifying the inescapable commitments, limitations, and consequences their choices entailed. Whichever is the case, the two lectures take one to a crossroad, and only say, "You may go this way or that; if you go in this direction such-and-such will be your road, and if in that, it will be so-and-so; and there will be such difficulties in going from the one to the other and such paths between them; choose."

Yet although Weber's thought comes to no definite conclusion, it surely points to one. He sought most of all a symbiosis of free, creative moral responsibility and technical mastery, either being senseless without the other. This necessarily implied a symbiosis between politics, the preeminent realm of the first, and science, the chief source of the second. Yet either was all too capable of encroaching excessively on, indeed destroying, the other, making action merely technical or merely sentimental. Symbiosis could not, therefore, simply mean combination. Moreover, the vocational cultures, as it were, of politicians and scientists were so different that they could neither personally cross nor collaborate across the boundaries of their callings without considerable strains and a high probability of ineffectuality. And in addition to that, both callings were, if anything, growing more divergent, as well as more life-absorbing for their practitioners: politics more organized, bureaucratized, specialized, professionalized, demanding, and fateful; science, through its very progress, more abstract, segmented, and evanescent. Hence, one is left with the impression that Weber considers a fruitful symbiosis most likely if politicians and social scientists work diligently and dutifully within their separate life-spheres, facing up to their quite different imperatives, keeping their distance, but recognizing the limitations of work in each calling as a condition to restrained and mutually sympathetic cooperation, if only at their margins.

For the social scientist this need be no counsel of resignation toward politics. Like anyone else, he can still be politically committed—provided that he acts out his commitments avocationally, not "in the name of science," in the usual market places of politics, and that he does not thereby neglect the stern duties of his vocational role, which he will, after all, have chosen freely and can freely choose to leave. More important, since the various vocations are all fragments of an interdependent whole, he can perhaps, in the final analysis, be more efficacious politically by doing as diligently as possible what he is most fit to do—which (unless he has mistaken his real bent) is the advancement and teaching of nomological knowledge—rather than by engaging himself intensely in a sphere so very different from his own. After all, social science can inform politics only to the extent that it can inform at all—that is, only to the extent that it has actually been developed.

That leaves the practical question of how social science, such as it is, might in fact inform political action, insofar as it has relevance. Weber says nothing specific about this. Perhaps he feels that if the pitfalls and vain pretensions afflicting their relationship are made plain, the problem will solve itself, which is surely improbable. However, here and there in Weber's writings there are hints as to how he would have social scientists influence politics in their professional capacities. They may do so through restrained publicist activities and equally restrained technical consultation. Best of all, they may do so by providing to students, who might choose politics as a career, decent specialized vocational training, provided that they do not delude them with any nonsense about there being a "science of policy." Weber considered this phrase an infelicitous result of the German universities' serving mainly as training schools for state officials and held categorically that there can be no special scientific preparation for policy making that differs from scientific training for any other purpose.[59]

Anyone who wishes to treat this position as an intellectualized response to purely personal problems in a special social setting can do so easily enough through the materials earlier provided. Yet the fact that a position suits a man's temper and justifies his life does not invalidate it, nor is an argument made irrelevant by the mere fact of being two generations old, least of all if a man had some understanding of continuing social forces.

From an exposition of Weber's thought, we turn therefore to an appraisal of its present pertinence.

THE CONTEMPORARY RELEVANCE OF WEBER

Does anything in contemporary politics or political science compel a revision of Weber's arguments and apparent conclusions? In particular, have recent trends in either sector increased the capabilities of political scientists to contribute to policy making in their professional capacities, either by collaborating across or actually crossing vocational boundaries?

The principal development in recent political science has been the growth of what is generally referred to as the "behavioral" persuasion. This involves in essence a wider, more intensive quest for "nomological" knowledge as Weber thought of it, based on methodological precepts derived from the natural sciences and the more positivistic social sciences. Surely that development has increased the capabilities of political scientists to contribute to policy in at least this sense: it has augmented considerably their stocks of knowledge and skills relevant to policy questions. Useful and instructive work has been done by contemporary "nomologists" in political studies on such subjects as the origins and resolution of conflicts in general and violent political conflicts in particular; conditions of political stability, especially in democracies and new nations; the conditions and prospects of certain kinds of engineered political change, such as "nation building"; the general structure of international systems and their specific potentialities for war and peace; decision making in crisis situations; and many others in a similar vein.

As for the skills acquired for purposes of such work, it may suffice to say that it is easy from any point of view to see the good, and difficult to see the harm, in political scientists learning new procedures for obtaining reliable data, processing them into findings, and testing the findings; and surely the same applies to their increasing mastery of the exact disciplines (statistics and mathematics) and the languages, perspectives, and methods of other social sciences. Many possibilities Weber attributed only potentially to the scientific study of politics (or any other social science) are actualities now, even though the ratio of actualities to possibilities is still puny and despite the fact that ever more "knowledge" is transcended, ever more rapidly, by progress in political inquiry, in the manner of all nomology.

So far, so good. But what of opportunities to bring such knowledge to bear on policy? Surely these too have grown in many respects. The easy informal relations Weber knew between politicians and academics—based mainly on class position and an attendant coincidence of tastes, education, residence, and circles of friendship and kinship—assuredly have declined, but in their place have developed numerous functional equivalents. An unparalleled number and variety of formal channels bringing political and other social scientists into the governmental machinery now exists. These include complex networks of consultantship, formal conferences, and task forces sponsored by governmental agencies; "in-house" research divisions of government departments that both carry out and sponsor professional study; research auxiliaries of such departments; and some full-time service by political scientists as departmental specialists. In addition, there has been a good deal of mobility, in both directions, between academic and governmental institutions, and in that sense at least a marginal fusion of the two vocations. The fact of that mobility is not unprecedented, but the amount of it certainly is. One should also note the growth of graduate training schools for the public service, providing opportunities to academics to devote themselves to policy-oriented teaching and research and to influence future "politicians" at an impressionable age and present ones in midcareer. Not least, as the business of government has become more complex and consequential, scientistic attitudes in politics and administration, as Weber expected, have concomitantly grown; and whatever the dangers of these attitudes, they do at least provide opportunities to social scientists to obtain a hearing among those who wield political authority. In fact, the channels between social science research and government are now such that, alongside in-house and auxiliary research establishments, there has even grown up a sizable industrial entrepreneurship of social science research tied to governmental contracts, as well as numerous academic social science research centers operating, in varying degrees, on public funds for public purposes. Over these preside a new bureaucratic species unknown to Weber, research administrators and promoters. Largely self-determining scholars, who are to science what the feudal nobles were in politics, still abound in the social sciences. But much more of the work of social research has been absorbed into bureaucratized research organizations, many of which depend on and promote massive governmental interest and subventions, and are, in the way of bureaucracies, highly efficient in turning out research and getting it into influential channels.

Thus far, then, even better. But there is another side to the matter which, in my view, is a great deal more important and strikingly bears out Weber's central arguments. The gist of it is that although policy-relevant political knowledge and formal channels for transmitting it to politicians have greatly increased, the *cultures* of politicians and political scientists have become so much more divergent and the *demands* of their separate roles so much more crushing that merely looking at the knowledge and the channels yields an altogether misleading picture of the actual relations between them.

The contemporary culture of political scientists is characterized, first, by a much greater sense of uncertainty than in the past. In part, this reflects their assumption of scientific attitudes along with scientific methods, and it is likely to persist. In part, it also reflects the fact that "behavioral" political studies, being young and rambunctious, have so far done more to unsettle old beliefs, to raise questions, to reveal areas of ignorance and partial knowledge, and to open new, still unattained, possibilities than to settle anything. This may be a temporary state of affairs, attendant on a large shift in methods and perspectives. Yet, there is already evidence to suggest that as scientific methods spread in political studies they will be characterized increasingly by the evanescence of knowledge, hence by the permanent tentativity intrinsic, in Weber's view, to all nomology—most of all in social studies.

In addition, the recent development of political science, also in the manner of all nomological study, has made it more abstract, more shadowy. Political studies, as Weber foresaw, have become more specialized and fragmented. Beyond this one need not be a mean opponent of the so-called "behavioral revolution" in our own field to see that its very accomplishments are predicated upon a growing estrangement from the living phenomena of politics. What, after all, is it to employ "indicators" as data if not to use the reflection as the real object? Or to study behavior by "simulating" it? Or to construct "models" as sources of knowledge? Or to discard the common vocabularies of politics and their meanings for technical conceptual schemes? Or to bury individuals in correlations? Or to treat responses to survey questions as living attitudes? Or to construct ever more general theories in which ever more vivid detail is lost? One may suspect that some of the resistance to behavioralism is due to just this fact and that it is for this reason that we are so strangely accused of fiddling among the flames.

The fact is, however, that what is going on in political science is precisely what the advance of nomological knowledge, hence technical mastery, requires. Tentativity, specialization, and conceptual and theoretical abstraction do not reduce the relevance of political study to public policy in principle. If anything, the opposite is the case—again, in principle. In fact, however, the politician's culture, largely unchanged since Weber's time (except for the maturing of then-embryonic tendencies), militates powerfully against the proper reception and utilization of the fruits of such study.

Politicians, working in bureaucratized machines, dependent on conformity to them and on popular appeals for their careers, pressed to make decisions highly consequential for society and for themselves, upon quick diagnoses of and responses to concrete pressures and conditions, want, understandably, hard certainties immediately applicable to complex concrete pressures. They shy away from studiously tentative abstractions with all their excess baggage of *ceteris paribus* clauses and caveats. In fact, like physicians, they often develop a sense of personal infallibility as a necessary defense against the inherent uncertainties and fatefulness of their work and therefore tend to be especially unresponsive to men with a carefully cultivated sense of their own and others' limitations. The resultant divergences in outlook are aggravated by growing differences in language and techniques of thought and work. And scientism in politics, being a corruption of the scientific culture precisely in regarding science as a solvent of uncertainties and necessities for choice, encourages mainly scientific quacks—persons who will produce a "system" for dealing with virtually any problem, if the customer is gullible and the fee is right; at least, it does so where there is no clear conception of the boundaries between what science must solve and politics must decide, of the sort that largely regulates the relations between politics and the natural sciences.

For these reasons, one may suspect that much relevant work in contemporary political studies gets no attentive political audience at all or gets it only at the margins of the policy process or only after intermediaries in or out of government have packaged (and distorted) it into a form more consistent with the politician's culture. And for the same reasons, it seems likely that political scientists least acculturated to the scientific culture get the most crucial and most attentive political audience.

Cultural strains affect not only the transmission and reception of messages from political scientists to politicians but also the very willingness of the former to use the channels of influence available and of the latter to grant different kinds of political scientists access to them. We have no systematic studies of the subject, but one's impression is that the willingness to become involved in policy processes (even if not a concern with policy in other senses) is unevenly distributed in the profession, with the behavioralists excluding themselves from direct involvement in politics more than other subcultures in the field. That exclusion, however, is not always self-imposed, but results also from the selectivity of politicians. This too is understandable, and perhaps inevitable. If it is natural for political scientists to opt out of policy processes on grounds of cultural strain, it is equally natural for politicians to recruit into their structures the more congenial, familiar, and supportive kinds of political scientists—not necessarily those who will nourish their biases, but those most like themselves in styles and modes of thinking and talking. Self-exclusion by certain political scientists thus is reinforced by the recruitment practices of the other side.

Exclusion does not always imply an absolute lack of access and participation. In many cases it manifests itself more subtly but with the same results: for example, in an unwillingness to continue interaction on one side or encourage continuation on the other, or in being put on a consultant roll but not asked actually to consult, or by one party making little effort to communicate intelligibly or the other little effort to understand correctly. These days not many political scientists of consequence fail to have any contact with government, but not a few find that after the initial interchanges the silences, on both sides, become longer, more frequent, and at last permanent.

Weber's analysis clearly points to, and explains, these cultural strains and their consequences. It also clarifies a second major dimension of the problem: the tendency for politicians and political scientists to become estranged because their roles grow more burdensome and life-absorbing, compelling the awful single-minded absorption in their special callings that the Puritans voluntarily assumed as a sign of grace.

Being an efficacious politician today requires a more "slow and arduous boring of hard boards" than Weber could have envisioned. The scope and complexity of governmental activities have grown enormously through the continuous expropriation of private spheres. So, concomitantly, have governmental structures and structures of political competition. So has the need for politicians both to balance complex pressures and interests to work effects through bureaucratic machines become more cumbersome and inert as they have grown larger and more settled and to act so as to safeguard their careers as a condition of personal income, deference, and security. To be a contemporary political scientist is not much less burdensome, at least if one is seriously committed to the calling. One assumes onerous teaching and administrative duties. There are massive pressures for research, by increasingly taxing methods, in an ever-widening set of contexts. One must get through an awesome and constantly growing quantity of publications and other materials to "keep up" with a discipline expanding its knowledge ever more rapidly and making it obsolete ever more swiftly. Constantly there are new languages to be learned, methods to be mastered, and theories to be appraised and tested. And all this is bound up with the political scientist's own income, security, and status, no less than his professional commitments.

Between committed politicians and political scientists, then, interactions may become more voluminous, but the very volume of interactions adds to their being more casual and superficial, for cultural reasons and reasons of personal economy. The question today, therefore, is not just who *will* listen and understand across vocational boundaries, but who *can:* who has the time and energy to listen and comprehend, and who the time and energy to speak, and speak intelligibly?

CONCLUSION

There may be workable remedies for these difficulties, as there are for others. Weber in no way supplies them to us. By the end of his life, despite incessant groping, he had not even worked out a fully integrated orientation toward science and politics for himself. But Weber's thought may help others to go further in that direction by laying bare, as it surely does, the more general and constant elements of the problem, identifying specific currents in politics, science, and their relations that any present position on the problem must still interrelate, and stating on these bases an explicit and thoughtful position against which to measure stances we take more implicitly and thoughtlessly.

This is not to say, however, that no further thought about the nature and roots of the problem is needed. One would like to see, as a condition for useful practical reflection, a considerable devotion of time and money by interested parties to the systematic study, with modern methods, of subjects like the following (about all of which we currently can only speculate and report impressions): (1) *the nature of the professional cultures of politicians and political scientists,* both of which vary over certain ranges; (2) the *channels and volume of interaction* among them; (3) *who* actually interacts in these channels on both sides, with what *frequency* and in what *manner*; (4) the *strains* that arise in the interactions; (5) *the nature and behavior of individuals and institutions that especially intermix the two vocations* (such as political scientists in actual public service and politicians recruited into academic careers); and (6) the *experience in public service of men who use training schools in public affairs as a springboard to their careers.*

Weber's reflections about our problem, however incisive, remained essentially uninformed by "nomological" study itself, as do ours. In this respect at least, we certainly can and should go beyond him, devoting science itself to the groundwork needed for fashioning useful bridges between political study and political activity.

ENDNOTE

It seems to me that this agenda for research on the issue still applies, in its entirety, in the 1990s.

NOTES FOR CHAPTER 2

1. Leo Strauss, "An Epilogue," in *Essays on the Scientific Study of Politics,* ed. H. J. Storing (New York: Holt, Rinehart and Winston, 1962), 327.

2. The principal sources of his views on the relations of social science and political activity are: (1) his early letters, collected in *Jugendbriefe* (Tübingen: J. C. B. Mohr, 1936); (2) his wife's invaluable biography, Marianne Weber, *Max Weber: Ein Lebensbild* (Tübingen: J. C. B. Mohr, 1926; rpt. Heidelberg: L. Schneider, 1950); (3) the methodological writings collected in *Gesammelte Aufsätze zur Wissenschaftslehre* (Tübingen: J. C. B. Mohr, 1922)—especially two essays, "The Meaning of 'Ethical Neutrality' in Sociology and Economics," and " 'Objectivity' in Social Science and Social Policy," both translated in *Max Weber on the Methodology of the Social*

Sciences, ed. Edward A. Shils and Henry A. Finch (New York: Free Press of Glencoe, 1949); and, above all, (4) two celebrated lectures delivered in 1918, "Politics as a Vocation" and "Science as a Vocation," both in *From Max Weber, Essays in Sociology*, trans. and ed. H. H. Gerth and C. Wright Mills (Fair Lawn, N.J.: Oxford University Press, 1946). Among the better commentaries on his views are: Karl Jaspers, *Max Weber: Eine Rede* (Tübingen: J. C. B. Mohr, 1921), and *Deutsches Wesen im Politischen Denken, im Forschen und Philosophieren* (Oldenburg: G. Stalling, 1932); Ernst Troeltsch, "Max Weber," in *Deutscher Geist und Westeuropa* (Tübingen: J. C. B. Mohr, 1925), 247ff.; J. P. Mayer, *Max Weber and German Politics* (London: Faber and Faber, 1944); Raymond Aron, *German Sociology* (London: W. Heinemann, 1957), part III; H. H. Gerth and C. Wright Mills, "The Man and His Work," Introduction, *From Max Weber*, 3–74; Leo Strauss, *Natural Right and History* (Chicago: University of Chicago Press, 1953); and Christoph Steding, *Politik und Wissenschaft bei Max Weber* (Breslau: Teildruck Marburg, Druck von W. G. Korn, 1932). Talcott Parsons's famous writings on Weber need not be cited here because they are almost exclusively concerned with the contents and techniques of his scientific work, not his reflections about the relevance of that work to public policy and political activity. A comprehensive bibliography on Weber up to 1949 can be found in H. H. Gerth, "Bibliography on Max Weber," *Social Research* (1949): 70–89.

3. Shils, foreword to Shils and Finch, *Max Weber on the Methodology of the Social Sciences*, iv.

4. "Politics as a Vocation," in *From Max Weber*, ed. Gerth and Mills, 126–127.

5. See, for example, Strauss, *Natural Right and History*, esp. chap. 2, and *What Is Political Philosophy?* (New York: Free Press of Glencoe, 1959), chap. 1.

6. Gerth and Mills, Introduction, *From Max Weber*, 44.

7. Ernst Troeltsch, *Max Weber: Ein Nachruf* (Tübingen: J. C. B. Mohr, 1926); Robert Michels, *Bedeutende Männer* (Leipzig: Quelle und Meyer, 1927); K. Jaspers, *Deutsches Wesen*.

8. Aron, *German Sociology*, 67–88.

9. Marianne Weber, *Ein Lebensbild*, 43.

10. *Jugendbriefe*, 121.

11. Marianne Weber, *Ein Lebensbild*, 173–174.

12. *Gesammelte Politische Schriften*, (Muenchen: Drei Masken Verlag, 1921), 8ff.

13. Mayer, *Weber and German Politics*, 45–46.

14. Marianne Weber, *Ein Lebensbild*, 236.

15. Ibid., 237.

16. For a full description in English of this phase, see Mayer, *Weber and German Politics*. The publicist writings are collected in the *Gesammelte Politische Schriften*.

17. See, for example, "Politics as a Vocation," in *From Max Weber*, ed. Gerth and Mills, 96–99.

18. Weber's own *verstehende Soziologie*, characteristically, was an attempt to make the best of both sides—neither entirely to identify nor utterly to separate the two realms of inquiry but, while identifying their fundamental differences, to find also points of overlap. The best discussion of its premises is still Alexander von Schelting, *Max Weber's Wissenschaftslehre* (Tübingen: J. C. B. Mohr, 1934).

19. See, for example, Gerth and Mills, Introduction, *From Max Weber*, 25.

20. Marianne Weber, *Ein Lebensbild*, 249.

21. Gerth and Mills, Introduction, *From Max Weber*, 30.

22. "Politics as a Vocation," in ibid., 77–78, 82–83.

23. Max Weber, *Wirtschaft und Gesellschaft, Grundriss der Sozialoekonomik* (Tübingen: J. C. B. Mohr, 1925), vol. 3, 619.

24. "Politics as a Vocation," in *From Max Weber,* ed. Gerth and Mills, 78. (It might be remarked, in passing, that to Weber this does not define all political systems but pertains rather to a distinctive type of political system developed in the West. The contrary has frequently been said by men who profess to be his followers.)

25. Ibid., 119.

26. Ibid., 121.

27. Ibid., 123–126.

28. "Bureaucracy," in ibid., 233.

29. See "Politics as a Vocation," in ibid., 87, 110.

30. See, for example, ibid., 115 and 117.

31. Ibid., 116.

32. Ibid., 117.

33. Ibid., 135.

34. " 'Objectivity' in Social Science," in *Weber on the Methodology of Social Sciences,* ed. Shils and Finch, 79.

35. Ibid., 57.

36. "Science as a Vocation," in *From Max Weber,* ed. Gerth and Mills, 193.

37. "The Meaning of 'Ethical Neutrality,' " in *Weber on the Methodology of Social Sciences,* ed. Shils and Finch, 143–145.

38. "Science as a Vocation," in *From Max Weber,* ed. Gerth and Mills, 143–145.

39. Ibid., 138.

40. Aron, *German Sociology,* 106.

41. "Science as a Vocation," in *From Max Weber,* ed. Gerth and Mills, 135.

42. "The Meaning of 'Ethical Neutrality,' " in *Weber on the Methodology of Social Sciences,* ed. Shils and Finch, 28–33.

43. "Science as a Vocation," in *From Max Weber,* ed. Gerth and Mills, 134–135.

44. Ibid., 140–141.

45. Emile Durkheim, *The Rules of Sociological Method,* 8th ed. (Chicago: University of Chicago Press, 1938), 1–13.

46. See especially Aron, *German Sociology,* 76.

47. "The Meaning of 'Ethical Neutrality,' " in *Weber on the Methodology of Social Sciences,* ed. Shils and Finch, 27–39.

48. Aron, *German Sociology,* 81.

49. " 'Objectivity' in Social Science," in *Weber on the Methodology of Social Sciences,* ed. Shils and Finch, 104.

50. Examples are theories of irreversible bureaucratization and differentiation, of the origins and transformation of charisma, of the antecedents of modern capitalism, and of the worldly effects of the historic religions.

51. Leo Strauss, *What is Political Philosophy?* 23.

52. " 'Objectivity' in Social Science," in *Weber on the Methodology of Social Sciences,* ed. Shils and Finch, 51–63.

53. "The Meaning of 'Ethical Neutrality,' " in ibid., 18–19.

54. Aron, *German Sociology,* 83.

55. Jacques Ellul, *The Technological Society* (New York: Alfred Knopf, 1964), 253.

56. For Weber's views on this matter, see especially "The Meaning of 'Ethical Neutrality,' " in *Weber on the Methodology of Social Sciences,* ed. Shils and Finch, 2–7, and "Science as a Vocation," in *From Max Weber,* ed. Gerth and Mills, 145–150.

57. " 'Objectivity' in Social Science," in *Weber on the Methodology of Social Sciences,* ed. Shils and Finch, 52–54.

58. Marianne Weber, *Ein Lebensbild,* 379.

59. "The Meaning of 'Ethical Neutrality,' " in *Weber on the Methodology of Social Sciences,* ed. Shils and Finch, 45–46.

THREE

A Perspective on Comparative Politics, Past and Present

Author's Note: This essay took stock of the history and condition of comparative politics in the early 1960s. Almost all of it remains pertinent now, although the final section needs much updating.

I called the essay a "perspective" because it is, in a way, a history of comparative politics, without being in any way a survey of writings in the field—not even of the most important writings.

The object of the essay was to illuminate the condition of the field by discussing the main phases in its evolution and the forces that have affected it, in both the present and the past. Had it been written as a conventional history, I would have dealt at length with many more writers, especially such great writers as Tocqueville, Marx, Weber, Mill, and Bagehot. I would have dealt more briefly, or not at all, with minor writers whose chief virtue is that they can illustrate, in an exaggerated way, the character of comparative political studies in their periods and not that they have made any important contribution to such studies. I would have taken some care to distinguish national differences in styles of analysis in the same periods, rather than speaking of comparative political studies only in overall terms. Such national differences have always existed and exist today: English writers on comparative politics, for example, were much less affected by what I call here the formal-legal style than others and have been less affected, perhaps for just that reason, by the contemporary reaction against that style. Finally, I would have taken greater pains to show the extent to which the predominant style of any one period is still practiced, with less em-

This essay originally was published as the introduction to *Comparative Politics: A Reader*, ed. by Harry Eckstein and David E. Apter (Glencoe, Ill.: Free Press, 1963), 3–32. Reprinted by permission of the publisher. Copyright © 1963 by The Free Press, a division of Macmillan.

phasis, in the periods that follow, although I try to make clear throughout that the development of comparative politics has not proceeded through mutually exclusive phases, but has involved instead a continuous heaping up of strata of analysis, if one may put it that way.

Since the distinction between comparative politics and other aspects of the study of politics is rather recent in origin, I should perhaps also point out that much of this essay provides a perspective on the whole study of politics, indeed of the social sciences, as well.

The field of comparative politics has a long and honorable past. That its pedigree reaches back as far as Aristotle is not unusual, since just about every discipline can, in one way or another, trace its origin to Aristotle. Comparative politics, however, has a particular right to claim Aristotle as an ancestor because of the primacy that he assigned to politics among the sciences and because the problems he raised and the methods he used are similar to those still current in political studies. From Aristotle stretches an impressive line of other Greats who can be numbered, without too much distortion, among the ancestors of the field: Cicero, Polybius, and Tacitus among the Romans; Machiavelli, among others, in the Renaissance; Montesquieu in the Enlightenment; and an imposing line of sages in the nineteenth century—Tocqueville, Marx, Mill, Bagehot, Mosca, and many more. The general analysis of political systems, the classification of their types, the study of the forms of their development, and the observation of the many varieties of actual political systems are concerns nearly as old as the history of recorded thought. These concerns have at least as time-honored a place in human thought as the concern with political morality.

Yet specialists in comparative politics seem today to be preoccupied, almost paradoxically, with questions we associate not with the maturity but with the infancy of a field of inquiry—questions about the fundamentals, the "first things," that govern the processes and ends of analysis. Such questions are raised only rarely in disciplines that have a highly developed tradition. If we are to understand the present state of comparative politics, we must know what these questions are and why they are being raised at this particular stage in the field's development.

THE PRESENT STATE OF COMPARATIVE POLITICS

Let us begin with the questions.

First of all, a host of procedural—perhaps one should say methodological and epistemological—questions are raised by contemporary students of comparative politics. What, they ask, is the nature of comparative method: how is it used, and what sorts of studies are not comparative?

What can be learned by comparisons, assuming that we know how to make them properly? Is the comparative method in the social sciences, for example, really an adequate substitute for experimentation in the natural sciences, as has sometimes been claimed? Can it be used at all in a field like political science—that is, are political systems really comparable—or is each system unique, so that each particular political system is best dealt with by configurative rather than comparative analysis, by constructing a special *Gestalt*, a "profile" as Heckscher has called it? Even if this conclusion is not necessary, does not the comparative method operate usefully only within certain limits: at a relatively low level of theoretical abstraction, where analysis is not very broad in scale but confined, at most, to limited periods in time, certain geographic areas, or similar types of political structure? And what do we mean by concepts like uniqueness, abstraction, similarity? Not only are questions raised about such basic issues, but also about the proper use of specific devices for comparative analysis: for example, the proper uses of ideal and real types, sampling methods, scaling techniques, and so on.

A second set of questions concerns the use of concepts in the field. These fall primarily into two categories: questions regarding the classification of political systems and questions regarding the elements of such systems.

In political science a bewildering variety of classificatory schemes is available. The most venerable of these schemes is still much in use and was never discarded (only amended, simplified, elaborated) from the time of the Greeks to the nineteenth century. It classifies political systems according to the number of participants in decision-making processes into monarchies, aristocracies, and democracies. Since the middle of the nineteenth century, however, schemes for classifying political systems have multiplied helter-skelter, every man his own taxonomist. Today an almost embarrassing number of such schemes exists, requiring choices we do not really know how to make.

Some writers on politics use schemes consisting of two basic types, not, as in the classic case, of three. Some of these two-term schemes consist of polar types, limiting a continuum along which actual systems may be ranged, while others simply provide two "boxes" into which actual systems are placed. An example of the "box" approach is the classification of systems, now widely used, into Western and non-Western types. The continuum approach is found in a large number of schemes—for example, the division of political systems into constitutional and totalitarian, traditional and modern, or agricultural and industrial types.

Some students of politics choose instead classificatory schemes consisting of three basic terms. Weber, for example, classifies political systems, according to the legitimations of authority dominant in them, into traditional, rational-legal, and charismatic types. The Marxists classify them, according to the dominant economic class, into feudal, bourgeois, and proletarian systems. Coleman, departing less from the classic typology, characterizes them either as competitive, semicompetitive, or authoritarian. Dahl uses the terms democracy, hierarchy, and bargaining systems. (The last are added, presumably, to accommodate his interest in economic systems in which not "decisions" but, so to speak, mutual "accommodations" are arrived at.) Still another series of writers uses four-term schemes. Apter, for example, labels governments as dictatorial, oligarchical, indirectly representational, and directly representational. Almond once constructed a scheme typifying political systems, obviously on a variety of bases, as Anglo-American, Continental European, totalitarian, and preindustrial.

We can find in the literature schemes even more complicated than these. Edward Shils, for example, has recommended a five-term typology, constructed specifically to deal with the analysis of "new" states: political democracies, tutelary democracies, modernizing oligarchies, totalitarian oligarchies, and traditional oligarchies. Coleman, in another classificatory proposal, has gone Shils one better by dropping one of his categories (totalitarian oligarchy, which, presumably, would not be omitted in the analysis of established as well as new states) and adding two others, "terminal colonial democracy" and "colonial or racial oligarchy." And this is only a partial list, a sample.

We have here a considerable *embarras de richesses*. We can explain why it exists and why it should have come into existence after the middle of the nineteenth century, particularly in very recent times, for this variety of classifications is obviously a reflection of the rapid development of modern social theory and the broadening of the range of materials in the social sciences. The important point, however, is that such a disconcerting wealth of classificatory schemes inevitably raises some fundamental questions: Which scheme is more useful than others for any given purpose and, even more basic, what is the use of any classificatory schemes at all? How ought such schemes properly to be constructed, and how can one distinguish, in principle, a good scheme from a bad one?

The same questions arise in regard to the elements of political systems, taking "elements" to mean the parts into which such systems are divided and out of combinations of which they are, for analytical purposes, constituted. Following early modern usage, we used to think of these elements primarily as three: legislative, executive, and judicial structures and functions; but lately a large variety of alternatives have been proposed and used. Apter, for example, thinks of political systems as consisting primarily of government, political groups, and systems of social stratification. The last he considers the aspect of the social setting most directly and most significantly related to politics. Each of these elements is then further divided and subdivided to arrive at a large series of components of politics, certain of which supposedly "cluster" in typical (frequently found) political systems. Governments, for example, are held to have a certain "format" and to depend for their very existence on five structural requisites: authoritative decision making, accountability and consent, coercion and punishment, resource determination and allocation, and political recruitment and role assignment. Lasswell presents a breakdown of political systems on the basis of seven functional variables (and explicitly because of his dissatisfaction with the classic separation-of-powers formula): intelligence, recommendation, prescription, invocation, application, appraisal, and termination. (The meanings of these anything but self-explanatory terms are immaterial to the present purpose.) Easton suggests that political systems have essentially two elements—inputs (demands and supports) and outputs (authoritative decisions)—while Almond provides a complicated breakdown of both inputs and outputs into seven so-called functional categories: four for the "input" function (political socialization and recruitment, interest articulation, interest aggregation, and political communication) and three for the "output" function (rule making, rule application, and rule adjudication—the classic formula, but restricted to only one aspect of political systems).

These also are only examples to which a good many others might be added, but they will suffice to illustrate the many different grounds on which a breakdown of political systems might be based—structural categories, functional categories, structural-functional categories, system requisites, elements of formal organization, elements of informal processes. They also show why questions should nowadays be in the air regarding the most basic aspects of such analytical breakdowns: their relative utility, their purpose as such, the "logic"—if there is any—of their construction.

To some extent, the answers to such questions depend on how one answers certain other basic questions that are also very much in the air these days. Is it, for example, more fruitful to treat political systems as autonomous systems or as systems embedded in other aspects of society? If we want to link politics with its larger setting, what aspect of that setting should we stress? Does social stratification really have the explanatory power Apter claims for it, so that we can safely dispense with the examination of other elements of setting? Or are the most significant links to be made with levels of economic development (as Lipset suggests), culture (as Beer implies), or personality (as political psychologists like Lasswell appear to argue)? Even more important for the way we break down and classify our data—and indeed also for our methods—what *is* a political system? What really is our subject matter? Is it "states"—governmental units possessing sovereignty—as the most venerable view in political science has it—or is it any power relationship (Catlin), any influence relationship (Lasswell), any system that allocates social values? And if the last, are we really interested in *any* such allocation or only, as Easton maintains, in *authoritative* allocations? That is to say, does government, in the traditional sense, remain our focus, or do we act upon the recommendations of a whole host of men, from Catlin to March, and examine in the construction of a truly general and comparative political science almost any interpersonal relationship, whether conventionally thought of as political or not?

Once we have dealt with such questions, a host of others, equally basic, remain. For example, what unit of analysis should we use in political studies? Should we use impersonal units, such as "roles" (clusters of expected behavior patterns revolving about a particular function) or "interactions" (acts and the responses they engender)? Or should we use a personal unit— that is, concrete individuals? Or superpersonal units, such as groups, institutions, or organizations (taking these in the specialized senses in which they are used in modern sociology)? What "perspectives" or "orientations" should we use in analyzing these units? Should we still emphasize, as we have traditionally emphasized, the study of formal constitutional structure or apply instead group theory, structural-functional analysis, the decision-making approach, communications theory—to mention only a few of the possible analytical approaches available to us? And what sort of "theories" do we want to construct through these approaches: empirical "laws," models, causal explanations, functional analyses, equilibrium theories, developmental theories, or still other, as yet unexplored, types of theories?

These questions—about methods, concepts, definition of the field and its elements and boundaries, units of analysis, analytical approaches, and types of theories—will be recognized immediately as the most important metatheoretical and pretheoretical problems arising in any field of inquiry. ("Metatheoretical" refers to theory about theory—methodology, for example. "Pretheoretical" refers to operations that must be performed before the construction of theory proper—that is, before the formulation of testable hypotheses and their testing.) I have listed them here, not because I have any intention of answering them or resolving disputes about them, but solely because they can immediately tell us something important about the present condition of comparative politics.

In most fields of inquiry, such questions, despite their obvious importance, are either not raised at all or are raised only by the way and by men, like the members of the Vienna Circle, who have a special taste for philosophy and fundamentals—and men who are usually more influential outside their fields than in them. Why then are they raised so much in comparative politics today? After all, students of politics, as I have stated, have had many centuries to reach settled conclusions about them. What is more, preoccupation with such questions, fundamental though they are (indeed just because they are fundamental), probably hinders more than it promotes substantive research. In a way such preoccupation involves a kind of vicarious experience of research. What then can explain the apparent paradox between the venerable age of the field and the infantile questions raised in it?

The answer is both simple and important. Some historians of science tell us that, despite the myth of steady scientific progress that we have inherited from the Enlightenment, the advance of science has not really been steady. Instead, it has been punctuated by revolutionary intervals in which the whole framework of scientific knowledge—all its basic, usually unspoken, assumptions—has come under heated debate: assumptions about the proper purpose of inquiry, about the nature of its subject matter, about what constitutes satisfactory scientific knowledge. Science always functions within a framework of such preconceptions, but the preconceptions are never opened to examination when a consensus on them exists; men do not argue questions upon which they are agreed. In such cases of consensus one may indeed get the impression of a steady unfolding of a shared perspective upon scientific work. When consensus breaks down, however—when a field is marked by dissent or is in transition from one framework of inquiry to another—the fundamentals always come to the forefront; the silent major premises cease to be silent. In such periods, if the breakdown of scientific consensus is broad enough, intensive philosophical exploration of a general sort occurs. If the breakdown is restricted to a narrow field, its practitioners will engage in metatheoretical and pretheoretical labors that, to others, may seem exotic and unrewarding, if not irrelevant to actual scientific work.

From this we can infer what is perhaps most basic about comparative politics today: that it is a field acutely in dissent because it is in transition from one style of analysis to another. For just this reason, it is a field in which many different styles of analysis are at present to be found. Because this is the case, we cannot give any simple account of comparative politics. Instead, to portray the character of the field today we must do three things: provide an historical account of its development, explain how it reached its present state of dissension, and expound the principal discontents and aspirations of its contemporary practitioners.

THE ORIGINS OF COMPARATIVE POLITICS

Periodization is always hazardous. Nevertheless, we can locate the beginnings of the modern study of comparative politics with fair precision at that point in time when political systems came to be conceived not as natural bodies ("corporations") but as artifacts, created by people and therefore subject to re-creation (reform) by people. In short, its earliest source, leaving the classics aside, is Renaissance political thought, most obviously that of Machiavelli; and it comes to its first full fruition in the Enlightenment, above all in the writings of Montesquieu.

Machiavelli and the Renaissance

When Burckhardt says that in the Renaissance the state came to be regarded as "a work of art," he does not mean that it was looked upon as something aesthetically pleasing; nor does he mean that political actions were considered to be self-justifying, like artistic creations, rather than subject, like works of morality, to ethical codes; and he certainly does not mean that politics was not regarded as a proper subject for scientific analysis. He means precisely what he says—that the state had come to be regarded as an artifact, something that was made rather than something that simply was; for just that reason, it came to be looked upon in the Renaissance and Enlightenment as a proper subject *in itself* for "reflection and calculation."

We can, of course, reflect on the behavior of natural objects that are only imperfectly subject to human control or not subject to it at all; the natural sciences do almost nothing else. But the more *unalterably* given we regard phenomena to be (that is, the less susceptible to human engineering), the more likely we are to be intellectually passive in regard to them, to dismiss "scientific" inquiry as futile or as an esoteric taste, or to subsume study of the phenomena to the larger contemplation of "being as such"—to metaphysics, ontology, or theology. It is no accident, therefore, that the study of politics through the broad-scale examination of political experience comes to the forefront just when we begin to talk about an "art" of governing and of "statecraft." From this standpoint we can also understand why comparative inquiries, conducted to establish generalizations about political behavior and not merely to illustrate them, came first to be carried on when natural law doctrines were on the wane. If one really believes in a natural law that rigidly governs all human relations, then one is likely either to look for it through abstract speculation upon first principles or, even more likely, through very narrow studies of experience, since any limited range of experience—a single government, for example—will then illuminate as much as very broad ranges of experience—and the analysis of very broad ranges of experience is the hallmark of genuinely comparative studies. The point of view most hospitable to such studies is one that sees social life as governed by necessary relations, knowledge of which can be used in controlling, at least to some extent, human affairs.

In the Renaissance this point of view emerged, although art was emphasized far more than nature, and this emphasis is important. If one studies a subject primarily because one believes in the necessity of human engineering in the area it comprehends, inquiry into it is bound to be of a particular kind. Inevitably it will focus upon the discovery of techniques through which such engineering can be effectively carried out: upon *Staatskunst*, not *Staatswissenschaft*. Machiavelli himself is the primary example. What makes a ruler successful? How can power be won, maintained, expanded? What arrangements and practices make a state powerful, stable, free, prosperous? These are the quintessential problems of the political technician, and they are precisely the problems that preoccupied Machiavelli.

Moreover, if one's purpose is to discover directly techniques of statecraft—if, that is, one proceeds from the very beginning with what we now call "policy-oriented" studies—the methods one uses are also likely to be of a certain kind. In all probability they will be "empirical" in the most literal sense of the term; that is, they will involve the examination of experience as if it were a record of trial and error, of a kind of thoughtless experimentation, in which some procedures are revealed to be conducive and others not conducive to certain ends.[1] If anything further is done with such "rules of prudence," it will be to infer generalizations about psychological propensities underlying the rules and to deduce further rules of prudence, not revealed directly by experience, from the psychological propensities. Crude inductions, crude inferences from the inductions, and crude deductions from the inferences will always characterize such direct inquiries into statecraft. Certainly they characterize Machiavelli's. *The Prince* and *Discourses* teem with examples.

Consider only one, by no means the most blatant—the argument against using mercenary soldiers (Chapter XII of *The Prince*). No Prince who relies upon an armed force of mercenaries, says Machiavelli, can ever "stand firm or sure"; such troops are "disunited, ambitious, without discipline, faithless, bold amongst friends, cowardly amongst enemies, they have no fear of God, and keep no faith with men." Why so? Because it is not a man's nature to die for another purely for the sake of a wage; because the more competent a mercenary leader, the more, having no deep bond of loyalty to a Prince, he is likely to aspire to the Prince's place or otherwise to overstep his powers. And what is the evidence for these assertions? The helplessness of the Italian cities before King Charles of France, the oppression of the Carthaginians by their mercenaries, the fickleness of Francesco Sforza toward the Milanese, and the successes, in contradistinction, of Rome, Sparta, and the Swiss. But what about the Venetians and Florentines, who seemed to do well enough with mercenary forces? No matter, for they were "favored by chance": the ambitions of their mercenary captains were diverted elsewhere, and these captains *would* have caused more harm if they had been *more* competent. And so it goes, in nearly every chapter.

Montesquieu and the Enlightenment

In the Enlightenment, such simple and disingenuous inductions, aiming at the discovery of political rules of prudence, still abound, along with deductive theories of the state influenced by Cartesian philosophy. In some writers of the Enlightenment, however, above all in Montesquieu, we can detect more modern and more sophisticated concerns, if not in method, then certainly in the problems raised and theories proposed. In many ways, *The Spirit of the Laws* is, in fact, a work astonishingly "modern."

To be sure, Montesquieu is interested, like Machiavelli, in using induction primarily for purposes of statecraft. What, after all, is his famous theory of the institutional conditions of freedom if not a rule of prudence based upon very limited and crude induction? But perhaps it would be more accurate to say that Montesquieu was interested not so much in statecraft, as Machiavelli would have understood the term, as in constitutional engineering—not in how rulers should behave but in how governments should be constituted. Unlike Machiavelli, whose argument proceeds from human nature, Montesquieu thought of right government primarily as a matter of sociology and ecology, of adjusting governmental structure to prevailing conditions. Hence, his interest in some very modern concerns: the relations of political systems to their physical environments, the role in politics of economic factors and of "manners and morals," problems of classifying political systems, and the like.

Any methodical arrangement of *The Spirit of the Laws* immediately gives it a contemporary ring, granted that such an arrangement must be largely imposed by others upon a study for which chaotic is a term of flattery. Take, as an example, the now widely followed scheme by G. Lanson. Montesquieu, according to this scheme, first considers the various types of government: their nature, their structural principles, and the conditions under which they arise and under which they tend to persist or decline (have "viability" or not, as we would say). He goes on to consider the functions of government, including provisions for the safety of the state (civil-military relations), the liberty of the subject, and the raising and expenditure of public monies ("resource allocation," in modern jargon). Then there follows a long series of chapters dealing with those aspects of their "setting" that condition political systems: ecological conditioning factors, such as climate, soil, and population; social institutions, such as the "relations between the sexes"; matters of culture (the "general spirit, the morals and customs of a nation," and religion); and economic conditioning factors (the "interrelation between commerce, morals, poverty, and the types of government"). Finally, there are some very scattered, but suggestive, hints at "developmental theory," at social dynamics no less than social statics.

Anyone au courant with modern comparative politics will recognize these topics as a large proportion of its stock in trade. And it is not only the topics that ring familiar, but also the way they are handled. Montesquieu's types of government, for example, are ideal types and quite consciously so in that they are logical structures based upon certain fundamental principles underlying the type, to which actual political systems only more or less correspond. Like modern sociologists, he thought of societies as being interconnected, as patterned structures, as "systems" the parts of which are interdependent in such a way that change in any one part leads to compensating changes in the others or to disintegration of the whole. Therefore, he produced an essentially mechanistic interpretation of social change, in distinction both to the voluntaristic theories prevalent in his time and the eschatological theories of history soon to be propounded. He has been called (by Meinecke, for example) one of the founders of "historicism," but this view is tenable only if we equate historicism with any theory of social change that assigns a role to involuntary social processes or if we use the term to denote any use of the "genetic" approach in social studies and not if we use it to describe grandiose theories of the meaning and goal of history. Montesquieu's modernity lay precisely in the fact that he worked at a nonvoluntaristic theory of social change without going over to the historicist extreme.

Was Montesquieu an aberration, a stranger to his own age? So it is often argued, but surely not correctly, for it is as plausible to regard him as the culmination of past trends of thought as to regard him as the precursor of writers still to come—not to mention other writers of his own time (such as Adam Smith, Hume, and Ferguson). Methodologically, a clear line runs to him from Descartes and through Malebranche. Montesquieu was certainly not the very crude empiricist that Machiavelli was,[2] but he understood what it means to assert the existence of "social laws" (as Machiavelli, with his constant harping on chance and fortune, never did). He understood that these laws are to be found by a combination of logic and observation, that proper induction requires the wide-ranging observation of many contexts, and that logic has at least an equal, if not prior, role to play in scientific analysis.

While Montesquieu's method originated in Descartes, his problems, in contrast, were posed largely by Machiavelli and Bodin. His approach to developmental theory may be quite original, but he wrote at a time when social mechanism was very much in the air and sophisticated historiography at least beginning, however little the latter was influenced by the former. His concern with the relations between governments and their settings, especially his concern with physical environment, was anticipated in a large number of "modern" thinkers, including Bodin and Chardin. And his far-ranging empirical work was certainly connected with the very broad outlook of his age: its belief in the uniformity of men beneath their cultural differences and its relative freedom from the nationalistic and provincial biases that predisposed subsequent thinkers to regard political systems as unique and incomparable.

In Montesquieu, then, and in the writings of lesser men of the Enlightenment, we can see emerging a comparative science of politics not so very different from that which present political scientists seem to want: a "science" aiming at the construction of a structural-functional analysis of political systems, a sophisticated typology of such systems, a set of broad generalizations about the links between polity, society, economy, and environment, and a set of mechanistic theories of political dynamics—all in embryo, of course, but, in many cases, in surprisingly sophisticated form. Between the late eighteenth century and the present, however, a number of forces intervened that sidetracked political studies from these paths, so that we can regard the intervening development of comparative political studies as an elaborate veering away from and return to the lines of analysis sketched, however embryonically, by Montesquieu.

HISTORICISM

Although Montesquieu's ideas had many antecedents, they undoubtedly were aberrations in the sense that very different ideas set the tone in social thought immediately after his time.[3] Not sociological historiography but rampant historicism—universal history, speculations on the first causes and final end of history—became the dominant style of social thought. This style (the style of Bossuet, Vico, and Condorcet rather than Montesquieu) affected the study of all social phenomena. In the study of political institutions interest now came to be centered primarily upon historical first principles, upon the "cunning of history," upon the construction of audacious developmental theories, unilinear in form, based on single determining principles and more often than not predicting the imminent universality of democracy—theories of change more organic than mechanistic in form. The best examples are obvious and familiar: Condorcet, with his belief in the simultaneous unfolding of reason and democracy; Hegel, with his belief in the unfolding of Reason and Freedom; Comte, with his belief in the unfolding of the scientific spirit (and, in contrast to the prophets of democracy, his prediction of the coming benevolent dictatorship of well-informed bankers); Marx, with his belief in the unfolding of utopia through class conflict.

Although historicism has long since become discredited, the field of comparative politics owes a great deal to this phase in Western social thought. In the first place, many of its concepts are still used and used fruitfully ("class," for example). Many of its problems are still raised, above all problems about the relations between politics and economic development, politics and education, politics and the "cultures" of societies. Historicist theories also directed attention, to some extent at least, to a broad panorama of political experience. Hegel, for example (among many possible examples), was anything but a parochial thinker; his ideas ranged widely, if not very accurately, over China, India, Persia, Judaea, Byzantium, and the Mohammedan world, as well as over ancient and medieval Western history. The historicists were also responsible for much of the subsequent interest in social dynamics—especially in evolutionary theory, which helped, much more than did the less fanciful Montesquieu, to counterbalance the voluntaristic biases of political historians. Most of all, interest in broadscale theory as such derives, in large part at least, from historicism.

But if the historicists bequeathed to subsequent students of comparative politics much to aim at and much to imitate, they also gave them much to overcome. Their broad-scale theorizing was mainly a matter of abstract and formal speculation upon the broadest conceivable questions; for the canons of accurate observation—for "content," in Hegel's terminology—they had a monumental disregard. Their data, in almost every case, were invoked merely to illustrate, not to test, their theories, so that one searches in vain in their works for a methodologically valid bridge between theory and data. In effect, their work engendered two interests that never really meshed: an interest in the construction of the most ambitious and contentless kinds of theories, on the one hand, and an interest in detailed and formless political history, a sort of political ethnography, on the other. They did not, however, engender (if anything, they discouraged) the sort of concerns that every young discipline ought to concentrate upon: the formulation and meticulous empirical testing of "middle-range" hypotheses and the tentative conceptual exploration of a field. The basic charge against the historicists is, consequently, that while they induced an interest in theorizing about wide ranges of data (the essence of any comparative study), both their theories and uses of data, and above all the way they related theory and data, ultimately proved sterile. They tried too early to do too much and so, in the end, contributed very little—except some interesting problems and theoretical approaches, and some very far-ranging misinformation.

Perhaps this explains why the historicists, in the final analysis, had a far greater influence upon politics (through the ideological impact of their theories) than upon political science. Concepts they used continued to be used; questions they raised continued to be raised; but the whole style of the historicists, their basic approach to social analysis, constituted only a swiftly passing phase in the development of social thought—granted the occasional appearance of throwbacks to the historicist era. A large number of forces converged in the later nineteenth century to discredit historicism: in the realm of philosophy, the rise of positivism and philosophical pluralism; in politics, the rise of nationalism; in social thought, the impact of cultural relativism; in the general climate of opinion, the reaction against the softer idealisms, the tough-mindedness and perhaps petty-mindedness that followed the great disillusion of 1848. All these conspired against theories inadequately grounded upon observation, blandly optimistic, and assuming a uniformity of development for every society and nation, so that in the end historicism came to be important not so much for the positive influence it exercised as for the reactions to which it led. Certainly this is the case if we confine ourselves to the history of the comparative study of politics.

REACTIONS AGAINST HISTORICISM

In the study of politics, the reaction against historicism took many different forms, each undoubtedly for good reasons, but each involving also a serious retrogression from the promising lines reached in the eighteenth century. Not Condorcet and his kind only, but Montesquieu and his kind as well, were rejected in the process.

Abstract Theory

One of the reactions against historicism was emphasis upon purely abstract political analysis, especially criticisms and defenses of democracy on the basis of deductions from metaphysical, ontological, psychological, and legal premises. This reaction has only a remote, though nonetheless significant, bearing on the study of comparative politics. Its relevance is, in gist, that in the post-historicist period, institutional and philosophical political studies, studies with "content" and studies with "form," became more rigidly separated than at any previous time in the history of political thought, a fact with the most momentous significance for the development of comparative political studies. Historicist thought, whatever its shortcomings, had at least one virtue: it joined, however unsatisfactorily, thought and data. The historicists did think about something, not just about thought. Even Hegel, who believed in the autonomy of formal thought from its content, at least undertook to fill the form with concrete matter in order to portray, if not to test, his formal theories. Those who reacted against historicism, however, did not initially attempt to improve upon what had been at best an uneasy marriage of fact and speculation. They resorted instead to outright divorce, so that in the wake of historicism (in the late nineteenth and early twentieth centuries, roughly) political thought tended to become, so to speak, increasingly subjective and the study of political objects increasingly thoughtless.

The contemporary study of politics as a separate field, and of comparative politics as a separate subdivision of the field, begins, unhappily, perhaps disastrously, at this very point in time. That fact tells us a great deal about one of the more remarkable, if not absurd, characteristics of the political science curriculum: the division of the field into the study of political thought and the study of political institutions and behavior. More to the point here, however, is that it tells us a great deal also about the development of comparative political studies in the post-historicist period.

Formal-Legal Studies

The separation of thought and data is at least partly responsible for a second reaction to historicism that does have a direct bearing upon comparative politics: the increasingly exclusive stress in the study of political actualities on formal political institutions—that is to say, on constitutional and legal structure (then called "public law"). Not all data lend themselves equally well to thoughtless treatment. Those that do so well are unequivocal data, easy to come by and subject to a minimum of interpretation; those that do so best are data that come to us, not in the usual way, inchoate and unordered, but in some already ordered form. And what data in political science present themselves in such a fashion—preprocessed, so to speak? Obviously two sorts: one, political thought itself; the other, formal institutional arrangements, prescribed in documents that are, in fact, mental constructs (and often bad hypotheses), but that can be treated as if they were raw data of political experience, for the political scientist does not invent them, but comes upon them, as he comes upon behavioral data of quite different sorts.

The emphasis in the study of politics upon formal-legal arrangements is thus a natural outgrowth of the positivistic reaction to historicism, simply because primitive positivism, in attempting to restrict the role of thought, naturally leads the analyst to steer clear of the more inchoate data. Primitive, unadulterated positivism insists upon *hard* facts, indubitable and incontrovertible facts, as well as facts that speak for themselves—and what facts of politics are harder, as well as more self-explanatory, than the facts found in formal legal codes? And what other facts are equally conducive to *Wertfreiheit* in analysis, to what purports to be hardheaded, ethically neutral empiricism? Perhaps this argument may seem strange today. Most of the self-labeled positivists in contemporary political science are concerned with precisely the sort of inchoate materials that their predecessors ignored: voting behavior materials, power and influence relations, elite structures, informal political processes, and so on. But this does not controvert the fact that the initial impact of positivism upon the field was to direct attention toward superficial facts, even pseudofacts; nor does it deny that the positivistic outlook as such creates, even today, a preference for the superficial over the profound.

The emphasis upon formal-legal structure that came to be the dominant empirical style of political studies in the late nineteenth century was not, however, due to the post-historicist dissociation of thought and data alone, although that dissociation alone may sufficiently explain it. One other factor that certainly made for emphasis upon formal-legal structure, especially upon constitutional documents, is simply that the nineteenth century was a great age of constitution making. In fact, one would be hard-pressed to find "constitutions," in the sense of elaborate formal-legal codes rationally devised to create political organizations and govern political processes, in a previous period.

If we go to earlier periods, we find constitutions in the Burkean and typically British sense of the term (constitutions as historical accretions of institutions and processes that can be stated in, but are not defined by, formal rules); we find one or two prophetic documents, like the *Instrument of Government,* as quaint in their own time as they are common later; and we find charters—bills and documents called "constitutions"—that are not constitutions in the modern sense at all, but either contractual agreements between princes and subjects (such as municipalities and social groups) or solemn and explicit declarations of historically evolved political relations. This discovery is hardly surprising, for the very idea of a constitution in the modern sense could not have occurred to anyone who regarded the political order as a "natural" thing and is, therefore, properly a product of a time when mechanistic social beliefs, coupled with faith in the powers of human engineering, displaced earlier organicist and historicist ideas. Of course, these beliefs alone were not enough to make political studies focus upon constitutional documents; the documents themselves had to be there to study—as indeed they were, in constantly growing numbers, in the late nineteenth century. But the prevalent mechanistic outlook and faith in social engineering of the period explain at least why constitutional codes were taken so seriously, by politicians and students of politics alike.

Inevitably, these beliefs and interests also left a deep mark on the virgin field of "political science." Indeed, the very fact that political science emerged in this period as a separate, autonomous field of study divorced from philosophy, political economy, and even sociology, may have created a tendency to emphasize the study of formal-legal arrangements, quite apart from any other factors moving the field in this direction. If a study becomes departmentally *sui generis,* it will try also to assume a subject matter and techniques of study that are *sui generis.* And what subject matter can be regarded as purely political? Political behavior, in the larger sense in which we now regard it, is touched upon by the subject matters of all sorts of other disciplines: those of sociology, social and individual psychology, cultural anthropology, and economics. If there is any subject matter at all that political scientists can claim exclusively for their own, a subject matter that does not require acquisition of the analytical tools of sister-fields and that sustains their claim to autonomous existence, it is, of course, formal-legal political structure. Its study, therefore, quite naturally became the focal point of the new discipline of political science in search of a *raison d'être*.

Perhaps we ought to add to this list of factors making for emphasis on formal-legal studies (it is an emphasis that requires a lot of explaining) still one other: the emphasis in the teaching of politics at this time upon "training"—training for citizenship and for public administration and preliminary training for the law. This emphasis was particularly great in the "new" states of Europe, above all in the newly unified Germany. Sigmund Neumann has pointed out that in the Bismarckian era, the German universities, once the centers of the fight for freedom, were "gradually transformed into guardians of training for leadership in important public offices, the judiciary, the bureaucracy, and the teaching profession." The "value-free" sociology of Weber and others is regarded by Neumann as one illustration of these tendencies; the emphasis on studies in formal public law may be considered another. To what were they due? Neumann attributes them to the regime's authoritarianism and German admiration for the Iron Chancellor's successes; but we can just as plausibly regard them as responses to the new state's need to socialize men into new political patterns: to inculcate in them civic loyalty and educate them to play roles in new administrative and legal arrangements. Perhaps this is an even more plausible interpretation than Neumann's, particularly when we take into account the emphatic interest in formal-legal codes in the United States. No authoritarianism, no admiration for successful *Realpolitik,* existed here to dampen the impulse to moral criticism in politics or the drive to uncover the deeper forces determining political actualities.

It is true, of course, that the German universities were extremely influential in America around the turn of the century, but the United States had also in common with Germany a tremendous problem in political socialization, due in one case to the creation of a new political system and in the other to mass immigration. In both cases, the agencies most readily available for dealing with these functional needs were educational institutions, especially institutions of secondary and higher education. Hence, there was a mushroom growth of civics courses providing indoctrination into citizenship and of courses preparing for participation, in one role or another, in the political structure—above all, courses in public administration, constitutional development, and public law. Courses in political "behavior," as we now use that term, could hardly have performed the same necessary function in either system—might indeed have been dysfunctional in both settings. And it *is* a fact that formal-legal studies were mainly German and American in origin, epitomized in the German case by the truly gargantuan collection of monographs appearing from 1883 on, the *Handbuch des Oeffentlichen Rechts der Gegenwart* (Handbook of Contemporary Public Law), and in the American case by a study of Woodrow Wilson's, based largely upon the *Handbuch,* which will be discussed presently.[4]

Configuration Studies

A third reaction against historicism in political studies involved a drift away from comparative studies of all sorts and toward "configurative" analysis—the analysis of particular political systems, treated either explicitly or implicitly as unique entities. Many political studies of the immediate post-historicist period exhibit a considerable narrowing of the analytical attention, a tendency to cover very little ground, and to cover it in great, often indiscriminate detail. This tendency not only restricted attention to one set of political data—formal-legal structure—but also was restricting in a geographic and historical sense. To some extent this narrowing of analysis in time and space may have been the result of the very emphasis on formal-legal structure, for such an emphasis necessarily makes one work within the compass of particular constitutional systems and is, for reasons already mentioned, appropriate only to a limited period in European history. We can see this narrowing influence of the formal-legal approach reflected even in some of the wider-ranging political studies of the post-historicist period, particularly in the large number of compilations of constitutional provisions then published and taken very seriously. But configurative analysis was also an outcome of some of the factors that produced the emphasis on formal-legal studies itself: the reaction against broad speculative theories of any sort; the influence of nationalism and its roots in the idea of national character, which logically implies that each nation is an analytically unique entity; the emphasis on citizenship training and vocational training in an age of rapidly expanding national bureaucracies.

This is not to say that only narrow political studies, confined to particular nation-states, were produced in this period.[5] There was no dearth of studies ranging over very wide territory indeed, but it is characteristic of these studies that their theoretical import should be almost inversely proportional to the range of material included. Generally speaking, they presented a wide panorama of political materials with a theoretical equipment restricted to little more than Aristotle's classifications of governments and to abstract speculations on abstract questions and with the materials arranged either in terms of the three basic forms of government, in chronological order, or in a combination of chronology and forms of government.

An example of this sort of political study—probably the most famous—is Wilhelm Roscher's *Politik,* written intermittently between 1847 and 1892, but chiefly in the last few years of this time span. The revealing subtitle, *Geschichtliche Naturlehre der Monarchie, Aristokratie und Demokratie* (Natural History of Monarchy, Aristocracy and Democracy), gives the whole work away. Its principal theoretical concern is with the proper classification of states, a question Roscher settled by adding a fourth category, Caesarism, to the three classical categories and by distinguishing among plutocratic, proletarian, and middle-class states (still well within the Aristotelian framework). The study is based upon an explicit rejection of the "idealistic" studies of the times—that is, purely abstract treatments like that of Fichte, who, in Roscher's own words, "conceived political science to have only the business of depicting a best state, so that reality appeared to him as real only in so far as it corresponded to the image of this best state." Roscher, on the contrary, sets out to do precisely what the idealists most disdained, namely, to present a *Naturlehre,* a set of "naturalistic descriptions" of the *Notstaaten* so despised by the theorists of the *Idealstaaten.* And this he does very largely, though not exclusively, in the manner of historical narrative within each of the classificatory categories he adopts.

The result is a work displaying, even by Germanic standards, a truly massive learning. Switzerland, Athens, Rome, Gaul—Egypt, Normandy, Sparta, Venice—Spanish America, Tudor England, the Hebrew State—Brahmanism, Buddhism, Jesuitism, Protestantism—Demosthenes, Henry VIII, Hannibal, Napoleon—the book is almost a political encyclopedia. In this it is reminiscent of nothing so much as the more extravagant historicist theories; but the history it presents is history without the "ism," a matter of content with very little form, a pointless display of interminable exactitudes. It is in such works that we see the real impact of the divorce of thought and data on the field of comparative politics, just at the time when its practitioners became conscious of having a separate disciplinary identity.

TWO SYNTHESES

Political ethnography, purely abstract speculations, formal-legal studies, and configuration studies—these are all different, even antithetical, reactions against historicism. But because they come from a single source, one should not be surprised to see them combined, however uneasily and in however ill-fitting a manner, in the large syntheses of political thought of the period. These "large syntheses" are not necessarily works of great merit. More often than not, in fact, such works are written by secondary figures, by those who ape the styles of the times rather than those who create them; but they do provide a very broad picture of the dominant fashions in analysis. Any number of such studies could be used to exemplify the immediate post-historicist period in comparative politics, but two may suffice here: one, published in 1878 by Theodore D. Woolsey, a former president of Yale, entitled rather grandiosely *Political Science, or the State Theoretically and Practically Considered;* the other, by his later Princeton counterpart, Woodrow Wilson, a work with the even more prolix title, *The State: Elements of Historical and Practical Politics: A Sketch of Institutional History and Administration* (1895).

Both Woolsey's and Wilson's subtitles, like Roscher's, tell us, in the typically ingenuous fashion of the late nineteenth century, the most basic things we need to know about their studies. Each portrays mainly two of the anti-historicist styles we have discussed, though in each may be found examples also of the others.

Woolsey's work, an ambitious and pretentious undertaking indeed, is in effect a combination of purely abstract speculations and purely concrete political ethnography. When Woolsey talks about the state "theoretically considered," he refers primarily to two of the three categories into which German writers on politics had by then come to divide political studies: *Naturrecht* (natural rights—sometimes *Staatsrecht,* public rights) and *Staatslehre* (theory of the state). The first of these, *Naturrecht* (Woolsey calls it the "Doctrine of Rights as the Formulation of a Just State") is, of course, concerned with normative theories of political freedom and obligation. This part of the study bears no relation to anything subsequently said in it, but it is justified in Woolsey's own mind on the ground that no state worthy of the name is unjust, that justice in the state mainly consists of the safeguarding of natural rights, and that, therefore, there is no point in discussing the state without discussing the theory of natural rights—a curious syllogism, to say the least, but one that does encompass in a flimsy way the bifurcation of theory and data that confronted Woolsey.

To this concern with natural rights is added a series of concerns that Woolsey himself identifies as *Staatslehre,* a veritable rag bag of ethical and nonethical questions: "Opinions on the Nature of the State and on Its Origins," "Theories of Sovereignty," "The Proper Ends and Sphere of the State," "The Organization of States" (whether the desire for it is instinctive or habitual, the need for a "constitution," the various departments of government, distinctions between representative and nonrepresentative systems), "Theories of Communism and Socialism," "Limits and Extent of the Punitive Power of the State," and sundry normative questions ("Can the Citizen's or Subject's Connection with the State Terminate?" "What Are the Limits of Loyalty and Obedience?" "What of Conflicts between Law and Conscience?").

All these problems, normative or not, are mainly discussed abstractly in the light of the abstract speculations of other political theorists. Politics "practically considered," however, turns out to be what the late nineteenth-century Germans understood by *Politik:* the large-scale historical examination of political institutions from earliest to modern times, mainly in terms of the classical categories; the formal examination of the "departments" and "institutions" of central and local government; and, at the very end, a few afterthoughts (one or two quite reminiscent of Montesquieu, whom Woolsey had obviously read but not really understood) on the influences of "Physical Causes on Politics," on "National Character," and on the "Causes of Political Change and Revolutions." In short, the whole book, save only for the very end, is either unmitigatedly abstract or pointlessly concrete, and the quotation cited from it on the relations of the study of rights and the state, which introduces the work, is a good indication of the way Woolsey relates theory to data throughout.

Woodrow Wilson's *The State* is admittedly his minor piece—though anything but a modest one, going on as it does through 1,287 sections, large and small. From our standpoint, however, it is much more worth examining than his more distinguished work, for two reasons: one, that it purports to be a text on politics of unprecedented scope, a summation of the empirical knowledge of the state in his time; the other, that it begins with large claims for comparative politics as the only proper approach to understanding political experience.

What is "comparative" politics to Wilson? Essentially, it signifies to him, as to Woolsey, a very detailed and far-ranging political ethnography primarily as historical narrative and secondarily through the depiction of contemporary formal-legal structure. About five-sixths of the work is devoted to such bald descriptions. Wilson begins the study with some questions about the probable origins of government—a fact whose significance we shall see later, but this subject, after a cursory consideration of evolutionary and early anthropological theories, soon takes him to the more congenial ground of classical history, where his political ethnography proper begins. The political institutions, first of Greece and Rome, then of "Teutonic Polity" in the Middle Ages, and then of German and French feudalism and monarchy are painstakingly examined; the chapters on them constitute the "institutional history" section of the work. The "practical politics" side of the study involves mainly an indiscriminate detailing of the formal-legal structures of French, German, Swiss, Austro-Hungarian, Swedish-Norwegian, British, and American governments. And all this, counting some historical discussions scattered throughout, takes up nearly a thousand sections.

Not until section 1,121 is any attempt made to draw any "comparative" conclusions. And what are these conclusions? Their modesty is perhaps as remarkable as the ostentatiousness of the data on which they are based. Essentially, Wilson distills from his materials three inferences: political change has taken the form of a very slow process of development from more primitive to more highly developed political organizations; modern political experience confirms the Aristotelian classifications, although modern monarchies, aristocracies, and democracies have some features not found in the ancient world; governments are all pretty much alike—denying the view of those (Wilson claims the great majority) who believe in the uniqueness of political systems—but there are differences between governments, due partly to unique historical backgrounds and partly to "nation-marks," an argument that immediately reinstates the belief in uniqueness, albeit in a milder form. Finally, in a sort of epilogue, Wilson considers some purely abstract questions in primarily an abstract way: sovereignty, the nature of law, the classification of the functions of government, political rights, whether society is greater than government, and so on. That is the total extent of Wilson's *summa*—for a *summa* in a way it is, a summation of all the dominant modes of political thought of his time.

POLITICAL EVOLUTIONISM

Undoubtedly this is an incomplete account of post-historicist studies in comparative politics. It has dealt only with dominant themes in American and German political studies. As a result, it necessarily is less than just to those writers who were, as some writers always are, out of tune with the dominant trends, who lagged behind the times or marched ahead of them. For example, Bluntschli, in his monumental (and much neglected) *Theory of the State*, begins with an explicit rejection of two "false methods," "abstract ideology" and "mere empiricism," and a special plea for methods of "concrete thinking," and lives up to this position at least to some extent (though Bentley denies it). We can no doubt find other important writers equally at odds with the tenor of the times. This is especially the case in regard to a school of writers who, more than any others, kept comparative politics alive throughout this largely anticomparative period, writers whose works have very wide scope, who combine theory and data almost on the scale of the historicists, and who are alluded to in almost every work on politics of the period, even the narrowest, most abstract, and most formal-legal—the political evolutionists.

Evolutionary studies might of course be considered a particular kind of historicism, and in some forms they do come close to what is nowadays (after Popper) generally meant by that term. Those evolutionary studies that posit some inevitable goal (such as democracy or perfect freedom) for the evolutionary process and a basic evolutionary principle (such as survival of the fittest, economic growth, progressive economic differentiation) as, so to speak, the "spirit" of the process are almost indistinguishable from historicist theories. Most evolutionists rejected, however, the too audacious, often ill-informed, theories of the historicists no less than did the pure philosophers, the formal-legalists, and the political ethnographers, although they rejected them in different ways and for different reasons.

Evolutionary theories about politics involved, in the first place, an empirical reaction against historicism in that the evolutionists paid meticulous attention to data that the historicists had on the whole treated only in the vaguest generalities—particularly primitive, early Western, and non-Western political systems. Evolutionism involved also a theoretical reaction against historicism. Instead of attempting to write universal history, including the future no less than the past, they concentrated upon much more limited problems—particularly the problem of the origin of the modern territorial state. As a general rule, they tried merely to find the processes and laws underlying the development of complex political systems. This is in every sense a more limited concern than that which motivated Condorcet or Hegel. At their best, evolutionary studies combined the respect for data of the ethnographers with the modesty in speculation of contemporary middle-range theorists. Granted that some of the theories the evolutionists produced look very peculiar nowadays—that is less the result of any dubious procedures on their part than of the fact that they proceeded from theoretical presuppositions and asked theoretical questions that have simply gone out of fashion.

Evolutionary Theories

What sort of theories did the evolutionists produce? Essentially two kinds: theories of sequence—the stages of political development—and theories of the moving forces behind the evolutionary sequences. The most common theory of sequence traced the origin of the modern state to a continuous process of social enlargement and complication beginning with the primordial family. Among many works arguing this point of view probably the most illustrious are Sir Henry Maine's *Ancient Law* (1861) and *Early History of Institutions* (1874), in which political life is depicted as beginning with the patriarchal family and proceeding through two intermediate units, the house and the tribe, before the territorially contiguous form of the state is reached. This argument is based on a meticulous examination of Hebrew, Greek, Roman, and Hindu history.

The principal alternative to this interpretation is one that traces the origin of the state not to the family but rather to the disintegration of primitive social forms—not to the growing size and complexity of social units but to the opposite, the gradual individuation of human beings, their extrication from collectivities in which individuality itself is absorbed into the larger unit. So, for example, Edward Jenks argued, in *A Short History of Politics* and *The State and the Nation,* both published toward the end of the period under consideration (1900 and 1919), that the proper sequence for the emergence of the territorial state is not Maine's, but rather from hunting pack to tribe, from tribe to clan, from clan to family, and from there to nonkinship units, individuals, and the state. In a sense, he reverses Maine's arguments.

As to the moving forces behind these sequences, a much greater variety of theories confronts us. Some evolutionists attributed the rise of the state, particularly the transition from the patriarchal family to the more extended political groups, to religious forces. The usual theory is that of Fraser's *Golden Bough* (for a political scientist's version, see Sir John Seeley's *Introduction to Political Science*, 1896), which traces the evolution of simple patriarchal authority through gerontocrats claiming a special skill in dealing with the world of spirits and through the rule of specialized magicians to that of the priest-king. Fraser's work was based largely on studies of societies with which Maine had not dealt in detail, such as ancient Egypt and primitive societies portrayed in early anthropological studies.

Another group of theorists, especially Oppenheimer in *The State* (1914), find the propelling force leading to the state not in religion but in force, in the building-up of gradually larger units through systematic conquest. Still another theory claims that the state comes into being through the impact of social differentiation on primitive social forms, especially through the appearance of vertical stratification. This view is argued, for example, by W. C. MacLeod in two works, *The Origins of the State* (1924) and *The Origin and History of Politics* (1921), studies in which Darwin, Marx, and early anthropology are all combined in a curious mixture.

A fourth theory linked the evolution of political institutions with economic changes, not so much in the style of Marx as in that of Rousseau's *Essay on the Origins of Inequality*. An example is Oppenheimer's *The State*, which, in effect, combines the conquest theory of the state with an economic theory of its origins. Oppenheimer argues that complex forms of government are made necessary by class distinctions based on wealth and that the institution of slavery to build up a labor force is the basic foundation of the state. ("The moment when the first conqueror spared his victim in order to exploit him is of incomparable historical importance. It gave birth to nation and state.") Some writers linked the development of the state with the development of pastoral pursuits, others with the accumulation of surplus wealth, still others with the development of the idea of property or population pressures upon resources and resulting wars of conquest or, as we have seen, social differentiation of any sort.

Finally, certain writers produced "diffusion" rather than "convergence" theories of the state. These theories argue, in effect, that the factors leading to the state did not produce it in different places through force of similar circumstances, but that the state came into being only once and in only one place through "natural causes" and then gradually spread, presumably because of its organizational superiority and through a process combining conquest and borrowing, to other societies, like ripples in a pool. For example, G. E. Smith and W. J. Perry, in *The Origin and History of Politics* (1931), place the origin of the state in Egypt around the year 5000 B.C. Here the state emerged, in their view, through a convergence of religious and economic forces never duplicated elsewhere. From Egypt it spread, by quite another sort of inevitability, to the rest of the world.

The Legacy of Evolutionism

Developmental theories of this sort have gone out of style in our age of models, "system" theories, and equilibrium analyses; and so they have about them a musty and archaic flavor, an ambience of crumbling volumes in the dark recesses of libraries and of vain debates long since resolved in irreconcilable disagreements. Yet the pursuit of such theories spans a period from mid-nineteenth century to a mere generation ago, a period that overlaps on one end with historicism itself and on the other with the comparative politics of our own time. In fact, the larger syntheses of political evolutionary studies still smell of fresh ink; the best-known perhaps is Book I of MacIver's *The Modern State,* first published in 1926 and reissued last in 1955, and Part II of E. M. Sait's *Political Institutions,* published first in 1938. Sait calls his study *A Preface,* a rather melancholy fact when viewed from the perspective of our time, for it is, in fact, an epilogue and a summing-up. This useful summing-up synthesizes all the divergent tendencies of nearly a century of evolutionary thought about politics, however, as witness the following extract:[6]

> The State is composed of three elements: people, government and territory. From the beginning, groups of people are bound together by the cohesive force of kinship and religion. The family is the primordial unit, which expands into sibs (*gentes,* clans) and the tribe. Among pastoral people, patriarchal discipline prepares the way for tribal government; tribesmen who are accustomed to give unquestioning obedience to their respective family heads naturally accept the authority of the council of elders or patriarchs and of the chieftain who rises out of the council. But the emergence of government— that is, an intensified regulative system—within the kinship group must be associated with economic causes, with the adoption of pastoral pursuits and the accumulation of surplus wealth. Property introduces all sorts of complications. There are disputes within the tribe to be settled; there are raids by avaricious neighbors to be repelled. The situation calls for individual leadership. Some member of the council, more energetic and enterprising than his fellows (and for that reason more wealthy), pushes his way to the front with or without the assistance of religious superstition. He, or some one who later essays the same role, is recognized as chieftain. Since the

qualities of leadership are likely to be inherited, the office becomes attached to a particular family and is transmitted like other forms of property. Government exists. But although the pastoralists may confine their wanderings within roughly determined geographical limits, they are still nomads.

The territorial State does not appear until population begins to press upon subsistence. Then one of two courses may be followed: new land may be acquired by migration or the old land put to more productive use. Fertile pasturage, when brought under cultivation, will support a much larger population; and the tribesmen have long been familiar with the possibility of raising grain and vegetables from wild seed. Rather than leave the region to which they have become attached, they supplement the prevailing pastoral economy with the rudiments of agriculture. Gradually the herdsmen become husbandmen. The transition takes place slowly, as, by trial and error or by the imitation of some neighboring agriculturists, the methods of tillage are improved and their potentialities realized. Along with the new system of production come great social changes: above all, the sharpening of class distinctions, the systematic resort to slavery, the emphasis placed upon military life (first for defense, then for conquest), and the establishment of monarchy. With settlement upon the land and the acquisition of fixed abodes, the original kinship tie gives way, naturally but stubbornly, to the new territorial tie.

In some such way the state arose.

Because evolutionary political studies have passed out of fashion, their importance is all too easily underrated, but they constituted a tremendously important phase in the development of comparative politics. Above all, they kept comparative study itself alive in a period when it was threatened from every direction. Along with political ethnography they helped to focus attention on political systems other than those of the West just when the academic emphasis on training exerted great pressure toward restricting the political scientist's span of attention. They posed genuine theoretical problems when political scientists were concerned mainly with depicting formal-legal structures. They kept alive a systematic interest in links between political institutions and other aspects of society and kept political science in touch with other social sciences, especially sociology and cultural anthropology, when the newly won departmental autonomy of the field produced attitudes threatening to cut it off from a vast range of relevant data and many useful theories. To be sure, they led in political studies to the consideration of a very limited range of problems, especially concern with the origin of certain widespread political forms and the attempt to discover common sources for similar political institutions in different societies—the chief purpose of E. A. Freeman's celebrated *Comparative Politics*. But that was better at least than no concern at all with problems requiring large-scale comparisons.

EARLY POLITICAL SOCIOLOGY

Anyone acquainted with political thought in the late nineteenth and early twentieth centuries will realize immediately that some formidable names that might have been mentioned in connection with the state of comparative political studies in this period are still missing from the picture, even after writers like Bluntschli and the evolutionists have been discussed. I refer to a number of men who loom very large in political science (not least in comparative politics) today, but who do not readily fit into any of the categories used here to characterize the political thought of their own time—men like Mosca and Max Weber, Pareto and Michels, the most illustrious of the early modern political sociologists. All constructed large-scale theories of politics, but theories certainly not purely formal in character. With the possible exception of Michels, they all ranged over wide sweeps of data, but not in the pointlessly empirical manner of the political ethnographers. They were more interested in actual power relations than in constitutional documents, more concerned with recurrent actual patterns of authority than with the inherited formal distinctions between types of government.

They did not restrict the subject matter of their studies to the state but branched out into all sorts of other political phenomena, from the government of political parties to that of private groups, and they explored systematically the impact on politics of its setting. In doing these things, they developed novel analytical perspectives for political studies, devised new concepts, proposed empirically relevant hypotheses, and developed unconventional techniques for applying comparative methods. They engaged, in short, in just the sort of conceptual, methodological, and theoretical explorations that would seem to be the major present concerns in comparative politics.

Why then have they been omitted from the story? Simply because only the *creation* of their works belongs to the period we have been discussing. Their impact on the field of comparative politics belongs to a later time, when the concerns of its practitioners had changed in such a manner as to make them more receptive to the sociologists' ideas. But this is not to say that political scientists in general simply ignored the political sociologists. They did read them and they did teach them, but only to some extent, and only in a way: they taught them as if they had been political "philosophers" in the then familiar sense, concerned primarily with abstract and normative political theory. Without exception, the early political sociologists were represented as "critics of democracy," "irrationalists," latter-day Hobbesians, who attacked the comfortable premises of the defenders of democracy, equality, and human reason—in short, as foils to men like Locke, Mill, and T. H. Green. Anyone who becomes familiar with the work of the early political sociologists today will realize that it was a travesty of their intentions, and indeed of what they actually said, thus to represent them, even though some of them—Mosca, for example—certainly invited such treatment by drawing large normative conclusions from their sociological studies. But basically the political sociologists were treated as they were, not because of anything they did themselves, but because the categories with which they dealt seemed naturally to place them, if not outside political science altogether, then in the area of political theory rather than in the political institutions division of the field. And this is something doubly regrettable, for it means that some of the most promising modern works on comparative political institutions and behavior were long misrepresented in the "political theory" courses, to which they were only indirectly relevant, while they were ignored in the comparative politics courses, on which they had a direct and important bearing.

No wonder that students of comparative politics had to rediscover, and even to relearn, the early political sociologists for purposes of their own work. No wonder either that this rediscovery is something quite recent. In my own undergraduate days Mosca, Michels, and Pareto were still represented mainly as abstract critics of the abstract bases of democratic ideology. I remember, with some horror and some relish, the comment of a venerable teacher (not a "theorist" by any means) on an undergraduate essay about Weber's political sociology: "An interesting analysis of a brilliant but obscure"—yes, obscure—"German thinker."

Today, of course, the names of Weber, Pareto, Mosca, and Michels are among the more luminous in the study of comparative politics. But before they could become this there had to be a reaction against the older conception of comparative politics and the actual lines of analysis pursued in the field. This reaction in fact occurred in the 1920s and 1930s.

"Informal" Politics

One of its first manifestations—not confined to comparative politics, but, in fact, appearing at first mainly in studies of American politics—was a growing interest in political parties and pressure groups. This interest is important because parties and pressure groups are not, strictly speaking, parts of legal-institutional structure and because they link politics to other social phenomena more closely than does the formal-legal framework of a political system. The reasons for the growing interest in "informal" political processes throughout the 1920s and 1930s are fairly obvious. Most obvious of all is the fact that parties and pressure groups by this time played a greater role in the politics of most states than they had before. Parties, in the sense we now think of them, developed rather late in the history of representative systems, however much the term itself might have been in use in earlier times. Large-scale, bureaucratized, intensely active pressure groups, especially great economic and other "interest" groups, also belong to a relatively recent period. This fact, however, while important, is not alone enough to explain the increased interest in parties and pressure groups, for the mere fact that something exists and plays an important role in politics does not mean that it will necessarily be studied by political scientists. The analyst's attention must first be prepared by operative preconceptions to seek out the data and to recognize them as significant. What theoretical influences, then, disposed political scientists to look intensively at party and pressure group activities?

One of these influences undoubtedly was political pluralism. By rejecting the idea of sovereignty and by intruding into the Lockean dualism of individuals and the state the concept of groups either mediating between them or coequal with the state, pluralism made all sorts of phenomena appear "political." Under the influence of the monistic theory of the state these phenomena had appeared extraneous to politics. To be sure, the pluralists argued mainly a normative case: that the state was only one social organization among many and that it had no special right to impose obligations upon individuals or their collectivities, that is, no special status above the other associations of society. But this normative position inevitably influenced the way politics was conceived for all theoretical purposes. In breaking down the distinction between the political and the social, the pluralists did not remove the consideration of politics from the study of society, but, quite the contrary, they invested all things social with political significance. Under their influence, one saw politics and government, power and authority, everywhere and in all social collectivities, but first of all, of course, in those collectivities most closely bound up with the state: pressure groups and parties.

There can be little doubt that the pluralistic point of view underlies, consciously or otherwise, the work of such men as Lasswell and Catlin, the undoubted pioneers in enlarging the subject matter of political science from the state to social relations as such. "The writer," says Catlin in the Preface to his *Principles of Politics* (1930), "sees no objection to calling the science of social inter-relations by the good Aristotelian name of Politics." Shortly thereafter, Catlin acknowledges his "profound debt" to Harold Laski, who was, at one time, perhaps the most celebrated of the normative pluralists. Politics he then defines as a particular kind of activity, "not as a thing," specifically as any act of human or social control. A broad definition indeed, but no broader than that with which Lasswell begins his famous *Politics: Who Gets What, When, How* (1936): "The study of politics is the study of influence and the influential," the influential being "those who get the most of what there is to get."

The growing emphasis on parties and pressure groups can also be attributed to a second major influence on political preconceptions: certain experiences made students of politics more aware than in the past of the great difference between constitutional forms and political reality. In America, the muckrakers had led the way toward the discovery of the "anonymous empire" of lobbyists and influence-wielders, conducting a kind of private government under the public facade of the Constitution and in interplay with formal authorities. This process seemed to the leading "group theorist" of them all, Bentley, to be the total sum and substance of politics.

Perhaps the most crucial experience leading to a disenchantment with constitutional forms was the fate of the Weimar Constitution, that professionally engineered document so widely acclaimed in its time, such a dismal failure in operation, which eventuated in the most extreme of totalitarian regimes. Some political scientists managed to cling to their preconceptions in the face of the Weimar experience (and the equally sorry operation of the French Third Republic) by claiming that it was all the result of faulty constitutional engineering. Many more, however, drifted toward the view that political processes are only imperfectly subject to control by formal rules and mainly the products of social and economic forces, of the interests and attitudes of the public and politicians, military officers and public officials, capitalists and trade unionists, and the like. Certainly these experiences helped to make political scientists aware that men like Marx and Pareto, Michels and Mosca, Wallas and Lippmann, did not belong merely among the abstract, primarily normative, political theorists, but that they could help one to reach a better understanding of actual political processes than could the constitutional lawyers and writers on formal political structure.

From this growing concern with informal political processes, political competition, semipolitical groups, and actual distributions of power, there naturally followed a growing interest in the links between politics and other aspects of society. From this in turn there followed a growing interest in systematic problem solving on the middle-range level rather than in the construction of mere morphology. "Political sociology" came by degrees to be reconciled with what had passed for political science. It is clear from the literature of the period that the crisis of democracy in Europe provided the main impetus toward this reconciliation—even more than the widespread influence of Marxism, which certainly had a greater impact on political activists than political scientists in these years.

THE SYNTHESIS OF DATA

The reaction that took place in the 1920s and 1930s against the older conception of comparative politics had also another important manifestation. There appeared in this period a number of studies that attempted to synthesize the findings of configurative studies in large-scale comparative works and, in the course of this synthesis, attempted also to reunite political theory and political data. These syntheses—the most weighty are James Bryce's *Modern Democracies* (1921) and C. J. Friedrich's *Constitutional Government and Democracy* (1937)—are fundamentally different from those of Woolsey, Wilson, and their kind, particularly in two ways. They do not present theory and data simply as cohabitants under a single set of covers but chastely separated. On the contrary, they bring the data directly to bear on the theories, making the resolution of theoretical issues turn at least to some extent upon the evidence of experience rather than exclusively upon the promptings of reflection. And they do not synthesize configurative studies by presenting broad historical narratives in the manner of Wilson (narratives in which each link in the chain still appears as something quite unique in whole or in large part). Rather—and this is especially true of Friedrich—they present data in terms of general functional and structural categories, which, by implication, are elements of all political systems, or of all political systems of a particular sort. Because of this presentation, they are much more obviously "comparative" in nature than Woolsey's and Wilson's syntheses. Perhaps these two tendencies—the reconciliation of theory and data and the use of generalized categories for the analysis of political systems—are still rather primitively developed in the work of Bryce and Friedrich. Perhaps also, the theories are still too much taken from purely abstract political speculations and the generalized categories from the existing corpus of formal-legal studies. This is saying no more than that their work was affected by studies already in the field, as any scientific work must be. There is much that is old-fashioned in both Bryce and Friedrich (and, of course, much more in Bryce than in Friedrich); but there is also much that is original and portentous for the future and much that is derived from the original studies of informal political processes of their own time. Bryce and Friedrich are in effect transitional figures in comparative politics; and just for that reason it is worth looking in some detail at both what is essentially old and what is essentially new in their studies.

BRYCE'S *MODERN DEMOCRACIES*

Bryce's *Modern Democracies* is in many ways a synthesis in the grand old manner, certainly in scope and to some extent also in content. Much of it consists of old-fashioned configurative studies of a large number of "democratic" countries: ancient Athens, the republics of Latin America, France, Switzerland, Canada, the United States, Australia, and New Zealand. In these configurative studies much space is devoted, in the established manner, to formal-legal structure. But quite apart from the fact that Bryce also gives considerable space to political parties and "the action of public opinion"—subjects not at all discussed by Wilson, whose index of seventeen pages does not even list parties, and discussed only cursorily, in the main abstractly, by Woolsey, who gives them twenty-five pages out of twelve hundred—the whole conception of the work makes it into something unprecedented, in idea, if not in every aspect of the way the idea is carried out.

The configurative studies that Bryce presents are in fact intended only to provide data necessary to achieve a broader analytical purpose. And what is this purpose? Basically, it is to solve a single substantive problem that ties together the whole prolix and often incoherent work and to solve it by applying a particular procedure that to Bryce is the only proper procedure for comparative analysis. Both of these aspects of his purpose, his problem and his method, furnish evidence of the transitional character of his work.

The basic substantive objective of *Modern Democracies* is to examine the plausibility of the justifications and criticisms of democracy on *empirical* grounds, to see what light actual experience sheds upon the abstract arguments used either for democracy or against it (in his time, chiefly for it). His object, Bryce explains in the Preface, is not to develop "theories" but to state facts and "explain" them. Explaining facts is of course precisely what most of us today understand by developing "theory," but to Bryce theory means something quite different, and significantly different. It denotes what he later refers to as the "systematic" approach: purely speculative thought, unencumbered by data. Such thought, he argues, leads only to "bloodless abstractions," based, more often than not, on supposedly self-evident propositions about man and society, which inevitably give rise to empirically false or dubious conclusions.

The usual procedure in arguments about democracy is, according to Bryce, to establish first certain natural human rights; to argue from these to the logical desirability of democracy (that democracy is "government upright and wise, beneficent and stable"); to posit certain propensities in the nature of man that make it possible to argue that "democratic institutions . . . carry with them, as a sort of gift of Nature, the capacity to use them well"; and then to deduce further a great many not at all self-evident propositions about the desirability of liberty and equality, the educatability of all men, the relations of literacy and political wisdom, the rightness of public opinion, and so on. Bryce himself wants nothing to do with such abstractions, nor with any discussions of schemes of political reform "on general principles." His aim is to subject all such assertions to a single question: are they borne out by political experience and, if not, what propositions fit such experience better? The whole work, then, is intended to be an antidote to abstract theory about questions that the abstract theorists had wrongly preempted from the empiricists.

Of course, this very definition of his problem means that the abstract theorists exercised a great influence upon Bryce's study, if only in that his own theoretical problems are derived from them. This fact alone gives the work a curiously old-fashioned tone. Like the abstract political theorists, Bryce is concerned with what is right or wrong with democracy and a host of subsidiary normative problems. (Does power corrupt? Does wealth? Can the arts and sciences flourish under democracy?) Since his data are in most cases not adequate to solve such problems, there is in his work, as in the older syntheses, still a considerable gulf between speculations and data, even though the basic aim is to bring the two together.

Furthermore, just as Bryce's problems are rooted in tradition, so also, in some respects, are his methods of dealing with them. Not only does he present his data in the first instance through a large series of configurative studies, but his whole conception of the relations between facts and theory is primitive and old-fashioned. Nowadays we certainly do not believe that facts speak for themselves, that we need only know them in order to know what follows from them. We believe that facts are dumb and slippery, that they reveal their significance only when we have set all sorts of cunning traps for them—when we have gathered them in various ingenious ways and subjected them to various complicated processing devices: experiments, carefully chosen samples, multivariate analysis, and the like. But Bryce's attitude to facts is essentially that of a methodological innocent, even though, like Machiavelli, he has more than the ordinary amount of shrewd common sense.

Basically, Bryce is the crudest sort of empiricist in that he believes, implicitly at any rate, that facts are really self-explanatory, and in that he decidedly belongs to the past rather than the present. So also he echoes the past, though in a different way, in his basic conception of "comparative method." *Modern Democracies* is indeed represented as a "comparative work"; in fact, its very first chapter, after the introduction, is devoted to an explicit discussion of comparative method, something surprisingly rare in the field. But comparative method to Bryce has only a very special and limited utility; it can yield no direct knowledge of anything he wants to know but only give a more solid grounding to those first principles from which all political positions must be deduced. Comparative method is not really intended by him to be an alternative to the "systematic approach." In the last analysis, he uses comparison only as a way of arriving at basic premises for systematic analysis, a way supposedly superior to the formulation of "self-evident" propositions. While, therefore, the basis of Bryce's arguments is certainly empirical, or meant to be empirical, the arguments themselves, once we leave his country studies behind, sound curiously abstract.

Methodologically speaking, Bryce is in effect both a crude empiricist and a reductionist of the most extreme sort. This combination explains all the essential characteristics of his work: why he is a theorist who uses almost no theoretical equipment and, even more important, why he carries out an explicitly comparative analysis in a basically configurative way. Bryce believes, in effect, that every concrete social pattern is something unique, something ephemeral and nonreplicable, and therefore that it can be adequately represented only by means of configurative analysis. But just because every concrete social pattern is a world unto itself, a precise social science must be based, he argues, upon psychology, upon the constants of human nature that underlie the varieties of social experience.

What then is the comparative method to do? Is it not, upon this view, irrelevant to social science? Not quite; comparative method, to Bryce, does have a role to play in social science, a psychological role: one uses it to discover the fixed characteristics of human nature by examining the differences in actual social phenomena. What we do in comparing is simply that we subtract from actual experience that which is seen not to be "fundamental" to it: anything due to "disturbing influences," such as the influence of race, "external" conditions, historical antecedents, and so on. We are then left, as a residue, with the human constants we need for a precise social science. For the sort of issues Bryce raised, this social science is necessarily deductive once the psychological premises have been established, but for the explanation of concrete social facts it yields a simple ad hoc empiricism. To explain any concrete behavior we simply combine the psychological constants with the unique disturbing influences bearing upon the behavior pattern—and there we are.

This sort of procedure is nothing original in Bryce's time—though there is no evidence that he knew anything of Pareto, with whose *Mind and Society* his *Modern Democracies* has much in common, not only in method but also, as a consequence perhaps, in manner: particularly in the disorganized presentation of great heaps of information in volume after interminable volume; the whole is sifted here and there for a very few dubious propositions of cosmic import. Psychological reductionism happened to be very much in the air in Bryce's time, not least in political studies. What is important in Bryce's version of it is his insistence on the actual analysis of political systems in order to discover relevant psychological constants, rather than proceeding from common-sense notions about human nature or "self-evident" propositions.

Whatever one may think of reductionism in principle, it is certainly a procedure difficult to carry out in practice. It is no small matter to try to find in the enormous varieties of concrete social life anything constant at all, except variety itself. And so it is not surprising that Bryce is, in the final analysis, not quite true to his method. He actually distills from his configurative materials not only psychological constants but also, with more emphasis and at much greater length, certain broad ad hoc generalizations about the essential bases of successful democratic government and the contingent circumstances that help or hinder its existence.

His argument comes down to this: Successful democracy, he thinks, requires a legislature rather like the British House of Commons up to the late nineteenth century. It should consist of illustrious men who command great respect and have a high sense of political responsibility, who are not divided into many antagonistic groups and yet not subject to great party discipline either, who are not mere speakers for constituents or parties and yet can easily be integrated into majorities for the expeditious discharge of business—a legislature devoid of caucuses, groups, opportunists, and the second-rate. The possibility of the existence of such a legislature depends on the general national character of a people. This character, in turn, Bryce treats not as a simple given fact but as the product of numerous conditioning factors that he never makes explicit but that keep appearing in his analysis: demographic and geographic factors (smallness is absolutely essential: only its great size keeps China from being a successful parliamentary democracy!); the ethnic, religious, and class diversity of a society; occupational structure and economic development (agriculture is conducive to democracy, while industry, because it generates occupational diversity and class conflict, and because wealth corrupts, is a threat to democracy); history (especially the gradual development of a desire for democracy and a tradition of self-government); and a mysterious factor he refers to as "racial qualities."

While most of the work thus deals with the "disturbing influences" that condition societies, some of it is devoted, as it must be, to the constants on which these influences work. Bryce's constants resemble those of Michels as much as his method resembles that of Pareto, again without any evidence of acquaintance with Michels's work. What Bryce really discovers is not any psychological constants at all but a sociological principle and certain principles subsidiary to it. This principle is the universal fact of oligarchy in politics. He finds it to be a universal fact because "organization is essential for the accomplishment of any purpose," because the majority takes little interest in politics and lacks sufficient knowledge to play a positive political role, and because the natural capacities of people are unequal. Democracy in its classic form, therefore, is a human impossibility; at most it can mean only the prescription of broad ends and the selection of leaders from among competing elites by the electorate. Bryce thus develops a very early version of Schumpeter's elitist argument in *Capitalism, Socialism and Democracy*, and couples it with some very pessimistic findings about the educability of people, the usefulness of mass media of communication, and the appetites for self-government and authority.

But this is not the place to go fully into Bryce's substantive findings.

The important thing is to note the ways in which he presents them and arrives at them. To sum these up: Bryce is, in the first place, still an abstract theorist, but one who insists on the empirical derivation of his first principles. He is also, by conviction, an exponent of configurative analysis, but he insists on using the data of configurative studies for broader theoretical purposes. Finally, he is also something of a middle-range theorist (insofar as he looks for the probable effects of particular conditioning factors like ecology, social structure, and economic structure on particular aspects of political behavior), but he assigns to such middle-range theories a relatively low importance compared with residual first principles and arrives at them through the crudest sort of empiricism. What we should note above all perhaps is that he insists that theories be fully grounded upon data and that data be presented always for theoretical purposes. Politics appears to him an activity embedded in all social relations yet not governed by any single transcendental principle. In these respects, his work represents a long step away from the world of historicism and its aftermath and toward the approach of Montesquieu, who was by Bryce's own admission, along with Tocqueville, the model he sought to emulate.

FRIEDRICH'S *CONSTITUTIONAL GOVERNMENT AND DEMOCRACY*

In one sense, perhaps, Friedrich's *Constitutional Government and Democracy* is more like the late nineteenth-century syntheses than Bryce's *Modern Democracies*. It is packed with discussions of the abstract political theorists that are in many cases not clearly integrated with the empirical parts of the study. Bryce at least derived from the abstract theorists his analytical problems; in Friedrich, references to the political "theorists" sometimes are little more than displays of erudition, albeit impressive erudition. In many important respects, however, *Constitutional Government and Democracy* takes great strides beyond *Modern Democracies*.

For one thing, there really is no purely configurative analysis in the book. Instead of presenting his empirical materials on a country-by-country basis, Friedrich organizes them in terms of a large number of structural and functional categories, under each of which theoretical speculations and data from a number of political systems (all Western) are given; the data are then sifted for theoretical significance. It is true that information under most of Friedrich's categories is itself presented in a country-by-country fashion, but the intent is clearly to go beyond configurative analysis; the country-by-country approach is used merely as a way of organizing the materials and not as the result of a belief in the uniqueness of each configuration. It should also be noted that many of the categories in terms of which the work is organized refer to formal-legal structure. That may, however, be the result simply of the nature of the materials available to

Friedrich rather than of a narrow conception of politics on his part. In any case, the study includes much comparative material on parties, interest groups, and media of political communication; and throughout Friedrich gives considerable attention to the interplay between political forms and social conditions. In *Constitutional Government and Democracy* we thus come upon a full-fledged modern comparative synthesis, although one which still leaves many theoretical strands dangling in empty abstraction and which is still deeply rooted in the formal-legal style of early political science—two facts perhaps inevitable, given the period in which it was written.

Just as the contents of the study and the way they are organized are a mixture of the new and old, so also is the methodology underlying it, although it is a methodology very different from that of Bryce. As we have seen, Bryce's methodology had as its object mainly the establishment of first principles on empirical grounds. The ultimate purpose of Friedrich's, on the other hand, is to defend crude empiricism in the direct (not the deductive) construction of middle-range theories, although in the course of establishing this position he passes over some of Bryce's methodological ground.

Friedrich is not nearly so optimistic as Bryce about the possibility of scientific precision in political science on any basis. In a methodological appendix that portrays exactly what he does in his substantive chapters (but that is omitted from the later editions of the work, since Friedrich himself no longer holds these views), he rejects the possibility of formulating "laws" about politics and argues that one can at most formulate only "reasonably accurate hypotheses concerning recurrent regularities" in political experience. A reasonably accurate hypothesis about politics seems to him doomed to be always a greatly inaccurate hypothesis. Why so? Because all social phenomena involve the operation of a great many variables, and the greater the number of variables bearing upon a subject, the more inexact generalizations and forecasts about it must be.

The proper method for such a subject matter, among all the methods available to us, is what Mill called the inverse deductive method, and this is simply the method of reductionism: the establishment of psychological constants by reasoning back from cultural variations to invariant underlying conditions. Here we seem to be back with Bryce. But—and this is the rub—to find the constant human nature underlying social experience, argues Friedrich, no complicated procedures are needed; psychology is fully available to common sense, for in talking about human nature we are only talking about ourselves, and therefore about data available to simple introspection! Friedrich is almost touchingly certain, in fact, that we already know almost everything worth knowing about politics and that any "partially inaccurate" notions we may have about the subject are easily corrected by deeper introspection and a wider inspection of data, for if psy-

chology is the basis of political knowledge, we need "only" look inward
to know politics, and if, despite this fact, inaccurate notions about politics
become established, the "facts" will soon disabuse us of these notions. In
this way, Friedrich, having ruled out scientific precision at the outset, then
makes things still easier on political scientists by holding that all "reasonably accurate" hypotheses in political science are immediately accessible
to common sense—anybody's common sense, though best of all the common sense of the well-informed political scientist. This "methodology" is
nothing more than an argument for ordinary shrewdness and nothing less
than an argument against "social science."

In the substantive chapters of the work Friedrich is faithful to these
views. Unlike many social scientists, he knows exactly what he is doing. His
actual method in *Constitutional Government and Democracy* (though not in
later works) is first to inspect a certain range of behavior (now broad, now
narrow) pertaining to one of his subdivisions of constitutional government,
then to generalize about it on the basis of common sense (that is, without
using any special technical apparatus), and finally to see whether the generalizations so arrived at, when reduced to psychological terms, are congruent with his own common-sense notions about human nature. He col-
lects a set of facts, reflects upon them, and checks the common-sense
plausibility of the reflections; this, in his view, is really all that social scientists can do fruitfully.

We get the quintessence of this procedure in the conclusion to his
chapter on electoral systems. "Proportional representation," Friedrich says
there, "has been found wanting and incompatible with parliamentary government"—as indeed it had to be, for the "natural" effect of P.R. is to
splinter political forces and thus prevent the formation of majorities on
which stable parliamentarianism depends. The Weimar Republic illustrates
the case. But if we look at all the other cases of P.R. that Friedrich cites—
Belgium, the Netherlands, Sweden, Norway, Denmark, Ireland—this conclusion seems by no means to follow. What then? Well, "there are special
factors to be considered in these several lands." Apparently, P.R. is not
incompatible with parliamentary government in constitutional monarchies,
or in small countries, or in countries with strong administrative traditions,
or in countries where a single emotional issue divides the electorate. And
"all this goes to show that the prevalent English and American opinion
against proportional representation is practically sound." What we get here
is in effect a generalization based on a single case, supported by common
sense, and then an almost model exercise in what to methodologists is one
of the cardinal sins: "saving the hypothesis" by enlarging it to cover all
the cases that seem to falsify it—in this instance, the great majority.

But it is too easy, and quite unjust, to be harsh on Friedrich from a
contemporary perspective. Despite the deliberate antiscientism to which

Friedrich adhered when he wrote the book, *Constitutional Government and Democracy* deals with a host of middle-range problems that simply cry out for more methodical treatment and includes a large number of theoretical propositions that have furnished issues to comparative politics for a long time now.

The objective that unifies the work is to determine the conditions of success of constitutional government (and, by the way, to develop, through the examination of existing systems, a set of maxims of constitutional prudence). In regard to this basic problem Friedrich chooses an essentially "cultural" solution—that is, the primary significance of what Bentley called "soul-stuff," political ideas and attitudes. Constitutional government and democracy, he argues, are threatened primarily by "intensity" in politics, especially intense disagreements over fundamental procedures and ultimate political objectives; intensity itself is measured by the extent of political enthusiasm ("consent") and animosity ("restraint") in a society. This broad hypothesis—which seems commonplace now but was not at all conventional twenty years ago—is the apex of a great many more limited generalizations: for example, that successful constitutional government requires a "balance of social classes" (whatever that might be), that "objective" heterogeneity in a society does not undermine constitutional government so long as there is a minimal unity of political outlook, that the number of parties in a representative system depends upon conditions prevailing in the system prior to the establishment of parliamentary government, that an inflexible constitution is to be preferred over a flexible one in societies that have no firm constitutional tradition but not in societies that have such a tradition—and many more, all based, of course, on artless inferences from very few cases.

At the end, we are left with three sets of theoretical ideas, two substantive and one procedural. First, the study presents what is in effect a set of requisites for successful democracy, many of them truistic, as they must be in view of Friedrich's method, but some not at all obvious. These requisites fall into two categories. One comprises organizational requisites, such as a responsible bureaucracy, an efficient diplomatic service, an effective judiciary with wide powers (including controls upon administration), a legislature organized for fruitful deliberation and not merely accurate representation and unlimited debate, some sort of separation of powers, functional or territorial, a neutral arbiter of constitutional disputes, and broad but rigidly defined executive emergency powers. The other comprises social and cultural characteristics: a viable economy, low intensity in politics, an effective constitutional symbolism, informative media of communication, and a high degree of political integration of economic and other material interests in society. Second, Friedrich presents a number of conditions that, while not requisites of effective democracy, do help to create a favorable climate for it: for example, a firmly rooted political tradition (its absence is not fatal because it can be overcome by proper constitutional devices), judicial review, the plurality systems of elections, and the existence of only two political parties in the system. And third, he provides throughout, chiefly by implication, a number of variables to use in the analysis of the functioning of all political systems, the most important of which are, in his view, political attitudes and constitutional structure, although he also resorts in places to factors such as social structure (note the requirement of a balance of social classes), history, and personality (that is, "leadership" as something that is not the product of any social forces).

All in all, then, *Constitutional Government and Democracy* is an early example of the functional approach to political analysis. It is a thoroughly comparative work, partly because a functional conception of a subject is in its very nature more conducive to comparative study than any structural definition. It is a study entirely devoted (leaving aside the generous references to traditional political theory) to the construction of middle-range theory about political institutions and behavior. In other words, its analyses are neither as all-encompassing as those of the historicists nor as narrowly restricted to configurative and formal-legal descriptions as those of the post-historicists. The middle-range theories presented deal mainly with the interplay of formal political processes with political parties and groups, and, in a still larger sense, with cultural, historical, and social forces. These are the "new" elements of the work. But *Constitutional Government and Democracy* has no real method (at most, an antimethodical methodology) and uses, geographically speaking, a rather limited range of data.

With Friedrich, however, we are at least to a large extent back in the world of Montesquieu's political sociology. We are not yet very far beyond it or in some respects even abreast of it. But it is no accident that it is Friedrich who really begins to synthesize political science with the political sociologies of Mosca and Pareto, Weber and Michels, to all of whom there are liberal references—though mostly critical references—throughout his study. What is still missing in his work is even that beginning of a systematic and rigorous approach that we can detect in *The Spirit of the Laws*.

POSTWAR DEVELOPMENTS IN COMPARATIVE POLITICS

By World War II, then, comparative politics was characterized by a reawakened interest in large-scale comparisons, a relatively broad conception of the nature of politics and what is relevant to politics, and a growing emphasis upon solving middle-range theoretical problems concerning the determinants of certain kinds of political behavior and the requisites for certain kinds of political institutions. Comparisons, however, were still made largely without the use of any special technical procedures; speculation and data were only beginning to be deliberately integrated. The subject-matter treated was still predominantly the sovereign state, indeed still mainly the formal aspects of Western nation-states. The concepts used for analysis were largely conventional rather than technical, no explicit conceptual schemes designed for theorizing were used, and some of the most important aspects of analysis were left implicit. The interwar period was one preeminently of ad hoc and common-sense theorizing. This brings us to our own time.

What have been the trends in comparative politics in the postwar period? The most basic have been four. First, the empirical range of the field has been greatly enlarged, primarily through the intensive study of non-Western systems, but also through research into aspects of politics previously little studied. Second, concerted attempts have been made to overcome the lack of rigor and system that characterized the field in the prewar period—to make it more "scientific," if the use of unconventional technical concepts, systematic analytic approaches, and rigorous testing procedures may be called scientific. Third, there has been much greater emphasis upon the political role of social groups (whether explicitly organized for politics or not) and upon social institutions that play a special role in molding political values and cognitions, loyalties and identifications—agencies of political "socialization." Finally, political systems have been analytically dissected and questions raised about them in terms of conceptual schemes largely imported from other social sciences, above all in terms of structural-functional analysis. These trends take us back full-scale at last to the political sociology of Montesquieu, and indeed greatly improve upon it.

I have not listed the trends here in any logical sequence, but neither have I listed them in a merely random way. Granted some unavoidable overlapping, they appear in the order in which emphasis upon them actually developed in the postwar period (save only for the fact that structural-functional analysis has played an important role throughout, but a constantly greater role as the trends unfold), and they appear in this order because each stage in the postwar development of the field helps us to understand why the next was embarked upon.

The Study of Non-Western Systems

The influences leading to the gradual extension of subject matter to non-Western systems are fairly plain. The most obvious of them is the fact that societies and areas that political scientists interested in current events could once safely ignore became important and obtrusive in the postwar period for a great many reasons: the emergence of many new states in non-Western areas, the impact of the Pacific and North African wars (which certainly made many Westerners intimately acquainted with areas previously regarded as merely exotic), and the fact that only the non-Western areas were uncommitted, or open to a revision of commitment, in the power conflicts of the cold war. There was, consequently, and still is, a considerable demand in the nonacademic world for specialized knowledge of these areas, and such a demand for expertise necessarily acts as an impetus toward its acquisition, most of all in a policy-oriented and training-oriented discipline like political science.

Yet it would be much too one-sided to regard the intense postwar interest in the developing areas merely as a response to postwar politics, even conceding that the most obvious academic influence that might have made for this interest, political evolutionism, had played itself out by this time. Why had not this great interest arisen much sooner? Perhaps because financial support for studies of premodern systems was harder to come by in the prewar period—and such systems are expensive to study—but financial support was scant at the time for almost all projects in the social sciences. Perhaps because international power relations centered heavily upon the European countries; but there was Japan to contend with in the East no less than Germany and Italy in the West, there were riots, demonstrations, and mass arrests in India, there were important upheavals in China and Turkey. There was much to study outside of the West.

Why then did so very few students of comparative politics turn to study other areas? The answer is, at least partly, that their aims and preconceptions as political scientists simply did not direct their attention toward them. Perhaps the most important factor responsible for this was the almost universal emphasis in political science upon the study of democratic institutions, then, and still, to be found mainly in the West. We must remember that even Alfred Cobban's pioneering study *Dictatorship: Its History and Theory,* which now may strike us as very antique, dates only to 1939. And why this emphasis on democracy? The answer was already noted by Bryce: because of an almost universal belief not only in the desirability and possibility but also the inevitability of representative democracy in the development of nations. After all, was not all of Western history itself indicative of this trend? Even the early Soviet Union did not raise any particular problem in this regard, for one could always take its doctrines at face value and persuade oneself to believe that it was itself tending in a democratic direction. So, in their larger-scale political works, political scientists wrote, if not about the modern democracies themselves, then about the Ur-democracies of the ancient world and the historical processes leading from them to the more fully developed democracies of modern times; but it seemed pointless and superfluous to write about contemporary predemocratic, obviously transitional, systems—certainly as long as the end of the transitional process did not seem problematic.

From this standpoint, the interest in non-Western systems in political science is closely bound up with the crisis of democracy in Western Europe, the emergence of Italian and German totalitarianism, and the brutalization of Soviet Communism under Stalin. The declining faith in the inevitability of democracy led not only to a general interest in authoritarian governments, as exemplified by Cobban's own work, but also to two other, and relatively new, interests: in the processes of political change and the forces governing it and in the social forces rather than the legal rules governing politics. All of these interests obviously helped to open the door to the study of nondemocratic, rapidly changing societies either lacking highly differentiated political systems and highly articulated formal-legal structures or possessing them only on the level of colonial authority.

Also as a result of the crisis of democracy, political scientists now undertook a more intensive searching of the early political sociologists in order to gain insights into the cause of the unexpected political experiences of the modern world, and through the works of the political sociologist—certainly through Pareto, Mosca, and Weber—they acquired at least a cursory acquaintance with a wider range of political systems than political scientists had normally possessed.

The great postwar interest in non-Western areas is therefore a reaction to prewar no less than postwar political conditions. At any rate, it is a consequence of certain modes of thought engendered by prewar political experiences. And it may also be regarded as a consequence of a trend more purely internal to the field—namely, the growing interest in middle-range theories as such. The connection here is really quite simple: configurative study is bound, by its very nature, to narrow the empirical scope of studies, and comparative study, for the purpose of formulating, and even more for testing, middle-range theories, is bound to broaden it. This is a truism, but for the present purpose an important one.

Scientific Rigor

Without slighting the role of external influences, therefore, one might reasonably have expected a broadening of the scope of comparative politics in the postwar period in any event. So also with the postwar interest in scientific method. Already in the 1920s and 1930s one can detect a certain unease about the looseness of analysis characteristic of the field. Bryce's chapter on comparative method is about a dubious version of it, but it *is* a chapter on the conditions of rigorous social analysis. Friedrich's epilogue on method is an apologia for his unscientific empiricism, but he does appear impelled to apologize for these aspects of his work. Certainly it is not difficult to see how formulations of middle-range theories about behavior within numerous contexts might lead the analyst, quite without other stimuli, toward increasing rigor of procedure and unconventional concepts and approaches; the moment one begins to question propositions like those which abound in *Constitutional Government and Democracy,* one can hardly avoid such matters, for it is precisely the lack of rigor and unconventionality that gave rise to the propositions.

But the postwar quest for a more rigorously "scientific" comparative politics is also due to certain "external" causes. It is certainly a reflection of the growing postwar cult of "behavioral" science throughout all the social sciences (taking "behavioral science" to denote (1) middle-range theorizing on the basis of (2) explicit theoretical frames of reference with the use of (3) rigorous, particularly quantitative, procedures for testing the theories). The "behavioral" approach has affected comparative politics primarily through the growing influence upon the fields of sociology and cultural anthropology, and this influence in turn may be attributed in large part (though not entirely) to the very fact of increasing interest in non-Western political systems. For one thing, when political scientists turned to the study of non-Western systems, they found other social scientists already occupying the ground, mostly cultural anthropologists but also a growing number of sociologists (or sociologically trained anthropologists); and so they naturally went to school with them and absorbed their techniques and style. For another, the theoretical equipment of political scientists, such as it was, generally failed them when they confronted political systems unlike the highly differentiated, formally organized, predominantly democratic or totalitarian systems of the West. For this reason also they went to school with social scientists who offered more appropriate theoretical tools and learned to use these tools.

The Emphasis on Setting

Just as the growing interest in non-Western political systems helped to engender a desire for going much further beyond common-sense propositions and common-sense testing procedures, so also it helped to produce—and much less obliquely—the present emphasis on the social setting of politics and on agencies mediating between the social and the political, such as political groups and agencies of political "socialization." Because political scientists found in such systems much less differentiation between the social and political—that is, few specialized organizations for political decision making or competition—they simply could not help seeing the extent to which the political is embedded in social relations in such systems, or suspecting that it might be so also in the more highly differentiated political system.

If they were indeed confronted by specialized political institutions and agencies, these, like the whole political system, were generally very much in flux—in process of coming into being or being altered. And when political processes are unsettled—when patterns of politics are in the making rather than functionally autonomous of the conditions creating them—the nonpolitical is always particularly obtrusive and apparent, as it was to political observers in Europe in the great age of revolutions from 1789 to 1848 and as it was in the era of the rise of totalitarianism. It is worth noting in this connection that the halcyon days of formal-legalism in the study of politics fell precisely in that relatively calm and settled period between the great revolutions and the totalitarian era.

Here again, however, we must add other factors leading in a similar direction. We must remember, for example, that interest in the broader setting of politics, and in its more informal aspects, was already well advanced in the prewar period, above all in studies of American politics. In fact, many of the concepts, methods, and interests now being applied in comparative politics came out of the intensive study of American politics in the interwar and postwar periods—not least because of a gradual awareness on the part of specialists in comparative politics that the study of American politics was far outstripping their own specialty. The great role of the Social Science Research Council's Committee on Political Behavior in stimulating interest in applying comparatively some of the insights and techniques developed in American political studies—not least, its important role in helping to bring into being the SSRC Committee on Comparative Politics, which has done so much to help advance the field in recent years—should certainly be mentioned here.

In a way, also, interest in the setting of politics flowed almost naturally from the desire for scientific rigor in the field. It did so in two ways. First, in so far as the pursuit of rigor led to the more intensive study and emulation of sociology and cultural anthropology, it also led to the introduction into comparative politics of broad frameworks of analysis that, on the whole, regard all social phenomena as interrelated and certainly do not concentrate on any functionally distinctive aspect of society as if it were divorced from all other aspects of it.

Second, it is on the whole much easier to develop theories subject to rigorous testing by taking certain social and economic categories and relating them to politics (for example, such easily measurable categories as wealth and economic development, demographic data, occupational distributions—even value-orientation data) than by taking the often unmeasurable "pure" phenomena of politics as such—especially in societies where electoral data, the most easily measurable of all purely political data, are nonexistent, unreliable, or beside the point. As the opponents of rigorous quantitative methods in political science never weary of pointing out, the phenomena of politics, as traditionally conceived, simply do not lend themselves well to rigorous (that is, statistical, logical, mathematical) treatment—

but this may (and did) as easily induce political scientists to conceive such phenomena differently as persuade them to give up rigorous methods altogether.

The influence of sociology upon comparative politics can be seen most clearly of all in the postwar emphasis upon a particular constellation of facts in the setting of politics, the facts that Montesquieu referred to as "the general spirit, the morals of a nation" and that have now come to be called "political culture." This term, as now used, refers in general to politically relevant values (purposive desires), cognitions (conceptions of the nature of reality), and expressive symbols, from language to visual ceremony. It refers in particular to the "internalized" expectations in terms of which the political roles of individuals are defined and through which political institutions (in the sense of regularized behavior patterns) come into being.

The emphasis upon such "cultural" data is clearly a reflection of the influence upon political studies of the currently dominant sociological frame of reference, the action frame of reference, evolved chiefly by Parsons and Shils, upon the basis of Parsons's interpretation of Weber, Durkheim, and Pareto. At any rate, the "political culture" approach has been pioneered in comparative politics chiefly by two writers who freely admit their debt to Parsons and Shils, Gabriel A. Almond (who may rightly claim to have originated the concept in political science) and S. H. Beer. It is mainly through this emphasis on "cultural" data that the study of political "socialization" processes has come to be of great significance in the contemporary field, for if the values, cognitions, and symbols defining people's political conduct are regarded as the primary substratum of their political behavior, then explanations of political behavior must stress ipso facto the processes through which values, cognitions, and symbols are learned and "internalized," through which operative social norms regarding politics are implanted, political roles institutionalized, and political consensus created, either effectively or ineffectively. This, essentially, is what we mean by political socialization.

At the same time, the concern with political culture helps to explain the emphasis upon the study of political groups, although this emphasis is also a continuation of prewar tendencies and a result of basing middle-range theories about politics upon hard, preferably measurable, facts. The vogue of the group approach to politics reflects the preoccupation with political culture simply in that there are very few societies, even among the most politically centralized, that have homogeneous political cultures, rather than being composed of a variety of political subcultures; certainly there are very few such societies among the emerging or rapidly changing states of the non-Western areas.

STRUCTURAL-FUNCTIONAL ANALYSIS

Throughout the postwar period, but particularly, as I have pointed out, in very recent years, students of comparative politics have also made increasing use of the perspectives and categories of structural-functional analysis. What precisely does structural-functional analysis denote in this case? The term certainly cannot be left without explication, even when used in discussions of the fields in which it originated, for structural-functional analysis seems to include a very large, perhaps all-comprehending, variety of analytical questions and procedures. One of its principal exponents, M. J. Levy, has even claimed that, as used nowadays by most sociologists, it is merely another term for "talking prose"—that the structural-functional theorists do nothing more than state in a particular language what everybody already states in other languages. That may be so, although it makes one wonder why a structural-functional language should then be used at all; but in the postwar study of comparative politics the term does refer to certain specific, though still somewhat heterogeneous, procedures and problems.

It refers, first, to the very definitions of politics: to what we conceive to be a political system. One can define a political system in two ways: either as a particular set of concrete organizations, such as "governments" or "sovereign states," or as any social structures that perform whatever we conceive to be the function of politics—that is, any social structures that engage in political activities.

The latter may be considered a structural-functional definition, and this kind of definition of the political system has become increasingly common in the field. We tend no longer to think of political systems solely as sovereign states and their formal subdivisions but as any "collective decision-making structure," or as any set of structures for "authoritatively allocating social values," or as structures that perform the function of "maintaining the integration of society," or as structures that perform the functions of "the integration and adaptation of societies by means of the employment, or threat of employment, of more or less physical compulsion"—and in many other ways in similar vein. Some of these structural-functional definitions, like the first two examples cited, simply define a special activity, whatever its effect upon the larger social unit in which it occurs. Others, like the last two examples, define an activity that is presumed to be a requisite of the viability of a larger social unit. The latter definitions are more strictly characteristic of the style of structural-functional analysis than the former, for the problem of the requisites of the viability of social systems, of their stability and efficient operation, is perhaps the most basic substantive concern of those using the structural-functional approach.

Just as we can define a political system in structural-functional terms, so also we can devise analytical breakdowns of political systems—construct schemes of the elements that constitute them—in such terms, and this again in two ways. One way is simply to define the subsidiary activities that go into the larger activity of politics. In effect, this is what Almond does in breaking down political function into four input and three output categories. The other way is to break down the political function into those subactivities and structures performing the subactivities that are required for the effective performance of the political function, as a viable political system is required for the effective operation of the larger social system. This is what Apter does in breaking down political systems into five "structural requisites," and this latter procedure also is more strictly characteristic of structural-functional analysis than the former.

The purpose of structural-functional definitions and breakdowns of systems is, of course, to allow one to state and solve certain problems in which structural-functional theorists are particularly interested and that are based upon their preconceptions of the nature of social life. For all intents and purposes, the problems typical of structural-functional analysis can all be subsumed under a single concern: the impact of any social structure or function upon the larger social unit of which it is a part (or, less frequently, upon any other structure or function to which it is related).

Social structures of functions can impinge upon social systems in a variety of ways. The structure or function under consideration may be a "prerequisite" for the larger (or related) pattern, in that it must exist before the larger pattern can exist. It may be a "requisite" for it, in that it is required if the larger pattern is to be maintained. It may be "eufunctional" if it helps the pattern to persist or "dysfunctional" if it helps to undermine it. Its operation may be "manifest" if it is intended and understood by the actors involved or "latent" if its operation is not intended and understood. Questions about such relations between structures or functions and larger social units are obviously not profoundly different from questions often raised in other terms. There is, for example, little difference between saying that something is a requisite or prerequisite for something else and saying that something is a necessary but not sufficient condition for (or cause of) another.

A distinctive preconception of societies does, however, underlie structural-functional analysis that gives to such questions an import, certain overtones, that they do not possess when raised in the language of causality or other theoretical languages. This preconception is that societies are mutually interconnected wholes, every aspect of which impinges upon every other and contributes something to the viability (or lack of viability) of the whole. Societies, upon this view, are equilibrated units that have a tendency toward inertia and change through the persistent or serious disturbance of any part of their equilibrium. They are "systems" in the technical sense of the term: hence the concern with their functional interrelations.[7]

It is this preconception of the nature of political systems, and of the way they fit into the larger social setting, that has gradually come to the forefront in postwar comparative politics. With it has come an emphatic interest in structural-functional problems, particularly problems regarding the requisites of any viable (stable, effective) political system or of the viability of certain kinds of political systems (for example, representative democracies) and problems regarding the functional consequences upon politics of other social patterns and upon nonpolitical patterns of political structures and activities.

What explains the present vogue in comparative politics of these preconceptions and problems? To some extent, of course, the very fact that social sciences in which structural-functional analysis is widely used have exerted an important influence upon comparative politics in the postwar period. But there are more deep-seated reasons.

Curiously enough, one of these deeper reasons is connected with the rapidly changing character of many contemporary non-Western systems—curiously enough, because structural-functional analysis is often accused of being a purely static approach to social science. It is so represented, however, for two bad reasons: one, the very concept of equilibrium is taken (erroneously) to imply immobility; the other, the major social scientists who have developed structural-functional analysis have in fact emphasized static over dynamic studies—most of them have worked in the anti-Marxist tradition, which assumes integration rather than conflict, and consequently inertia rather than constant motion, as the "normal" state of society. But this fact represents a coincidence rather than a logical relation. Indeed, structural-functional analysis, as depicted here, seems perhaps to lead logically (if it leads logically to anything at all) to theories about the coming into being, transformation, and breakdown of societies rather than to static analyses of fixed social states.

Rather than arguing that structural-functional analysis has a logical affinity to static analysis, one should argue that it is likely to produce a particular approach to social dynamics, different from that produced by theories like Marxism or evolutionary theory—an approach that always sees social change as a transition from one static, equilibrated state to another. Marxist and evolutionary theory are perhaps more *inherently* dynamic than structural-functional analysis in one sense: one cannot imagine, in terms of them, any fixed states, any equilibria other than dynamic equilibria, at all. For the structural-functional analyst, a fixed state is entirely possible and even necessary, although it does not rule out the analysis of changes of state.

At the same time, however, theories like Marxism and evolutionary theory make it difficult, if not impossible, to think of rapid, cataclysmic changes in society; note, for example, the great difficulties created for Marxist theorists by the doctrine of "permanent revolution." Such theories lend themselves chiefly to a conception of orderly, constant flow in social phenomena: one thing leads, never very rapidly or abruptly, to the next, and the whole flow is conceived, but only for heuristic purposes, as a series of "stages" through which societies must always pass in their life-histories. But structural-functional analysis makes it perfectly possible to think in terms of very broad and rapid changes, of one society skipping the stages of growth passed through by another or embarking very rapidly upon a new course of growth, through some large-scale change, however brought about, in one of the functional elements of society. It makes it possible to think of rapid transformations, revolutionary breaks, innovations, and metamorphoses, while other, supposedly more dynamic, approaches make it possible only to think of flows and phases.

Precisely these two characteristics of structural-functional analysis—that it leads to a conception of social change as a process from static states to other static states and offers the possibility of explaining very broad and rapid changes—make it attractive for those concerned with contemporary non-Western political systems. With what kinds of social dynamics do these systems confront us? Certainly not with orderly and constant flow. In such systems one always seems to begin with very static traditional societies, hardly changed in essential respects for centuries—societies exhibiting "fixed states" in any reasonable meaning of the term. And from such beginnings one always seems to proceed to the swiftest and most large-scale changes: from tribalism to the nation-state, from agrarian subsistence economics to modern industrialization, from feudalism to socialism; hurricanes of change strike the societies and swiftly transform them in ways that elsewhere took generations, even centuries.

Perhaps we shall find that this is not really an accurate depiction of what is happening in the "developing" areas. Perhaps the large-scale changes that appear to be occurring in them are merely surface phenomena under which more gradual processes of social flow proceed. But rapid metamorphosis from relatively unchanging states does *seem*, to naked observation, to be the essence of their contemporary history. For that sort of dynamism a theoretical approach at once static and dynamic is obviously the most appropriate.

Thus, the very study of rapidly changing political and social systems creates a predisposition toward structural-functional analysis, not despite but precisely because of its affinity for static theory. And thus also the present emphasis on social setting and on theoretical rigor in comparative politics has induced an increasing use of structural-functional analysis and directs the analytical attention, more perhaps than any other approach, to the whole web of relationships of which politics is a part: the social phenomena on which politics impinges and those phenomena that impinge upon politics. Structural-functional analysis is the preeminent approach to the study of social interconnections. The emphasis on rigor has induced structural-functional analysis because it at least offers the possibility of something more than crude, unsystematic description and induction, without committing the theorist to a premature, perhaps vain, search for social "laws" or for "grand theories" in the historicist manner.

Nor does it commit him to a quest for sufficient "causes" in a realm where multicausality and multivariation operate to such an extent that necessary—or favorable—but insufficient conditions of phenomena are perhaps all we can ever hope to find. Structural-functional analysis, from this standpoint, is the preeminent approach to what I have called middle-range theories—theories that go beyond mere description and common-sense generalizations, that are based upon some explicit theoretical frame of reference, that permit some rigor in formulating and testing hypotheses, and that yet do not present ironclad laws or total interpretations of the meaning of social life. Talcott Parsons, whose name is perhaps the most famous of those associated with structural-functional analysis in the contemporary social sciences, defends the approach precisely on this basis:

> It may be taken for granted that all scientific theory is concerned with the analysis of elements of uniformity in empirical processes. The essential question is how far the state of theory is developed to the point of permitting deductive transitions from one aspect or state of a system to another, so that it is possible to say that if the facts in A sector are W and X, those in B sector must be Y and Z. In some parts of physics and chemistry it is possible to extend the empirical coverage of such a deductive system quite widely. But in the sciences of action dynamic knowledge of this character is highly fragmentary, though by no means absent.
>
> In this situation there is danger of losing all the advantages of systematic theory. But it is possible to retain some of them and at the same time provide a framework for the orderly growth of dynamic knowledge. It is as such a second best type of theory that the structural-functional level of theoretical systematization is conceived and employed.
>
> In the first place completely raw empiricism is overcome by describing phenomena as parts of or processes within systematically conceived empirical systems. The set of descriptive categories employed is neither ad hoc nor sheer common sense but is a carefully and critically worked out system of concepts which are capable of application to all relevant parts or aspects of a concrete system in a coherent way. This makes comparability and transition from one part and/or state of the system to another, and from system to system, possible.[8]

COMPARATIVE POLITICS TODAY: AN APPRAISAL

Because the postwar tendencies in comparative politics are illustrated and analyzed fully in many other essays and books, I conclude this essay without further describing and evaluating these tendencies. And yet, in a sense, we cannot really "conclude" it, for in the contemporary development of the field nothing has really been concluded. It would be nice if we could say that the study of comparative politics, after its many vagaries and tergiversations, had reached at last a new consensus upon concepts, methods, and analytical approaches capable of yielding a broad and precise science of political institutions. It would be nicer still if we could point to the actual existence of such a science. But there is a great distance still to go before this point is reached, and we are unlikely to reach it without further serious modifications of the field. Given its present state, it is quite inevitable that we should end on a note of ambiguity and suspended judgment, primarily for three reasons:

1. The field is today characterized by nothing so much as variety, eclecticism, and disagreement.
2. Disagreement and divergences are particularly great in regard to absolutely basic preconceptions and orientations (in terms of which one *recognizes* "scientifically" valid findings).
3. The tasks contemporary practitioners of comparative politics (especially the more radical ones) have set for themselves are so many and so difficult that they are unlikely to achieve satisfying results without further important changes in their approaches.

Dissent

It should not be supposed that in describing the four main tendencies in present-day comparative politics—structural-functional analysis, the quest for scientific rigor, concern with non-Western systems, and concern with the broader setting of politics—we have in fact described the whole field of comparative politics in the postwar period. Not at all; we have only described what is new and progressive in a field that is in fact to a large extent old-fashioned and conservative. It is important to realize that the stages in the development of comparative politics described here did not unfold in an orderly and episodic manner. In the manner of all things historical, these stages overlapped one another, each leaving within the contemporary discipline a certain residue, a particular style of analysis incongruent with other styles in the field.

In the contemporary field of comparative politics, we can in fact find, not two, but three quite distinctive styles; indeed we can sometimes find them in the writings of a single individual. One is the predominantly formal-legal, morphological, essentially descriptive, and configurative style of the immediate post-historicist period. In any of the established texts in the field (Ranney, Hertz and Carter, Cole, Zink, Neumann) that is essentially what will be found. If any approach is today dominant in the field, it is still this one. The second is middle-range theory based upon common-sense concepts and methods—crude empiricism, unguided by any rigorous procedures or explicit analytical frames of reference. That is what one finds in most of the deliberately comparative and problem-solving works of the present day, like Duverger's *Political Parties,* Rossiter's *Constitutional Dictatorship,* or Friedrich and Brzezinski's *Totalitarian Dictatorship and Autocracy.* The third is the broad and self-consciously systematic style distinctive to the postwar period.

The Concern with Fundamentals

This coexistence in the field of three quite different styles accounts, as pointed out at the beginning, for the present concern in comparative politics with a multitude of pretheoretical and metatheoretical problems. These problems were not raised in earlier times—or not raised with such intensity and by so many people—simply because no one saw anything problematic in them. Political scientists *knew* the proper subject matter of their science: the state. They *knew* what it was most essential to deal with in studying this subject matter: public law. They *knew* how to classify political systems, how to divide them into parts, the nature of the basic units to be used in analysis, and what sort of a finding was a satisfactory and trustworthy finding. Today, precisely because of the variety of approaches in the field, we are not at all sure about these and other basic matters, and so we spend almost as much time and effort in thinking about the field of comparative politics as we spend in the comparative study of politics.

Nowhere are this self-concern and self-criticism more apparent, and nowhere are the depth and intensity of intradisciplinary disagreement more clearly revealed, than in the two general works about the study of comparative politics so far produced in the postwar era, Gunnar Heckscher's *The Study of Comparative Government and Politics* and Roy C. Macridis's *The Study of Comparative Government.* Macridis and Heckscher—the first speaking for what is essentially "modern" in the field, the second for what is essentially "traditional"—disagree not so much about whether comparative politics is to be a "science," as may appear to be the case in the readings, but—and this is much more serious—about what a political science, properly speaking, ought to be; and that is the deepest and most frustrating disagreement that can arise in any discipline.

Macridis and Heckscher can speak for themselves; there is no need here to reproduce their arguments. In any case, all the essential issues their arguments raise, explicitly or implicitly, are sketched at the beginning of the essay. But it is essential to note one fact about their disagreements: not only do such arguments impede the development of the field by distracting its practitioners from substantive tasks, they also impede the development of the field because, while such issues are unsettled, one cannot even determine when a field has been developed. All science involves building upon tacit assumptions and silent premises; and this means that the moment such assumptions and premises are made explicit by being argued no science can be said to exist. In such cases one can only have methodology and metaphysics, only prolegomena to study, research designs, conceptual proposals, and the like—preliminaries that now in fact afflict comparative politics in astounding volume. But one cannot have that heaping up of tested theoretical findings ("cumulative research," in the wishful jargon of modern social science) that we generally think of as science.

Would it then be better not to raise questions regarding basic preconceptions? In the final analysis, it is unnecessary to answer this question one way or the other because we simply have no choice in the matter. Pretheoretical and metatheoretical concerns become significant in fields of inquiry under certain conditions; they arise because it is necessary that they should arise, and once they have arisen they cannot be wished away. One can operate with agreed preconceptions or one can disagree about preconceptions, but one cannot operate without any preconceptions. Therefore, when preconceptions are being questioned, one can only let the questioning take its course until some general understanding is reached, or, better, one can try, by procedural argument or substantive research, to influence others to accept one's own preferred preconceptions and thus contribute to the outcome of the questioning. In one way or the other—by argument or example—some dominant opinion will sooner or later become established, but in the meantime one can only leave the analysis of the field open-ended or indulge in prophecy.

The Need for Simplification

What kind of a comparative politics, then, is likely to emerge out of the present disorder in the field? Whatever the final product, one thing seems certain. Even if we confine ourselves to the postwar developments in comparative politics, it seems improbable that a coherent discipline could be built upon concerns so various and complicated as are the present concerns of comparative politics. The most obvious need in the field at present is simplification—and simplification on a rather grand scale—for human intelligence and scientific method can scarcely cope with the large numbers of variables, the heaps of concepts, and the mountains of data that seem at present to be required, and indeed to exist, in the field.

Consider what the contemporary practitioner of comparative politics is supposed to know in order to be au courant with all the mainstreams of his field. He is supposed to be at once a political scientist, a logician, and a methodologist. He is supposed to know a good deal of sociological, anthropological, social-psychological, and general systems theory. His knowledge must (ideally) extend not merely to a specific country, nor even a particular region or type of government, but over the whole universe of political phenomena. He must not only know contemporary politics, but be something of a universal historian as well. And there is even a suggestion that his familiarity with political behavior should extend not only to nation-states but to every social relationship in which authority is exercised, or influence wielded, or the allocation of social values carried out. Certainly, the study of public law, in which scholars of the past made rich and busy careers, has become a mere fraction of all the things he is supposed to study. He must also learn all about informal politics, relate politics to its setting (ecological, social, economic), and be able to deal adequately with attitudes and motivations, with culture and socialization processes. These, obviously, are absurd demands to make even of the highest intelligence, the most retentive memory, the busiest industry, the most versatile manipulator of the skills of social science. They are demands that could conceivably be met by a sensible division of labor in the field, but such a division of labor presupposes some agreement on what is being divided, an accord (which we do not possess) on the desirable nature and direction of inquiry. The fact that at present it is very difficult, perhaps impossible, for any specialist in the field to know just how his work fits into any broader picture makes it necessary for everyone to work essentially according to his own lights, in terms of what he conceives to be the ultimate destiny of the field.

Dissent on fundamentals is thus reflected in lack of focus and definition in regard to "circumstantials" in the field, and in a way this is to the good. In the past, comparative politics had clearly defined boundaries only at the cost of too narrow and perhaps too inconsequential a concentration on subject matter, formal-legal structure. Any workable approach to the field, particularly at a time when we are concerned largely with relatively undifferentiated political systems, was bound to depart from such a rigidly constricting focus. But what have we to put into its place? If the answer is that we must deal with everything instead, that nothing can be omitted, then we are lost just as surely—indeed, more surely.

The basic need of the field at present, therefore, is focus and simplification. While we can detect searches for simplified approaches in the contemporary literature about the field, these are so far *only* searches. What is more, the usual tack taken in analytical writings on comparative politics is to throw into proposed schemes everything considered in any sense relevant to political study. Thus, students of comparative politics today confront a profoundly serious problem, even a dilemma. They must not focus on formal-legal studies only; we know that from long and disappointing experience. Yet they must not deal with *everything* else—and formal-legal data to boot. They must somehow limit inquiry. Yet the most obvious way to limit political inquiry is to focus on the most obviously political thing there is, as political scientists did in the formative years of their field—namely, formal-legal structure. What, then, are we to concentrate upon? We do not know as yet; that is to say, we are not agreed upon a solution.

ENDNOTE

This essay, as stated, was written at a still early stage of the "revolution" in comparative politics, but a good deal before the Terror of the Grand Theories discussed in chapter 1. Readers who wish to be brought more fully up to date on that subject might look at Oran R. Young, *Systems of Political Science* (Englewood Cliffs, N.J.: Prentice-Hall, 1968), and James A. Bill and Robert L. Hargrave, Jr., *Comparative Politics: The Quest for Theory* (Columbus, Ohio: Merrill, 1973).

As I wrote in chapter 1, it seems to me that we have now settled down to a fundamental choice between perspectives to follow in macropolitical inquiry: between culturalist and rationalist points of departure. It would take far too much space here to explain the reasons for this and the exact nature of the perspectives. My greatest regret in the academic work I have done remains, however, the fact that the envisaged "test" of the more fruitful path to follow, also discussed in chapter 1, was never done. Had it been, we might not now be afflicted, as we are, by attempts to join what, at the basic theoretical level, should be dissociated—attempts that have had results something very like the mess Tycho Brahe, a fine astronomical data-gatherer but a timid and messy theorist, made of his attempt to join Ptolemaic to Copernican astronomy.

In general, I have taken the culturalist tack (for reasons), but I should mention that I do not regard culture as independent of objective structure, though I also do not regard it as merely superstructural. Culture has to come from something, and that, no doubt, is something objectively structural. And it must adapt to structural objective changes (see chapter 7, below). It is, in Paretian terms, a derivative from "residues." But that view does not provide an easy answer to the question of what to emphasize in our theorizing. In chapter 7, I try to make the point that the culturalist tack can be made more fruitful than theory based on "deeper" structural factors because of cultural "inertia." Still, no conclusive test of the position exists.

Simplification has also occurred in another, more encouraging, way: a gradual shift toward macropolitical theories of the middle range (e.g., in

Lipset; in the literature on contemporary peasant wars and, more generally, collective political violence; in Inglehart, et al.). From the weight of such work, if not more directly, a result about the value of culturalist or rationalist perspectives might gradually emerge.

NOTES FOR CHAPTER 3

1. I use the word "empirical" here in its conventional sense, not technically—that is, not with specific reference to the British school of "empirical" psychology and epistemology.

2. I refer to Machiavelli's "method" as viewed from the perspective of social science. I refer to neither the quality of his work as such nor the aptness of his method when viewed in the light of his avowed aims—which were *not* primarily to produce social science.

3. These ideas set the tone in social science, but certainly did not monopolize it. That Montesquieu's style of thought was not without influence in succeeding generations can be seen most clearly perhaps in Tocqueville's works, although Tocqueville was far from typical of his own period. Large-scale comparative studies flourished also in this period in fields somewhat peripheral to social science: comparative geography, comparative philology, comparative religion, and comparative jurisprudence: a brief treatment of these, with references to more comprehensive works, is given in Fritz Redlich, "Toward Comparative Historiography: Background and Problems," *Kyklos: Internationale Zeitschrift für Sozialwissenschaften* II (1958): 362–389. Redlich points out that these fields were influential upon some of the earliest nineteenth-century writings in comparative politics, above all E. A. Freeman's *Comparative Politics* (New York, 1874).

4. The emphasis on formal-legal studies undoubtedly varied in this period from country to country, depending on special considerations—whether, for example, the study of politics was an autonomous branch of university life, whether there were serious problems of political socialization, whether the country concerned had a written constitution—although in the field as a whole there was a strong trend toward such studies. Perhaps the main exception to the trend can be found in Great Britain. Here there was no written constitution to analyze; here also the common law tradition, in contrast to the continental Roman law tradition, directed attention to usage and other "informal" aspects of politics. British politics was exceptional and so also, perhaps necessarily, was British political science. Bagehot's *English Constitution* is certainly not a formal-legal study; nor, in the strict sense of the term, is Dicey's *Law and Opinion*. Yet even British political studies were not totally out of the mainstream of development in the field, certainly not so much that we can consider nineteenth-century formal-legal political studies merely a continuation of a long-standing emphasis upon public law in Roman law countries. For one thing, theory in Britain in this period reflects the subjectiveness of political thought everywhere, not only in the case of the political "idealists" but even among the utilitarians. Informal political processes were widely neglected—Bagehot, for example, talks about "party," but, unlike the monarchy, it is not considered deserving of a special chapter. Lacking a constitutional document, British writers on

British government tended to treat actual behavior as if one could read formal-legal rules into it and as if one had "explained" it when the formal rules it implied had been made explicit. In this connection, it is worth noting that this period is not only the great period of continental constitution making, but also that of the great codifications of procedure in Britain. Thus, in Britain, there is some tendency toward turning the study of politics into the study of public law, while on the continent the latter practically swallowed the former. British writers did, however, keep alive in this period a broader and more analytical tradition in political study. In this way, they may have contributed to the later revulsion against formal-legal studies.

5. Nor is it to say that narrow, and largely formal-legal studies have nothing to be said for them. Many of them set standards of scholarliness, solidity, and resistance to fads that contemporary practitioners of comparative politics might well emulate.

6. E. M. Sait, *Political Institutions: A Preface* (New York: Appleton, 1938), 135.

7. Most contemporary structural-functional theorists treat this as a point of view from which to analyze societies, not, as was once the case, as gospel truth. The reader interested in the differences between contemporary and the older functionalism should read R. K. Merton, *Social Theory and Social Structure* (Glencoe, Ill.: Free Press, 1949), chap. 1.

8. Talcott Parsons, *The Social System* (New York: Free Press of Glencoe, 1951), 20.

FOUR

Case Study and Theory
in Political Science

Author's Note: One aim of the attempt to overhaul comparative politics was to make it more theoretical. Before the 1950s comparative politics consisted almost entirely of studies of particular cases (polities or aspects of them); many of these were highly learned, but not theoretical. Even the major texts in the field were collections of case studies: usually Britain first; then France and Germany; in some cases, also, a smattering of Italy and Sweden; and, for contrast, the Soviet Union. This was the genre in which I was formed, and thus I have always found intensive case study congenial.

One can readily understand why, to achieve "theory," highly extensive large-*n* studies using aggregate statistics (that is, studies in the manner of Gurr, Hibbs, or the *Cross-Polity Survey*) would be used, despite sacrificing intensive knowledge of the cases covered. I have not been much impressed by their results. Usually they have been complex, weak, and much-qualified by ill-fitting variables. And, although alienated from the configurative case studies prevalent in the field before, I *was* impressed by the import of single or limited observations, critical for theory, in the "hard" sciences or, in sociology, by the theoretical case-method as used by Michels, Malinowski, or Whyte.

This led to reflections on "extensive" versus "intensive" studies for purposes of building theory; to reflections on what the process of theory building is about: and about the roles that case studies, which come in a number of varieties, might play in the process.

This essay first appeared in *Handbook of Political Science*, ed. by F. I. Greenstein and N. W. Polsby (Reading, Mass.: Addison-Wesley, 1975), 7: 79–138. Reprinted by permission of the publisher; copyright © 1975 by Addison-Wesley Publishing Company, Inc.

The essay that resulted has been widely used and cited, and I have received much positive feedback about it. That would be gratifying, if it were not for an irony. The essay has widely been taken to vindicate case studies of the old, accustomed mode, when even a minimally careful reading should make clear that I attack that mode and make the case only for certain, rather rare, kinds of case study, especially for a kind that hardly exists at all as yet: "crucial case-study."

I have by now come around to a somewhat modified view of that argued here: that "matched comparisons" of cases carefully selected for theory—a kind of "strong inference" procedure—are even more telling for theory. Alexander George has argued for that method cogently in the abstract; Ronald Dore's inspired comparison of virtually identical electrical industries in Britain and Japan is a good case in point. (Dore keeps the fact that his superb, apparently idiographic, descriptions have a theoretical purpose well-concealed by stating it only in his preface, but the purpose both exists and is well-served by the case studies.) Matched comparisons of properly selected cases serve especially well the experimental methods of both agreement and difference. But single case study also, as I argue here, can have powerful, even conclusive, theoretical results.

INTRODUCTION

The extent to which certain kinds of study are carried out in the field of political science seems to be a poor indicator of their perceived utility for building theories.

The type of study most frequently made in the field is the intensive study of individual cases. Case studies run the gamut from the most microscosmic to the most macrocosmic levels of political phenomena. On the microlevel, we have many studies of conspicuous political personalities (political leaders such as Lincoln, Stalin, Gandhi), and of particular leadership positions and small leadership groups (the American presidency, the British cabinet, the prime minister in British government, the operational code of the Soviet leadership, and so on). At the level of political groupings, the literature of the field teems with studies of particular pressure groups, political parties, party systems, revolutionary and protest movements, and political "elites," on both the national and local levels. More abundant still are studies of individual polities in all corners of the world and at many stages of history and development. Many of these treat polities as overall macrocosms; many deal with their subsidiary organizations (administrative apparatuses, legislatures, judiciaries, systems of local government), or with their programs and policies, or their particular electoral, legislative, executive, or judicial decision processes. Beyond that level, one finds a similar profusion of case studies of transnational phenomena: specific processes of and organizations for transnational integration, particular "systems" of international politics, particular crises in international relations, and the like.

The abundance of examples is such that it seems pointless to provide bibliography. Precisely because the genre is so common, political scientists can easily construct a representative list of examples for themselves. If not, a brief visit to the political science section of the library will serve. It is not much of an exaggeration to say that the case study literature in the field comes close to being coterminous with its literature as such.

This plenitude of case studies is not associated with any perception that they are a particularly useful means for arriving at a theoretical understanding of the subject matter of political study. Most political scientists who do case studies appear to have no views at all, or only ambiguous views, on the role that case studies can play in theory building. For them, the case study is literally a genre, not a method. If they do express views on the subject, they usually disparage the genre as a method—for instance, by holding that case studies can at most stir up becalmed theoretical imaginations. One might explain this apparent paradox by holding that political scientists do not place a high value on theory building. No doubt this is true for many of them. But it is much less true nowadays than it used to be, and the volume, or proportion, of case studies in the field has not notably decreased.

It is in order, therefore, to raise three questions: What general role can the case study play in the development of theories concerning political phenomena? How useful is the case method at various stages of the theory-building process? And how is case study best conducted for purposes of devising theories?

I intend here to propose answers to these questions that run sharply counter to the now conventional wisdom in political science, especially in the division of the field we call "comparative politics." The quotation marks no doubt give the dénouement away. Readers are supposed to conclude that "comparative" studies are by no means necessary (and often not even wise strategy to follow) in pursuing the objective for which they are usually conducted: the discovery of valid generalizations about political phenomena. Indeed, I hold that the conventional wisdom has things virtually upside down. Case studies, I will argue, are valuable at all stages of the theory-building process, but most valuable at that stage of theory building where least value is generally attached to them: the stage at which candidate theories are "tested." Moreover, the argument for case studies as a means for building theories seems strongest in regard to precisely those phenomena with which the subfield of "comparative" politics is most associated: macropolitical phenomena, that is, units of political study of considerable magnitude or complexity, such as nation-states and subjects virtually coterminous with them (party systems or political cultures). More precisely, the abstract brief in favor of the case study as a means of building theories seems to me to hold regardless of level of inquiry, but at the macrocosmic level practical research considerations greatly reinforce that brief.

Extensive argument is necessary to make these points. But while the fun is in arguing against conventional views (especially if, as in this case, they seem truistic), arguments do not make sense, and counterarguments are unlikely to be apropos, unless major terms are first defined. In political science the safe bet usually is that even widely used concepts are not widely understood in a uniform, unambiguous manner. Readers must therefore bear with me for a while as I clarify some basic terminology.

DEFINITIONS

Case Study and Comparative Study

1. The conception of case study commonly held in the social sciences is derived from, and closely similar to, that of clinical studies in medicine and psychology. Such studies are usually contrasted dichotomously (as if they were antitheses) to experimental ones, which furnish the prevalent conception of comparative study. Contrasts generally drawn between the two types of study cover virtually all aspects of inquiry: range of research, methods and techniques, manner of reporting findings, and research objectives.[1]

As to *range of research:* Experimental studies are held to be conducted with large numbers of cases, constituting samples of populations, while clinical studies deal with single individuals, or at most small numbers of them not statistically representative of a populous set. Experimental studies thus are sometimes said to be "extensive" and clinical ones "intensive." These adjectives do not refer to numbers of individuals alone, but also involve the number of variables taken into account. In experimental studies that number is deliberately and severely limited, and preselected, for the purpose of discovering relationships between traits abstracted from individual wholes. Clinical study, to the contrary, tries to capture the whole individual—"tries to" because it is, of course, conceded that doing so is only an approachable, not an attainable, end.

As for *methods and techniques:* The typical experimental study, first of all, starts with, and adheres to, a tightly constructed research design, whereas the typical clinical study is much more open-ended and flexible at all stages. The clinical researcher may have (probably must have) in mind some notions of where to begin inquiry, a sort of checklist of points to look into during its course, or perhaps even a preliminary model of the individual being studied; but actual study proceeds more by feel and improvisation than by plan. Second, the techniques most commonly associated with such inquiry in the case of "collective individuals" (i.e., social units) are the loose ones of participant observation (simply observing the unit from within, as if a member of it) and *Verstehen* (i.e., empathy: understanding the meaning of actions and interactions from the members' own points of view). The typical techniques of experimental inquiry, per contra, are those rigorous and routinized procedures of data processing and data analysis concocted to ensure high degrees of "nonsubjective" reliability and validity—the techniques of the statistics texts and research methods primers.

Reports of the findings of clinical study are generally characterized as narrative and descriptive: they provide case histories and detailed portraiture. Such reporting might therefore also be termed synthetic, while that of experimental studies is analytic, since it does not present depictions of "whole" individuals but rather of relations among components, or elements, of them. Beyond description, clinical studies present "interpretation"; beyond raw data, experimental ones present rigorously evaluated "findings."

It follows that the *objectives* of the two types of study also differ. That of experimental study is generalized knowledge: theoretical propositions. These may certainly apply to individuals but never exhaust the knowledge it is possible to have of them. Being general they necessarily miss what is particular and unique, which may or may not be a lot. The objective of clinical study, however, is precisely to capture the particular and unique, for if anything about an individual whole is such, so must be the whole per se. It is conceded that in describing an individual configuration we may get hunches about the generalizability of relations not yet experimentally studied, but only hunches, and even these only by serendipity.[2] Clinical study is therefore associated more with action objectives than those of pure knowledge. In the case of single individuals, it aims at diagnosis, treatment, and adjustment; in that of collective individuals, at policy. This association of clinical study with adjustive action is based on the assumption that therapy and policy can hardly proceed without something approximating full knowledge of its subjects, however much general propositions may help in proceeding from clinical knowledge of a case to the appropriate manipulation of a subject. Clinical and experimental objectives draw near, asymptotically, as "pure" knowledge becomes "applied" (i.e., in engineering models), but application is merely a possible extension of experimental knowledge while generally being an intrinsic objective of clinical research.

2. Anyone familiar with the modern history of comparative politics (see chapter 3) will realize that its development since the early 1950s involves

a transition, or shift, from the clinical to the experimental mode of study. Macridis and Brown criticized the old "comparative" politics for being,[3] among other things, noncomparative (concerned mainly with single cases) and essentially descriptive and monographic (not substantially concerned with theory and, at least in aim, wholistic); and they imply that it had a dominant therapeutic objective: to find ways of diagnosing the ills of un-stable democracies and making them more stable. Such studies, conform-ing to the model of clinical research, still abound, but the proportion of those conducted in accordance with that of experimental study has steadily grown, as has the proportion of monographic studies seeking, somehow, to tie into the other variety.

However, while the distinction between clinical and experimental stud-ies is useful for contrasting the old and new comparative politics, it does not serve nearly so well in distinguishing the case study from other modes of research. At best, it can provide an initial inkling (but only an inkling) of the differences among them. Certainly this chapter, which argues in favor of case studies, is not by any stretch of the imagination to be taken as a defense of the kind of work Macridis assails and the field has down-graded. The distinction offers a useful denotative definition of case studies in the social sciences (that is, what people usually mean by the term) but a far from useful connotative and generic one (how the term ought to be used if it is not to raise serious difficulties of meaning and classification and not to define merely one of numerous types of case study).

3. The essential objections to equating case study with clinical and com-parative study with experimental inquiry all revolve on one basic point: nothing compels the clustering (hence, dichotomization) of the various characteristics used to distinguish clinical and experimental studies. Al-though that clustering in fact occurs very frequently in the social sciences, it does so chiefly because of dubious beliefs and assumptions. At most, the characteristics have a certain practical affinity; for example, the fewer the cases studied, the more intensive study may be, other things being equal. But no logical compulsion is at work, and the practical considera-tions often are not weighty.

We may certainly begin with the notion that case studies, like clinical studies, concern "individuals," personal or collective (and, for tidiness of conceptualization, assume that only one individual is involved). From this, however, it does not follow that case studies must be intensive in the clinician's sense: nothing like "wholistic" study may be attempted, and the researcher may certainly aim at finding relationships between preselected variables—unless he assumes, a priori, that this is foolish. The research may be tightly designed and may put to use all sorts of sophisticated re-search techniques. (An excellent example is Osgood and Luria's "blind analysis," using the semantic differential, of a case of multiple personality.)[4] Its results need not be cast in narrative form, and its objective can certainly be the development of general propositions rather than portraiture of the particular and unique; nor need case studies be concerned with problems of therapeutic action when they go beyond narration, depiction, and subjective interpretation.

The same applies, *mutatis mutandis,* to studies of numerous cases, even leaving aside the fact that the cases need not be, and often are not, very numerous and certainly not a "sample." This leaves a large residual no-man's-land, even from the standpoint of numbers, between the clinical and experimental. Studies of numerous cases can also take into account numerous variables. Modern data-processing capabilities have, in fact, encouraged a kind of omnibus approach even to cross-national research, à la Banks and Textor,[5] in which anything one can think of is cross-tabulated and correlated with just about everything else. Even before these capabilities existed some comparative works treated the various aspects of complex whole, like polities, as comprehensively as any clinical investigation.[6] Studies of numerous cases also leave room for improvisation in research. They are not always tightly designed, do not always use rigorous research techniques, are sometimes reported in the descriptive vein, often have few or no theoretical pretensions, and also often seek direct answers to policy and other action questions, not answers that amount to the deduction of applied from pure theory.

These points of overlap and ambivalence in the distinction between the clinical and experimental have led to a concerted attack on the dichotomy in psychology itself. One typical attack argues that the dichotomy originates in an archaic and absurd *Methodenstreit* between "mechanistic" and "romantic" views of human nature.[7] Another argues that experimental modes of study can also be used profitably in research into single cases; this is the theme of a notable book of essays, $N = 1$.[8] This work implies the most important definitional point of all: if case study is defined as clinical study in the traditional sense, then we not only construct a messy generic (not necessarily classificatory) concept, but also foreclose the possibility of useful argument about case study as a tool in theory building. The definition answers the question: case study and theory are at polar opposites, linked only by the fortuitous operation of serendipity.

4. This attack on the conventional idea of case study serves a constructive as well as destructive purpose. It provides ammunition for later arguments against highly restrictive views concerning the role of case study in theory building and also points the way toward a better, and simpler, definition of what case studies are.

An unambiguous definition of case study should proceed from the one sure point that has been established: case study is the study of individuals. That is about as simple as one can get—but, because of one major problem, it is too simple. The problem is that one person's single individual may be another's numerous cases. Take an example: In order to help break down the dichotomy between the clinical and experimental, Davidson and Costello reprint a study by Chassan on the evaluation of drug effects during psychotherapy.[9] Chassan argues for the greater power of single-case study over the usual "treatment group" versus "control group" design—in this case, for determining the relative effects of tranquilizers and placebos. Readers can catch the flavor of his argument through two of his many italicized passages:

> The intensive statistical study of a single case can provide more meaningful and statistically significant information than, say, only end-point observations extended over a relatively large number of patients.
>
> The argument cited against generalization to other patients, from the result of a single case intensively studied, can actually be applied in a more realistic and devastating manner against the value of inferences . . . drawn from studies in which extensive rather than intensive degrees of freedom are used.

And so on, in the same vein. The whole paper is an object lesson to those who seek theoretical safety only in numbers. But there is a catch. Chassan studied only one patient, but used a large number of treatments by drug and placebo: "frequent observations over periods of sufficiently long duration." The individuals here are surely not the patients, although they may be for other purposes; it is each treatment, the effects of which are being compared. It is easy enough to see the advantages of administering different treatments to the same person over a long period (hence, safety in small numbers of a sort), as against using one patient per observation (although it is to Chassan's credit that he pointed them out in contrast to the more usual procedure). But n, despite the title of the book, in this case is not one.

If this problem arises with persons, it arises still more emphatically with "collective individuals." A study of six general elections in Britain may be, but need not be, an $n = 1$ study. It might also be an $n = 6$ study. It can also be an $n = 120,000,000$ study. It depends on whether the subject of study is electoral systems, elections, or voters.

What follows from this is that ambiguity about what constitutes an "individual" (hence "case") can only be dispelled by not looking at concrete entities but at the measures made of them. On this basis, a *"case" can be defined technically as a phenomenon for which we report and interpret only a single measure on any pertinent variable.* This gets us out of answering insoluble metaphysical questions that arise because any concrete entity can be decomposed, at least potentially, into numerous entities (not excluding "persons": they differ almost from moment to moment, from treatment to treatment, and consist of highly numerous cells, which consist of highly numerous particles, and so on). It also raises starkly the critical problem of this essay: what useful role can single descriptive measures (not measures of central tendency, association, correlation, variance or covariance, all of which presuppose numerous measures of each variable) play in the construction of theory?

If case study can be thus defined, *comparative study is simply the study of numerous cases along the same lines, with a view to reporting and interpreting numerous measures on the same variables of different "individuals."* The individuals, needless now to say, can be persons or collectivities, or the same person or collectivity at different points in time, in different contexts, or under different treatments. And the term "measure" should of course here be treated with latitude: it might be a highly precise quantity (34.67 percent of all Britons always vote Labour) or a rather imprecise observation (the British Labour party is now a chronic minority party).

Theory and Theory Building

We will be concerned with the utility of case studies in the development of theories in macropolitics—their utility both in themselves and, to an extent, relative to comparative (n = many) studies. While nearly everyone in the field at the present time agrees that the development of good theories is the quintessential end of political inquiry, conceptions of theory, and of the processes by which it may be developed, vary extremely in our field. This makes unavoidable a definitional exercise on theory and a review of the normal steps in theory building.

1. Two polar positions on what constitutes theory in our field can be identified. While positions range between them, they have recently been rather polarized, more often on, or very near, the extremes than between them.

On one extreme (the "hard" line on theory) is the view that theory consists solely of statements like those characteristic of contemporary theoretical physics (or, better, considered to be so by influential philosophers of science). A good summary of this view, tailored to the field of political science, is presented in Holt and Richardson's discussion of the nature of "paradigms," [10] but even better sources are the writings of scientist-philosophers such as Kemeny, Popper, and Hempel.[11]

Theories in this sense have four crucial traits: (1) The concepts used in them are defined very precisely, usually by stating definitions in terms of empirical referents, and are less intended to describe phenomena fully than to abstract from them characteristics useful for formulating general propositions about them. (2) The concepts are used in deductively connected sets of propositions that are either axioms (assumptions) or theorems deducted from them. (3) The object of the propositions is both logical consistency and "empirical import," that is, correspondence to observations of phenomena. And (4) empirical import is determined by tests themselves deduced from the propositions, and these are designed to make it highly probable that the propositions will flunk the tests because confidence in propositions is proportionate to the stiffness of the tests they manage to survive. In our own field, theories of this type are sometimes called "formal theories," mainly because of the large role of formal deduction in their elaboration; and economics is generally taken as the nearest social science model for them, not only in general form but also in regard to substantive "rationality" axioms.[12]

On the other pole (the "soft" line), theory is simply regarded as any mental construct that orders phenomena or inquiry into them. This qualifies as theory many quite diverse constructs, including classificatory schemes that assign individual cases to more or less general classes; "analytic" schemes that decompose complex phenomena into their component elements; frameworks and checklists for conducting inquiry (e.g., the "systems" approach to macropolitics, or "decision-making" checklists for the study of foreign policy formation); any empirical patterns found in properly processed data, or anything considered to underlie such patterns (e.g., learning processes or class position).

2. If the term *theory* were always prefaced by an appropriate adjective, wrangling about these, and less extreme, positions could be avoided. But this would not take us off the hook of having to specify how "good theory" as an objective of inquiry in our field should be conceived. The best position on this issue, it seems to me, is neither hard nor soft but does come closer to the hard than the soft extreme. It rests on two major premises.

The first is that it makes no sense whatever to call any mental construct a theory. Such constructs differ vastly in nature and purpose, so that they can hardly be considered to be of the same species. With some of them, not much more can be done than to assign names to phenomena or to order one's filing cabinets. And it can be demonstrated that, strictly speaking, the soft position compels one to regard as theory any statement whatever in conventional or technical discourse.

Second, it makes little more sense to restrict the term to constructs like those of theoretical physics, or those abstracted from that field by philosophers of science. While such constructs have proved extremely powerful in certain senses, one may doubt that they alone possess power (even in these senses). If constructs like them are not attainable in a field such as our own at its present stage of development (which is at least an open question, since constructs like them have in fact not been attained), commitment to theory in such a narrow sense may induce one to forego theoretical inquiry altogether. Most important, theories in the "hard" sense are a particular form developed, over considerable time, to realize the purposes—the motivating goals, animus, telos—of an activity; and while they do this very well, it does not follow that they are absolutely required for realizing these purposes.

Consequently, even if the constructs of theoretical physics are taken as a model, it seems unwise to restrict the notion of theory entirely to such constructs. It seems better to label as theory any constructs designed to realize the same ends and formulated with the same animus as those that characterize the fields in which hard theory has been developed—leaving open, anyway provisionally, the forms such constructs may take consistent with reasonable achievement of the ends. On this basis, theory is characterized by a telos, or animus, of inquiry rather than by the particular form of statements. The only requirement (which, however, is far from soft) is that the forms of theoretical statements must be conducive to the goals of theoretical activity.

Such a teleological conception of theory requires that the goals be made explicit. They can be characterized under the following headings: *regularity, reliability, validity, foreknowledge,* and *parsimony.*

a) The quintessential end of theorizing is to arrive at *statements of regularity* about the structure, behavior, and interaction of phenomena. "Regularity" here means, literally, "rulefulness": the discovery of rules that phenomena observe in the concrete world, as players do in games or logicians in logic. Such regularity can exist in many senses. The rules may describe simple relations among variables without specification of their exact nature; or they may describe sequences like causal paths or historical and genetic patterns; or they may be statements of the conditions of persistence or efficacy of structures. The rules may also be more or less "ruleful." They may be "probability statements" that permit no inferences about individual cases but only more or less confident ones about sets of them, or they may be "laws" in which probability is at unity. Both of these can further vary in "rulefulness" according, for example, to the number and significance of variables held constant or ignored, or whether they state necessary, sufficient, or both necessary and sufficient conditions if causal sequences or conditions of viability or performance are specified.

b) The animus of theoretical inquiry requires not merely empirical rules, but also that the rules be as *reliable and valid* as possible. Reliability exists to the extent that inquirers, proceeding in the same manner, arrive at the same results; validity to the extent that a presumed regularity has been subjected, unsuccessfully, to tough appropriate attempts at falsification. Not all presumed or discovered regularities are subject to tests of reliability and validity, and certainly not to equally tough ones: for example, a statistical inference about a set of cases observed by a researcher that cannot be restudied at all or in much the same way can never be reliable and is unlikely to be valid (i.e., successfully tested). Hence, just as concepts become theoretical by being used in regularity statements, so such statements become theoretical if they are subject to tough reliability and validity tests.

c) *Foreknowledge* is the correct anticipation, by sound reasoning, of unknowns (whether the unknown has or has not yet occurred). Theory not only does, but needs to, aim at that objective, because the toughest, hence most conclusive, test of any rule is the correct deduction from it of unobserved experience. In most cases, theories are shaped to fit observations already made, and this is fine, so long as observations are not deliberately selected to fit theories. The manner in which theories are shaped to fit observations does tell us something about their probable validity. But generally there are numerous rules that fit well any body of observations and numerous techniques that yield different results when the question of degree of rulefulness arises. Even if this were not so, all we can really learn from rules shaped to fit knowns is that they hold (in some degree) for the cases observed under the whole complex of conditions prevailing when they were observed, not that they hold for all such cases, under all conditions or under other precisely specifiable conditions. Only foreknowledge, in the sense above, can provide confidence that the regularities are less tenuous.

The objective of foreknowledge has been neglected in recent political science studies because of a fixation on the power of sophisticated data processing to yield valid rules (rather than just rules likely to be validated). Even more, it has been neglected because of a belief that foreknowledge always involves literal prescience of events in the future of the natural world, which, in view of the complexity of macropolitics, seems as near to impossible as anything can be. In fact, theoretical foreknowledge rarely takes the form of prescience. More often it involves experimental prediction (anticipating, by correct reasoning from presumed regularities, the results of activities in which variables are fully controlled), or concrete prediction (anticipating, by such reasoning, what will occur in the natural world if and only if specified initial conditions obtain), or forecasting (anticipating, by such reasoning, the probabilities of specified events occurring, given the initial conditions that do obtain). These types of foreknowledge all fall short of prescience and are not all equally conclusive for theory. The failure of a single forecast, for example, is generally (not always) less conclusive than that of an experimental prediction, although repeated forecasting failures are pretty definitive. All, however, give an essential insight into validity that the mere fitting of regularity statements to known data can never provide.

It should be evident that constructs exactly like those of theoretical physics are not needed for foreknowledge: certainly not for every type of it. All that is required of theory in the generic sense is that some unknown be strictly deducible from the posited regularities, whether the unknown is the outcome of an experiment, or the probabilities of natural events under obtaining conditions, or the occurrence of natural events under conditions specified by the theorist.

d) The notion of *parsimony* is hard to define precisely. The philosophers of science seem themselves to have had inordinate trouble with the concept. I take it to mean that regularity statements are parsimonious in proportion to (i) the variety and number of observations they order; (ii) the number of discrete theoretical constructs (i.e., constructs not strictly deducible from one another) used to order a constant volume and variety of observations; (iii) the number of other theoretical constructs subsumed to or derivable from them; and (iv) the number and complexity of variables used in the statements. On this basis, regularity statements are never parsimonious or unparsimonious (although the concept is often used dichotomously) but always more or less so, especially since trade-offs among the criteria of parsimony are possible.

The ideal of parsimony is to an extent aesthetic, but a high degree of it is required by the objective of foreknowledge and thus hangs together with the general animus of theoretical inquiry. The reason is simply that regularity statements can be made so cumbersome and complex that nothing (or, much the same, too many different things) can be strictly deduced from them, even when the cardinal sin of hypothesis saving is not committed. A case in point is Easton's "systems analysis" of macropolitics.[13] By my reading, Easton identifies at least twelve crucial stresses that can arise in the political system's input-conversion-output-feedback cycle, each potentially fatal and each capable of being more or less reduced ("managed") by different adaptations to stress. Since the stresses can occur in various combinations and sequences, deducing what may ensue from any given initial condition in a polity becomes a matter of permutation, and $12! = 479$ million (approximately); hence, any state of political affairs can lead to something like half a billion subsequent states of affairs without violating Easton's theory. Given that fact, the probability of correct forecasting of any sort seems low. So does that of finding a unique solution for why any given state of affairs exists, or that of failing to account for anything within the terms of Easton's theory. This is precisely why parsimony is essential: only a high degree of it can ensure that regularity statements may fail, and therefore also succeed. [14]

Theories can, of course, be more or less powerful, or "good," depending on the rulefulness of regularity statements, the amount of reliability and validity they possess, the amount and kinds of foreknowledge they provide, and how parsimonious they are.[15] The animus of theoretical inquiry is constantly to increase their power to some unattainable absolute in all these senses. And while that absolute might have a unique ideal form to which the forms of theoretical physics might provide a discerning clue, it should be evident that it can be approached through many kinds of formulations, and always only approached. This is why "theory" is better conceived of as a set of goals than as statements having a specified form.

At the same time, no mental construct qualifies as theory unless it satisfies the goals in some minimal sense. This minimal sense is that it must state a presumed regularity in observations that is susceptible to reliability and validity tests, permits the deduction of some unknowns, and is parsimonious enough to prevent the deduction of so many that virtually any occurrence can be held to bear it out. If these conditions are not satisfied, statements can still be interesting and useful; but they are not "theory."

These are the sort of constructs we want about macropolitics. It should be evident that the pivotal point in the whole conception is that regarding foreknowledge: validity is held to depend on it, parsimony is mainly required for the sake of establishing validity, and regularity statements are not an end unless valid. Any general appraisal of the utility of a method of inquiry must therefore also pivot on that point, as will my brief for the case study method.[16]

3. It should also be evident that foreknowledge is most closely bound up with the testing of theories and that the process of theory building involves much that precedes testing and some activities subsequent to it as well. It follows that modes of inquiry might be highly serviceable at one state of the process but not at others, and this also must be considered in arguments about them.

a) The process of theory building, needless to say, always begins with *questions* about experience for which answers are wanted—and raising questions, especially penetrating ones, is anything but a simple matter; indeed it is perhaps what most distinguishes the genius from the dullard (for whom common sense, the sense of ordinary people, leaves few mysteries). It is also an ability that, conceivably, could be sharpened or dulled by various modes of inquiry.

b) Questions, to be answered by theories, must usually be restated as *problems* or *puzzles*. This is a complex process that I have discussed elsewhere,[17] and it consists essentially of stating questions so that testable rules can answer them (which is not the case for any and all questions) and determining what core-puzzles must be solved if questions are to be answered. A familiar example is the subtle process by which Weber arrived at the conclusion that the question of his *Protestant Ethic* ("Why did modern capitalism as an economic system develop spontaneously only in the modern West?") boils down to the problem "what engenders the (unlikely) attitude of continuous, rational acquisition as against other economic orientations?"

c) The next step is *hypothesis:* formulating, by some means, a candidate-solution of the puzzle that is testable in principle and sufficiently plausible, prima facie, to warrant the bother and costs of testing. Like the formulation of theoretical problems, this initial step toward solving them generally first involves a "vision," then the attempt to state that vision in a rigorous and unambiguous form, so that conclusive testing becomes at least potentially possible. The candidate-solution need not be a single hypothesis or integrated set of hypotheses. In fact, a particularly powerful alternative is what Platt calls "strong inference" (and considers characteristic of the more rapidly developing "hard" sciences, such as molecular biology and high-energy physics): developing a set of competing hypotheses, some or most of which may be refuted by a single test.[18]

d) After that, of course, one searches for and carries out an appropriate, and if possible definitive, *test.* Such tests are rarely evident in hypotheses themselves, especially if questions of practicability are added to those of logic.

Testing is, in a sense, the end of the theory-building process. In another sense, it is not: if a test is survived the process of theorizing does not end. Apart from attempting to make pure knowledge applied, one continues to keep an eye out for contradictory or confirmatory observations, continues to look for more definitive tests, and continues to look for more powerful rules that order larger ranges of observations, or the same range more simply, or subsume the tested rule under one of a higher order, capable of subsuming also other tested rules.

We now have the basic conceptual equipment needed to discuss sensibly the usefulness of case studies in the building of theories in our field, both in general and at different stages of the theory-building process. The scene-setting has been long, and perhaps tedious, but nothing in political case studies (which are many) or writings about them (which are very few) suggests that the stage is overstocked with props. Others may, of course, argue for different constructions of the props—in which case, they will also reject much that follows.

OPTIONS ON THE UTILITY OF CASE STUDIES: AN OVERVIEW OF THE ARGUMENT

The Options

In taking positions on the value of case studies for theory building, both in themselves and relative to comparative studies, one can choose between six, not all mutually exclusive, options. These have been derived from a review of actual political case studies, the scant methodological literature about them (and counterparts in other social and behavioral sciences), and my own reflections on unconsidered possibilities. They are listed in order of the value seen in case studies, especially as one progresses along the path of theory building—a progression in which, arguably, intuitive vision plays a constantly decreasing role relative to systematic procedure.

Option 1 holds case studies and comparative studies to be wholly separate and unequal. They are separate in that the two modes of inquiry are considered to have so little in common that case studies are unlikely to provide more than a severely limited and crude basis for systematic comparisons (e.g., variables of major importance in "n = many" studies might be wholly ignored in studies of pertinent cases or might not be treated in readily comparable ways, and so on). The two modes of study are unequal in that only comparative studies are associated with the discovery of valid theories; case studies are confined to descriptions and intuitive interpretations.

Option 2 desegregates case studies and comparative studies, but hardly lessens their inequality. It holds that the two modes of inquiry draw near (asymptotically) in the interpretation of cases, because such interpretations can be made only by applying explicit or implicit theoretical generalizations to various cases. Case study, however, remains highly unequal because it is certainly not required, nor even especially useful, for the development of theories. There is an exception to this principle, but it is very limited. One never, or, at least very rarely, has all the theories needed to interpret and treat a case; hence, something in the process of case interpretation must nearly always be left incomplete or to intuitive insight (which is why the two modes may approach closely but not intersect). Any aspects of case interpretation in regard to which theory is silent may be regarded as questions on the future agenda of theory building, as any intuitive aspects of interpretation may be regarded as implicit answers to the questions.

Option 3 grows out of the exception to Option 2. It holds that case studies may be conducted precisely for the purpose of discovering questions and puzzles for theory and discovering candidate-rules that might solve theoretical puzzles. The idea is simply that, if subjects and insights for comparative study are wanted, case study can provide them, and that case study might be conducted precisely for that purpose and perhaps satisfy it by something less chancy than serendipity or at least by affording larger scope to serendipitous discovery than studies that sacrifice intensive for extensive research. This still confines the utility of case study to the earlier stages of theorizing and makes it a handmaiden to comparative study. But it does tie case study into the theory-building process by something less contingent than possible feedback flowing from the "clinician" to the "experimentalist."

Option 4 focuses on the stage in theory building at which one confronts the question whether candidate-rules are worth the costs (time, effort, ingenuity, manpower, funds, etc.) of testing. It holds that, although in the final analysis only comparative studies can really test theories, well-chosen case studies can shed much light on their plausibility, hence whether proceeding to the final, generally most costly, stage of theory building is worthwhile. This clearly involves something more than initial theoretical ideas. It begins to associate case study with questions of validity, if only in the grudging sense of prima facie credibility.

Option 5 goes still another step further, to the testing (validation) stage itself. It might be held (no revelation forbids it) that in attempting to validate theories, case studies and comparative studies generally are equal, even if separate, alternative means to the same end. The choice between them may then be arbitrary or may be tailored to such nonarbitrary considerations as the particular nature of theories, accessibility of evidence, skills of the researcher, or availability of research resources. A corollary of this position is, of course, that case studies may be no less systematic in procedure and rigorous in findings than comparative studies.

Option 6 is the most radical from the comparativist's point of view. It holds that case studies are not merely equal alternatives at the testing stage, but, properly carried out, a better bet than comparative studies. It might even be extended to hold that comparative studies are most useful as preliminary, inconclusive aids to conclusive case studies: that is, the former may suggest probabilities and the latter clinch them. (Beyond this, of course, lies the still more radical possibility that comparative studies are good for nothing, case studies good for everything. But all inquiry suggests that this is wrong, and while the history of ideas also suggests that the unthinkable should be thought, there is no point in doing so unless a good case can be made for Option 6.)

Arguments on the Options: An Overview

The options discussed above tell us how we might answer the first two questions posed in the introduction to this chapter, while the answer to the third depends on the others. Since the answers to be proposed are complex and the manner of the presentation is far from simple (being intended to present others' views as well as my own), I will outline them before arguing them, as a sort of map to the discussion.

1. First of all, a taxonomic point should be emphasized. This is that "case study" is in fact a very broad generic concept, whether defined

technically as "single-measure" study or by the simpler "single-individual" criterion. The genus can and, for our purposes, must be divided into numerous species, some of which closely resemble, some of which differ vastly from, the model of clinical study. The species that need distinction are: *configurative-idiographic studies, disciplined-configurative studies, heuristic-case studies, case studies as plausibility probes,* and *crucial-case studies.* There may be still other types, but these five occur most frequently or are of most consequence to us.

Two things are notable about these species. They are intimately associated with the options on the utility of case studies in theory building: each option is linked to a special type of case study (except that options 5 and 6 make no difference to the type of case study used). And as the utility attributed to case study increases, especially in progression through the phases of theory building, the associated type of case study increasingly departs from the traditional mode of clinical research and, except for numbers of individuals studied, increasingly resembles that of experimental inquiry.

2. As for choice among the options, and associated types of case study, it seems that the modal preference of contemporary political scientists is the third and/or second (not so different, except in nuance, that they preclude being chosen in conjunction); that few choose the fourth (more for reasons of unfamiliarity than methodological conviction); that options 5 and 6 are not chosen by anyone, or at least by very few. The evidence for this is mostly what political scientists actually write, reinforced by reactions to a preliminary version of this paper by a pretty fair cross-section of fellow professionals and a desultory poll among colleagues and students (only one of whom chose any option beyond the third, and that only because he reckoned that no one would list other possibilities unless up to tricks).

The prevailing preferences seem worth challenging on behalf of the options more favorable to case study. The latter appear to be rejected (better, not considered) for reasons other than full methodological deliberation, more as a result of overreaction against one weak type of case study than because of full consideration of the whole range of alternatives. In consequence, potentially powerful types of case study are neglected, and case studies are carried out less rigorously than they might be. Arguably, as well, this incurs liabilities in the conclusiveness of theories and the definitiveness of findings.

I propose to conduct the argument to this effect by evaluating each option, and associated type of case study, seriatim. In gist, my argument runs as follows:

a) Option 1 is hardly worth arguing against. Its basic premise—that comparative and case studies are, for all intents and purposes, antithetical—has been exploded for good and all by Verba in our field,[19] and has been widely attacked in other social sciences as well.[20] Nevertheless, it is worth discussing because the type of case study associated with it was once dominant (and is still fairly common), and still provides the most widely prevalent notion of what case study is all about and of its potential for theory building.

b) All the other options are tenable, but only because there are different types of case study that have different power in regard to theory building, and because the utility of case studies is not fully determined by logic (abstract methodology) but depends also on practical considerations (e.g., characteristics of one's subject matter).

c) Options 2 and 3 identify perfectly legitimate uses of case study and methods of carrying them out. They are implicit in a host of meritorious political studies, but these studies do not come near exhausting the utility of case study for theory building. Case studies may be used not merely for the interpretative application of general ideas to particular cases (i.e., after theory has been established) or, heuristically, for helping the inquirer to arrive at notions of problems to solve or solutions worth pursuing, but may also be used as powerful means of determining whether solutions are valid.

d) Option 4 deserves special consideration for two reasons. It identifies an objective for which case study of a particular type is eminently serviceable and which can be of vast importance in theory building, but which is rarely pursued, by case study or other means. In addition, the utility of case study for that objective prepares the ground for arguing the case for the more radical options remaining.

e) Option 5 will be held to state the logically most defensible position: to attain theory in political inquiry, comparative studies and case studies should be considered, by and large, as alternative strategies at all stages, with little or nothing to choose (logically) between them. Since that argument will be most difficult to sustain—at least against the conventional wisdom—for the testing stage, the argument will concentrate on the type of case study suitable to it.

f) When practical considerations are added to logic, option 6 seems still more sensible, at least for studies of politics on the macrolevel. Case study is generally a better choice than comparative study for testing theories in macropolitics, but the type of case study useful for this purpose requires a kind of prior knowledge for which preliminary comparative study (of a limited kind) may often be useful or even necessary. This amounts to saying that comparative study can, in some circumstances, be treated as a handmaiden to case study, not vice versa, and thus, in a sense, stands the popular option 3 on its head.

Before working through all this in detail, I want particularly to emphasize two points. First, nothing that follows should be regarded as an attack on the utility of comparative study in theory building, simply because case studies are defended. (Some readers of an early draft of this essay concluded from this that comparative and case studies were not distinguishable after all. This is wrong: they have been distinguished. The point is that, logically at any rate, the distinction is not necessarily consequential for theory building.) Comparative studies have proved their utility. To the extent that they are invidiously evaluated vis-à-vis case studies, this is done on two grounds only: on practical grounds of limited applicability and because "n = many" studies invite avoidable errors of method (psychological, not logical hazards) in theory building that case studies are more likely to preclude.

Second, it is not to be inferred that just any case study will do for the purposes of theory building. Some readers of a draft of this essay concluded that it constituted a defense of "traditional" political studies against the "behavioralists." This is ludicrous, but it occurred. *The discussion presents an argument for both case studies and for carrying them out in a particular way.* Since the type of case study for which it argues is very demanding, implying great rigor of thought and exactitude of observation, it is hardly "anti-behavioralist"; and since that type of case study, to my knowledge, is as yet virtually nonexistent in our field, the argument can hardly be "traditionalist."

TYPES AND USES OF CASE STUDY

Configurative-Idiographic Study

1. In philosophy and psychology a distinction has long been drawn between nomothetic (generalizing, rule-seeking) and idiographic (individualizing, interpretative) types of, or emphases in, science. The philosophic progenitor of this terminology (and, in part, the ideas that underlie it) is Windelband,[21] the most notable contemporary defender of the distinction is Gordon Allport.[22] Idiographic study is, in essence, what was earlier described as clinical study and configurative-idiographic study is its counterpart in fields, like macropolitics, that deal with complex collective individuals. (Verba calls them configurative-idiosyncratic studies, but the difference in terminology is of no consequence.)

The configurative element in such studies is their aim to present depictions of the overall *Gestalt* (i.e., configuration) of individuals: polities, parties, party systems, and so on. The idiographic element in them is that they either allow facts to speak for themselves or bring out their significance by largely intuitive interpretation, claiming validity on the ground that intensive study and empathetic feel for cases provide authoritative insights into them.

If configurative-idiographic studies are made from philosophic conviction, then the following assumptions usually are at work:[23] (a) In the study of personalities and the collectivities they form, one cannot attain prediction and control in the natural-science sense, but only "understanding" (*verstehen*)—and thus, from understanding, limited, nondeductive conceptions of probable futures and prudent policy. (b) In attaining understanding, subjective values and modes of cognition are crucial, and these resist quantification. (c) Each subject, personal or collective, is unique, so generalizations can at most be only about their actions (persons) or interactions (collectivities). And (d) the whole is lost or at least distorted in abstraction and analysis—the decomposition of the individual into constituent traits and statements of relations among limited numbers of these; it is "something more" than an aggregate of general relations, rather than "nothing but" such an aggregate.

As already stated, configurative-idiographic studies were long the dominant mode of case study in political science. They still are common, although harder nowadays to distinguish from other types of case study in the field because, as Verba points out,[24] homage is now often paid to the behavioral "revolution" in the field by using "some systematic framework to preface or organize the chapters of such studies and by including new variables and aspects of political systems" in them—frameworks and variables, that is to say, developed for nomothetic purposes.

2. Configurative-idiographic studies are certainly useful, and, at their best, have undeniably considerable virtues. They may be beautifully written and make their subjects vivid. They may pull together and elegantly organize wide and deep researches. The intuitive interpretations they provide may be subtle and persuasive and suggest an impressive feel for the cases they treat.

Their most conspicuous weakness is that, as Verba puts it, "they do not easily add up"—presumably to reliable and valid statements of regularity about sets of cases, or even about a case in point.[25] This is plain in regard to sets of cases; the summation regarding them is at most factual (information about similar subjects, e.g., legislatures, parties, etc., in different contexts) and, because of idiosyncrasies in fact collecting and presentation, rarely involving even the systematic accumulation of facts. Anyone who has used secondary sources for compiling comparable data on numerous cases knows this to his pain, and, even more painfully, that inventories of interpretative propositions culled from case studies usually contain about as many distinguishable items as studies. The point is less plain, but just as true, for regularity statements concerning individual cases. The interpretations, being idiosyncratic, rarely come to an agreed position, or even to a point of much overlap. For example, in the configurative-idiographic literature on France there seems to be overlap on the position that there are "two Frances," but nearly everyone has his own conception of what they are and where they are found. This situation is hardly surprising: in configurative-idiographic study the interpreter simply considers a body of observations that are not self-explanatory, and, without hard rules of interpretation, may discern in them any number of patterns that are more or less equally plausible.

The criticism that configurative-idiographic study does not add up to theory, in our sense, is mitigated by the fact that its capability to do so was never claimed by its exponents; in fact it is often explicitly repudiated. What is really troublesome about configurative-idiographic study is the repudiation itself (i.e., the claim that case study in the behavioral and social sciences can only be idiographic) and its consequences for the way in which the nomothetic utility of case studies in these fields is regarded.

For a thorough refutation of the idiographer's position, and a broad attack on the distinction between the nomothetic and idiographic itself, readers should consult Holt.[26] His argument, in gist, is (a) that both the position and distinction have "peculiar origins"—misunderstandings of Kant by lesser German philosophers and "romantic" assumptions prevalent during the early nineteenth century ("Teutonic ghosts" raised against classical ideas and styles) that led to unreasonably sharp lines between nature and mechanisms on one hand and behavior and organisms on the other; and, more important, (b) that none of the postulates of idiographic study, as outlined above, withstands examination. As for the consequences of the claims of idiographers, the most stultifying has been the association of nomothetic study in macropolitics with study different from that favored by idiographers in all respects: not only study based on more systematic methods of collecting and processing data and on explicit frameworks of inquiry intended to make for cumulation, but "comparative" (i.e., multicase, cross-national, cross-cultural) studies.

If case study could only be configurative-idiographic in character, then the conclusions that case studies and comparative studies are wholly antithetical and that theories about politics require comparative study, or are unattainable, could not be avoided. But case study need not have that character, and the comparativists themselves have pointed the way to other varieties—without, however, overcoming a fundamental bias against case study of any kind in theory construction, largely anchored to the archetype of such studies in our field.

Disciplined-Configurative Study

1. The comparativist's typical reaction to the theoretical poverty of configurative-idiographic studies is to hold that, while theories cannot be

derived from case interpretations, such interpretations can, and should, be derived from theories. "The unique explanation of a particular case," says Verba, "can rest on general hypotheses."[27] Indeed, it *must* rest on them, since theoretical arguments about a single case, in the last analysis, always proceed from at least implicit general laws about a class or set to which it belongs or about universal attributes of all classes to which the case can be subsumed. The logic involved has been succinctly stated in Hempel's discussion of "scientific" explanation, the essence of which is the explanation of particular phenomena (in my terms "case interpretation") "by showing that [their] existence could have been inferred—either deductively or with a high probability—by applying certain laws of universal or of statistical form to specified antecedent circumstances."[28] Those who consider this the only way of interpreting cases scientifically hold that the theoretical bases of case interpretations should always be made explicit, and that ad hoc additions to a framework of case interpretation should always be made as if they were general laws, not unique factors operating only in the case in point. The bases of case interpretation, in other words, should be established theories or, lacking them, provisional ones, and such interpretations can be sound only to the extent that their bases are in fact valid as general laws.

Case studies so constructed are "disciplined-configurative studies." The terminology is Verba's, who recommends such studies to us. Studies of this type are in fact very common in contemporary political studies—although, because of our disciplinary *embarras de pauvreté* in regard to validated, or even provisional, "general laws," they more frequently involve the application to cases of frameworks of inquiry, hopefully intended to help knowledge become nomothetic, not deductions from theory in any strict sense of the term.[29]

Disciplined-configurative studies need not just passively apply general laws or statements of probability to particular cases. A case can impugn established theories if the theories ought to fit it but do not. It may also point up a need for new theory in neglected areas. Thus, the application of theories to cases can have feedback effects on theorizing, as Hempel recognizes. In addition, it is unlikely that all aspects of a case can be nomologically explained. As in the field of engineering, where general theories are applied to achieve conscious ends in particular circumstances, there are nearly always elements of prudence, common sense, or "feel" in case interpretations. Theory building, however, aims at the constant reduction of those elements, by stating notions that fit particular cases as general theoretical rules and subjecting them to proper theoretical tests.

In essence, the chain of inquiry in disciplined-configurative studies runs from comparatively tested theory to case interpretation, and thence, perhaps, via ad hoc additions, newly discovered puzzles, and systematized prudence, to new candidate-theories. Case study thus is tied into theoretical inquiry—but only partially, where theories apply or can be envisioned; passively, in the main, as a receptacle for putting theories to work; and fortuitously, as a catalytic element in the unfolding of theoretical knowledge. This is, of course, still close to the clinician's conception of his role, and configurative studies that are disciplined in intent are not always easy to distinguish from unadulterated idiography. The two types are often intermixed and easily blend together.

2. The essential basis of Verba's argument about the relations between general theory and particular case interpretation is surely correct. If the interpretations of a case are general laws correctly applied to the case, the interpretations may be valid or invalid, depending on whether the laws are valid; otherwise, their validity simply cannot be known at all. Moreover, if cases are complex, the number of possible alternative interpretations, equally plausible because not at variance with the facts of the case, is usually vast, so that undisciplined case interpretation in much-studied cases usually yields large inventories of quite different propositions, none of which is clearly superior to any other. Preferences among them depend on personal tastes or general intellectual fads.

This point can be illustrated by a long quote from an essay of mine on the causes of revolutions. Studying the etiology of internal wars, I argued,

> poses a difficulty . . . how to choose among a rare abundance of hypotheses which cannot all be equally valid nor all be readily combined. This problem exists because most propositions about the causes of internal wars have been developed in historical studies of particular cases (or very limited numbers of cases) rather than in broadly comparative, let alone genuinely social-scientific, studies. In historical case studies one is likely to attach significance to any aspect of prerevolutionary society that one intuits to be significant, and so long as one does not conjure up data out of nothing one's hypotheses cannot be invalidated on the basis of the case in question.
>
> That most studied of all internal wars, the French Revolution, provides a case in point—as well as examples in abundance of the many social, personal, and environmental forces to which the occurrence of internal wars might be attributed. Scarcely anything in the French *ancien régime* has not been blamed, by one writer or another, for the revolution, and all of their interpretations, however contradictory, are based on solid facts.
>
> Some interpreters have blamed the outbreak of the French Revolution on intellectual causes, that is to say, on the ideas, techniques, and great public influence of the *philosophes* (who were indeed very influential). This is the standard theory of post-revolutionary conservative theorists, from Chateaubriand to Taine, men who felt, in essence, that in prerevolutionary France a sound society was corrupted by a seductive and corrosive philosophy.
>
> Other writers have blamed the revolution mainly on economic conditions, although it is difficult to find very many who single out as crucial the same

conditions. The revolution has been attributed to sheer grinding poverty among the lower classes (who were certainly poor); to financial profligacy and mismanagement on the part of the government (of which it was in fact guilty); to the extortionate taxation inflicted on the peasants (and peasant taxation verged upon brutality); to short-term setbacks (which actually occurred and caused great hardship) like the bad harvest of 1788, the hard winter of 1788–89, and the still winds of 1789 which prevented flour from being milled and made worse an already acute shortage of bread; to the over-abundant wine harvests of the 1780s (one of the first historic instances of the harmful effects of overproduction); to the increased wealth and power of the bourgeoisie in a society still dominated to a significant extent by aristocrats, the growth of the Parisian proletariat and its supposedly increasing political consciousness, and the threatened abrogation of the financial privileges of the aristocracy, particularly their exemption from taxation—all unquestionable facts producing manifest problems.

Still another set of writers locates the crucial cause of the revolution in aspects of social structure. Much has been made, and with sufficient reason, of the fact that in the last years of the *ancien régime* there occurred a hardening in the lines of upward mobility in French society—for example, a decline in grants of patents of nobility to commoners and the imposition of stringent social requirements for certain judicial and administrative positions and the purchase of officerships in the army. This, many have argued (following Mosca's and Pareto's famous theory of the circulation of elites), engendered that fatal yearning for an aristocracy of wealth and talent to which the *philosophes* gave expression. Much has also been made, with equal reason, of popular dissatisfaction with the parasitic life of the higher nobility, with its large pensions and puny duties, its life of hunting, love-making, watch-making, and interminable conversation.

And much has been attributed to the vulnerability of the privileged classes to the very propagandists who wanted to alter the system that supported them ("How," asked Taine, "could people who talked so much resist people who talked so well?"), reflected in the Anglomania which swept through the higher aristocracy toward the end of the *ancien régime* and in the rush of many aristocrats to the cause of the Americans in their war of independence.

There are also certain well-founded "political" explanations of the French Revolution: that the revolution was really caused by the violation of the tacit "contract" on which the powers of the monarchy rested (a contract by which the aristocracy surrendered its powers to the monarchy in return for receiving certain inviolable privileges), or that the revolution was simply a successful political conspiracy by the Jacobins, based on efficient political organization. Personalities, needless to say, get their due as well: the revolution has been blamed, for example, on the character, or lack of character, of Louis XVI (who was in fact weak, vacillating and inconsistent), the supposed immorality of the Queen (who indeed was the subject, justly or not, of many scandals), the effect on the public of the dismissal of Necker, and, of course, on the "genius," good or evil, of unquestionable geniuses like Mirabeau, Danton, Marat, and Robespierre.

We could take other internal wars and arrive at the same result—similarly large lists of explanations, most of them factual, yet inconclusive. The more remote in time and the more intensively analyzed the internal war, the longer the list of hypotheses. . . .

How can this embarrassment of interpretative riches (one hesitates to say theoretical riches) be reduced? If the examination of any single case allows one to determine only whether an interpretation of it is based on facts, then broad comparative studies in space and/or time are needed to establish the significance of the facts on which the interpretations are based. Was a blockage in the channels of social mobility a significant precondition of the French Revolution? We can be reasonably confident that it was only if it can be shown that elite circulation and political stability are generally related. Was the Chinese population explosion really an important cause of the Chinese revolution? Surely this is unlikely if demographic pressures do not generally affect the viability of regimes.[30]

The argument of this passage still strikes me as correct. However, the operative sentence in the last paragraph should have read that "valid theory is needed to establish the significance of the facts on which the interpretations are based," leaving open the extent to which the formulation of valid theories requires "broad comparative studies." For the problem here is one of case interpretation, not theory building, and the possibility that sound bases for case interpretation might be furnished by case studies themselves cannot be dismissed, unless one assumes (as Verba does, and as I did) that no types of case study other than the configurative-idiographic or disciplined-configurative varieties exist. But this, as will soon be evident, is far from the case—and concedes far too much to idiographers or those who, opposing idiography, nevertheless accept the dichotomy between the clinical and experimental that ultimately gives rise to idiographic studies.

It remains to add a point insufficiently stressed in writings on disciplined-configurative studies. The application of theories in case interpretation, although rarely discussed, is not at all a simple process, even leaving aside the question of how valid theory is to be developed. Such applications only yield valid interpretations if the theories permit strict deductions to be made and the interpretations of the case are shown to be logically compelled by the theories. In the case of revolutions, for instance, it is not enough to know that a regularity exists and that a case somehow "fits" it (i.e., does not manifestly contradict it). One should also be able to demonstrate, by correct reasoning, that, given the regularity and the characteristics of the case, revolution must have occurred, or at least had a high probability of occurring. Not all theories permit this to be done, or at least equally well. For example, a theory attributing revolution to aggressions engendered by social frustrations will hardly fail to fit any case of revolution, nor tell us exactly why any case of it occurred. Unless it specifies precisely how much and what sort of frustration engenders revolution, on whose part, and under what complex of other conditions,[31] the frustration-aggression theory of revolution, applied, say, to the French Revolution, can yield about as many plausible case interpretations as can configurative-idiographic study (there having existed many sources of frustration in the *ancien régime,* as in all regimes).

This point brings out a major utility of attempting disciplined case interpretation. Aiming at the disciplined application of theories to cases forces one to state theories more rigorously than might otherwise be done—provided that the application is truly "disciplined," that is, designed to show that valid theory compels a particular case interpretation and rules out others. As already stated, this, unfortunately, is rare (if it occurs at all) in political study. One reason is the lack of compelling theories. But there is another, which is of the utmost importance: political scientists reject, or do not even consider, the possibility that valid theories might indeed *compel* particular case interpretations. The import of that possibility, assuming it to exist, lies in the corollary that a case might invalidate a theory, if an interpretation of the case compelled by the theory does not fit it.

But this goes too far ahead, toward a crucial argument that will require much discussion below. The point for the present is merely that exponents of disciplined-configurative study have insufficiently considered both the difficulties and promises of the relations between general theories and particular case interpretations.[32]

Heuristic Case Studies

1. Disciplined-configurative study assumes that "general laws" are available. It is not thought of as a part of the process of theory building as such, except in that the interpretation of cases may lead to ad hoc, serendipitous additions to existing theories in order to cover puzzling aspects of a case. However, the feedback effect in Verba's recommended sequence of inquiry can be isolated from the rest of the sequence and case study deliberately used to stimulate the imagination toward discerning important general problems and possible theoretical solutions. That is the essence of heuristic case studies (heuristic means "serving to find out"). Such studies, unlike configurative-idiographic ones, tie directly into theory building and therefore are less concerned with overall concrete configurations than with potentially generalizable relations between aspects of them; they also tie into theory building less passively and fortuitously than does disciplined-configurative study, because the potentially generalizable relations do not just turn up but are deliberately sought out.

Heuristic case studies do not necessarily stop with one case, but can be conducted seriatim, by the so-called building-block technique,[33] in order to construct increasingly plausible and less fortuitous regularity statements.

This technique is quite simple in principle. One studies a case in order to arrive at a preliminary theoretical construct. That construct, based on a single case, is unlikely to constitute more than a slim clue to a valid general model. One therefore confronts it with another case that may suggest ways of amending and improving the construct to achieve better case interpretation; and this process is continued until the construct seems sufficiently refined to require no further major amendment or at least to warrant testing by large-scale comparative study. Each step beyond the first can be considered a kind of disciplined-configurative study, but is better regarded as heuristic case study proceeding with increasingly refined questions and toward increasingly more specific ends. It is important not to confuse the whole process with comparative study. The latter seeks regularities through the simultaneous inspection of numerous cases, not the gradual unfolding of increasingly better theoretical constructs through the study of individuals. Of course, comparative studies can also employ the building-block technique by successively refined theories through a series of multicase studies.

Heuristic case studies should also not be confused with pedagogic ones, which abound in politics and closely related fields. Pedagogic cases in politics generally have the aim of teaching policy and administrative skills by putting students into the positions of policymakers and administrators through detailed narrative accounts of real action problems. They are derived from case-method teaching in the law and business schools and are most akin to configurative-idiographic studies, except that the idiography is supplied by students, under the guidance of pedagogues assumed to possess special practical wisdom or experience. Theory is not supposed to emerge, and to my knowledge never has emerged, from them.

2. The claim that theoretical puzzles and insights can be usefully (perhaps most usefully) sought in case study is the standard defense of case study by theory-oriented social scientists. Equally commonplace is the belief that this is all that case study can usefully accomplish in the process of theory building. Consequently, studies of this type abound in political science and have recently crowded or displaced configurative-idiographic studies as the predominant species (no actual frequency count has been made); and there has been little exploration of case studies that might take one beyond the stage of hypothesizing. In many cases, such studies are carried out in light of preconstructed checklists of variables or frameworks of analysis, such as the "functional" framework associated with Almond and his associates. As one might expect in case study oriented toward theory, these frameworks focus attention on special variables, but not so narrowly as is common in extensive experimental work.

The justification for heuristic case studies runs as follows: (a) Theories do not come from a vacuum, or fully and directly from data. In the final analysis they come from the theorist's imagination, logical ability, and ability to discern general problems and patterns in particular observations. (b) There are ineffable differences in such imaginative and other abilities, but various aids can be used to stimulate them: among them, the printouts from data banks or other comparative studies (which, however, never obviate the use of theoretical imagination, e.g., for interpreting the printouts into proper regularity statements and for determining what data banks should contain or how comparative studies should be designed in the first place). (c) The track record of case studies as stimulants of the theoretical imagination is good. (d) One reason it is good is precisely that, unlike wide-ranging comparative studies, case studies permit intensive analysis that does not commit the researcher to a highly limited set of variables, and thus increases the probability that critical variables and relations will be found. The possibility of less superficiality in research, of course, also plays a role here.

3. Arguments in favor of heuristic case studies surely have merit. Whatever logic might dictate, the indubitable fact is that some case study writers in macropolitics have come up with interpretations notably incisive for their cases and notably plausible when taken as generalizations for sets of them, with or without the benefit of special frameworks or approaches. See, for example, the works of such men as Tocqueville, Bagehot, Halévy, Bryce, and Bodley, or, in another field, anthropologists too numerous to mention.

Nevertheless, one may argue that too much is made of heuristic case studies, for two related reasons. One is that those who defend them sometimes seem to do so simply because they can see no more ambitious function to be served by case study. The other is that, not wishing to make other claims but to defend case studies, they claim too much for such studies as heuristic tools, especially in comparison to "n = many" studies. Scenting a valid claim, they exaggerate it—and miss the possibility that a more persuasive brief might be based on a greater sense of limitation at the heuristic stage of theory building and a lesser one at others.

The point that case studies are good for more than getting clues will concern us later. But the anticipation of that point in the previous section can be supplemented here by a further suggestive argument. Case studies intended to serve a heuristic function can proceed much in the manner of "clinical" study, that is, with a minimum of design or rigor, and tackle any case that comes to hand. In that event, however, nothing distinguishes the study from configurative-idiographic study, except the researcher's hopes and intentions, and results can only turn up by good fortune—which the bright will seize and the dull miss, but which the researcher can do nothing to induce. The alternatives are to use at least a modicum of design and rigor in research and not to choose just any case on any grounds but a special sort of case: one considered likely to be revealing, on some basis or other. The suggestive point in this for later argument is not that case study may often depart markedly from the archetype of clinical study (although that is noteworthy), but that *certain kinds of cases may be regarded as more instructive for theory building than others*. Actual heuristic case studies seem in fact generally, even if often just implicitly, to make that claim for the cases selected. The grounds are often obscure, and the claim often seems *post hoc* and intended to disarm charges of idiography. The point nevertheless remains that the brief for heuristic case study is strong only to the extent that cases especially instructive for theory, and subject to rigorous inquiry, can be identified. And if that possibility exists, then the further possibility arises that some cases might be especially instructive also at other stages of the theory-building process.

If the prevalent emphasis on heuristic functions is too modest, in what senses does it also exaggerate? First of all, the fact that case study writers have often spawned ideas notable as generalizations proves nothing. The Tocquevilles or Bagehots might have been successful in spawning plausible theories without writing case studies, since their imagination and incisiveness clearly matter more than the vehicles chosen for putting them to work. If they had used comparative studies they might have been even more successful, and more successful still if they had had available modern technology for accumulating, coding, storing, and processing data—not to mention the fact that they do always make implicit, sometimes explicit, use of comparisons in their case studies (e.g., Bagehot's contrasts between Britain and America, Tocqueville's between America and France), even if only to demonstrate that factors used to interpret their cases do in fact differ in different cases. Moreover, for every case study that has notably succeeded in spawning theory, there are scores that have notably failed— and this does not refer to idiography alone. Case study certainly furnishes no guarantee that theoretical abilities will be awakened or sharpened. And comparativists have been at least as successful in spawning theories as configurativists; for every Tocqueville or Bagehot we can produce an offsetting Aristotle, Machiavelli, Mosca, Pareto, or Weber.

Second, the benefit of being able to take into consideration more variables in case study incurs the cost of highly circumscribed breadth of inference. And it is probable that the number of hypotheses suggested, hence also the number of invalid ones to be pursued, will be proportional to the number of variables considered. Heuristic case studies have a demonstrable tendency, as in the case of studies of the French Revolution, to spawn a crushing and chaotic number and variety of candidate-generalizations, or hypercomplex multivariate theories, especially when these studies are made by imaginative people. And, unlike comparative studies, they cannot even yield initial clues about the generalizability of relations selected from all those that constitute the case—unless, to repeat, the case is considered, on some good basis, especially revealing for sets of phenomena, that is, one for which breadth-of-inference problems may be claimed to be slight.

These problems have led some to identify "grounded theory" (theory that is initially derived from observations, not spawned wholly out of logic and imagination) with comparative inquiry rather than case study.[34] The reasons for doing so are rather convincing. But the more sensible position surely is that, if we are really only concerned with the initial formulation of candidate-theories as a phase of theoretical inquiry (and not theory leaping full-blown out of data), case study is useful but by no means indispensable, as also is comparative study or any other exercise of the theoretical imagination. It is manifestly more useful for some people than others. It also would be generally more useful than it has been if more case studies were deliberately undertaken as exploratory means for arriving at candidate-theories, rather than simply allowing these to occur fortuitously, and if special characteristics of heuristically instructive cases could be specified and something like a heuristic "method" could be developed.

If nothing more were to be said for case studies than that they may be helpful in initially formulating candidate regularity statements, we could only conclude that there is no special reason for either making or not making such studies. It follows that if there is a strong justification for case studies as tools in developing theories, it must be found in the special utility of such studies at some later stage of the sequence of inquiry by which theories are established, or, at a minimum, their availability as reasonable alternatives to comparative studies during the later, no less than earlier, stages of the theory-building process.

Plausibility Probes

1. After hypotheses are formulated, one does not necessarily proceed immediately to test them. A stage of inquiry preliminary to testing sometimes intervenes and ought to do so far more often than it actually does in political study (or in other social sciences). It involves probing the "plausibility" of candidate-theories. Plausibility here means something more than a belief in potential validity plain and simple, for hypotheses are unlikely ever to be formulated unless considered potentially valid; it also means something less than actual validity, for which rigorous testing is required. In essence, plausibility probes involve attempts to determine whether potential validity may reasonably be considered great enough to warrant the pains and costs of testing, which are almost always consider-

able, but especially so if broad, painstaking comparative studies are undertaken.

Such probes are common in cases where costly risks have to be run. These probes are roughly analogous to the trials to which one subjects a racehorse before incurring the costs of entering and preparing it for a major race: success cannot be guaranteed, but some kind of odds (ratios between certain costs and probable benefits) can be established. The simple principle at work is that large investments in less likely outcomes are worse propositions than large investments in more likely outcomes. Here the analogy between theorizing and horse racing becomes a little specious, for in probing the plausibility of a theory we can hardly expect to know much, or anything, about previous performance or to have exact estimates of probability like those given by a stopwatch. But we do not lack means for at least getting a reasoned, not merely intuitive, "feel" for the odds against a theory.

At a minimum, a plausibility probe into theory may simply attempt to establish that a theoretical construct is worth considering at all, that is, that an apparent empirical instance of it can be found. I take that (together with heuristic objectives) to be the purpose of Dahl's influential study of power in New Haven.[35] Dahl, as I read him (contrary to some other interpreters of his work), wants to establish that power in democracy may be "pluralistic," or may not be "monolithic," not that it must be the former and cannot be the latter. The study certainly succeeds in that regard, although it would succeed even more if New Haven had been selected for study because it is typical of a specified class of cases.

Some ways of surmising the plausibility of a theory beyond that minimal point are nonempirical, and since they entail only the cost of thought, these should generally be used before, or instead of, empirical probes. We may have confidence in a theory because it is derived logically from premises that have previously yielded valid theory in a field or because it is derived from premises contrary to those that have led to major failures. We may also have confidence in a theory if it is able to account for both strengths and weaknesses in existing relevant hypotheses or otherwise seems to organize considerable volumes and varieties of unexplained data. An example of both these methods of estimating plausibility is furnished by those passages of my monograph on stable democracy that show the grounding of its main proposed regularity statement in (as I then thought) validated psychological theories and those that try to show how the strengths and weaknesses of three alternative hypotheses, all rather powerful yet flawed in certain ways, can be explained by the main proposed regularity statement (see chapter 5). Demonstrating logically that proposed regularity statements can potentially explain data not yet explained, and/or provide a common foundation for previously validated but quite discrete and unconnected hypotheses, and/or extend assumptions found powerful in some areas to other areas, all create presumptions in favor of testing the statements independently, even by costly means.

Plausibility probes can also be directly empirical, that is, in the nature of preliminary, rather loose and inconclusive, but suggestive tests before more rigorous tests are conducted. Such probes confront theories with lesser challenges that they must certainly withstand if they are not to be toppled by greater ones. If, for example, it were posited that democratic power structures are normally monolithic (which is in fact often done in political theories) and one had strong reason to believe that New Haven was unlikely to be a deviant case (which is also arguable), then Dahl's study of its power structure would establish much more than that the counteridea of pluralism in democratic power is not completely vacuous. It would cast serious doubt on the posited regularity. Such empirical probes are especially important where nonempirical probes yield very uncertain results, and there is also reason to use them, as additions to others, as cheap means of hedging against expensive wild-goose chases, when the costs of testing are likely to be very great.

2. There is no reason why empirical plausibility probes should not take the form of modest or rather diffusely designed comparative studies, as preludes to more ambitious and tighter ones. Indeed, most systematic comparative studies in macropolitics make more sense as plausibility probes (or as "heuristic comparative studies") than as what they are generally claimed or regarded to be: that is, works presenting definitive results. Almond and Verba's *The Civic Culture* is surely a case in point. The sample of cases covered by the study is hardly large and dubiously representative; the regularity statements about "democratic stability" emerging in its final chapter could certainly be made more exact, are mainly afterthoughts imputed to the evidence, and are hardly conclusively compelled by that evidence. But they seem sufficiently rooted in data and reasoning to warrant their statement in more precise form and their thorough testing, preferably by logically deduced predictions about findings in a project specifically designed not to get interesting data but to get those crucial to establishing the validity of the work's central propositions. (One may consider it reprehensible that so many comparativists are willing to stop where only that much, or little more, has been accomplished, and then go on to other, still merely plausible, ideas on different subject matter. We have no right to bewail the fact that others do not take up our ideas if we ourselves drop them far short of the point to which they could be taken.)

The essential point for us is that, as empirical plausibility probes, case studies are often as serviceable as, or more so than, comparative ones— and nearly always a great deal cheaper—a prime consideration in probing plausibility. The economic case for them is strongest where required information is not readily available in aggregate data or good secondary sources and is intrinsically hard to get. Case studies can certainly serve the purpose well if well selected, that is, if they are such that a result, for or against a theory, cannot readily be shrugged off. It is true that case studies have been little used in political studies as plausibility probes, but this is largely due to the fact that the idea of any sort of plausibility probe is foreign to the field, plus the fact that comparative studies to amass data from which finished theories supposedly emerge have been its dominant contemporary genre. (Comparative studies as plausibility probes are equally uncommon, except only in the sense that some of them appear better tailored for that purpose than the purposes they pretend to serve.)

Because of the rareness of plausibility probes in the field, an example may be more instructive than abstract discussion. The example I shall use involves my work on governmental performance, following up my monograph on stable democracy (chapter 5). Self-advertisement is not intended, and no claims about the quality of the work are made. But cases in point are, as stated, rare; and the work in question illustrates well the circumstances under which probing plausibility becomes important and case study is useful to that end.

As to circumstances that indicate the advisability of plausibility probes: After first formulating the hypotheses on stable democracy (see chapter 5), I thought it imprudent to plunge immediately into concerted testing, even assuming that an argument for more than minimal potential validity had already been made. Although the propositions were simple and parsimonious, there is unfortunately no close relationship between the simplicity of propositions and the ease or economy of testing them; in this case, in fact, the effort required was bound to be immense. Concepts used in the propositions had to be more precisely and rigorously formulated. Virtually all the data required to test them had to be produced by extensive fieldwork: one could certainly not base cross-national research into "congruence" among authority patterns (the main independent variable used in the hypotheses) on conveniently available statistical annuals and the like. This called for resources—time, language skills, historical and cultural knowledge—that a single scholar never commands. Consequently, it would be necessary to involve others in the work, an effort likely to fail, or to be wasteful, while ideas are still little more than mildly plausible. Furthermore, testing the propositions would not be possible without developing an elaborate scheme of concepts for getting at the multifarious facets of authority relations: concepts unambiguously defined, standardized to apply to interactions in virtually all kinds of social units, and operationalized to make field observations reliable and some sort of measurement of resemblances among authority patterns possible. To relate the independent variable to levels of governmental performance (the main dependent variable), it was necessary also to develop a set of categories and techniques for reliably determining different levels of such performance. And all this done, a large number of taxing field studies had (as it then seemed to me) to be carefully designed, thoroughly carried out, rigorously processed, and their results collated. Under such circumstances it surely is reasonable, even imperative, to seek some decent, however inconclusive, estimate of probable success before any concerted attempt at testing, better than that provided in the initial work.

As to the utility of case studies as plausibility probes: Several things were done to arrive at that estimate,[36] but the most important was a study of Norway. That country was selected in part for extraneous reasons (language, personal connections, the high development of social research in the country). The main reason for selecting it, however, was that Norway seemed somehow critical for the theory to be tested, in the sense that the theory could hardly be expected to hold widely if it did not fit closely there. The theory purported to account for high, but not necessarily low, levels of governmental performance—and such performance had been outstandingly high in Norway for a long time on all the criteria initially used to gauge it. Moreover, the theory related social (i.e., nongovernmental) structure to governmental performance, but selected from all facets of such structure one special aspect that intrinsically could remain unchanged while all or most others changed, or, conversely, could change while others remained constant. As it happens, there had been virtually no significant change in governmental structure, but much in social structure, in Norway since late in the nineteenth century. Two things consequently had to be found if the theory were to be considered plausible. The proposed correlates of high governmental performance had to be unmistakably present in high degree and the aspect of social structure selected for emphasis had to be constant over time despite considerable other changes in Norwegian society. Neither was known in advance and both were in fact the case, or so it seemed; hence confidence that the theory might withstand concerted comparative study was greatly increased, to a level more in line with expected costs. The essential point is that Norway seemed to have special characteristics particularly illuminating for the theory: in short, it appeared to be a specially instructive case, of the sort that might be particularly useful for heuristic inquiry but that is more readily identified if candidate-theory already has been formulated.

3. The study was not conclusive for the theory; it merely strengthened its prospects. One reason for its inconclusiveness was that the methods

used in it were less rigorous, and the research less thorough, than they might have been, precisely because economies are a major consideration in probing plausibility. Another reason was the prevalent belief that the study of a case could, at most, yield a subjective estimate of the theory's plausibility, simply because it was case study, hence that no massive research assault on it, which would long postpone comparative inquiry, was needed or even justifiable.

And here again we come to a critical possibility. If studies of well-selected cases, no less than comparative studies, can serve the purposes of plausibility probes (the idea of which is, after all, to form estimates of probable validity), could they not also serve, painstakingly selected and rigorously carried out, as tests of validity itself, with similar economies in the work required? The possibility should at least be entertained and the case for it argued, since the potential practical gains could be enormous. It arises, at bottom, from the obvious fact that cases are not all equal in their import, even for the modest purposes of heuristic exploration. The question is whether their inequality extends to the point where certain types of cases, and modes of case study, can serve to test theories for validity—the step most demanding on rigor and in which breadth-of-inference problems seem most damaging to case studies.

To explore this question further, we shall have to look more closely at a suggestion made in the discussion on disciplined-configurative study: that if theory can compel particular case interpretations, then particular cases could invalidate or confirm theories.

Crucial-Case Studies

1. The position that case studies are weak or useless for testing theories rests, at bottom, on the mistaken application of a correct principle—a principle that applies more, but still imperfectly, to the discovery of theories in data than to their testing.

We can think of theory formulation as a process that leads one to postulate a curve or line to which observations of reality are expected to correspond; and we can think of theories as valid if the curves or lines that best fit relevant observations in fact match the theoretical expectation, or, put in a different manner, if the points yielded by measurements of relevant observations fall on or very near the postulated curve at logically specified locations. The principle that seems to rule out case study for the purpose of finding valid theory is the elementary one holding that any single instance of a relationship yields only one observed point, and that through any single point an infinite number of curves or lines can be drawn. (A less abstract variant of this principle is the argument above that any number of different explanations, not contrary to fact and thus at least minimally plausible, can be offered for any political event.)

The principle is, as stated, incontestable. But we are not constrained to conclude from it that comparative studies are indispensable to the development of valid theories and case studies useless for the purpose, unless we inject between the premise and conclusion a major fallacy that apparently dies hard: the inductive fallacy. The essence of that fallacy is the belief that theories, being contained in phenomena, can be fully derived from observations by simple inspection or, at any rate, sophisticated data processing. This is fallacious in several senses that should be disentangled, although the fallacies are all of a piece and usually all committed at once.

a) One aspect of the fallacy involves confusion between the discovery of candidate-theories and their testing: in deriving theory from observations ("grounded theory") one may be tempted to think that curves suggested by comparative data are themselves valid theories. This hazard is not logically inherent in comparative study, but contemporary political science, among other fields, suggests that it is extreme in practice, most of all where the behavioral sciences' model of experimental study is closely followed. Such study, regardless of how punctiliously carried out, cannot, in and of itself, reveal general laws guaranteed to be valid. It only provides more or less powerful clues as to what they are, that is, helps to discover them. In some cases these clues may be so powerful that testing may seem superfluous or not worth the cost, but this is highly exceptional.[37]

Strictly speaking, generalizations directly inferred from data only hold (probabilistically) for the phenomena observed under the conditions prevailing during observation. If the observations are voluminous and accurate, and if the conditions of observation are highly various or controlled, then one may have very high confidence that the curve that best fits the observations in fact manifests, in graphic form, a valid theory. Nevertheless, the element of surmise in going from data to theory always is considerable, and the "epistemic gap" between them, as Northrop calls it, ineluctable. And such great limitations usually exist, in practice, on the volume, accuracy, and variety or control of observations (including, of course, the obvious limitation that we cannot observe the future) that the risk in identifying an empirical generalization with a theoretical rule usually cannot be defended unless special testing of the presumed rule is carried out.

b) A second aspect of the fallacy concerns the discovery of candidate-theories in the first place. It is the principles that give rise to empirically discovered curves that constitute theories, not the curves as such: these only represent the principles, that is, show them at work. When an empirically grounded curve has been drawn, therefore, the principles it expresses must still be elucidated. Often this is not much of a problem, and statistical techniques (like causal path analysis) can help solve it. Nevertheless, curves can deceive as well as instruct, regardless of such techniques; and they most resist the discerning of *simple* regularities governing phenomena because the data from which they are constructed usually express all the complex interactions of factors in the concrete world, or sometimes even the laboratory. Nature, as Bacon knew, is a tough adversary capable of innumerable disguises. More than routine method is often required to strip off these disguises.

It seems, in fact, unlikely that the more powerful laws of physical science could have been discovered (their testing aside) by the mechanical processing of observations, however "sophisticated." Certainly one is struck by the small role played by systematic comparative observation in both their formulation and critical testing—in effect, by the thorough lack of correspondence between the psychologist's and physicist's conception of "experimentation." As illustration, take that touchstone of ancient, modern, and contemporary physics: conceptions of gravity and the closely associated law of the velocity of freely falling objects.

The Galilean challenge to the Aristotelian conception of free fall (the heavier the object, the faster it falls), accepted as gospel for nearly two millennia, did not grow out of observation at all but out of a simple "thought-experiment" (simple in retrospect, but apparently not at all obvious until performed). In gist (and with apologies for a layman's bowdlerization): if Aristotle is correct, then two bricks of the same weight, dropped at the same instant from the same height, must strike the ground at the same instant. If the two bricks are dropped side by side, as if cemented, the rate of fall of each must be the same as if dropped separately; but if cemented, they would be twice as heavy as a single brick and must therefore drop much faster; hence, since both conclusions cannot be right, the theory must be wrong. And the only way to square the two conditions logically is to make the weight of the falling objects irrelevant to acceleration in free fall, with the relevant variables being only the gravitational forces that account for falling and, possibly, the duration of the fall.

There is no observation here at all (and much doubt even about whether Galileo ever climbed the Tower of Pisa to check out, by a single "probe," the plausibility of his conclusion). Had systematic comparative measurements been used, anomalies in the Aristotelian conception would certainly have turned up, at least in the fall of objects "heavy" above a certain threshold. But if a well-chosen sample of objects had been dropped from a well-selected sample of heights under a well-selected sample of wind and other conditions, the likely conclusions would surely have been something like this: that the whole process of falling, like macropolitical phenomena, is "immensely complicated and cannot be accounted for by one or two simple causes";[38] that weight is a factor (as it is at certain heights and other conditions); and that weight, size, shape, and density of object, and wind conditions account for such and such a (no doubt high) percentage of the variance in rates of fall, singly or in various combinations. A radical, deductively fertile simplification of the whole complex process might, but almost certainly would not, have emerged.

The Galilean notion was widely disputed until a crucial experiment could be conducted to check it out. Objects of different weights did demonstrably fall at different, sometimes vastly different, rates. So the Galileans' extraneous factors, having no place in the law, remained other people's favored explanatory variables. Only with the invention of the air pump, about 1650, was a definitive experiment possible: dropping a heavy object (coin) and a light one (feather) in an evacuated tube. Again, no systematic comparative measurement was used, only a single experimental observation that foreclosed weaseling out by ad hocery to Galileans and Aristotelians alike.

Newton's theory ($F \propto mm'/r^2$) was certainly suggested by observations of the movement of astronomical bodies (although Singer argues that all Newton's laws are quite abstract and not concerned directly with phenomenal observations),[39] but the value of the universal gravitational constant G, needed to convert the expression of Newton's theory into an equation, was worked out initially by Lord Cavendish (in 1798) through a single experiment and the measurement derived from it. And Einstein's theory could certainly not have been derived from quantitative analysis of observations, while its conclusive test involved a single critical phenomenon: the deflection of light as it passed close to the rim of the sun.[40]

Comparative observations may be significant in fleshing out basic conceptions of regularities (e.g., determining that the velocity of freely falling objects is described by $s = gt^2$, or measuring any specific value g). But they are far from necessary, and quite likely to deceive, when these basic conceptions—critical variables and their basic relationship—are to be formulated.

c) The inductive fallacy has a third facet, pertaining exclusively to testing. It might be conceded that discovering and testing theories are different processes, but not that testing requires data different from those that help in discovery. The analysis of data may be so convincing that one might not consider it worthwhile to test rules derived from them but, despite this, the experiences in light of which theories are constructed cannot be used again as tests of them. Testing involves efforts to falsify, and anything giving rise to a theory will certainly not falsify it; nor will any body of replicated observations do so, if replication indeed is faithful. (Replication pertains to reliability, not validity.) The object of testing is to find observations that must fit a theory but have a good chance of not doing so. Nothing that suggests a theory, therefore, can also test it.

2. Having established a need for the independent testing of theoretical

curves (on the grounds that the discovery and testing of theories are intrinsically different activities, that no method of discovery can guarantee validity, that even painstakingly gathered and analyzed data can deceive, and that data which suggest regularities cannot also validate them), we come to the crux: the argument of the fifth option that, *in principle, comparative and case studies are alternative means to the end of testing theories, choices between which must be largely governed by arbitrary or practical, rather than logical, considerations.*

Comparative studies can certainly be used to test theories. If we use them for this purpose, our object, as stated, is to demonstrate that a curve that fits their results well in fact closely coincides with a curve postulated by theory, however that may have been worked out. In the case of a law like that of the velocity of falling objects, for example, one might try to demonstrate that the curve yielded by a set of observations sustains the expectation that the postulated law is an increasingly better predictor as one increasingly approximates the conditions under which the law is considered to hold absolutely.

However, there is available (not necessarily in all cases, but in many) an alternative to that rather cumbersome procedure, and it involves a kind of case study. One can use a well-constructed experiment, conducted to simulate as closely as possible the specified conditions under which a law must hold, and compare its result with that predicted by the law. In the history of science the decisive experiments have been mostly of that kind, a fact that makes one wonder how the comparative observation of unmanipulated cases could ever have come to be regarded as any sort of equivalent of experimental method in the physical sciences. (The main reasons are, by my reading, the influence of J. S. Mill's *Logic,* the intuitive decision reached by some influential contemporary social scientists that their regularity statements must unavoidably be "probabilistic" in form, origin, and testing, and the fact that much experimentation in the physical sciences is simply hopeful fishing for regularities in masses of data.) And if a well-constructed experiment can serve the purpose, then so may a well-chosen case—one that is somehow as crucial for a theory as are certain experiments, or indeed natural observations, in the physical sciences.

This argument is not at all impugned by the incontestable principle regarding the relations between points and curves with which we started. For there is another principle about those relations that is equally incontestable. This is that any given point can fall only on an infinitesimal fraction of all conceivable curves: it will not fall on any of the curves, the number of which is also infinity, that do not in fact pass through the point. (A less abstract variant of this principle is that for every plausible explanation of a political event, there is an infinite number that are not even minimally plausible.) The fact that a point falls, or does not fall, on a curve, therefore, is not at all insignificant. If the curve is not constructed to pass through the point but preconstructed to represent a theory, and if, given the nature of a case subsequently examined, we can predict, according to the theory, that it must fall on, or very near, the curve at a specified location, the fact that it does so is of the utmost significance, and its location far from the predicted point will impeach the theory no less than the tendency of several points to describe a divergent curve. At any rate, this is the case if the bases for predicting the location of an unknown point are really compelling—which is the object of crucial case study. In such case study, the compelling instance "represents" a regularity as, in comparative study, a sample of individuals "represents" a population.

3. Crucial case study presupposes that crucial cases exist. Whether they do or not in macropolitics can hardly be settled abstractly. All one can say on the subject is the following: *(i)* If they do not, no reasonable alternative to testing theory by comparative study exists. *(ii)* The inability to identify cases crucial for theories may not be the result of their nonexistence but of the loose way theories are stated, their relative lack of what we earlier termed "rulefulness." *(iii)* Any a priori assumption as to their nonexistence manifestly is a self-fulfilling prophecy, and it is difficult to see with what compelling reasoning such an assumption might be justified. *(iv)* If that reasoning rests on the inability to use controlled laboratory experiments in macropolitics, it suffices to point out that crucial measures in the physical sciences can be of natural observations (as, for example, the confirmation of Einsteinian relativity). And, obviously most important, *(v)* both hypothetical and actual examples of (apparently) crucial observations in the social sciences, including observations of complex collective individuals can be found—and would almost certainly be found more often if deliberately sought more often.

A more important question, therefore, is how a crucial case can be recognized. What guidelines can be used?

The essential abstract characteristic of a crucial case can be deduced from its function as a test of theory. It is a case that *must closely fit* a theory if one is to have confidence in the theory's validity, or, conversely, *must not fit* equally well any rule contrary to that proposed. The same point can be put thus: in a crucial case it must be extremely difficult, or clearly petulant, to dismiss any finding contrary to theory as simply "deviant" (due to change, or the operation of unconsidered factors, or whatever "deviance" might refer to other than the fact of deviation from theory per se) and equally difficult to hold that any finding confirming theory might just as well express quite different regularities. One says difficult and petulant because claims of deviance and the operation of other regularities can always be made. The question is therefore not whether they are made but how farfetched or perverse the reasons for them (if any) are.

Generally speaking, "must-fit" cases are those that naturally have the characteristics of a well-designed experiment, so that mere forecasts must be as accurate as concrete, or even experimental, predictions. The case of Norway, as discussed above, is a case in point, if what is claimed about it is indeed true: that is, that governmental performance has been continuously high while social structure has thoroughly changed. The case would also be in point if social structure had remained nearly constant while a substantial change in level of governmental performance had occurred. But it may be admitted that such cases, naturally paralleling the artificial controls of the laboratory, will not commonly occur and that one will need unusual luck to find them out economically even if they exist.

An alternative is to focus inquiry on "most-likely" or "least-likely" cases—cases that ought, or ought not, to invalidate or confirm theories, if any cases can be expected to do so. The best-known example in political study probably is Michels's inquiry into the ubiquitousness of oligarchy in organizations, based on the argument that certain organizations (those consciously dedicated to grass-roots democracy and associated ideologies, representing classes whose interest lies in such democracy, having highly elaborate and pure formal democratic procedures, and leaders from the same social strata as the membership) are least likely, or very unlikely, to be oligarchic if oligarchy were not universal. (One may argue with Michels's choice of social units, his methods, or his findings,[41] but the principle of the idea is surely sound.) Another example is Malinowski's study of a highly primitive, communistic (in the anthropological sense) society,[42] to determine whether automatic, spontaneous obedience to norms in fact prevailed in it, as was postulated by other anthropologists. The society selected was a "most-likely" case—the very model of primitive, communistic society—and the finding was contrary to the postulate: obedience was found to result from "psychological and social inducements." A similar example is Whyte's study of Boston slum gangs,[43] collective individuals that should, according to prevailing theory, have exhibited a high level of "social disorganization," but in fact exhibited the very opposite.

The "least-likely" case (as in Michels) seems especially tailored to confirmation, the "most-likely" case (as in Whyte and Malinowski) to invalidation. Methodological purists will find this a curious sentence. They will find it odd because philosophers of science deny the distinction between confirmation and invalidation. The philosophers are right to the extent that they argue that nothing can categorically prove theories in the manner of logical proofs, but that some findings may categorically invalidate them. But to the working scientist the distinction between confirmation and disconfirmation does have meaning, even if logic compels one ultimately to equate "validates" with "fails to falsify." There is a difference in nuance between saying "this can't be so if a theory is weak" and saying "this must be so if a theory is powerful." Per contra, of course, any most-likely case for one theory becomes a least-likely case for its antithesis, and vice versa (e.g., the Boston slum was a least-likely case for the ubiquity of social "organization"), so that the distinction is one of research design and objectives rather than the inherent characteristics of a case. For the same reason, crucial case study obviously proceeds best when a case is treated in both senses and confronted with both theory and countertheory.

Cases that are extreme on pertinent measures can usually be regarded as crucial in the sense of being least-likely and most-likely cases. If, for example, one holds that democratic stability is directly proportional to level of economic development and inversely proportional to rate of economic growth ($S_d \propto E_d/E_r$), a very high value of S_d (as in Norway) should predict a high value of E_d and a low value of E_r. If either is not the case, then grave doubt is de rigueur; and if both are not, then the theory simply cannot be right. The same holds, of course, if the starting point is the economic variables, or if one starts with extremely low stability (as in Republican Spain). And this logic follows, in particular, if the extreme measure is of change on the stability measure: a marked change, for example, from instability to stability. This appears to have occurred in Germany, which was highly unstable during the Weimar Republic but, by one calculus, ranks third out of twenty only to New Zealand and Sweden (with a score of 112.56 on a range from 118.42 to 67.19) in the post-World War II period.[44] (This measure is not greatly at odds with a different and more complex one of change in German "political performance" made by Gurr and McClelland.[45] If, in that case, a relatively low level of E_d and high level of E_r turned up, and the regularity statement were not rejected, any theory at all could be saved, presumably by casually adding explanatory factors or casually dismissing cases as "deviant."

Measures need not always be extreme to be considered crucial for theory, nor will any extreme measure do as well as any other. It depends on the theory and the circumstances of the case that provides the measure. For example, I have proposed elsewhere that (1) high governmental performance requires congruence between the government's authority pattern and the authority patterns of other social units in the society; that (2) other specified factors also affect performance levels; and that (3) the effects of congruence on performance are considerably greater than those of the principal other factors, which, by and large, work only to depress fractionally the level of performance predictable from congruence.[46] If all these propositions are valid, any case of very high performance becomes crucial: it must permit accurate predictions about the independent variable, congruence. But a less extreme case may still be crucial, if a marked change in performance has occurred and noncongruence factors remain constant or change little (no doubt hard to know in advance of intensive study), or (not so hard to know) if a positive change in performance is considerable enough to make it very unlikely that it has anything to do with increased congruence but only expresses the amelioration of other factors that previously depressed performance. For this purpose, a change from near the bottom to somewhere near the middle of a scale may suffice, although the more considerable the change the better.

These arguments about most-likely and least-likely cases, cases in which some pertinent variables change and others remain constant, extreme cases of most kinds and some that are not extreme, have a bearing on the question whether crucial cases may be found in macropolitics. It seems rather unlikely that all cases should be equally unlikely or likely, equally changeable or constant in all respects, equally short of extreme values on pertinent variables, and equally modest in change on the variables. More and less crucial cases should therefore be available en masse, and some of the more crucial ones identifiable without taxing preliminary studies—on their face value or because the special work required has already been done, even if for other purposes. The possibility, of course, remains that a particular theory, even if suitably stated, cannot be confronted by a clearly crucial case, or that such a case can only be found by wide-ranging preliminary observations and measures of many cases. But these prospects should now appear less daunting than might have been the case, and not at all inevitable.

4. To this point, the discussion has presented the case only for option 5: that case and comparative studies are best conceived as equally useful, alternative means for testing theories. The utility of case study and the weaknesses of comparative studies have been stressed only because the reverse is far more common in our field.

If logic does not intrinsically favor one method or another, the method to be used must be selected for other reasons, that is, out of practical, prudential considerations. One such reason may be the unavailability of clearly crucial cases. But assuming that not to be the case, probable costs and benefits become the pertinent calculus. On that calculus rests the case for the sixth option on case study, which pertains only to macropolitics. Inquiry into macropolitical units involves problems of scale and of sound comparison that point strongly toward crucial case study as the preferable method; the same considerations might also apply to stages of inquiry other than testing but are less telling there since rigor is at a lesser premium.

The most manifest practical advantage of case study is, of course, that it is economical for all resources: money, manpower, time, effort. The economies are not strictly equal to $1/n$, where n is the number of cases studied comparatively, since some resources usually have to be devoted to the identification of crucial cases, and some work needed to prepare rigorous case study is similar to that required by rigorous comparative studies. But even so they are likely to be considerable. This economic advantage is especially important, of course, if studies are inherently costly, as they are if units are complex collective individuals. Sociologists of knowledge might note, in this connection, that the growth of comparative studies coincided with the influx of unprecedented research monies and other facilities (research institutions, crowds of postgraduate students) into political study, and that my revisionism coincides with a sudden shrinkage in these factors. If that shrinkage compels us to develop less costly means to the same ends, it will be a blessing in disguise.

A second practical advantage involves access to the subjects of study. Samples of macropolitical units are always likely to be poor and highly uncertain in result: small in number (the population being small) despite the likelihood of a sizable range of variation. If, as is usually the case, they consist of contemporary cases, they are also bound to be a badly biased sample for all cases relevant to general laws. These problems in principle are compounded by practical problems of access resulting from the political exclusion of researchers (as in Burma), the inaccessibility of subjects in other cases, the lack of local research facilities (e.g., survey research organizations), and language problems for foreign researchers, among many other factors. As a result, contemporary comparative studies in macropolitics predominantly have one or more of three characteristics: (1) small numbers of cases chosen by intuition or for convenience; (2) the use, in wide-ranging studies, of readily available, aggregate data that are often quite untrustworthy and dubious indicators of traits they supposedly represent; or (3) think-pieces based on discussions of cases by "country-experts" in light of a common framework that are usually not at all well coordinated. Crucial case study may, of course, also suffer from problems of access. However, since crucial cases rarely appear singly, the likelihood of being unable to study properly even one of them seems considerably smaller than the likelihood of working with poor samples in comparative studies or that of having to tailor theoretical research to practical possibilities rather than the far more desirable vice versa.

A huge practical problem in comparative research involves special knowledge of the cultures being studied. The arguments made by the German exponents of the view that the *Naturwissenschaften* and *Kulturwissenschaften* are ineluctably different, and the arguments of the clinicians inspired by them are surely right insofar as they hold that "social facts," personal or collective, are embedded in widely varying, even in each case unique, cultural systems of meaning and value, and that one can neglect these only at great peril. Their position may not imply that "social laws" are therefore unattainable, but they do imply that the cultural sciences impose a requirement of special cultural "understanding" that does not exist in natural science. Crucial cases can often be selected to satisfy this requirement for individual researchers, and it is always possible to acquire a great deal of cultural *Verstehen* in the course of in-depth study of a case if one does not already possess it. Even if we reject the notion of a special inherent requirement for cultural science, this point can still be made to rest convincingly on the question of special language skills and special historical and sociological knowledge of cases, for lack of which comparativists are often justly criticized.

At the very least, one can obviously, if other things are equal, go more deeply into a single case than a number of them and thus compensate for loss of range by gains in depth: to that extent, at least, the clinicians have a foolproof case. In crucial case study, the advantages of traditional scholarship, as displayed in configurative-idiographic studies, can thus be combined with those of modern technique and rigor. And it is also more possible to apply in crucial case study certain techniques developed in social science for overcoming the imperfections of single measures, especially the "triangulation of imperfect measures" technique developed in social psychology and applied, impressively, by Greenstein and Tarrow in political socialization research.[47] (As an aside: the problems of *Verstehen*, depth, and imperfect measures are especially great in research into "political culture"; hence, it is rather astonishing to find that exponents of the political culture approach should also be devoted comparativists.)

Specialists in macropolitics have tried to overcome these problems by spawning general frameworks to be applied by different individuals in different cases or by deliberately organizing group research, hoping that the results will add up to coherent comparative study. The results have been uniformly disappointing. The frameworks have not been widely taken up, except as terminology, or have been widely butchered, and a whole volume could be written on the difficulties and meager results of different organizational frameworks for group research. At least until macropolitics develops a consensual paradigm, there seems to be no adequate collective substitute for the work of isolated researchers or, much the same, small and intimate teams of close collaborators.

At this point it should be clear that the practical advantage of crucial case study does not lie merely in resources. Case studies yield methodological payoffs as well. This is in large part due to the fact that they help avoid difficulties that are hard to reduce or abolish in cross-cultural research. Not the least of these are two related difficulties not yet mentioned: the problem of the proper cross-cultural translation of research instruments, a subject rapidly becoming a methodological field in itself and one that absorbs ingenuity and thought better devoted to theory construction and testing themselves. In addition, if we conduct crucial case studies, we are far more likely to develop theories logically and imaginatively, rather than relying on mechanical processing to reveal them. More important still, we are more constrained to state them tightly and in proper form, suitable to testing: that is, in a manner that permits their deductive and predictive application to cases. Sloppiness in the forms of theory compatible with the criteria developed in the section on "definitions" above is not inherent in comparative studies (certainly not in the "disciplined" variety), but crucial case study involves far more compelling practical demands for the proper statement of theories, or else exposes far more manifestly when theories are not properly stated: that is, when nothing— or a great number of different things—can be deduced for any case from regularity statements about it.

More thought, more imagination, more logic, less busy work, less reliance on mechanical printouts, no questions about sampling, possibly firmer conclusions (including that extreme rarity in political study, the conclusively falsified hypothesis), fewer questions about empathy: these surely establish a heavy credit. It remains to see whether any debits may cancel it out.

OBJECTIONS TO THE ARGUMENT
AND REPLIES TO THE OBJECTIONS

A number of arguments that might be, or have been, raised against my brief for crucial case studies should now be considered. None seem unanswerable, except in ways not very damaging to the argument. But others may see more merit in the objections than in the ways they are answered— and it is also possible that the really telling objections have been missed, or subconsciously avoided to restrict discussion to those that can be answered. The most telling objection of all, of course, would be that crucial cases simply are not available in macropolitics, but that has already been ruled out as unlikely for most, or many, theories. It is true that the literature of political science is not rich in crucial cases, but neither does it abound in efforts to find them; the most likely reason is that the very idea of crucial case study is alien to the field.

Objection 1

Comparative studies have the advantage over case studies of allowing one to test for the null hypothesis that one's findings are due to chance. Case studies may turn up validating or invalidating results fortuitously, not because theories are actually valid or invalid, but because one cannot determine by single measures whether or not this is so.

Answers. (a) The possibility that a result is due to chance can never be ruled out in any sort of study; even in wide comparative study it is only more or less likely. Now, it is surely very unlikely that, out of all possible states of affairs (which normally are vastly more than the two faces of a coin and sometimes approach infinity), just that predicted by theory should fortuitously turn up in a case carefully chosen as crucial for the theory, and also improbable that in such a case the predicted result should, just by chance, be greatly out of line with actual observation. The real difference between crucial case study and comparative study, therefore, is that in the latter case, but not the former, we can assign by various conventions a specific number to the likelihood of chance results (e.g., "significant at the .05 level"). Thus, if a theorist posits that democratic stability varies directly with level of economic development and inversely with rate of economic growth, and finds a case of extreme instability with high E_d and low E_r, he cannot rule out plain bad luck, but the presumption that he has an invalid theory surely is vastly greater.

(b) Any appreciable likelihood of unlucky chance findings in a crucial case study arises from the fact that very short-run fluctuations generally occur in any measure of a variable. (Think of air temperature, or rainfall, or the climate of a marriage.) For example, a polity generally high in performance will probably experience some peaks and troughs in its level, and peaks and troughs will also occur in variables used to explain levels of performance. If we then measure a dependent variable at a peak and an independent variable at a trough, a deceptive result will certainly be obtained. But the remedy is obvious: observe over a reasonable period of time.[48]

(c) There is, of course, also a possibility of observer bias in the observation of a case (seeing only what one wishes to see), hence of misleading, if not literally fortuitous, measures. That problem exists also in comparative studies, but not so acutely because of the prophylaxis provided by statistical measures of significance. But again, simple remedies are available. The most obvious is to recognize that falsifying a theory is to be reckoned as success rather than failure, and thus to redefine what one generally wants; knowing what is valid tells one more than knowing what is not, but knowing something to be invalid does signify progress and often provides very powerful clues as to what is valid. It is true that the reward structure of the social sciences overvalues positive findings, especially in publication—which may be why methods that maximize the probability of some sort of positive result (e.g., multiple regression) are so widely used. But such prizing of positive results, however tenuous, indicates scientific immaturity or insecurity and ought not to be perpetuated. It works like Gresham's law: bad theory crowds out good. (In fact, the question most frequently, and fearfully, asked about the preliminary version of this paper was: "What do you do if a prediction about a crucial case fails?" Answer: You publish the result—if editors permit and the failure is informative, as it is almost bound to be—and you go on, trying to do better.) Apart from that fundamental point, the problem of observer bias arises more in configurative-idiographic studies than in the more rigorous varieties of case study—hence the stress on it in existing critiques of case study[49]—and can certainly be reduced in the study of collective individuals by the same methods used to reduce it in comparative studies, such as the correct sampling of the microunits that constitute the case.

(d) In crucial case studies a powerful substitute for the null hypothesis can be put to work: testing for a theory's "countertheories," that is, likely alternative solutions if a theory is invalid, or a theory's "antithesis," if one is available. (This can also be done in comparative research, but practical considerations make it more feasible in case study, especially if theory and countertheories cannot be tested by exactly the same data.) The process of testing simultaneously for alternative hypotheses ("strong inference") has been held persuasively by John Platt as the correct way to put Baconian empiricism to work and, also persuasively, as the hallmark of the most rapidly developing hard sciences (high-energy physics and molecular biology). An example (not yet acted upon) from my own work on the relations between governmental performance and resemblances among governmental and other authority patterns may again provide a useful illustration of the procedure. "Congruence" theory rests, at bottom, on psychological learning theory in general and some of its specific variants. Since learning theory emphasizes the operation in behavior of gradually internalized orientations (something like habit, although not in the crude sense of the term), its obvious countertheory is one that postulates rational calculations in the light of one's current life-situation, untrammeled by the accretive influences of past learning: in short, an "economic" model of behavior. A theory of political performance could be rigorously developed on that basis.[50] A crucial case study can readily be designed not only to determine whether a case lies off a predicted point on one curve but also whether it lies on, or nearer, a predicted point on a crucial countercurve. Since only one case is involved, the cost of doing both will not be much greater than that of performing one operation alone. Several advantages accrue. We may not merely establish that a theory is false but also why, at bottom, it is false, and what sort of theory would serve better. Furthermore, a finding near a predicted point on one curve but far off such a point on the countercurve, adds to one's case enormously. One may thus not only shed special light on one's theory, but also more general light on the more fundamental bases for further theory construction. And if both theories are confirmed, a false contradiction is exposed; if neither is, the same result is obtained, or sloppy deduction is unmasked. All this takes one far beyond the mere void of statistical nullness.

Objection 2

If preliminary comparative studies are required to identify crucial cases (e.g., cases extreme on pertinent measures, or highly changeable on a measure, or having the characteristics of natural experiments), the practical advantages of case study are severely reduced. And if they are severely reduced, certain practical advantages of comparative studies, such as their ability to provide data for reanalysis or simply data from numerous contexts, tend to tip the scales in their favor.

Answers.   (a) Independent comparative study is not always required to identify crucial cases, simply because in an ongoing discipline the evidence needed to identify a crucial case often is already available. One may want to recheck that evidence or try to improve on it, but that is not tantamount to starting from scratch.

(b) Even if one starts from scratch, comparative studies specifically designed to uncover crucial cases can be very limited in scope, even confined to a single variable, and so much reduced in costs of all kinds. (For example, in the case of congruence theory, one might not initially do research on both performance and congruence, but on performance alone—a fact which, if realized earlier by the author, would have saved funding agencies much money and him much effort and time in designing research projects and carrying them out.) Common knowledge, no less than disciplinary knowledge, can also reduce problems of sampling in the search for such cases. For example, if the object were to discover a long stable polity, it would take more than ordinary ignorance to include, say, Germany in the search. Comparative studies to uncover crucial cases thus have little in common, in regard to required breadth of study or data requirements, with comparative studies as currently conducted.

(c) The fact that comparative studies provide "extensive" data from many contexts can be offset by the usual claim for "intensive" study: that it can provide more varieties of data (and is likely to do so not only if study is clinical but also if strong inference procedures are used). Such data, moreover, are as much subject to reanalysis as any others. They may not suit well the purposes of others, but then neither might those produced by comparative study; and virtually any body of data has import for a variety of purposes.

Objection 3

Several crucial case studies are always better than one. Some degree of additional safety is always provided by additional numbers. If therefore the intent is to be conclusive, crucial case study ends as comparative study anyway.

Answers. (a) The basic problem here again is the equation of success with confirmation. A single crucial case may certainly score a clean knock-out over a theory (as Galileo's thought-experiment would have, had it been a real experiment, and as the falling feather and coin in the evacuated tube later did). The problem arises only if confirmation occurs. Because distrust is a required element of the scientific culture, confirmation only eggs us on to allay our own always remaining doubts and disarm those of carping adversaries: and thus we may want to know whether a theory that fits crucial case X also fits cases Y and Z, assuming these are also crucial, and whether, despite precautions and great unlikelihood, chance has tricked us after all. But the further examination of other cases can be restricted much more than in comparative studies that rest their case on sampling, and in such studies "added confirmation" may also be deemed advisable—in fact, is necessary if the studies merely establish curves rather than matching them.

(b) Conceivably, the most powerful study of all for theory building is neither the presently common form of comparative study (of cases studied randomly, or intuitively selected, or simply studied because they seem readily available or accessible) nor the study of single crucial cases, but, so to speak, "comparative crucial case studies." The case for such studies, however, is strong only to the extent that the most crucial cases available are not very crucial, so that high confidence in the results they yield needs the increment of other crucial case findings. Thus, the feather and coin falling in a vacuum leave virtually no doubt to the skeptic or the inquirer devoted to the tested theory, while a case of change in governmental performance highly unlikely to be due merely to the disappearance of performance-depressing factors, as against the factor posited to be re-quired for high performance, probably leaves enough doubt to both to make desirable a further study or two of equal import. The study of such a more tenuous case might also, in some instances, be considered an es-pecially powerful "plausibility probe," warranting the (costly) comparative testing of a probabilistic hypothesis like that logically implied in the con-gruence theory of governmental performance:[51] that "in all cases, the correlation between performance and congruence will be high." The com-parativist may treat any and all crucial case studies as plausibility probes, warranting the costs of using his favored method. The notion of the crucial case study was, after all, devised largely from that of the plausibility probe. The point is that he need not do so, unless the crucial case falls far short of the ideal.

Objection 4

Crucial case studies turn out to be comparative studies in disguise. For instance, when dropping a coin and feather through an evacuated tube we take two simultaneous measures and compare them; or, when studying the correlates of a change from low to high governmental performance we again take two measures at different points in time and compare them. The distinction between comparative studies and case studies thus vanishes, along with that between the clinical and experimental modes of inquiry.

Answers. (a) Not all crucial measures are like that. Observing the deflection of light near the rim of the sun compares nothing with anything (unless it is claimed that it compares deflection with nondeflection). The same holds true if only high governmental performance, not change toward it, is the critical observation.

(b) It is by no means sophistic to maintain that the supposedly dual measures above are single measures, that is, measures of the amount of change in performance between an earlier and a later period or the amount of difference in the rate of fall of two objects. Such changes and differences can be used as points on a curve no less than measurements of static conditions at a particular point in time, and thus satisfy the exacting technical definition of case study.

(c) Measures of "more than," "less than," and "equal to" do presuppose two anchoring measures (see also Objection 5, Answer (d) below), but are not to be confused with comparative measures of samples, and $n = 2$ always suffices to establish them. Thus the distinction between case studies and comparative studies is watered down little, even if points (a) and (b) are disregarded.

Objection 5

Social science, especially on the macrolevel, does not have available measures precise and discriminating enough to make the sort of predictions needed for crucial case study.

Answers. (a) If this is true, the fact must bedevil comparative studies as much as any others, unless there is some magic by which many poor measures are equal to one that is good. Numerous poor measures can, of course, cancel one another out, or increase confidence in any one of them. But they can also make for increased distortion, that is, reinforce one another, and will certainly do so if a measuring instrument contains a consistent bias.

(b) What gospel ordains that social measures must be highly inexact and undiscriminating? That of experience? Perhaps; but perhaps only because of the prevalent assumption that nothing precise can be done in social study—surely a self-fulfilling prophecy if ever there was one. And while there is research there is hope: most of the natural sciences had to live long, and managed quite well, with rather imprecise measures too, and ours have been improving.

(c) Highly discriminating measures are *not* required to put crucial case study to work. If the measure to be predicted is, let us say, the level of democratic stability in postwar Germany, it is not necessary to be able to say that the level is at 112.56 (à la Hurwitz), with reasonable assurance that it is not then at 112.57. It may quite suffice to say that the measure must come out somewhere between 8 and 10 on a ten-point scale, either because theory permits or because of recognized possible error in a measuring technique. The possibility of disconfirmation then still exists, and is, after all, about four times as likely as confirmation. There must, of course, be a limit on imprecision. The minimum requirement is that measures must not be so inexact that any measure considered to validate (or invalidate) a theory could also, because of inherently possible measurement error, be taken to imply the opposite. If we cannot do much better than that in the social sciences, we might as well not measure at all, in any kind of study. Therefore, arguments about imprecision impugn quantitative social science, not crucial case study only.

(d) If no more than a single point is measured, however, crucial case study does presuppose interval measures (even if measurement techniques do not allow discrimination between minute intervals). If only ordinal measures are available, then (and only then) one must have two measurements to confirm, or invalidate, the prediction that a variable will have a higher, or lower, value at one time than another, or under one condition than under another. Ordinal measures only state "more than," "less than," or "equal to," and that always requires two points of reference, as stated above. And, as also already stated, this still concedes next to nothing to comparative study, and perhaps nothing at all if the predicted measure is interpreted as the measure of a difference of some discernible magnitude.

Objection 6

Crucial case studies cannot confirm multivariate theories, in which one deals with one dependent and several independent variables. The social sciences (especially on the macrolevel, where crucial case study is most advantageous) deal with multivariate phenomena: phenomena in which a variety of determinants converge upon observed experience.

Answers. (a) Again one wants to know: What gospel ordains that social phenomena must be multivariate, or decisively more so than any others? One might answer, the phenomena themselves: look, for instance, at all the factors associated with revolution, or authoritarian political behavior, or political instability, or nonvoting. True—but not decisive, and quite probably pernicious. In the natural sciences, too, "causes" converge in phenomenal experience, but notable successes have been achieved in cutting through the phenomenal complexities to simple theoretical constructs that are powerful tools in explaining particular occurrences or, by engineering, for bringing them about. (For example, the law of velocity of freely falling objects consists of one dependent variable, velocity, and one independent variable, time, gravitational force being a constant; but actual "falling" depends on many more factors, although some operate only with infinitesimal effects.) The problem of multivariate complexity largely dissolves if theory is thought of as a tool of explanation of the behavior of concrete individuals rather than as total explanation. And the probable perniciousness of the assumption that theories must be multivariate if phenomena are resides precisely in the fact that then they will be, thus missing beautiful and powerful simplicities, even if they might be found.

(b) Multivariate theories do *not* necessarily rule out crucial case study in testing, provided that one does not simply list independent variables that affect a dependent variable (*x* has some relationship to *a, b, c, . . . n*) but specifies precisely the relationship of each to the dependent variable and their effects on one another. Newton's theory of gravity, for example, is multivariate: the dependent variable, gravitational force, is determined by two independent variables, mass and distance. But it specifies a direct relationship to one and an inverse relationship to the square of the other. Given the constant necessary to turn these ideas into an equation, predictions can be made for any case that may conclusively confirm or invalidate. The problem then lies more in the way multivariate theories are stated than in multivariation as such. The job of avoiding that problem is immensely difficult (most of us probably need not apply) but it ought to be tackled, even though here again the prevalent reward structure of the social sciences discourages the attempt to do the better work that is more likely to fail, or to be perceived as failure.

(c) A real problem is that a case finding may be the result of complex "interaction effects." The careful choice of a case may allow one to discount that as a probability, but never altogether, and the fact that the problem might also queer comparative findings (more factors are nearly always interacting than a research design takes into account or allows one to separate) does not abolish the difficulty. The only sensible response is to treat the possibility as reason for continued doubt of some magnitude or other, and thus for further research. If the findings confirm a theory, that simply implies that one might want additional assurance in another pertinent instance. The point here is exactly the same as that regarding the possibility of "chance" results. If the findings disconfirm, and one has strong prior reasons to consider a hypothesis valid (e.g., because of various sorts of estimates of plausibility), the sensible course is simply not to give in all at once but to try another crucial test. In neither case is comparative study the required solution. The responses simply involve added confirmation, or added disconfirmation, by further crucial case study. And studies of additional cases for added assurance are not, strictly speaking, "comparative" studies.

Objection 7
Crucial case studies cannot test probabilistically stated theories.

Answers. (a) Agreed.

(b) Theories need not be probabilistic, and the more powerful are not, even if the occurrence of phenomena is. Here, once again, the difficulty lies in confusion between theory as a tool of explanation and theory as the full explanation of concrete events. (That confusion is especially reprehensible in this case because probability statements, inherently, are not total explanations either.) The position rests also on two further fallacies: that if something is true probabilistically of a numerous set of cases, then the probability of its being true is equal for each individual in the set (which is true only in rare cases, like tossing fair coins); and that no mere probability can be deduced from a "law" (it can, to the extent that the conditions under which a law is supposed to hold absolutely do not in fact exist, or to the extent that a law treats variables as constants).

(c) Probability statements are used more often than they need be in political study because of the uncompelled belief that they must be, which works, like other methodological assumptions, as self-fulfilling prophecy.

Objection 8
Even if all these objections are answerable, it is highly suspicious that so many should arise. Case study seems more susceptible to challenge than comparative study, in regard to which most of these problems are not even raised.

Answer. The essential difference here is not the volume of issues, but that the issues differ because the methods differ. Moreover, comparativists have only recently begun to raise important difficulties inherent in their method, especially on the macrolevel. But, in a relatively short time, an impressive number of difficulties in the method have turned up. After all that has recently been written about difficulties in comparative cross-national study, or even in microlevel studies—problems concerning the selection and proper number of cases, the feasibility and trustworthiness of research instruments (like survey research schedules), the comparability of data, or the utility of various data processing techniques and modes of inferring regularities from numerous data (e.g., various types of significance tests, attributions of causal paths to correlations, attributing longitudinal characteristics to synchronous data)—it is impossible to take seriously the position that case study is suspect because problem-prone and comparative study deserving of benefit of doubt because problem-free.

CONCLUSION

Case study in macropolitics begins in idiography and is rooted in the traditional conception of clinical study. In recent years the position that case study cannot be "nomothetic" has been increasingly attacked in psychology, the very field that made the distinction between idiographic and nomothetic study sharpest and most insuperable. But the notion of nomothetic case study has not been taken far. If not conceived as the application of established theory to case interpretation, it has merely been represented as case study in which rigorous methods, similar to those of "experimental" study, are used and/or in which individual experience is used to help find clues to general theories. If more has been claimed, as by Chassan, it has turned out that the term case study ("n = 1" study) is indefensibly applied, by confusing a case with a concrete person rather than a measure.

My object has been to take the argument for nomothetic case study far beyond this point, following up clues provided by examination of more modest arguments in favor of it. The point has been to relate "n = 1" studies to all phases of theory building and particularly to stress the utility of case study where rigor is most required and case studies have been considered least useful. Comparative studies have not been attacked, except on practical grounds in limited fields of inquiry; nor is it claimed that appropriate case studies are always available for all theoretical purposes, and absolutely not that any kind of case study will serve all purposes. The types of case study are numerous, and that recommended for going beyond formulating candidate-theories is extremely rare in our field or related disciplines.

The argument thus is mainly abstract. There is no track record worth mentioning. But if the horse is run, the results just might be astounding—or, possibly, abysmal. The point is that trials seem in order, not in place of but alongside comparative researches.

It should be evident that case study can be nomothetic only if cases are not selected for the theoretically trivial reasons that nowadays predominate in their selection: because one knows the language, finds a culture congenial to live and work in, can get money for study in it through an affluent area program, considers the case important for foreign policy or otherwise publicly marketable, finds it exotic, and the like. Considerations of congeniality or publicity are well and good if other things are equal, not otherwise. And not the least advantage of crucial case studies is that they may permit one to study intensively attractive or convenient cases without sacrifice of disciplinary conscience.

ENDNOTE

Chapter 8 deals with a methodological subject, the observation of "subjective" culture and thus might well have been included in this part of the book. It is not because it is best read as a companion piece to chapter 7, for reasons explained in the introduction to that chapter. It should be noted, however, that chapter 8, like the essay on case study, emphasizes the critical significance of *testing* in proper procedure. We do not subject theories to tests—especially our own theories; and there has been distinctly less emphasis on that aspect of method than others, especially data gathering and processing, and, to a lesser extent, conceptualization and operationalization. These are all important, but they fall far short of genuine "results" if not severely tested. Chapter 8 not only reiterates that argument but also tries to make a more novel point: testing is significant also for obtaining reliable and valid data of certain kinds, not just as the final stage of rigorous theoretical inquiry.

NOTES FOR CHAPTER 4

1. See W. H. Riley, *Sociological Research: A Case Approach* (New York: Harcourt, Brace, and World, 1963), 32–75.

2. R. K. Merton, *Social Theory and Social Structure* (Glencoe, Ill.: Free Press, 1962), 103.

3. R. C. Macridis and B. C. Brown, eds., *Comparative Politics: Notes and Readings* (Homewood, Ill.: Dorsey, 1955).

4. C. E. Osgood and Z. Luria, "A Blind Analysis of a Case of Multiple Personality Using the Semantic Differential," *Journal of Abnormal and Social Psychology* 49 (1954): 579–591.

5. A. S. Banks and R. B. Textor, *A Cross-Polity Survey* (Cambridge: MIT Press, 1963).

6. H. Finer, *The Theory and Practice of Modern Government,* rev. ed. (New York: Holt, 1932); and C. J. Friedrich, *Constitutional Government and Democracy* (New York: Harper and Brothers, 1937).

7. R. R. Holt, "Individuality and Generalization in the Psychology of Personality," *Journal of Personality* 30 (1962): 377–404.

8. P. O. Davidson and C. C. Costello, $N = 1$: *Experimental Studies of Single Cases* (New York: Van Nostrand Reinhold, 1969).

9. Ibid., 214–232.

10. R. R. Holt and J. M. Richardson, *The State of Theory in Comparative Politics* (Minneapolis: Center for Comparative Studies in Technological Development and Social Change, University of Minnesota, 1968).

11. J. G. Kemeny, *A Philosopher Looks at Science* (Princeton, N.J.: Van Nostrand,

1959); K. R. Popper, *The Logic of Scientific Discovery* (London: Hutchinson, 1959); C. G. Hempel, *Aspects of Scientific Explanation* (New York: Free Press, 1965).

12. A. Downs, *An Economic Theory of Democracy* (New York: Harper & Row, 1965); W. H. Riker, *The Theory of Political Coalitions* (New Haven: Yale University Press, 1962); J. M. Buchanan and G. Tullock, *The Calculus of Consent* (Ann Arbor: University of Michigan Press, 1967); R. L. Curry, Jr., and L. L. Wade, *A Theory of Political Exchange* (Englewood Cliffs, N.J.: Prentice-Hall, 1968).

13. D. Easton, *A Systems Analysis of Political Life* (New York: Wiley, 1965).

14. This statement may be quantitatively unjust to Easton: The point is not to single him out for criticism but to make a general argument often violated in political studies. The possible injustice to Easton arises from the fact that it would be possible, logically and/or empirically, to rule out many combinations and sequences—although, by my reading, Easton has not done so—and there are quite a few to rule out before his framework could permit confident forecasting or unique accounts of existing states of affairs.

15. The power of theories can also be assessed by another criterion, not included in the text because it strikes me as something for which theorists generally hope, rather than something at which they consciously aim. This is "deductive fertility": not just unexpected knowledge but knowledge in unexpected areas, that is, reliable and valid accounts of observations outside the original fields of interest. That criterion can, of course, be consciously pursued when one asks whether a single regularity statement can account for observations that several separate ones cover, or whether the separate regularities can be deduced from a higher-order rule.

16. The foreknowledge criterion also seems pivotal for economic theorists. Thus, Friedman writes: "The belief that a theory can be tested by the realism of its assumptions independently of the accuracy of its predictions is widespread and the source of much of the perennial criticism of economic theory." It seems pivotal as well in contemporary philosophy of science, for the emphases on the deductive elaboration of propositions and parsimony are mainly attributable to the stress on nonintuitive foreknowledge (i.e., foreknowledge that is not prophecy or clairvoyance, but rigorously deduced from "rules") as the crucial test of theories. I agree with these positions, except for holding that the ends sought do not manifestly require a unique form of theory. For a somewhat different "hard," but not overdemanding, view of theory—also based on natural science models but making central "generality" (i.e., range of applicability) and parsimony (i.e., the number of factors needed for complete explanation of a class of events)—see A. Przeworski and H. Teune, *The Logic of Comparative Social Inquiry* (New York: Wiley, 1970).

17. H. Eckstein, ed., *Internal War* (New York: Free Press, 1964), introduction.

18. J. R. Platt, *The Step to Man* (New York: Wiley, 1966).

19. S. Verba, "Some Dilemmas in Comparative Research," *World Politics* 20 (1967): 111–127.

20. Holt, "Individuality and Generalization," and Davidson and Costello, $N = 1$.

21. W. Windelband, *Geschichte und Naturwissenschaft*, (Sigmaringen, Germany: Thorbecke, 1982).

22. For bibliography, see Holt, "Individuality and Generalization," 402.

23. Ibid., 388–397.

24. Verba, "Some Dilemmas," 112.

25. H. Kaufmann, "The Next Step in Case-studies," *Public Administration Review* 18 (1958): 52–59; T. H. Lowi, "American Business, Public Policy, Case-studies, and Political Theory," *World Politics* 16 (1964): 677–715.

26. Holt, "Individuality and Generalization."

27. Verba, "Some Dilemmas," 114.

28. Hempel, *Aspects of Scientific Explanation,* 299–303.

29. I take the following to be leading examples: D. E. Apter, *The Gold Coast* (Princeton: Princeton University Press, 1956) and *The Political Kingdom in Uganda* (Princeton: Princeton University Press, 1961); G. A. Almond and J. S. Coleman, eds., *The Politics of the Developing Areas* (Princeton: Princeton University Press, 1960); R. A. Dahl, ed., *Political Oppositions in Western Democracies* (New Haven: Yale University Press, 1966); S. M. Lipset and S. Rokkan, *Party Systems and Voter Alignments* (New York: Free Press, 1967); and L. Pye and S. Verba, eds., *Political Culture and Political Development* (Princeton: Princeton University Press, 1965).

30. H. Eckstein, "On the Etiology of Internal Wars," *History and Theory* 4 (1965): 133–163.

31. T. R. Gurr, *Why Men Rebel* (Princeton: Princeton University Press, 1970).

32. If the essence of disciplined-configurative study is its application to cases of preestablished theories or to tools for building theories, we can distinguish four subspecies of this type of case study. They are quite different and need to be differentiated. (1) *Nomological case studies,* as they might be called, are studies of the sort Verba has in mind: studies that interpret cases on the basis of theories considered generally valid. (2) *Paradigmatic case studies* involve the application to a case of a preestablished framework, or checklist, for analysis, such as Almond's functional framework or the decision-making framework used in some studies of foreign policies. In (3) *methodical case study* rigorous methods associated with experimental study are applied to the study of individual cases, as in the studies reprinted in Davidson and Costello's *N = 1.* In (4) *therapeutic case study* validated theories and rigorous methods are used to diagnose problems and difficulties and to arrive at likely ways of eliminating or reducing them. (The labels used here are mine and arbitrary; they seem apt for the types.) The first subspecies is uncommon in all the social sciences, except economics, for reasons mentioned in the text. The third is common in psychology, the fourth more common in psychiatry than in other human sciences. In political science, the second subspecies predominates, exceeded in frequency only by configurative-idiographic studies.

33. H. S. Becker, "Social Observation and Case Studies," *International Encyclopedia of the Social Sciences* 11 (1968): 232–238.

34. B. G. Glaser and A. L. Strauss, *The Discovery of Grounded Theory, Strategies for Qualitative Research* (Chicago: Aldine, 1967).

35. R. A. Dahl, *Who Governs?* (New Haven: Yale University Press, 1961).

36. Harry Eckstein, "Authority Relations and Governmental Performance," *Comparative Political Studies* 2 (1969): 269–325.

37. These statements do not imply that *acting* on clues provided by empirically drawn curves is foolish. Usually it is wise—for example, not smoking if one wants to keep one's health—and often nothing better is available for making prudent decisions. The preeminent function of statistical analyses, as Wallis and Roberts emphasize, is in fact to help one to make wise decisions in the face of uncertainty. Hence such analyses are best used to help cope with problems of action (e.g., traffic

control problems, public health problems, problems of increasing agricultural yields, and the like) in which valid theories provide no better guide than plain statistics and in regard to which common sense is inadequate. As the field of statistics has become more and more powerful for this purpose, statistical findings have become increasingly confused with theories, but the distinction remains.

38. Verba, "Some Dilemmas," 114.

39. C. Singer, *A Short History of Scientific Ideas* (London: Oxford University Press, 1959).

40. J. R. Newman, ed., *The Harper Encyclopedia of Science* (New York: Harper & Row, 1963). This discussion provides a particularly splendid example of the process of theory building. The process begins with the perception of a puzzle—in this case in the logical implications of a theory. (The puzzle might also have been discovered in the actual behavior of objects). A "vision" of an alternative way of looking at experience then occurs. The vision is transformed into a rule. Then a critical test of both rule and alternative is sought. The test may not be available immediately, but its general nature is apparent in the theory. If it confirms the theory, inquiry is not ended, but resumes with the discovery of new puzzles and/ or alternatives.

41. See J. R. Willey, *Democracy in the West German Trade Unions: A Reappraisal of the "Iron Law"* (Beverly Hills: Sage, Professional Papers in Comparative Politics, 1971).

42. B. Malinowski, *Crime and Custom in Savage Society* (New York: Harcourt, Brace, and World, 1926).

43. W. F. Whyte, *Street Corner Society* (Chicago: University of Chicago Press, 1943).

44. L. Hurwitz, "An Index of Democratic Stability," *Comparative Political Studies* 4 (April 1971): 41–68.

45. T. R. Gurr and M. McClelland, *Political Performance: A Twelve-Nation Study* (Beverly Hills: Sage, Professional Papers in Comparative Politics, 1971).

46. H. Eckstein, "Authority Relations and Governmental Performance," *Comparative Political Studies* 2 (1969): 269–325.

47. F. I. Greenstein and S. Tarrow, *Political Orientations of Children: Semi-Projective Responses from Three Nations* (Beverly Hills: Sage, Professional Papers in Comparative Politics, 1971).

48. What constitutes a reasonable period of time for observations cannot be specified even in general terms. It depends on what one is studying, and it can generally be determined only by a combination of reasoning and reflection on findings. "Reasonable" time spans make it unlikely that findings will be distorted by fortuitous short-term events. For example, I have argued, upon reasoning, that valid measures of performance require observations of polities over about a ten-year period at the least. Gurr and McClelland in *Political Performance*, an empirical follow-up study, suggest, upon evidence, that a shorter time span might be serviceable for certain measures of performance.

49. H. S. Becker, "Social Observation and Case-study," *International Encyclopedia of the Social Sciences* 11 (1968): 232–238.

50. For example, R. Rogowski, *Social Structure and Stable Rule* (Princeton, N.J.: Center of International Studies, Monograph TR-3, 1969).

51. Eckstein, "Authority Relations," 282.

PART III

Political Stability

FIVE

A Theory of Stable Democracy

Author's Note: This paper is the watershed that divided my academic life into two rather distinct parts. I have described both its prehistory and a good deal of its aftermath in an extensive monograph, *The Natural History of Congruence Theory* (University of Denver: Monograph Series in World Affairs, vol. 18, no. 2, 1980). Here I will be a good deal briefer.

Prehistory first. In 1959, when I began teaching at Princeton, I inherited two courses on modern democracies from Gabriel Almond. As a faithful revolutionary in comparative politics, I decided to teach the courses in a "problem-oriented" way, the problem chosen being how to explain stability and instability in democracies. At that time, the pertinent theoretical notions we had were largely concerned with formal-legal aspects of the structure of government, such as electoral systems and the way executive-legislative relationships were defined. In 1959 Lipset had published *Political Man;* his theories about relationships between levels and rates of economic development and political stability were also widely known. Kornhauser, a couple of years before, had published *The Politics of Mass Society,* in which the principal variable related not to stability, but to the tendency to join political mass movements. This could be related to stability, in the manner of Tocqueville, through the variable of intermediate associational structures in societies. Not associated with any particular individual was the idea that religion was a critical variable: Catholic countries could not be stable democracies; only Protestant countries could. There also existed an "evolutionary" explanation. It was held, in essence,

This essay first appeared in *Division and Cohesion in Democracy: A Study of Norway* (Princeton: Princeton University Press, 1966), Appendix B, 225–288. Reprinted with permission of the publisher. Copyright © 1966 by the Princeton University Press.

that if unavoidable, thus universal, problems like national identification, distribution, participation, and so on, are solved successively, then governments will be stable and politics moderate. If, however, they occur simultaneously, as in that prototype of unstable democracies, Germany, the opposite will occur. In the air at the same time, as always, were two vague theoretical notions involving consensus and homogeneity. Stable government was thought to follow from a high degree of consensus, particularly on what were called fundamentals, as against merely circumstantial matters. Homogeneity theory held, of course, that the more alike people are the less likely they are to be at each other's throats.

To become more fully acquainted with the literature I compiled an "inventory" of ideas pertinent to the problem. Most of these were buried, as offhand interpretations, in mostly descriptive case studies. The full inventory contained about 150 theoretical propositions: there was no lack of ideas but, on the contrary, an embarrassment of riches. Weeding seemed manifestly needed, as well as statements of general propositions that had wide applicability. So, as a next step, I reviewed the inventory to see if it contained patterns that might be the basis of more general propositions.

Something immediately became evident. There seemed to be two general schools of thought about the problem. In one case, the stability or instability of democracies was treated as dependent on the way they were endogenously constituted. In the other, the explanatory variables were external to government; governments were held to be, in one way or another, superstructural (on a vast variety of substructural variables, not only economic factors).

For several reasons, which would consume too much space to explain here, I thought both approaches deficient. Still, it seemed unlikely that governmental structure should have no significance at all and just as unlikely that the social contexts of governments should have no significant bearing on their performance. Yet, it seemed "obvious" that explanatory variables must be either endogenous or exogenous. The categories surely exhausted all the possibilities. So I worked, as best I could, with what existed—until a third possibility somehow came to mind. Governments are patterns of authority. Other social units also have authority patterns: modes of governance. Here, then, was a factor both endogenous and exogenous, and also neither: a possible "linkage-variable" that might connect governments and their contexts, and through which brute contextual factors could work effects upon governments (and vice versa). Polities and other social units, in fact, are most alike in that all have patterns of authority; that alone made it likely that "private" governments (as Charles Merriam called them) would affect public ones through the commonality of modes of governance.

And so, I wrote the article that follows—not as a final word, but as a first attempt (an "explanation sketch") needing elaboration theoretically, conceptually, and operationally. I have been at elaboration, off and on, alone and with collaboration, ever since. The later period started with the attempt to examine the theory's plausibility for costly further work—I had hoped it would lead to a comparative test—in a country about which I knew almost nothing, except that observations in it had to support the theory. The country was Norway, and the result of inquiry there was a book that I had not intended to write, *Division and Cohesion in Democracy* (1966). Other publications that followed include the following:

1. "Authority Relations and Governmental Performance," *Comparative Political Studies* 2 (October 1969): 269–326. A more elaborate, more precise, statement of the theory.
2. *Political Performance* (Beverly Hills: Sage Monographs in Comparative Politics, 1971). An attempt to lay the groundwork for the dependent variable of the theory. The attempt is carried forward and empirically applied in a companion monograph by Ted Robert Gurr and Muriel McClelland.
3. With Ted R. Gurr, *Patterns of Authority* (New York: Wiley, 1975). A full presentation of my work, with Gurr and others, in trying to bring congruence theory to a decisive test, but a work more concerned with the study of authority relations in general than congruence theory only. Also contains a full list of others' work related to congruence theory.
4. *Support for Regimes: Theories and Tests* (Princeton: Center of International Studies, Research Monograph 44, 1979). This presents my view on how congruence theory may decisively be tested.

For as long as men have studied politics they have tried to discover connections between political life and its social setting. In this search one aspect of social life has been strangely neglected—strangely, because it is the element of social life most obviously and immediately relevant to political behavior on the governmental level; I refer to authority patterns in nongovernmental social relationships, in families, schools, economic organizations, and the like. We have propositions about the relations between politics and geography, politics and economic organization, politics and social stratification, politics and religion, politics and child training, politics and role structure, politics and education. But, beyond allusions to the subject, we have no general propositions about the relations between politics on the governmental level and politics in nongovernmental social structures. Under any circumstances this would be a serious omission, for it stands to reason that if any aspect of social life can directly affect government it is the experiences with authority that people have in other spheres of life, especially those that mold their personalities and those to which they normally devote most of their lives. The omission is all the more serious when one considers that the propositions now available for relating society and polity are all, in one way or another, highly imperfect, however much some of them may be supported by evidence and logic. Certainly none has as yet been established so rigorously as to have led to even a moderate consensus among political scientists, nor has any line of analysis yet proved so promising that political scientists can feel easy about leaving other possibilities unexplored.

There is another reason why one should be mystified by the lack of propositions relating governmental authority to other forms of social authority. For some time now numerous developments in political science seem to have been converging on just such propositions. One such development is what the political philosophers call pluralism: the belief that the state has neither a moral nor a practical monopoly upon political authority. Another is the belief that political science must concern itself with a subject matter broader than the state for methodological reasons: for example, on the ground, stated by Catlin already thirty years ago, that political science, if it is to be a true science, must have a subject matter which is simple, general, commonplace, and frequent of occurrence—the state, as we know it, satisfying none of these criteria, while the "act of control," in whatever context it may occur, allegedly satisfies them all.[1] Still another development leading in the same direction is the growing concern of political scientists with power and influence relations as such. Finally, political scientists, and others, have been concerned for many decades now (since Mill, at least) with the possibilities of private despotism in a context of public liberty and with "informal" politics within the context of constitutional law.

These trends have in fact produced a small number of studies dealing with the politics of nongovernmental structures[2]—a surprisingly small number, considering the enormous variety of cases available. They have also produced many exhortations to political scientists to produce more such studies, by, among others, Merriam, de Jouvenel, and Dahl.[3] But while political scientists have not entirely neglected to study nongovernmental relations as political structures, and while they have certainly not neglected the possibilities of social determination of the operation and fate of governments, no one seems even to have thought of systematically linking the first interest to the second, of producing propositions which explain certain facts of public authority on the basis of certain facts of nonpublic authority. I can think of only one good reason for this omission—namely, that the modern idea of the state has so tenacious a hold even on those who disavow it that they tend not to think of private authority when they are concerned with public authority, but think of it only when they are not concerned with states at all. However that may be, propositions linking the two do not yet exist, and the present paper seeks at least to begin remedying this state of affairs.

Despite its title, it presents only an idea, not a full-fledged theory. Nevertheless, it seems to me worthwhile stating the idea now, even in an obviously rudimentary form. The main reason for this emerges from the conclusion of the paper: before the idea can claim to be a full-fledged theory, so much theoretical and empirical work still needs to be done that it might be years before one could say much more about the subject than can be said about it now. In the meantime, I hope that the present statement of the idea will provoke others to look into it, so that its theoretical and empirical elaboration will not be a job falling only to myself. There is more than enough work here for all who may have an interest in it.

CHARACTERISTICS OF STABLE DEMOCRACY

A theory should always begin by defining its subject. In the case of stable democracy this might seem to be a simple matter, but the concept actually raises one or two knotty problems.

Ordinarily we mean by a stable democracy one that has demonstrated considerable staying power, a capacity to endure, without great or frequent changes in pattern. On this basis, the French Third Republic, to take a simple and familiar example, was certainly a stable democracy; like M. Talleyrand in the French Revolution, "it survived," longer at any rate than any other French constitutional order, and longer than many other constitutional orders elsewhere. Yet this example also indicates why a definition of stability as mere longevity will not quite do, even if we could agree on just how long a democracy must endure to be considered stable. Taking the term in this sense, a system may be stable because of its own effectiveness or simply because of the ineffectiveness (or bad luck) of its opponents; it may persist, as did the Third Republic, for no better reason than that it never quite manages even to collapse, despite much opposition and many hairbreadth escapes. But this sort of tenuous survival surely requires an explanation different from that required by the persistence of a constitutional order because of its capacity for adapting to changing conditions, for realizing political aspirations and holding fast allegiances. The first can be explained only on the basis of particular historical circumstances (or "accidents")—the misjudgments of a MacMahon, the untimely relations of a Boulanger with his mistress, the timely realization of the Communists that helping the Fascists would not expedite the proletarian revolution. The second requires an explanation, not in terms of fortuitous circumstances, but in terms of settled social and political con-

ditions; it is, therefore, for political science the more interesting phenomenon, and indeed the only one political science can really handle. The
theory of this paper, consequently, does not concern itself with stability
merely in the sense of endurance, but stability in a more complicated sense.
Endurance is a part of it, but only a part.

What else does the concept imply? First of all, it implies effective decision making—"effective" not in the sense of right action on the basis of
some particular scheme of values, but in the basic sense of action itself,
any sort of action, in pursuit of shared political goals or in adjustment to
changing conditions. The political order must not be "immobilistic," for
immobility can lead to desired results only by inadvertence, if at all. A
government must govern, whatever else it may be supposed to do, otherwise it is not a government at all; and on this criterion the Third Republic,
for all its staying power, certainly comes out badly. In addition, we can
hardly call a government a stable democracy unless it is genuinely "democratic," and this implies that it must satisfy at least two conditions. One
is that democratic structures must not be mere facades for actual government by nondemocratic structures; the decisions of government, which
make it "effective" and perhaps capable of survival, must come from the
democratic process, at least in large part. On the basis of this criterion
the Third Republic comes out badly again, for it was a government carried
on in normal times mainly by a nearly autonomous bureaucracy ("the
Republic on top, the Empire at bottom") and in times of crisis mainly by
temporary dictators armed with *plein pouvoir;* it was, in effect, largely a
system of democratic politics and nondemocratic government. The second
condition is that elections in such systems must decide, in some basic way,
the outcome of the competition for power and policies; for what else can
one mean by democracy? On this basis, too, the Third Republic fares badly,
for its elections decided very little, compared with the traditions of the
bureaucracy, the whims of parliamentary dictators like Laval, Chautemps,
and Daladier, and the irrepressible *trasformismo* of the Radicals, the party
always indispensable to governments and always in power, whatever the
outcome of elections.

The term "stability," when applied to democracies, thus implies three
conditions: persistence of pattern, decisional effectiveness, and authentic-
ity. And barring the sort of large good fortune that saved the Third Republic repeatedly upon the point of extinction, we may be sure that these
three conditions hang closely together. The Third Republic, in fact, is the
only case that does not completely illustrate this fact—it would indeed be
strange if there were many others, for the sort of accidents that preserved
it have only a slight statistical probability. In other cases—the Weimar
Republic, for example, or the Fourth Republic, or pre-Fascist Italy—the
interdependence of all three conditions is clearly revealed. Governmental

paralysis, particularly in the face of crisis, is generally a prelude to the demise of democracy. It always leads, even before the end of the formal representative system, to government by freewheeling bureaucrats, or parliamentary dictators, or inconsequential minority leaders like Facta and von Papen. And even if a democratic system survives in form by surrendering power to its adjuncts or to a minority, it cannot in that case be said to survive in fact; nor is it then likely, on the evidence, to survive for long in form. That is why all three conditions can be sufficiently stated in a single adjective, *stable* democracy, without any cumbersome additional ones (e.g., "effective").

THE PROBLEM OF STABLE DEMOCRACY

Certain conditions obviously favor stable democracy, so obviously in fact that no decent theory ever stops with them. When someone says, for example, that democracies tend to be stable if they enjoy wide support,[4] that individual has obviously not said very much, and probably nothing that we really want to know. Neither is it very instructive to be told that a highly integrated party system (like the British) is more conducive to stable democracy than a fragmented party system, or that a climate of moderation and pragmatism in politics is more favorable to it than one of extremism and ideological dogma.[5] There is in fact a well-known syndrome of conditions connected with stable democracy which is practically synonymous with the term, in that it would be difficult to imagine the one without the other. This syndrome of conditions includes, above all, consensus on the form of government, a high degree of political pragmatism, and a certain kind of party system: either a two-party system or a larger number of parties possessing to a high degree what the Germans call *Koalitionsfähigkeit* (coalition capacity, to be very literal). These conditions do "explain" the existence of stable democracy, but only in a very superficial way: the same way that the statement, "X pulled the trigger of a loaded revolver while pointing the muzzle at himself," explains how X came to commit suicide. In both cases, the explanation we really seek is one step further removed. We do not really want to know what sort of political party systems and climate of opinion favor stable democracy. We really want to know what conditions underlie the requisite syndrome of favorable conditions, whatever it may be, for only on this level of the problem are the answers not obvious.

Getting beyond the obvious in regard to the problem of stable democracy requires also that we do not dwell very long on the general functional and structural requisites of viable social systems that sociologists and general systems theorists have so far managed to establish, even though these requisites are meant explicitly to explain the stability or instability of systems.[6] We could, of course, discuss the collapse of democracies like the Weimar Republic, pre-Fascist Italy, or the French Fourth Republic in terms of these requisites; and keeping them in mind will certainly help us to look for and to find certain important weaknesses and malfunctions in these political systems. But the use of system requisites is also unlikely to lead us to the desired level of explanation. To some extent these categories will merely help establish the fact that the political systems mentioned do indeed fit our definition of unstable democracy: for example, that they failed to "maintain" the democratic "pattern" by the surrender of power to nondemocratic adjuncts of the system. To some extent, they will only lead us to the more familiar truistic theories stated earlier: to lack of "integration" in party systems, for example, or lack of "conformity" to the norms of the democratic polity on the part of many of its members. To some extent they will lead us to certain symptoms rather than preconditions (effects rather than causes) of instability: for example, the inadequate "adaptation" of fluid social resources through faulty economic policies, as in the constantly misshapen budgets of the Third and Fourth republics; or the failure of basic mechanisms of accountability and consent, as in the virtually unchecked use of decree powers by parliamentary autocrats; or the failure of a government's structure of coercion, as illustrated by the unconstrained violence in pre-Fascist Italy by D'Annunzio's orgiastic nationalists, pillaging peasants and workers, and Mussolini's own *fascisti*. In every democratic system that has failed, we do find a failure to satisfy some of the system requisites that men like Parsons, Levy, and Apter have proposed; if nothing else, this means that their claims to have established truly general categories are not invalidated. But the fact remains that these categories simply do not get us to the level of the problem with which we are concerned in this case.

Our real problem is not to find whether system failures have indeed occurred in unstable democracies or to link their occurrence to manifestly unfavorable conditions. We need to discover the deeper, or more remote, conditions that rule out or make possible stable democracy, either directly or by bringing into being the obviously deleterious or obviously favorable conditions discussed above.

THE CONGRUENCE OF AUTHORITY PATTERNS

The Universality of Authority

To solve this problem, a theory is required that, up to a point, is also a *general* theory of governmental stability. Since democracy is a special kind of government, it seems plain logic that a theory of stable democracy should consist of two parts, one stating the general conditions that make governmental stability probable, the other stating the particular conditions required to make democracies stable. These particular conditions should of course be special instances of the more general conditions that produce governmental stability. It may be that no general theory of governmental stability can really be developed, that every kind of government is sui generis in this regard; but at this stage of inquiry we have no reason whatever to think that this is the case. Hence the first proposition of the present theory is in fact a proposition about the stability or instability of any governmental order, whatever its special character. This proposition concerns the nature of, and the relations among, the different authority patterns in a society.

In every society we can discover numerous authority patterns, both attitudes regarding authority and, to use Lasswell's terminology, authority "practices." Certainly this is so if we use the term "authority" in its broadest and most conventional sense, to denote relationships of superordination and subordination among individuals in social formations, relationships in which some members of the formation take decisions and others treat the decisions as binding. In this simple sense of a hierarchy of wills, the state certainly has no monopoly upon authority. It may be quite possible, and even useful, to distinguish between the authority of the state and other kinds of authority; and it is easy enough to define authority in a way that will confine it arbitrarily to the state. But as the term is used here, authority in some form is a characteristic of practically any persistent social aggregate, at least in that certain actual practices of subordination and superordination will be found in such aggregates, and probably also in that there will exist in the society as a whole and in its subunits certain dominant notions as to how such practices *should* be conducted. Authority exists not only in the state itself, but also in parties and pressure groups, in economic organizations, in various kinds of associations, in schools and families, even in friendships, bands, clubs, and gangs. We can discover it in any set of social relations which, in the not too happy jargon of social psychology, is "cooperatively interdependent"[7]—that is, very simply, not competitive. The only persistent social relations in which we are pretty certain not to find it are "competitively interdependent" relations, like the bargaining relations that take place in a free economic market or in international politics—granted that a certain amount of bargaining can be an aspect of authority relations as well, and a certain amount of authority sets limits to the scope and content of bargaining.

I assert this universality of authority patterns in noncompetitive social relations, not because it is absolutely necessary to my theory to assert it, but because it is a palpable fact. All that is necessary to the present theory, however, is that authority should exist in *some* social relations other than those of formal government, particularly in those social relations, like the family or economic organizations, which one finds in any society; and this assertion will surely not be disputed by anyone without some sort of re-definition of authority.

The Idea of Congruence

Stated very briefly, the first proposition of the theory I would suggest is that *a government will tend to be stable if its authority pattern is congruent with the other authority patterns of the society of which it is a part.* The crucial term in this proposition is of course "congruence," and it needs to be defined, particularly since, as used here, the term is not at all self-explanatory.

Authority patterns are congruent, in the first place (but only in the first place), if they are identical (that is to say, since we are dealing not with an abstract geometric universe but real life, if they very closely resemble each other). An example of congruence in this sense is furnished by the authority patterns in British government and British political parties, at any rate if we accept the standard analyses of the latter by Beer and McKenzie.[8] Both patterns consist of a curious and very similar mixture of democratic, authoritarian, and, so to speak, constitutional elements; this despite the fact that British government can be traced back to the eras of medieval constitutionalism and royal absolutism, while political parties are, in almost every respect, creatures of a much later period, the era of the mandate; and this also despite the fact that the formal constitution of the Labour party makes it seem very different from both the Conservative party and the British governmental structure.[9] In both government and parties, the idea of the mandate is formalized and paid considerably more than lip service, in one case in the House of Commons, in the other in the Annual Conferences. In both cases, however, the leaders actually enjoy long tenure in office and a great deal of autonomy, even though the autonomy of the Conservative Leader rests on formal rules and that of the Labour Leader "merely" on actual practice; in both cases, moreover, the idea of the mandate is contravened by the fact that the leaders are widely *expected* to govern, in the sense of taking personal policy initiatives and sometimes even acting contrary to opinion in the rank and file. In both cases, too, this autonomy of leadership is mitigated by the expecta-tion—on the part, incidentally, of both elites and masses—that authority will be exercised "constitutionally"; that is to say, that it will be exercised, if not in conformity with written documents, then at least within a frame-work of widely accepted and well-understood limits and rules, including, for example, the rule that authority inheres always in a collective structure, whether this structure is provided for in a formal constitution, as in the Labour party, or not, as in the Conservative party and the governmental machinery. In addition to these absolutely fundamental resemblances, there are also many less basic, although no less striking, similarities between

British government and parties. For example, both Parliament and the parliamentary organizations of the parties have largely an advisory and exhortatory role in decision-making processes; in both Parliament and the party conferences, the leaders are given certain traditional privileges in debates (they speak longer, for example, and more frequently); in both government and parties, bureaucracy plays an indispensable but subordinate and unusually self-effacing role, even in this age of massive government and massive parties; and, of course, government and party leaders entirely coincide, a fact that the Weimar parties show to be by no means inevitable in a parliamentary system.

The essential patterns of cabinet government, and the essential attitudes on which it is based, thus all have their counterparts in the major British parties. In fact, it has been argued, cogently I think, that cabinet government on the British model compels a certain correspondence between party structure and governmental structure, certainly while a party is in power, and therefore also perhaps while it is in opposition and presumably aspiring to power. Cabinet government could not otherwise work at all on a party basis; hence the anxieties of many English citizens when the Labour party strays, as it infrequently does, from the model of the cabinet system and acts as if it really believed in its formal constitution. But this argument should not be taken to mean that British parties cannot help but have a structure similar to that of British government. "Compel" does not in this case mean "cause." The argument means merely that British government can work smoothly only if such a congruence of governmental and party structures exists, not that things could not actually be otherwise. There are plenty of parliamentary systems in which the same logic holds, but few in which the same congruence can be found.

The most extreme and plainest form of congruence, then, is identity. Mixing metaphors, we might speak in this case of isomorphic authority patterns. But identity cannot exhaust the meaning of congruence when applied to social phenomena, for it is difficult even to imagine a society in which all authority patterns closely resemble each other. Certainly such a state of affairs is impossible in a democracy. Some social relations simply cannot be conducted in a democratic manner, or can be so conducted only with the gravest dysfunctional consequences. Take, for example, those social units which link different generations—families and schools. An infant cannot be cared for democratically, or a child brought up and schooled democratically. Families and schools can be permissive, but this is merely to say that they can be authoritarian in a lax and lenient manner. Families and schools can also carry on a certain amount of democratic pretense, and indeed more than pretense, and when they do so on a large scale, that fact is not without significance; but by and large they cannot carry such simulation and imitation of democracy to very great lengths, if they are not to produce warped and ineffectual human beings. One of the most basic and indispensable functions in any social system, the socialization function, must therefore always be to some extent out of tune with democratic patterns and potentially at odds with them. The same point applies, almost as obviously, to certain relations among adults. We have every reason to think that economic organizations cannot be organized in a truly democratic manner, at any rate not without consequences that no one wants; and we certainly know that capitalist economic organization and even certain kinds of public ownership (like the nationalization in Britain of industries absolutely vital to the health of the whole economy) militate against a democratization of economic relations. The case of military organizations is even plainer in this regard, and the case of public bureaucracy just as clear. Again, there can be some simulation and imitation of democracy in firms, or public offices, or military units, but only within rather narrow limits. Precisely those social relations in which most individuals are engaged most of the time—family life, schools, and jobs (most kinds of jobs)—are the least capable of being democratically organized. To expect all authority relations in a democracy to be identical would therefore be unreasonable, and we could probably demonstrate the same thing, in other ways, for other kinds of governmental structures. In any complex society, but above all in democracies, we must expect some heterogeneity in authority patterns, even if we deal only with fundamental patterns and not circumstantial details.

In that case, however, one can still speak meaningfully of a congruence of authority patterns if the patterns have a certain "fit" with one another— if they dovetail with, or support, the governmental pattern, however indirectly. One way in which they can do this is by the partial imitation of the governmental authority patterns in other social structures. Democratic (or other) pretenses, if taken seriously and carried far, may have important consequences for the operation of the governmental structure, even though they are pretenses. Furthermore, structures like economic or military organizations may, in some cases, willingly incur certain functional disadvantages for the sake of acting out norms associated with governments in their substantive decision-making processes. For instance, capitalistic economic organizations, which play a great deal at democracy and permit certain deviations from the logic of the double-entry ledger in order actually to carry on certain democratic practices, may be said to be more congruent with democratic government than those that stick closely, both in ritual and process, to the economically most rational practices.

In view of this, we might be tempted to say that authority patterns are congruent if they have, not everything, but something in common. But if the equation of congruence with identity makes demands that are too great, its equation with mere resemblance, however slight, does not demand enough. On the first basis, we shall almost never find a society in which authority patterns are really congruent; on the second, we shall assuredly not find any in which authority patterns are incongruent. However, by congruence I do not mean any resemblance at all among authority patterns. Where authority relations are not all highly similar, the term refers rather to a particular pattern of resemblance among them, one that makes stringent requirements, but not requirements impossible to fulfill—a pattern of *graduated resemblances,* so to speak.

To grasp the concept of graduated resemblances, one must think of societies as being composed of segments that are more or less distant from government. Governments themselves are adult structures, and for this reason families, for example, are more "vertically" distant from them, in terms of age levels, than schools, and schools more distant from them than purely adult structures. In the same way, adult structures may be "horizontally" segmented, so that some appear close to, others distant from, government. Parties, for example, ordinarily are situated closer to government than pressure groups; among pressure groups certain types may be particularly closely involved in government or parties; and all pressure groups are located more closely to government than nonpolitical organizations. These are very rough breakdowns; in some concrete cases, moreover, it may be difficult to make unambiguous distinctions, and the same social structures will not always fall into the same positions in every society. But none of this affects the definition: that social authority patterns are congruent, either if they are very similar, or if similarity to the governmental pattern increases significantly as one approaches the governmental segment itself.

On the basis of these explications of the term "congruence," we can now restate the first proposition of the theory. *Government will be stable, (1) if social authority patterns are identical with the governmental pattern,* or *(2) if they constitute a graduated pattern in a proper segmentation of society,* or *(3) if a high degree of resemblance exists in patterns adjacent to government and one finds throughout the more distant segments a marked departure from functionally appropriate patterns for the sake of imitating the governmental pattern or extensive imitation of the governmental pattern in ritual practices.* Conditions (2) and (3) are both, of course, looser and less demanding versions of condition (1); all refer to a basic need for considerable resemblance in authority patterns if government is to be stable, particularly in those segments of society which impinge directly on government. Condition (3) may be regarded, in this way, as the minimum required for governmental stability (and the minimum meaning of congruence), but perhaps the most that can be realized in relation to some particular pattern of government. By the same token, *governments will be unstable* (and the authority patterns of a society incongruent) *if the governmental authority pattern is isolated* (that

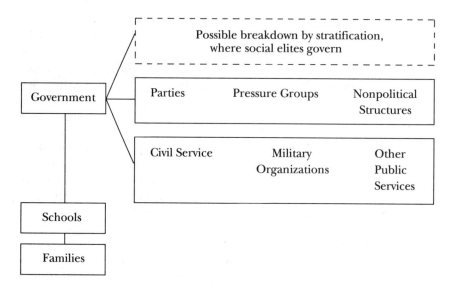

is, substantially different) *from those of other social segments, or if a very abrupt change in authority pattern occurs in any adjacent segments of society, or if several different authority patterns exist in social strata furnishing a large proportion of the political elite* (in the sense of active political participants). In the last case, congruence with the authority patterns of a particular part of the elite—say, a particular social class—may be quite possible, but congruence with the overall authority patterns of a society is logically out of the question.

Two Examples: Great Britain and Germany

To make these propositions less abstract, let us look at two concrete cases that illustrate them: contemporary Britain and Weimar Germany.

We have already seen how closely the authority patterns of government and political parties resemble one another in Great Britain and that this resemblance helps to make effective the processes of cabinet government. One can similarly find great resemblances in authority patterns between British government and other aspects of British social life. As one moves away from the governmental segment these resemblances do decline, but never markedly or in a very abrupt manner.

For example, there is a quite striking resemblance in the authority structures of government and pressure groups, a resemblance also required for effective cabinet government, at least in this age of the social service state (as I have pointed out in another work).[10] This resemblance is perhaps greatest in the case of groups constituted almost exclusively for political purposes (that is, in "attitude groups"),[11] but it also exists to a surprising extent in functional organizations, like professional and economic organizations, which go in for politics only as a more or less important sideline. Among such functional organizations, moreover, the resemblance to government is particularly great in groups most directly involved in governmental and party affairs, for example, trade unions, large-scale employers' organizations, cooperative societies, and the like. It is true that, on the whole, involvement by the group in nonpolitical affairs, such as economic bargaining, tends to decrease resemblance to the governmental pattern. Also, certain nonpolitical activities (for example, economic activities as against those of professional associations) act as inhibitions on too great an imitation of the governmental pattern. But throughout the whole universe of British pressure groups, resemblance to the governmental pattern is quite surprisingly great, even in organizations where, for functional reasons, one would least expect this.

British pressure groups tend to follow more or less closely, but ordinarily very closely, a certain ideal-typical authority pattern, which will immediately ring familiar to anyone acquainted with British government and parties. At the apex of this authority pattern, one usually finds a ceremonial figure who symbolically represents the group, perhaps presides over important meetings, and makes solemn speeches, but occupies a largely ritualistic and honorific position—although in a few cases ceremony and "efficiency" may be combined, as it is also in the leadership of the Conservative party. Under this figure, there generally is a council or executive committee, a collective body that usually exercises the real decision-making power, at least so far as higher decisions are concerned; more often than not this body is dominated, despite pretenses of collective decision making, by its chairman and a small handful of especially powerful members. Under the council, one generally finds a large number of other collective bodies— functional committees—with overlapping memberships; the dominant roles on these committees are played by the more powerful figures on the council. The functional committees and council are formally considered "responsible" to large annual conventions (a conference, or representative meeting, or whatever it may be called), which are always supposed to exercise the ultimate decision-making power, but generally act only as bodies acclaiming the leaders, occasionally criticizing them, and very infrequently making substantive contributions to policy; nevertheless, the leaders take care not to deviate too far from the public opinion of the convention and at the very least put up a show of responsiveness to the rank and file. Finally, there are a number of paid, full-time officials, a secretary and the assistants, who administer the organization's activities, play an extremely important role in regard to all affairs and an all-important role in regard to routine business, work closely and unobtrusively with the chairman and other important council members, generally get their way, but know when to stay in the background and when not to press their views. Throughout this structure operate norms typical of all public authority in Great Britain: that decision making must be carried out by some sort of collective leadership, which is both responsive to the mass of the organization and, to a large extent, autonomous of it, which is expected to behave according to some sort of code well-understood in the group but normally not explicitly defined, and which, although resting to some extent on an elective basis, enjoys great tenure of office, often for as long as the leaders want to keep their positions.

In short, in the typical British pressure group we find the same mixture of basic authority forms that characterizes British government and parties, as well as imitations of less basic British authority practices, from the ubiquity of committees to ceremonial headship. This resemblance of the pressure-group pattern to the governmental pattern even extends to very minor matters, such as styles of debate at the annual conventions (directing remarks at the presiding officer, referring to other speakers in a florid and impersonal fashion, rarely delivering set speeches), or ways in which motions are introduced and processed, or ways in which orders of speakers are determined. We find this pattern, in almost every aspect, in a professional association like the British Medical Association,[12] in a trade union like the National Union of Teachers, and in an employers' organization like the Federation of British Industries.[13] Names may differ—the B.M.A. has an Annual Representative Meeting and a Council, the N.U.T. a Conference and an Executive, the F.B.I. an Annual General Meeting and a Grand Council—but the substance is the same, in structural forms and in actual practices.

In nonpolitical adult organizations, from friendly societies and clubs to business organizations, smallness of scale and functional considerations generally lead to significant departures from these forms and practices, but in the vast majority of cases one finds in these organizations at least a great deal of imitation, if only as ritual, of the governmental pattern. Even small-scale neighborhood clubs, like the many lawn tennis and social clubs that dot the landscape of middle-class England, generally have their committees and secretaries, their relatively inconsequential elections and stable oligarchies, their formalities, petty constitutionalisms, and ritualistic annual meetings; and still more is this true of larger clubs and friendly societies, like the famous snob clubs of Pall Mall and that holiest of holies, the Marylebone Cricket Club. It may be easier in such small organizations for elites to maintain themselves in authority, and also for members to participate in decision making, if they wish, but the essential forms and actual patterns of authority do not differ very much from the great political associations.

In business organizations, greater departures from the typical pattern occur, but even in such organizations there is usually some acting out of the governmental forms (most conspicuously, much reliance on committees, both on the level of management and among workers). In business organizations, however, congruence with the authority patterns of the political organizations may be found mainly in seemingly inconsequential patterns of behavior, some of which have driven countless American efficiency teams, taking as their frame of reference behavior strictly "rational" in economic terms, to uncomprehending distraction—such as the tendency of British executives to keep civil service hours, and above all their tendency to carry on endless consultations instead of reaching quick and independent decisions. The general tone of relations among bosses and workers is also relevant here, although this is a matter difficult to deal with very explicitly. The typical British boss, like any other boss, is an authoritarian figure, but he is rarely an overbearing tyrant or a stern taskmaster. More often than not, he is a paternalistic authoritarian, in the general style of the British upper classes in relation to the British lower classes. It would not occur to him to be on intimate terms with his workers. Neither would it occur to him that his position might entitle him to treat his workers in an insulting manner, or to claim special privileges over them outside of the business organization, or that his functionally specific authority might extend to other aspects of his workers' lives.

Business organizations depart to a rather great extent from the governmental pattern, not only for obvious functional reasons, but also because of a fact just touched upon: they bring into close relation members of the upper and lower social classes. Wherever this occurs in British life, the authoritarian elements of the authority pattern tend to become enlarged and the democratic elements diminished. This is so not only in relations between economic bosses and their workers, but also between domestic servants and masters, enlisted men and officers, and members of the Administrative Class and other classes in the civil service. While all of these relations are governed by a high sense of propriety and functional limitation (by constitutionalist norms), those among members of the higher levels tend to be quite surprisingly democratic, or at least consultative and comradely; here again we might note the ubiquity of committees at every conceivable level in the higher civil service, the unusual use of staff committees in the military services, and the easy relations among officers of all ranks in military regiments, especially in elitist regiments like the Guards. But between members of the Administrative Class and their underlings, officers and their men, managers and their hired help, relations are highly nonconsultative and certainly not comradely; the observance of propriety and functional limitations in these cases is complemented by a considerable separation of individuals from each other, a general lack of contact among them for purposes other than functional ones.

All this is quite in keeping with a governmental pattern that is as markedly elitist as the British. In general, the governmental authority pattern is conformed to most in Britain in relations among members of the upper classes; it is conformed to less in relations among members of the lower classes and least in interclass relations. In other words, the more important the role in government that members of a social stratum are likely to play, the more their relations tend to be molded in the governmental pattern; and this is just what one would expect in a system like the British.

British schools and family life are at least partly responsible for this state of affairs. Family life in the lower strata is much more authoritarian than in the upper strata; there is less reasonableness, less consultation, less courtesy, less formality, more punishment, and more arbitrariness. Although even in the lower classes we can find no counterpart of the menacing paterfamilias of certain continental European families, the matriarchs whom Young and Willmott found in Bethnal Green or the arbitrarily despotic fathers depicted in working-class novels,[14] like those of Lawrence and Sillitoe, have no upper-class counterparts. The same thing applies to schools. A marked change of atmosphere occurs as one moves from the secondary modern and technical schools to the grammar schools and public schools, especially the latter. Of course, even on the upper levels, British schools, like British government itself, tend to be rather authoritarian—more so, certainly, than schools in the United States—but relations among masters and pupils involve also a great deal of rather formalized good fellowship (in school games, for example) and a strict adherence to well-defined codes of conduct, while behavior among pupils is modeled to a remarkable extent on the political system. A case in point is described in Duff Cooper's book of memoirs, *Old Men Forget*. In Cooper's days at Eton, and possibly still today, debates were conducted in a manner obviously a carbon copy of House of Commons procedure, even though political questions were never discussed. A motion would be introduced, and any one of the students attending ("the House"!) might be called upon to captain the discussion; prior to "business," questions would be asked as in the Commons, and boys referred to one another as "honorable members" rather than by name. Not always do we find quite such faithful copies of governmental patterns in the higher educational institutions, but the governmental style is noticeable in almost every case; indeed, British politics has a readily recognizable style precisely because politicians are brought up to it practically from the time they wear rompers. Again, this is not to imply that relations among public school boys or grammar school boys are remarkably democratic or egalitarian; it would be absurd to call the prefect systems of British schools egalitarian. But then neither is British government remarkably egalitarian. And British schoolboys do enjoy an unusual degree of freedom from the direct supervision of their elders, a great amount of self-government, even though it is self-government modified by relatively well-defined authoritarian relations among themselves.

British life thus illustrates the congruence of social authority patterns in all its aspects and degrees. There is a great resemblance between the authority pattern of government and those most closely adjacent to it, parties and pressure groups. Between government and those authority patterns that least resemble it intervene authority structures that are to a fairly large extent like the governmental structure. At no point in the segmentation of British society is there any abrupt and large change in authority patterns, and throughout one finds at least some imitation of governmental forms. And resemblance to the governmental pattern is greater in elite structures than in those of the nonelite. This does not validate the present theory, but it does support it in the case of perhaps the most stable of all modern political systems.

For support from the opposite end of the spectrum, we might look at one of the least stable of all modern governments, the Weimar Republic. How did the authority patterns of interwar Germany differ from modern Britain? Basically, in two ways. On the one hand, the German governmental pattern was much more one-sidedly democratic, at any rate if we confine analysis to the level of parliamentary representation and decision making and do not take into account the instrumental adjuncts of government, bureaucracy, the military, and the judiciary. On the other hand, social life, including life in parties and political interest groups, was highly authoritarian and relatively little "constitutionalized" compared with Britain. Not only were society and polity to some degree incongruent; they existed in unprecedented contradiction with one another. And on the basis of the theory of congruence, in consequence, the Weimar Republic could only have been what indeed it was: nasty, brutish, and short-lived—unless, like the Third Republic, it had been more lucky than any political order can expect to be.

Democracy, in interwar Germany, was, for all practical purposes, isolated at the level of parliamentary government, but at that level it was organized in an almost absurdly pure and exaggerated manner. Weimar Germany was governed by a Reichstag chosen on the basis of universal suffrage and by means of one of the purest systems of proportional representation ever devised. The chief of state was a plebiscitary president, and an effort was made, through run-off provisions, to assure that he would have the support of an absolute, not merely a relative, majority. Ministers were easily removable both by the popularly elected Reichstag and popularly elected president, and government was conducted on the basis of a very lengthy and detailed bill of rights. The Weimar constitution was proclaimed in its day as the most perfect of all democratic constitutions, and for good reasons.

This unalleviated democracy was superimposed upon a society pervaded by authoritarian relationships and obsessed with authoritarianism. In his study of interwar German films, *From Caligari to Hitler,* Siegfried Kracauer has pointed out that a morbid concern with despotism, with raw power and arbitrary will, was a characteristic alike of reactionary and revolutionary German films, most obviously in films like *Caligari, Waxworks, Dr. Mabuse,* and *Mädchen in Uniform.* That the Germans should have been deeply preoccupied with naked power, large and petty, is hardly surprising in a society democratized on its parliamentary surface, but shot through with large and petty tyrants in every other segment of life. Compared with their British counterparts, German family life, German schools, and German business firms were all exceedingly authoritarian. German families were dominated, more often than not, by tyrannical husbands and fathers, German schools by tyrannical teachers, German firms by tyrannical bosses. Insolence, gruffness, pettiness, arbitrariness, even violence were so widespread that one could certainly not consider them mere deviations from normal patterns. In a sense, throughout the whole of German interwar society one finds authority patterns that in Britain are confined to the nonelite strata, but even among the lower classes in Britain authority relations are not quite so arbitrary or so unrelenting as they were in Weimar Germany, nor afflicted by such omnipresent intimations of violence.

Families, schools, and occupational contexts are the most basic (that is, the most absorbing and demanding) segments of life, and the patterns existing in them are bound to affect all other social relations. But perhaps a high degree of authoritarianism in these patterns would not matter from the standpoint of democratic government if there were interposed between them and government certain institutions having mixed authority relations—institutions that might mediate between the pervasive despotism of the primary segments and the pure democracy of government, so that individuals would not be tossed abruptly from stark domination in one segment of life to stark liberty in another. But nothing remotely like this was the case in Weimar Germany. Political parties in imperial Germany had served as the principal model for Michels's iron law of oligarchy, and their internal political characteristics persisted in the Weimar period; at a later date, German political parties served as the chief illustration for Hermens's argument that proportional representation with the straight list system inevitably makes for a highly centralized and oligarchical party structure. Associational life in Weimar Germany presents, if anything, an even sharper contrast with Great Britain. Quite apart from the fact that the great interest groups were intimately involved in the party system—every major interest, economic, religious, or sectional, had a party of its own—the main associations offering men opportunities for escape from loneliness or from the primary social relations were extraordinarily authoritarian in structure. Germany was not a country of hushed snob clubs and demure whist drives, of jolly good fellowship and darts in the public bar, but a country of paramilitary organizations, trade union militants, beer hall conspirators, grimly serious *Turnvereine* and systematically joyful *Gesangvereine*. This, of course, is something of an exaggeration. Not all German associations were highly authoritarian in structure, and we have reason to think that there were important differences among the various regions of Germany in this regard—southern Germany, for example, being on the whole less monotonously authoritarian than northern Germany. But while any simple picture of any complex society will exaggerate and overemphasize to some extent, the essential picture of pervasive authoritarianism in German secondary associations given here probably does so relatively little. At the very least, we can say that life in German associations was much more authoritarian than it is in the great majority of democracies. Associations thus formed no bridge between government and the primary and occupational groups; if anything, they formed a barrier to their reconciliation. Certainly it is in organizations like the *Stahlhelm*, or the *Freikorps*, or the SA and SS, that we find the greatest contrast to the pattern of plebiscitary government.[15]

The same argument applies to the instrumental appendages of the parliamentary system, the civil and military service. Just as the imperial German parties had inspired Michels's theory of universal oligarchy, so the Prussian civil service, which persisted in form and to a large extent even in personnel under Weimar, had served as the chief model for Weber's ideal type of bureaucracy, with its emphasis upon "hierarchical subordination" and "the distinct social esteem" of the official. To these characteristics, which are by no means found in anything like pure form in other modern countries (e.g., Britain), we might add another that innumerable works on German bureaucracy have remarked upon: its recruitment from the more authoritarian elements in German society and its open sympathy, throughout the Weimar period, for reactionary and authoritarian movements.[16] As for the military, so frequently has the antagonism of its patterns and attitudes to the Weimar system been pointed out that nothing more need be said on this subject.

We have in the case of the Weimar Republic a government violently contradictory to all nongovernmental aspects of life. However, it would not be strictly accurate to say, as so many have said, that the Germans were simply thoroughgoing authoritarians who just had no use for political democracy, that in Germany governmental democracy was imposed upon a country that provided no basis at all for it, so that the first talented and lucky authoritarian to come along could easily demolish the whole structure. There is every reason to think that the great majority of Germans were convinced democrats during the Weimar period and even before—

in their attitudes toward government. Imperial Germany was one of the first countries to have universal suffrage, and the fact that prodemocratic, liberal, center, and socialist parties consistently won somewhere between 80 and 90 percent of the vote in elections before World War I is therefore a matter of some importance. This voting pattern, furthermore, continued under the Weimar Republic right up to the ill-starred elections of the early 1930s; the right-wing Nationalists (the DNVP), the party that best fits the stereotype of the unmitigatedly authoritarian German, rarely polled more than 10 percent of the vote. Consequently, when one says that there was no basis for democracy in interwar Germany, one says something much more complicated than that Germans did not really want a governmental democracy. One says that Weimar Germany could provide no proper basis even for a governmental system that the great majority indeed wanted, while imperial Germany, ironically, did furnish a proper basis for a type of government the great majority did not seem to want. Had the German taste for authoritarianism been absolute, the Germans would probably have constructed after World War I a much more stable, though not a purely democratic, government. The trouble was not that the Germans were so one-sidedly authoritarian; the trouble was rather that they were—and perhaps had always been[17]—so remarkably two-sided (i.e., incongruent) in their political beliefs and social practices. Profound ideological commitment to governmental democracy is not a sufficient basis for stable democracy; in fact, it can be worse, in the long run, than a more qualified commitment to democracy.

One more point regarding the incongruities in Weimar authority patterns may be worth mentioning. Although the constitution of the Weimar Republic was democratic to an unprecedented degree, it did contain some authoritarian elements. The executive, as in Britain, was given an unlimited power of dissolution; and under Article 48, the article that played such a villainous role in the legal destruction of German democracy, the president, with the cooperation of a chancellor appointed by himself, could wield enormous emergency powers, including the virtually absolute suspension of civil rights and a nearly unlimited power to govern by decrees. But these authoritarian elements of the constitution were reserved for particular periods when regular parliamentary processes no longer operated; contrary to the British case, they were not built into the everyday management of government. They were no part of the normal pattern of governmental authority. The constitution really left nothing to choose between absolute democracy in "normal" times—rare enough in the Weimar period—and an absolute lack of it in times of crisis. As a result, government was carried on not only in contradiction with society, but even in a sort of contradiction with itself; periods of pure parliamentary democracy alternated at a rapid rate with periods of practically unchecked executive dictatorship, much as in the last years of pre-Fascist Italian democracy and during the 1930s in France.

Motivational Basis of the Theory

In addition to the fact that it seems to fit the most unambiguous cases of stability and instability, the theory of congruence has, prior to any concerted testing, one other important point to recommend it: it leads one immediately to the motivational (or psychological) links between the variables it relates. This is important. Any generalization about human behavior obviously lacks an important element of plausibility if it makes no sense in terms of what we know about human motivations. Conceivably societies may involve certain purely mechanical relations that require no motivational explanation at all, but follow simply from the fact of interaction, whatever may underlie it; but even theories about competitive interdependence seem always to proceed from particular views of probable human conduct. In any event, to ask *why* certain relations exist in social life is always to ask what there is about one state of society that induces behavior leading to another.

Such motivational connections between different aspects of social life are by no means easy to see whenever one finds a positive correlation between social variables. Take the correlation between democracy and economic development. A positive relation of some sort seems to exist between the two, but why exactly should it? The only link which readily suggests itself is that a high degree of economic development leads to a high degree of economic satisfaction and thus reconciles people to their condition of life, including their government. But this does not tell us why it should reconcile them particularly to democracy, and, what is more, militates against the obvious fact that economic satisfaction is always relative to economic expectations—expectations that might conceivably outstrip any rate of economic growth and any level of economic development. This is not to say that there is no link between democracy and economic development at all, but only that the motivational link between them is not readily apparent from the correlation itself and probably very indirect, if indeed it does exist.

The motivational basis of the theory of congruence, however, is quite readily apparent. This is due to the fact that the conditions described by the term "incongruity" are very similar to the conditions denoted by two other concepts of social science that, appropriately enough, denote both certain social conditions and certain psychological states or propensities to act: the closely related concepts of anomie and strain.

Anomie exists, in its purest form, whenever there is a complete breakdown of a normative order governing action, when individuals lack clear and commanding guidelines to behavior, do not know what is expected of them, and are thus compelled to rely solely upon their egos, their "rational" calculations, to inform their conduct. Anomie, in this sense, may be more or less acute and more or less widespread in a society; it may extend to few or many, important or unimportant, phases of life, and it may be found in society generally or only in certain of its members. It is always disturbing, but becomes, in its more acute form, unbearable; the actual responses to it depend, however, not only upon its acuteness but also upon the extent of its diffusion throughout a society. At its less acute levels, it manifests itself in merely annoying, possibly even constructive, anxieties, and the resort to perfectly innocuous means of relieving them. But in its more intense forms it has been linked, on the individual level, with serious functional disorders (even suicide), and, on the social level, with mass movements in general, particularly movements of religious fanaticism and political movements of a chiliastic and highly ideological character—in general, with movements that provide people with a sense of orientation, a sense of belonging to a bearable social order, or merely with the opportunity for escaping from the dilemmas of everyday life or submerging themselves in some comforting collectivity.

Anomie may result from many conditions. In individuals, it may be the result of inadequate socialization, or rapid mobility from one stratum of society to another, or transplantation from one culture to another, or indeed any important change in one's condition in life. In societies it may result from any social change (especially rapid change) requiring important adjustments in conduct, or from a widely successful attack upon traditional norms, or from large-scale mobility.

Among these many conditions that can give rise to anomie, the condition of "strain" is perhaps the most common in any complex society. "Strain" is used here in a technical sense; it refers, not to the utter lack of settled guides to behavior, or to ambiguous norms, but to ambivalent expectations—that is, the coexistence of different, perhaps even contradictory, norms of conduct in regard to a particular set of actions or an individual's actions in general.[18] We may speak of strain whenever people are expected to conform to different, but equally legitimate, norms of conduct—as, for example, when an individual simultaneously performs some roles involving universalistic norms and others involving particularistic norms, or some roles permitting affective responses and others demanding affective neutrality; and strains are of course particularly acute if a single role makes contradictory normative demands. Strain thus exists for a doctor who is sexually attracted to a patient.

Incongruity between the authority patterns of a society, like any other incongruity among social patterns, is an obvious source of strain, and through strain of anomie, and through anomie of behavior potentially destructive to the stability of any pattern of government. This seems obvious; yet one cannot let the argument go at that. Conflicting expectations inevitably exist in any highly differentiated society, and are perhaps given in the very nature of the human condition, for human beings are inherently multifaceted. One can no more imagine a bearable existence that is utterly devoid of affect than one that consists only of emotional responses; pure and complete universalism is unattainable, people being what they are, and pure and complete particularism leads to chaos and gross inefficiency in any kind of social life. It is not, therefore, the simple absence of strains that distinguishes an integrated and stable society from one that is unintegrated and unstable, but rather the successful reduction and management of strains that can never be eliminated. How then can strains be "managed," in order to prevent them from leading to acute anomie?

Perhaps the only reliable way is through the institutionalized segregation of roles—through preventing one role as much as possible from impinging upon, or even being mentally associated with, another, if the other makes conflicting normative demands. Such segregation of roles is in fact a feature of any society that is functionally differentiated to a high degree; it may be physical (note, for example, the fact that the doctor's office and domicile are generally separate) or psychological—that is, achieved only through the widespread mental disjunction of particular roles. Why then should not incongruities in authority patterns be similarly manageable through segregation? Why should it matter, for example, that authority is strong in one context and weak in another?

A number of things need to be said about this issue. First, the theory here sketched does not assert that *any* disparity among authority patterns is disastrous; it only asserts that disparities of a particular kind and degree have fatal consequences; I have already argued that the very notion of congruence encompasses certain kinds of disparities. Some disparate authority patterns can be tolerated well enough—anyway, without serious anomic consequences; the argument here is that *incongruent* patterns cannot be tolerated, partly because they are, by definition, patterns in which disparities are particularly stark and great, and partly because strains arising from incongruent authority patterns are not alleviated by "intermediate" patterns that help to reconcile the starkly disparate patterns in relatively distant segments of society. In any case, no one would argue that all strains can be managed equally well; and, obviously, the greater the strain, the more unlikely it is to be successfully managed.

Another point to bear in mind is that managing a strain is not the same thing as abolishing it; when we manage strains, we merely reduce them to a tolerable level, or, without reducing them, in some way accommodate ourselves to their existence. The strains, however, persist, and may at any time lead to behavior modifying the social relations that give rise to them. What is more, certain kinds of strains are hard to reduce or tolerate, and strains among authority patterns, in my view, are of this type. The reason is precisely that authority relations are nearly universal in social relations, aspects of almost every social role, a fact that makes it inherently difficult to segregate authority patterns from one another. Whether a person is acting the role of parent, teacher, boss, or politician, that individual is almost always in some context involving authority; the operation of authority is one of the more inescapable facets of life. Not so for an individual playing both the affective spouse and affectively neutral professional, or both the particularistic parent and universalistic boss. In these cases, not only the structures but the functions also are different. There is, in other words, a crucial difference between performing different functions in different ways and performing the same function in different ways; conflicts of the latter sort obviously impose incomparably the greater psychological burden. Imagine, on the one hand, doctors who are expected to take a coldly scientific attitude toward their patients and a warmly unscientific attitude toward their spouse; imagine, on the other, doctors who are expected to administer only to their wealthy patients but wash their hands of others, or who are supposed to help friends and kin but let strangers suffer, or to alleviate the pains of adults but not those of children. In the latter cases strain is bound to be the more severe, whatever grotesque value system might be used to legitimate such behavior—and functioning in incongruent authority relations is like the latter cases rather than the former.

This is not to say that an individual cannot rule in one context and be ruled in another. Although such a duality of positions does create strains which, apparently, are unmanageable by some people, most of us do just that most of the time. The question here is one of operating in conflicting authority patterns, not of occupying different positions in similar authority patterns. When one is subordinated in one pattern of authority, one may in fact learn very well how properly to be dominant in a similar pattern of authority, but being tossed back and forth among radically different authority patterns is another matter.

To some extent, however, it may be possible to segregate even very disparate patterns in the performance of the same or similar roles through highly rigid institutionalization. The likelihood of this is small, but not absolutely zero. Human ingenuity in ridding life of strains, or in creating the delusion that strains do not really exist, is very great. Political science itself furnishes a striking example of how far such delusions may go, in the long-held, and still carefully nurtured, belief that authority is characteristic only of the state, not of anything outside the state. This belief is quite modern in origin and has been dominant mainly in the liberal West. Why has it been dominant there? Has it become established only because of the development of political science departments in search of some subject matter entirely their own? Or because of the effects of the theory of sovereignty? Or because of the gradual development of functionally differentiated, specialized structures of government? Or is it really a delusion that keeps liberal democrats from having to face up to the inevitable lack of real democracy in nongovernmental phases of social life? On the face of it, the notion that authority is a property solely of the state is so absurdly untenable that the compulsions making for it among eminently sensible people must be very great indeed. And that lends credence to the view that the notion performs neither an academic, nor a legal, but a psychological function: that it helps preserve the myth of democracy by keeping people from having to face up to, and incorporate in their political theories, uncomfortable disparities between governmental and nongovernmental life. In this connection, note that it has been mainly those out of sympathy with classical democratic ideas who have maintained a different position: pluralists, like Laski and Cole; Marxists, most obviously; and power theorists, like Lasswell and Michels.

Undoubtedly, individuals are able—and must be able—to make bearable, by all sorts of devices, even the most crushing strains. Under one condition, however, we can be sure that the chances of successful role segregation are not merely small, but practically zero: if nongovernmental social relations are themselves highly politicized—that is to say, if they are greatly concerned with governmental politics. One of the characteristics of life under the Weimar Republic was that social formations, in addition to being extraordinarily authoritarian, were concerned, to an extraordinary extent and with extraordinary fervor, with matters of government; many voluntary societies—even some of the least of gymnastic or choral groups—seemed to have some sort of governmental ideology, or even some affiliation with political parties or movements. Where this is the case, it is obviously much more difficult, indeed impossible, to segregate discrepancies in expected behavior, for the simple reason that government itself cannot then appear as a segregated social context. And in a democracy some politicalization of nongovernmental life is always unavoidable, even necessary; how otherwise could there be any political competition? Democracy presupposes, at the very least, some organized party life, and party life tends to draw into politics all sorts of other social units; it diffuses governmental politics throughout society, now more, now less, but always to some extent, and thus makes the management of strains by role segregation particularly unlikely.

My purpose here is not to show that strains arising from incongruent authority patterns cannot be managed or tolerated under any circumstances. Rather it is to show that, among the manifold strains of life in a complex society, such strains are unusually, perhaps incomparably, difficult to manage, so that it seems logical for people to try and cope with them by reducing them at the source, that is, ordinarily, by changing the governmental patterns under which they live. Even if this is not granted, however, one fact is surely beyond doubt: societies possessing congruent authority patterns possess an enormous "economic" advantage over those that do not. In the more extreme cases, like Great Britain, individuals are in effect socialized into almost all authority patterns simultaneously (even if they belong to the nonelite strata), while in highly incongruent societies people must repeatedly be resocialized for participation in various parts of social life. For society, then, congruence in regard to authority patterns, at the very least, saves much effort; for individuals, it saves much psychological wear and tear resulting from uncertainty and ambivalence. In that basic and indisputable sense, the congruent society starts with a great advantage over the incongruent society; and we have many reasons to think that it enjoys greater advantages still.

If it is true that incongruities among authority patterns can be reduced only at the source (in democracies, and perhaps other systems of government as well), and if it is true that such incongruities are particularly hard to bear, then all sorts of things that are otherwise mysterious become more comprehensible. To cite only one example: perhaps these points explain why in totalitarian systems such massive efforts are made to accomplish seemingly trivial, even self-destructive, ends, particularly efforts to reshape all social relations, from the family up, in the totalitarian image—or else to destroy them. "What rational balance sheet," asks Inkeles, speaking of early Soviet attacks on family and church, "would have led a group of leaders who were concerned first and foremost with preserving their power to attempt that particular diversion of energy with its obvious consequences of social resentment and popular hostility"?[19] His own solution is that the Soviet leaders' actions can be explained only by their messianic visions of an utterly transformed society; the theory of congruence, however, provides a still more logical explanation, even if it was only felt in some intuitive way, not grasped in the sense in which it is stated here, by Soviet leaders.

But the subject here is democracy, not totalitarianism; and for the analysis of democratic government another important deduction can be made from the proposition that strains due to ambivalences in authority patterns can be relieved only by reducing the ambivalences themselves: there must always be *some* strains among authority patterns in a democracy. Such strains will be nonexistent only if a society's authority patterns are identical, a condition quite unrealizable in a democracy, as we have seen. Obviously, however, they can be kept at a relatively low level if the society provides sufficient opportunities for learning patterns of action appropriate to democracy (if, that is, a good many of the authority patterns in a democracy are significantly democratized); and this will be all the more the case if the

more congruent patterns are directly associated with government or involve mainly interactions among the political elite. And there is also a
second possibility: strains might be kept within tolerable limits in democratic governments which have certain characteristics rather than others—
there are, after all, many varieties of democracy.

This is a subject better dealt with under the second theory we require,
a theory that specifies the particular conditions which must exist if democracy, rather than government in general, is to be stable.

BALANCED DISPARITIES IN THE GOVERNMENTAL PATTERN

What are the special conditions that democracies must fulfill if they are
to be stable? Undoubtedly one could list here a massive catalog of social
characteristics that favor stable democracy, but if we confine ourselves to
conditions not merely favorable but indispensable, to necessary conditions,
we can deal with this question rather briefly. The most essential special
requirement of stable democracy can in fact be deduced from the theory
of the congruence of authority patterns—as indeed ought to be the case,
since special theories should always be derivable from general theories. If
governments tend to be stable when social authority patterns are congruent; if a great many social relations cannot be organized on a purely
democratic basis without seriously dysfunctional consequences; and if some
of these relations resistant to democratic structure exist in social segments
adjacent or close to government; then it follows that *governmental democracy
will tend to be stable only if it is to a significant extent impure—if, in short, the
governmental authority pattern contains a balance of disparate elements, of which
democracy is an important part (but only a part).*

To forestall a tempting, but unjustified, retort to this proposition, it
should perhaps be pointed out immediately that I am not now asserting,
after arguing that governmental stability requires congruent authority patterns, that stable democracy requires an incongruent authority pattern
after all. The notion of congruence applies to the relations between governmental and nongovernmental authority patterns, while the present
point relates only to governmental patterns. It asserts merely that intolerable strains between governmental and nongovernmental patterns are
likely to be avoided if the governmental pattern is not extremely, that is,
purely, democratic.

One could even argue that the very minimum definition of congruence
cannot be satisfied in a pure governmental democracy. Not only are the
primary and occupational relationships of social life inhospitable to democratic organization, but we have every reason to think that associations,
parties, and pressure groups also resist democratization after a point—not
to mention the still more obvious cases of the civil and military service.

Parties, for example, are competitive organizations—Michels called them fighting organizations[20]—which can hardly afford the luxuries of plebiscitary democracy; so are pressure groups. Associations in general are rarely very democratic, if only because of the relatively low rate of participation by members in their affairs, in the great majority of cases[21]—not to mention functional requirements that act as barriers against democratization. The iron law of oligarchy seems to hold pretty well, which is not to say that democracy must always be a chimera in any form. It follows that between a governmental pattern as purely democratic as that of Weimar Germany and any kind of social life, even in the least authoritarian of political cultures, there are bound to be glaring, perhaps insurmountable, disjunctions. Governmental democracy, of course, is never really pure in practice; but, as the case of Weimar shows, it can come close, certainly in the forms and myths of authority, if not quite so readily in actual practices.

It is certainly curious how often one finds mixtures of heterogeneous characteristics, sometimes even contradictory characteristics, in stable democracies. Take Great Britain once more as the obvious and most essential case in point. British government and British authority beliefs, as already pointed out, are a mixture of all the elements out of which governmental authority can be concocted: popular government, the government of an autonomous elite, and government under an impersonal law; and none of these elements is clearly dominant over the others. British government combines (in a surprisingly easy fit) authority, responsibility, and responsiveness—the dominion of rulers, rules, and the ruled; for this reason there is something in British government to which every aspect of British social life, whether permissive or compulsive, traditional or modern, can have an affinity. Nor is this mixture of basic authority patterns the only balance of disparities that British government contains. We find in it a similar mixture of ceremonial and "efficient" institutions, of sober business and gaudy show. We find in it also a mixture of integration and pluralistic competition. Authority is concentrated in the cabinet, but the cabinet, being a collective entity, is itself a pluralistic structure and, under modern conditions, functions less as a single, cohesive unit than through a large number of committees and subcommittees, formal and informal, permanent and ad hoc; normally this structure works slowly, by patient bargaining and consultation, like all polycentric structures, but the myth of the fusion of authority can accommodate on occasion swift and autonomous action, by a prime minister or an inner cabinet. So also the monolithic character of the disciplined mass parties is balanced by a highly pluralistic universe of active and influential pressure groups, acting, by and large, directly upon government, rather than through the instrumentalities of the parties.

Not least, British politicians strike a most remarkable balance between dogmatism and pragmatism in their behavior. They tend to be neither absolute ideologists (in the manner of most Weimar politicians) nor utterly unprincipled opportunists (in the manner of the "trasformists" of pre-Fascist Italy); parliamentary behavior in Britain is characterized neither by unstable maneuvering for power nor by intransigent insistence upon ideals. K. B. Smellie has said that British politicians, while not unprincipled opportunists, are nevertheless "hard to work up to the dogmatic level"—suggesting that they are, on the average, men of principle, but lukewarm, phlegmatic, and tentative in the principles they hold. This, however, is not what I want to suggest at all. What is involved here is not a matter of temperament. The crucial point is rather that dogma and principle are concentrated upon some aspects of government and kept almost entirely out of others. In essence, the British invest with very high affect the procedural aspects of their government and with very low affect its substantive aspects; they behave like ideologists in regard to rules and like pragmatists in regard to policies. Procedures, to them, are not merely procedures, but sacred ritual. Neither the Tories nor the Whigs appear to have the slightest difficulty in stealing one another's clothes; yet in Britain any procedural reform, even the slightest and most sensible, seems to run into the most intractable and irrational obstacles. Massive evidence for this point is provided by the heaps of fruitless proposals on parliamentary reform, piled up both by private individuals (from Jennings to Crick)[22] and by Select Committees. Herbert Morrison's *Government and Parliament* contains some particularly arresting examples, especially in regard to the complex, time-devouring, and needlessly repetitious financial procedures in the House of Commons. This explains not only why the British fit neither the extreme model of the Weimar ideologists nor that of the Italian "trasformists," but also why they do indeed sometimes behave as if they were ideologists in regard to policy. They do so when policy problems appear in procedural guise, as in the case of the House of Lords crisis of 1909–1911, and more recently (and not on the governmental level) in the Labour party disputes over nuclear weapons.

The theory of congruence gives us one reason, but only one of several, for the assertion that such balanced disparities are necessary if democracy is to be stable. Others are perhaps even more obvious. Democratic governments require a healthy element of authoritarianism not only for the sake of congruence between government and other aspects of society, but for the even simpler reason that a representative government must govern as well as represent—must satisfy two values that, on the evidence, are not easily reconcilable. This point can in fact be stated in a much less truistic form and tied in with the motivational basis of the theory of congruence sketched above. That strains in the definition of political roles can produce governmental instability seems manifest; but can governmental stability also be affected by nonpolitical strains? There is at least a possibility that acute anomie, in whatever segment of life it may appear, will have destructive consequences upon government, and not only because it may alienate people from their general condition of life. If intolerable strains exist in some social relations, but not in authority patterns, it is particularly likely that attempts will be made to manage the existing strains through governmental means; it seems natural that individuals should attempt to modify unacceptable relations through whatever relations they accept. But if government, under these conditions, is incapable of realizing important special changes through political direction, it will itself become identified with the unbearable aspects of social life. Hence, a particular need for some measure of authoritarianism in the governmental pattern, or, to put the same point slightly differently, a high capacity to control social relations toward desired ends. This capacity is always necessary—it is inherent in the governmental function; but it is particularly necessary if society needs a solvent for nonpolitical tensions.

We could rest this point, and others, on an even simpler psychological basis: human beings just are not one-sided. They have superegos and libidos as well as egos. For that reason, as Bagehot so clearly saw, a government that provides no food for the sentiments, a purely businesslike, perfectly rationalized government, is unlikely to get very much support and likely to engender a rash of hysterical social movements to satisfy the instincts it neglects. And as Bagehot also clearly saw, a government that provides no clear and focused leadership, no easily recognized source of directives for conduct, is equally unlikely to succeed. The superego requires such a definite source of directives, even if only an imaginary one, just as the libido requires that it be invested with high affect; and a political system also requires it for operational purposes, above all in times of crisis. These two points may explain why constitutional monarchies seem to work better than parliamentary republics, and why presidential government seems preferable wherever monarchy no longer exists—two very old theories of political science.

We might speak in this connection of a second kind of "strain" that can afflict human behavior—strain that results from overconcentration on any pattern of behavior satisfying to only one aspect of the human psyche. Certainly we can regard the compulsive ritualism of political movements in the Weimar Republic as attempts to satisfy needs frustrated by the insipid matter-of-factness of the Weimar government; and we can regard the American penchant for giving officers of private associations stately titles (high potentate, grand marshal, sultan, and the like) in the same light. Indeed, one could argue that strain, in one sense or the other, is a condition inherent in human life, for anything that decreases strain in the first sense tends to increase it in the second. And if this is true, then it is clear that a stable government is never one lacking in strains, but one that strikes a tolerable balance between disparate strains, between strains resulting from the existence of inconsistent norms and strains resulting from overconsistent norms. This lends support to the still older theory of political science that mixed government is the most stable form of government—and puts it also in a new light.

As for the need to balance pragmatism and ideologism in politics, an explanation not quite so manifestly relevant to the present theory is required. A high degree of pragmatic behavior in politics is obviously desirable because it makes possible political integration, either on the party or the parliamentary level. Because of the great multiplicity of interests existing in any modern society, both a two-party system and stable coalition government presuppose a great deal of compromise, and compromise in turn presupposes a relatively low degree of affect and dogma in political competition. Pragmatic attitudes in politics also help to keep political problems in proper focus and on a proper level of significance, and thus facilitate rational and relevant decision making. Political ideologies tend to elevate even the most minor matters to major importance, so that energies tend to be dissipated upon insignificant questions while great problems go begging for solution; they invest everything with "world significance," to translate literally an untranslatable German word. But if too much principle can kill a government, so can the lack of any principle at all. Spiro has pointed out,[23] quite rightly, that too unprincipled an approach to politics will lead to a lack of consistent and long-range policies, to an eclectic flitting to and fro from policy to policy, which may prove destructive to a government by setting it internally at cross-purposes; what is wanted is "programmatic" government, and this must of necessity blend principle with pragmatic adjustment. One can add to this another, perhaps still more serious point. Pragmatic politics, absolutely unburdened by affect and principle, can lead to only one kind of political behavior: sheer opportunism—mere maneuvering lacking any higher purpose. That is what Italian politics was like before Giolitti's grant of universal suffrage, and, judging from the works of Mosca and Pareto, opportunism did more than anything else to discredit democratic institutions in Italian minds. Nor should one overlook that the most unprincipled and adaptable politician is likely also to be the most cynical (and effective) manipulator of symbols for unscrupulous ends; Richard Rovere's fascinating analysis of McCarthy provides a perfect case in point. And just as ceremony feeds the emotions, so principle feeds the superego—narrows the range of decisions requiring "rational" adjustment, and thus makes pragmatic reasoning a more tolerable burden. In this last sense, a proper balance between commitment and moderation is part and parcel of those manifold counterweights that preserve a tolerable balance of strains in social life.

RELIGION, ECONOMIC DEVELOPMENT, AND MASS SOCIETY: AN APPRAISAL OF OTHER THEORIES

No attempt will be made here to test the theory I have sketched directly by broad-scale, comparative analysis; but, as pointed out at the beginning, one can to some extent test a theory indirectly by viewing it in light of other, well-substantiated theories. If the latter can be subsumed to the theory proposed, that is certainly a powerful argument for it. If one can show on the basis of a proposed theory *why* certain other correlations between variables hold, that is a still more powerful argument for it. And if one can show that the theory not only explains such correlations but also explains why they are not better correlations, then one has as cogent a case as can be made for it, short of direct testing.

The propositions I should like to consider in light of the present theory are the following: (1) that countries with large, or predominant, Catholic populations do not produce stable democracy; (2) that a high degree of economic development correlates positively with stable democracy; and (3) that stable democracy correlates positively with vigorous associational life in a society and negatively with "mass societies," societies in which people are highly individuated or in which very strong primary group attachments exist. The first proposition has been stated in a great many sources, but perhaps most strongly and unequivocally by certain French writers, for example, André Gide and Raymond Aron. The second has been argued most strongly by Lipset.[24] The third comes from Kornhauser's *The Politics of Mass Society.*[25]

These three propositions hold up very well; certainly they are the best propositions about the basic conditions of stable democracy available at present. Other propositions—for example, those relating stable democracy to integrated party systems or to a high degree of political consensus— may hold up even better, but deal with the subject on a much more superficial (or at any rate, a different) level. But however cogent, each of the three propositions leaves something to be desired when properly tested. For this, there may be several possible explanations. One possibility is that the phenomenon which the theories are meant to explain may be "multicausal" and that certain additional factors must be invoked in each case to make the theories entirely satisfactory. Another is that imperfections in the correlations arise because of the operation, in some cases, of accidental circumstances, the sort of circumstances which, I have argued, led to the longevity of the French Third Republic. Here is also a third possibility, namely, that the conditions singled out in the propositions are not directly responsible for the stability or instability of democracies, but are linked to these only through some other condition—a condition that they either help to bring about or of which they are frequently a manifestation. My argument is that the last is indeed the case: that religion, economic development, and a society's structure of participation affect the stability of democracy only insofar as they affect or reflect relations among its patterns of authority. This is the preferable explanation of the imperfections of the three theories for several reasons: first, because in each case it can in fact be shown that the theories hold to the extent that they are special cases of congruence theory and fail to hold to the extent that they are not; second, because we can never tell when our subject matter intrinsically requires complex explanations (as distinguished from complex explanations that are required merely because we cling to highly imperfect hypotheses); and third, because it is very unlikely that fortuitous circumstances could account for the whole combination of conditions here identified as stable democracy, even if they can account for the mere survival of a political order.

Democracy and Catholicism

The proposition that countries with large, or predominant, Catholic populations tend not to be stable democracies certainly contains some truth, but the correlation between stable democracy and Catholicism is highly imperfect. For one thing, it is by no means established that predominantly non-Catholic countries tend to be markedly more stable democracies; it may be that stable democracy is simply very rare, no matter what a society's religious composition, in which case the failure of most predominantly Catholic countries to produce it indicates a condition pertaining to humanity, not just to such countries. Even granted that the most conspicuously stable democracies have existed in largely Protestant countries, some uncomfortable facts remain. Among the more stable democracies are several with very sizable Catholic populations, for example, Australia, Canada, Switzerland, and the United States. At least one almost exclusively Catholic country, Ireland, is a highly stable democracy. Present-day West Germany, with a government verging upon hyperstability, is much more highly Catholic than was the unified Germany of the Weimar Republic. And there are even some reasonably stable Latin American democracies, like Costa Rica and (until very recently, and perhaps still today) Uruguay.

Furthermore, most of the familiar arguments used to link Catholicism with unstable democracy (arguments used to *explain* the supposed correlation) simply do not stand up to close examination. Catholicism, being a highly dogmatic religion, is supposed to make for ideological intransigence in politics, yet nothing more pragmatic or accommodating can be imagined than political behavior in Italy before World War I or the attitudes of the French Center of the Fourth Republic described by Leites. Catholicism, being authoritarian in structure, is supposed to engender a preference for highly authoritarian government, yet in France it appeared rather to engender a preference for near anarchy. Catholicism, by intruding clerical issues into political life, is supposed to prevent the consensus required in a highly integrated political system, yet nothing more consensual could be imagined than Italian politics in the postunification era.

It is reasonable to suspect, therefore, that if the imperfect correlation between Catholicism and unstable democracy does indeed represent some sort of causal relation—if it is not just a spurious correlation—then Catholicism must frequently be associated with some other factor, which can also exist in non-Catholic countries, which need not invariably exist in Catholic countries, and which leads more invariably to unstable democracy than Catholicism itself. The moment the question is viewed in this way, it becomes apparent that the theories proposed here can make very good sense both of the correlation and of its imperfections.

Catholicism, by subjecting its adherents to a highly authoritarian relationship, and one which involves extremely powerful psychological sanctions, certainly does nothing itself to reinforce democracy. Potentially it always threatens to introduce an incongruity into a democratic society, so that in any democracy there exists a fair probability that Catholicism will have dysfunctional consequences. But no more than a fair probability. If a democracy is sufficiently hedged about with authoritarian elements, the incongruity between government and church need not be very great. Moreover, if the church does not play a very important role in the associational life of a society, or if between church and government there exists a multiplicity of less authoritarian associations, even associations with a religious tinge, the incongruities will be diminished, in the sense of being mediated and reconciled. Whether or not Catholicism will inhibit or undermine stable democracy depends, therefore, not only on the inherent characteristics of Catholicism, but also on the nature of the governmental pattern and the vigor (and particular characteristics) of associational life in a society. This is why there neither is nor could be a very close correspondence between stability of democracy and size of Catholic population, and yet why there is some such correspondence.

Catholics certainly have no difficulty in acting as constructive democratic citizens in countries offering the chance to participate in a large variety of nonecclesiastical associations, particularly in countries like the United States and Switzerland, perhaps even Britain, where they account for a large but not predominant part of the population. It has been argued, of course, that in these countries Catholics are a minority (although a very large minority) and that this makes all the difference in the effect they can have on politics. Perhaps so, though obviously a group comprising from 20 to 40 percent of the population can affect the political life of a nation a great deal; but this hardly explains why Catholics themselves should be relatively unaffected by Catholicism in these countries—why, for example, they should not themselves be markedly more authoritarian or ideological in political behavior, but fit instead so easily into the overall political culture of their society. Nor are Catholics a crashingly discordant element in what we might call "authoritarian democracies," like the *Kanzlerdemokratie* of the Bonn Federal Republic and the cabinet system of Britain. The real trouble lies in societies that combine a large Catholic population with a very pure democracy and in which nonsectarian associational life is poorly articulated. France of the Third and Fourth republics, for example, had not only a predominantly Catholic population but also one of the world's most unmitigated democracies and, relatively speaking, an unintensive associational life; such as it was, moreover, a good deal of its associational life was directly centered upon the Church. From this standpoint, the Fifth Republic ought to be a good deal more stable than the Third and Fourth, just as the German Federal Republic has been more stable than Weimar Germany. Certainly Gaullist France should be more stable than postwar Italy, a system that, under the understandable impression that pre-Fascist Italy was destroyed by Mussolini and not by its own weaknesses, had hedged against the possibility of excessive executive authority much more than it had provided against an insufficient amount of it. It is, of course, too early [in 1965] to assess the stability of the Fifth Republic, but just because of that—and because of the inauspicious circumstances of its beginning in near revolution and charismatic rule (always the most transient form of rule)—it provides a good test case for the future assessment of the theory.

A Catholic country, in short, requires a democracy more modified by authoritarianism, and perhaps also by unquestioned "principle," than countries in which certain other religions predominate. Yet Catholic countries are also less likely to possess such modified democracies than others. Where the Church has been powerful enough to resist reform, it has generally also been powerful enough to delay liberal government and to assure that revolution would be required to establish it. Nowhere has the Church been able entirely to withstand the liberal wave. But in many places, by delaying change, it has contributed to the abrupt imposition of highly advanced democracy upon highly traditional societies and, by requiring revolutionary change, prevented that blending of modern and premodern forms that is the secret of stable democracy in Britain; also, by requiring revolution, it has prevented the persistence of unquestioned principle in the course of major change and instead made everything subject to "rational" debate. Catholicism thus has tended to prevent precisely those conditions that might make it compatible with stable democracy. This, even more than the inherent disparity between Catholic and democratic patterns, explains why Catholic countries so often (and yet with such signal exceptions) are unstable democracies.

Democracy and Economic Development

If there is a close connection between democracy and economic development—if stable democracy and a high degree of economic development
are positively correlated—then still another link may exist between the
stability of democracy and the religious composition of society, for the
connection between religious attitudes and economic development seems
now to be well established. But is there really a close connection between
democracy and economic development?

The evidence suggests strongly that there is. Lipset, for example, found
a positive correlation of sorts between stable democracy (in *his* sense of
the term) and almost every conceivable index of economic development.
Average per capita income in European and English-speaking stable democracies he found to be (in 1949 and 1950) $695, in unstable democ-
racies only $308. Stable democracies had one doctor for every 860 persons,
unstable democracies one for every 1,400 persons. There were 17 persons
per motor vehicle in one case, 143 in the other; on one side, there were
205 telephones, 350 radios, and 341 newspapers per 1,000 persons, on
the other only 58 telephones, 160 radios, and 167 newspapers. Stable
European democracies had a male agricultural population of 21 percent,
European dictatorships one of 41 percent. No less than 43 percent of the
population in stable European democracies lived in urban areas (cities
over 20,000), but only 24 percent did so in European dictatorships. And
so on. These findings are supported by Coleman (in the Conclusion of *The
Politics of the Developing Areas*), countries with "competitive" political systems in the developing areas coming out much better, on the indices used
also by Lipset, than "semi-competitive" and "authoritarian" countries.[26]
And Deutsch's[27] work also lends credence to the thesis, since the great
majority of the countries located at the highest extreme of economic development in his "country profiles" are also stable democracies—for example, Switzerland, Australia, New Zealand, Sweden, Norway, Denmark,
the United Kingdom, and the United States.

This is a lot of evidence—but far from conclusive. If we look, not at
overall averages, but at specific cases and at ranges of economic differences
among countries in the same governmental categories, it becomes apparent
that we have here a rather weak correlation, not a strong one. A few
countries that have been anything but paragons of democratic stability
rank quite high in economic development. France, Venezuela, and the
USSR (not to mention Kuwait) rank high now, and Weimar Germany did
in its own day. It is true that the half-dozen countries that are most highly
developed are also stable democracies, but difficulties seem to arise only
a very little below their level. And the ranges between the most and the
least developed stable democracies, as well as the most and the least de-

veloped unstable democracies (and nondemocracies), are enormous. The least developed stable European democracy had, according to Lipset, an average per capita income of $420, the most developed European dictatorship one of $482. Stable democracies have as many as sixty-two persons per motor vehicle, dictatorships as few as ten; one has as many as 46 percent of males employed in agriculture, the other as few as 16 percent; in one case as few as 28 percent of the population live in cities, in the other as many as 44 percent. Such overlaps, varying in size, but all large, are found for every index.

It follows that between the great extremes of economic development and economic underdevelopment is a large no-man's-land where apparently any governmental order, from stable democracy to totalitarianism, can exist—and at the great extremes there are not many cases. That stable democracy is not found at the very lowest levels is, of course, not surprising. At that level of underdevelopment the more obvious requisites for any democracy at all, stable or unstable—a certain minimum level of literacy, information, and communications—are not satisfied. But beyond that extreme, in the higher and intermediate ranges of economic development, everything is puzzling and indeterminate, if one assumes a simple correlation between democracy and economic level.

Lipset himself seems well aware of this, for his theory does not stop with economic development, but also uses a large number of other factors to explain the stability or instability of democracies: rapidity (rather than level) of economic development; "legitimacy" (that is, acceptance of a regime as right for a society), with special emphasis on the support of conservative groups; religion; historical development; and governmental structure. By adding all these conditions to qualify the correlation with economic development, the theory can be made to come out right in every case, but so could any theory whatever; the whole procedure smacks of the familiar methodological fallacy of "saving the hypothesis." Moreover, the theory that finally emerges from all these modifications is extremely complicated, to say the least. It does not blatantly violate the rule of parsimony, for it is not established that a simpler theory with equal explanatory power is available; but it is very cumbersome to use and the significance of any of its variables almost impossible to establish, owing to the number of variables alleged to be independently capable of producing unstable democracy.

For these reasons alone one ought to look for another way to deal with the imperfections of the correlation, and such a way is provided by the present theory. Like religion, we can regard economic development as an aspect of society that correlates with stable (or unstable) democracy only insofar as it has an impact upon the congruence of authority patterns in society and the balancing of disparate patterns in government—as it does frequently (hence the positive correlation) but certainly not always (hence its imperfections).

That this is probably the right way to proceed is suggested by the most important modification Lipset himself makes in his theory. Not only the *level* of economic development seems to him to be associated with the performance of democracies, but also the *rate* of economic development; very rapid economic development, he argues, has consequences inimical to democracy, but more gradual economic development supports it. On the evidence, this is a very strong argument—and exactly what one would expect on the basis of congruence theory. Rapid industrialization from a traditional base, whatever its long-run effects, obviously introduces into society profound incongruities, particularly if it is imposed by direction, in one form or another. If economic development is relatively slow, strains between the economic and other sectors of life can be kept at tolerable levels by the gradual adaptation of other social institutions to the slowly evolving industrial economy. Nor is this the only reason why rapid economic development has political consequences different from gradual economic development. In the course of rapid economic development, the social order (appearing, as it must, as a barrier to development) is usually attacked in all its aspects, and in that process even aspects of social life which are, if not perfectly, then at least sufficiently, compatible with a modernized economy may be uprooted. Even if social life is not coercively uprooted by those who want to industrialize rapidly, it may nevertheless be uprooted by revolutionary violence resulting from the great strains attendant upon rapid industrialization. In either event, the outcome is the same: society and government will not consist of that mixture of modern and premodern patterns, that blending of disparities, which is characteristic of the more stable democracies. Furthermore, rapid industrialization usually occurs, for obvious reasons, at a relatively late stage in the history of industrialism; because of this, the desire for rapid economic modernization is likely for manifest historical reasons to be accompanied by expectations of relatively advanced democracy. Rapid industrialization in nontotalitarian countries will therefore tend to be accompanied by the creation of especially pure democracies, and these are always more tenuous than impure democracies; and if democracy is achieved by revolution, the result is, of course, the same. Worst of all, the sudden creation of an advanced democracy will abruptly liberate men politically, while the exigencies of rapid industrialization will subject them, in the short run, to unprecedented disciplines and compulsions. In this way, rapid industrialization not only unsettles the social order in general, but tends to create particularly great strains between government and other aspects of social life.

The theories of congruence and balanced disparities can thus account comprehensively for the deleterious impact upon democracy of rapid industrialization. But what of the positive correlation between economic development and stable democracy in general? If rapid industrialization is indeed inimical to democracy, and if it leads, as it must, to the attainment of relatively high levels of development in relatively little time, then surely this correlation is rather puzzling—until one remembers that the most advanced industrial societies (at present, or at any rate when Lipset collected his data) are precisely those which developed industry most gradually but still lead the field because of their early start. In these countries— Great Britain, the United States, Switzerland, Sweden, and Canada—industrialization was associated with the relatively slow growth of populistic democracy and the gradual adaptation, never complete displacement, of preindustrial patterns, or else the forming of society itself simultaneously with the growth of industry and democracy. When this is realized, it becomes apparent that level of economic development, the moment one goes beyond extreme underdevelopment, matters only because speed of economic development matters; and from this it also follows that the present theory can account for Lipset's general proposition, no less than for the supposed modification of it which he introduces. This is because the modification is, in fact, the really crucial theory.

Economic development thus correlates very imperfectly with stable democracy because certain forms of development produce precisely those incongruities and imbalances that endanger democracy. That is why some very highly developed countries are unstable democracies or not democracies at all. But economic development need not produce these deleterious consequences and has not produced them in the (currently) most highly developed countries—that is why there is, nevertheless, a positive correlation between level of economic development and stable democracy. Indirectly, in the ways Lipset mentions, industrialization may even create conditions favorable to democracy, provided it is achieved in the right way. It is even more likely, however, that the two are associated simply because their roots lie in the same historical conditions—that is to say, because the processes of industrialization and democratization coincided and did not, while both were being achieved gradually, frustrate one another.

If this is so, then it would clearly be unwise to base on the correlation any optimistic predictions about the future impact of industrialization upon the stability of democracies. The only predictions that seem to follow from this analysis are that late industrialization is, in the typical case, likely to have political consequences directly opposite to those of early industrialization and that rapid industrialization is particularly dangerous to democracy if, paradoxical though it may seem, it is accompanied by rapid democratization.

Democracy and Mass Society

The third theory I wish to consider has now become associated mainly with William Kornhauser—although Kornhauser himself acknowledges the great role played in its formulation by such diverse people as Jacob Burck-hardt, Gustave Le Bon, Ortega y Gasset, Karl Mannheim, and, above all perhaps, Emile Durkheim, Emil Lederer, and Hannah Arendt. This theory attributes unstable democracy primarily to "mass society," a technical term denoting societies without a vigorous corporate life, societies in which elites have "direct access" to nonelites, and nonelites to elites, owing to the weakness or absence of organizations mediating between government and primary social relations. Such societies leave people "naked" before the state, and the state naked before people, unlike "pluralistic" societies, in which sovereign and subject are separated by many autonomous social formations, through which each must act upon the other.

With this theory we can deal rather more briefly than with the others, not because it is transparently bad, but, on the contrary, because it is so very well established. The theory of mass society is by all odds the best substantiated of the theories we have considered and just because of that requires the least reinterpretation. Kornhauser supports it with truly mas-sive evidence—evidence which shows not only that the more unstable de-mocracies fit the model of mass society but also that the most apathetic and extremist antidemocrats, even in stable democracies, are found among the most "socially isolated" members of all classes and walks of life, among the "nonparticipants" who exist, in greater or smaller numbers, in any society. Kornhauser, in other words, not only links variables on the social level, but also, by looking at individual behavior in a great variety of con-texts, shows that these relations have a clear and definite motivational basis. All that is necessary here, therefore, is to show that the theory of mass society is intimately related to the theory I have sketched—indeed, it is almost the same—and that the very slight imperfections which exist in it are attributable to the very slight ways in which it departs from the present theory.

That the two theories are closely related should be manifest without long explication. If it is true that democratic government is inherently and profoundly in tension with the primary and occupational relations of social life, then it follows from the present theory that vigorous interactions upon the "intermediate" (or secondary) levels are required to produce congruity of authority patterns in democracies. Only a wide variety of intermediate associations can keep the inherent contradictions between democracy and life at the primary social levels from directly leading to insupportable strains; only intermediate associations can provide opportunities for learn-ing democratic behavior patterns.[28] This is even more important than the fact, of which Kornhauser makes a great deal, that such associations act as buffers against overbearing rulers, for while this fact may explain why vigorous associational life can be a barrier to totalitarianism, it does not explain why it should be particularly compatible with stable democracy; after all, impeding totalitarianism is not at all the same thing as facilitating stable democracy—there are unstable democracies and nontotalitarian autocracies as well. Kornhauser's emphasis upon the protective effect of secondary associations seems therefore to miss the really crucial relation between associational life and stable democracy—except in one sense. Kornhauser argues that associations not only act as buffers shielding the ruled from their rulers, but that they also work in the opposite direction: they provide the rulers with a certain autonomy from the ruled, while still subjecting them to exigent social pressures. If this is so, and it seems cogent, then it is apparent that a vigorous associational life not only permits authority patterns to be congruent, but leads also to one of the balanced disparities that democracy seems to require—a balance between governmental autonomy and dependence, "democracy" and "authoritarianism."

The two theories thus closely fit one another. Do they in any way differ? The answer is that in one way they clearly do: if a society has a vigorous associational life, but if the associations themselves are highly undemocratic, then, upon my theory, democracy should not be stable, and upon Kornhauser's, it should (at any rate, one condition making for unstable democracy—large-scale, illegitimate, antilibertarian movements—should not exist). It is, of course, perfectly possible for intermediate associations to be as undemocratic as primary groups, or even more so. It is improbable, but not impossible—and it has happened. Weimar Germany is itself a case in point, though admittedly there are not many others, for intermediate associations resist absolute authoritarianism nearly as much as they resist utter democracy. But the Weimar example suggests that, insofar as the two theories differ, congruence is the more powerful—for it is just in improbable cases like Weimar Germany that the theory of mass society fails to hold.

In this connection it is worth noting that, in a book teeming with apposite evidence, data relating to Germany are conspicuously sparse and inapropos. Some of the evidence intended to show unintensive associational life in Germany actually relates to the Bonn period;[29] some of it shows that German associations tend to be engaged in politics to an unusual extent, not that there is a scarcity of associations or of participation in them;[30] and the rest either shows what is true of all societies, that participants are disposed more favorably to democracy than nonparticipants, or that certain other conditions unfavorable to democracy existed in Weimar days. In actual fact, life upon the secondary levels was very vigorous in the Weimar period—and very incongruent with democracy. One might perhaps argue that large-scale participation in illiberal organizations was itself a response to social atomization, but this would be transparent sophistry, for it implies that illiberal associations simply do not count when one evaluates the extent to which a society is atomized, a position for which there can be no possible justification. If only mass movements like the Nazi and Communist parties had existed at the intermediate levels in Weimar Germany, such an argument would be sensible enough, but in fact one finds at those levels a great many organizations—most of them of a piece, from the standpoint of authority relations.

CONCLUSION

However easily other theories can be subsumed to, and even improved by, the theory I have proposed here, it should be admitted that at this stage the theory is still little more than plausible. It is deficient, most obviously, in that no rigorous validation of it has been undertaken; the data used here illustrate the propositions, but do not validate them. Moreover, before the theory can be adequately tested, much more theoretical work is required. Testing the theory will not be just a matter of looking at the relevant data. For one thing, to test the theory we need a much better set of categories for classifying authority patterns than we now possess. Terms like democratic, authoritarian, and constitutionalist may do in the initial formulation of the idea, but for any large-scale comparative analysis a more discriminating and less ambiguous set of categories seems required. Such categories ought to be applicable to any kind of authority pattern, not just to government, a point that rules out many of the typologies now in use in political science. It is also necessary to find ways to measure with some exactness the extent to which different kinds of authority are present in actual cases, so that degrees of correspondence and disparity between authority patterns can be precisely established and, even more important, so that the very idea of congruence can be given a more precise formulation. In addition to measurable categories of authority, we need such categories for different types and degrees of instability; we need to relate types and degrees of instability to types and degrees of incongruence and imbalance; and, not least, we should be able to establish direct connections between incongruence and imbalance of authority patterns and the obvious conditions and system failures associated with unstable democracy.

Apart from these tasks, a staggering amount of empirical work still seems required before validity can be claimed for the theory. Because of the traditional emphasis on the state in political science, and on nonpolitical matters in other social sciences, studies of authority in general social life are pitifully meager and, for the most part, inadequate. Political scientists have charted little more than the visible part of their world; the massive infrastructure of political life is still largely *terra incognita.* This applies even to the data given here about authority in British and German life. By and large, these data are derived from my own and other people's personal impressions and from allusions to the subject in works not directly concerned with the rigorous and intensive investigation of authority relations.

In short, almost everything needed to establish the theory still needs doing, and an enormous amount of work is required if these things are to be done. Hence the claims made for the theory here are modest. Nevertheless I do make some claims for it. I claim that it is at least plausible; I claim that it fits what is known about the more obvious cases of stable and unstable democracy; I claim that it can make still more convincing propositions about stable democracy which are already convincing to a degree; and I claim that it not only relates variables but gives immediate insight into the motivational forces which link them. Not least, I claim that the theory can account for a crucial fact not yet touched upon—perhaps the most important fact with which the study of democracy confronts us. This is that stable democracy is immensely difficult to achieve and has in fact been achieved only in very few cases—that it is unstable democracy, not stable democracy, which is, by any reasonable measurement, the "normal" case.

Every aspect of the essay suggests how very tenuous and improbable are the foundations of stable democratic government. Stable democracy requires congruence of authority patterns between government and segments of social life that resist democratization; it requires balances of contradictory behavior patterns, in such a way that the balances do not lead to undue strain and intolerable anomie; it requires a certain similarity among authority patterns, but not to the extent that basic human needs are thwarted. Surely, if these conditions are indeed required, then the existence of a stable democracy requires much explaining, while unstable democracies practically explain themselves. Perhaps this is why writers like Lipset find so many factors that can of themselves prevent stable democracy and none that can of themselves assure it. What, after all, is a complex multicausal explanation if not an assertion that a great many factors must coincide if a phenomenon is to exist—and that its existence is, for that reason alone, improbable?

Given the evidence of our times, this seems a most appropriate conclusion. The age when we had some reason confidently to expect the universal reign of democracy (and, more than that, the end of fundamental political change, because of a supposedly inherent affinity of human nature to democracy) ended with Bryce—and the trials of Weimar. For our own world we need a more pessimistic approach to democratic government, one not based upon the bland assumption that people are natural democrats, but one that directs attention to those calamitously improbable combinations of circumstances which actually make democracy work.

For the present purpose this is certainly the most important deduction that can be drawn from the theory. But still larger implications, which might be briefly indicated, follow from it. One could argue, for example, that the conditions which make stable democracy improbable also make stable totalitarianism improbable: not only is totalitarianism a very "pure" governmental system but also one fundamentally incongruent with certain functionally indispensable social relations. By the same token, semiauthoritarian government—government in which strong, preferably ascriptive, authority is mitigated by adherence to impersonal rules, paternalistic benevolence, institutionalized channels of representation, and a vigorous corporate life—is bound to be the most stable of all possible governments, owing precisely to its impurity and easy congruence with primary group patterns. This corresponds to Weber's view that "traditional" authority is the most stable of his three ideal types.

But still more convincing would be the deduction that, while degrees of stability, or rates of change, may vary, no form of government can be inherently stable—if only because no form of government can escape the dilemma of managing some strains by increasing the probability of others. The present theory leads logically to an inherently dynamic conception of government, in which strains (and, through strains, change) are the rule rather than the exception; stable governments, upon this view, are the product of "accidental" (extremely improbable) conjunctions of conditions that do sometimes, but rarely, occur in actual societies. Such a dynamic view of governmental change—a view positing change as normal and constant, but, unlike Marxism and other historicist theories, specifying no concrete content or goal for the process of change—seems, on the face of it, more in tune with the manifest testimony of history than theories that take stability for granted and attribute change to external, rather than immanent, conditions. But this takes us far beyond the subject of stable democracy and obviously requires a more thorough treatment than can be given here.

NOTES FOR CHAPTER 5

1. G. E. G. Catlin, *Principles of Politics* (London: Allen and Unwin, 1930).

2. R. A. Dahl, "Business and Politics: An Appraisal of Political Science," *American Political Science Review* 53 (1959): 1–34.

3. C. Merriam, *Public and Private Governments* (New Haven: Yale University Press: 1944); B. de Jouvenel, *Sovereignty* (Chicago: University of Chicago Press, 1957); Dahl, "Business and Politics."

4. S. M. Lipset, *Political Man* (New York: Doubleday, 1960), 77; H. J. Spiro, *Government by Constitution* (New York: Random House, 1959).

5. C. J. Friedrich, *Constitutional Government and Democracy*, 2d ed. (Boston: Ginn, 1941).

6. D. E. Apter, "A Comparative Method for the Study of Politics," *American Journal of Sociology* 64 (1958): 225–227; M. J. Levy, Jr., *The Structure of Society* (Princeton: Princeton University Press, 1952), 149–197; T. Parsons, *The Social System* (Glencoe, Ill.: Free Press, 1951), 167–177.

7. M. Deutsch, "A Theory of Cooperation and Competition," *Human Relations* 2 (1949): 129–152.

8. S. H. Beer, "Great Britain: From Governing Elite to Organized Mass Parties," in *Modern Political Parties*, ed. S. Neumann (Chicago: University of Chicago Press, 1956); R. T. McKenzie, *British Political Parties* (London: Heinemann, 1955).

9. We can treat this breakdown of authority patterns into democratic, authoritarian, and constitutionalist patterns, at least as a first approximation toward a useful typology of authority patterns. *Democracy* in this case refers to the rule of numbers, hence its equation with the idea of the mandate; it denotes a high degree of participation in decision making, regularized choice between competing political elites, and the transmission, usually not very precisely, of instructions from the political "mass" to the political "elite." *Authoritarianism* refers to limited participation in decisions by the mass and to a high degree of autonomy and a low degree of formal precariousness of position on the part of the elite. *Constitutionalism* refers to the subjection of the elite to a broad and highly explicit impersonal framework of rules, procedural and substantive, where this framework of rules operates as the principal limitation on the autonomy of the elite. We might say that democracy involves the rule of a dependent elite, authoritarianism the rule of an autonomous elite, and constitutionalism the rule of law; but this is such a great oversimplification that it can only serve as shorthand to help one keep the vital distinctions in mind.

10. Harry Eckstein, *Pressure Group Politics* (London: Allen and Unwin, 1960).

11. A. Potter, "Attitude Groups," *Political Quarterly* 29 (1958): 72–82.

12. Eckstein, *Pressure Group Politics*.

13. S. E. Finer, "The Federation of British Industries," *Political Studies* 4 (1956): 61–82.

14. M. Young and P. Wilmott, *Family and Kinship in East London* (London: Routledge and Kegan Paul, 1957).

15. K. D. Bracher, *Die Auflösung der Weimarer Republik* (Stuttgart and Düsseldorf: Ring-Verlag, 1956), 128–149, 165–169, 199–208.

16. Ibid., 174–198.

17. K. W. Deutsch and L. J. Edinger, *Germany Rejoins the Powers* (Stanford: Stanford University Press, 1959), 12–14.

18. T. Parsons, *Social System*, 253.

19. A. Inkeles, "The Totalitarian Mystique," in *Totalitarianism*, ed. C. J. Friedrich (Cambridge, Mass.: Nomos Series, 1954).

20. R. Michels, *Political Parties* (Glencoe, Ill.: Free Press, 1956), 46–49.

21. S. M. Lipset, M. A. Trow, and J. S. Coleman, *Union Democracy* (Glencoe, Ill.: Free Press, 1956), 46–99.

22. Sir I. Jennings, *Parliamentary Reform* (London: Cambridge University Press, 1934); B. Crick, *Reform of the Commons* (London: Weidenfeld and Nicholson, 1959).

23. Spiro, *Government by Constitution*, 189.

24. Lipset, *Political Man*, chap. 2.

25. W. Kornhauser, *The Politics of Mass Society* (Glencoe, Ill.: Free Press, 1959).

26. G. A. Almond and J. S. Coleman, *The Politics of the Developing Areas* (Princeton: Princeton University Press, 1960), 579–581.

27. K. W. Deutsch, "Toward an Inventory of Basic Trends and Patterns in Comparative and International Politics," *American Political Science Review* 54 (1960): 34–57.

28. Authority, of course, is not the only kind of social relation found in many social contexts. But not all types of social relations are universal or near-universal in societies. I suggest that the degree of success with which strains can be managed through role segregation is inversely proportional to the diffusion of social relationships among various social contexts: the more roles resemble one another, the less strains among them can be reduced.

29. Kornhauser, *Politics of Mass Society*, 170–171.

30. Ibid., 88.

PART IV

Change, Development, Revolution

SIX

The Idea of Political Development:
From Dignity to Efficiency

Author's Note: The articles in this section deal with political change, usually the obverse of political stability. Obviously, the absence of conditions that make for the latter also may be assumed to make for change, but this is too facile. For one thing, we can say nothing about kinds of change by such reasoning. Furthermore, certain kinds of change (discussed in chapter 3) may involve the adaptation of the polity to changed conditions and thus denote in fact a kind of stability: the maintenance of a pattern, to whatever extent may be possible, if context changes.

One thing that must be known then if political change occurs is whether it results from a polity's malfunctioning or whether it happens in the nature of things: especially, whether it is "normal" developmental change—as germination, maturation, decay, and termination are normal organic changes.

During the 1960s and 1970s a large literature on political development grew, for reasons that are surely obvious. In the article that follows I tried to do three things: (1) to point out the considerable shortcomings of that literature; (2) to define the traits of proper "developmental theory," following the ideas of the aboriginal developmental theorists who wrote during the nineteenth and early twentieth centuries; and (3) to sketch a theory of political development that had those traits and also seemed plausible. The theory precipitated considerable feedback, most of it gratifying. It was also examined, again with gratifying results, in a conference on comparative law, in which the legal systems of societies at different levels of development were contrasted on the basis of the theory.

Originally published in *World Politics* 34 (1982): 451–486. Reprinted by permission of Princeton University Press. Copyright © 1982 by the Princeton University Press.

In chapter 1, I wrote that my German experience pervades my work. It may be well hidden in the theory, but it is there just the same: chiefly in the notion that totalitarianism, as what I here call "political society," may be regarded as a developmental stage, already latent in "elementary" political life, and not an aberration. It is all too easy and comfortable to think of totalitarianism as aberrant. The grotesque features of the Nazi version may well be so. But that does not mean that the general phenomenon is no more than a kind of madness. Nor is it to say that there may not be a "democratic" form of totalitarian government. That, however, is too large a subject to be dealt with here—except to remark that recent changes in "political societies" (Eastern Europe especially) may be dramatic, but far less vast than they seem: perhaps they are only changes from one to another kind of political system in its full (total) development.

From one point of view, the study of political development is a major area of achievement in recent political inquiry; from another, which matters more, it is a conspicuous failure.

What has been achieved is great and rapid growth. The study of political development, in contemporary form, started barely two decades ago.[1] In short order, an extraordinary boom occurred in publications on the subject. By 1975, a standard overview listed over two hundred pertinent works. Accretion became especially rapid after 1964, though it seems to have "peaked out" (at a high level of production) in the early 1970s.[2]

The negative side is that the result is mostly muddle. The study of political development has all the traits of too-rapid, jerry-built growth, and of its concomitant, "decay."[3] The muddle is especially pronounced where it does the most harm: in regard to the very meaning of political development. Even scholars who were conspicuous in pushing the boom along are now viewing the matter of definition with dismay. Thus, Huntington and Domínguez start their review of the literature with remarks about loaded and wishful definitions—an "alarming proliferation" of them—and the consequent "superfluity" of much work on political development.[4] It stands to reason that, if a concept is encumbered with many meanings, theories using it also will vary alarmingly because they are not about the same thing.

The study of political development thus is at a critical juncture. One can let it decay further or, not much different, choose to abandon it— Frank Lloyd Wright's prescription for what to do about Pittsburgh (and, I think, Huntington's for political development). Or one can try a project in conceptual and, through it, theoretical renewal. In this essay, I develop a basis for renovation. Abandonment might, of course, be the wiser course. But the present conceptual muddle in studies of political development seems to me due to avoidable causes; the early explorers of the subject were getting at something worth getting at—if it was attainable.

CRITICAL ANALYSIS OF THE
CONCEPT OF POLITICAL DEVELOPMENT

The reasons for the muddle about the meaning of political development start with a strange inversion of the proper and usual relations between concepts (labels), objects, and subjects.

Normally, one begins with observations or ideas (or both). Concepts are used to make statements about them: "messages" that convey information. In making statements, difficulties may arise. More or less misinformation, or "noise," may be conveyed. Unless conventional language has been seriously abused, the fault can hardly lie in the words. Messages will be unclear to the extent that observations or ideas are crude or fuzzy. To achieve greater clarity, it is usually not to the point to revise the definitions; the obvious remedies are more exact observation and more lucid thought. The exceptions that call for abandonment are concepts that turn out to be vacuous because they label ignorance itself—like "phlogiston" or "having the vapors."

If, then, one asks what a concept means, the answer ought simply to be that it means what it is intended to mean. If disputes about the labels we ourselves have devised concern meaning as such, one can be sure that something went wrong at the first move. But, in point of fact, nothing is more discussed and debated among specialists in the study of political development than what the concept means. Huntington and Domínguez put their finger on the reason in pointing out that scholars first became concerned with a "thing" called political development, and that this concern "naturally" led them to try to define what the thing is.[5] Trying to find a proper bottle to attach to a label had a predictable result: the "alarming proliferation" of meanings mentioned earlier. One sees this best in overviews of the literature on political development, which generally present lists of meanings—lists that tend to be lengthy as well as different from one another.[6]

Why this topsy-turvy procedure of putting concepts before meanings? The explanation seems to me apparent in the actual unfolding of studies of development since the early fifties. At first, the term "development" became fashionable policy language for describing economic differences between Western (and other) societies and the assumed aspirations of Third World countries. In the economic sense, the concept was reasonably informative: it referred to levels of material abundance and processes of raising the levels. When political scientists appropriated the label, they also referred to assumed aspirations in the Third World and differences between it and the West; they then searched for a special content for the concept. Since "political abundance" has no immediately apparent meaning, the results were bound to be odd and eclectic.

The search for a political version of abundance is most evident in attempts to define political development in terms of capabilities—levels of them; "crises" regarding them; changes in them; various capabilities (as in Almond and Powell); or some particular kind (as in Organski).[7] This tack, however plausible, turned out, at best, to be problematic. Because capabilities are potential, it is intrinsically difficult to be precise about them. More important, the notion of capability only removes the problem of definition by one step. We now ask: Capability to do what, and how?

In most cases, the definition of the "thing" called political development was sought in a manner even more likely to lead to conceptual entropy. From the outset, development was, as stated, a norm-laden concept, distinguishing "us" from "them," Western achievements from non-Western aspirations—much like the earlier, less euphemistic word *civilization*. The difficulty here is not just parochial bias, but the tendency to conceive political development simplistically—as what exists in the West and had gone on in its history (especially its recent history), and what was sought to be replicated, or was bound to occur, in "backward" societies. Since a great many things have gone on in Western history, scholars were virtually compelled to choose for emphasis some aspect, or aspects, of Western history. They could—perhaps had to—choose by opinion. And so we get eclectic catalogues of meanings, which, taken altogether, simply spell Western history.

Thus, political development has been especially associated with increasing democratization; with growing bureaucratization; with the professionalization of politics (what Weber called living "off," not "for" politics);[8] with the formalization of politics (actions based on explicitly prescribed legal rules); with the decline of ascription and the rise of achievement in political roles; with the growing clarification and resolution of political jurisdictions (the gradual vanishing of parallel or overlapping functions, like those of the Church, principalities, and other traditional corporations, and the clearcut rank-ordering of roles and structures, contrasted to the messy lack of hierarchy produced by infeudation).[9] The very fact of the building of nation-states has also been equated with political development ("nation-building" once was the most common meaning), as has the increased penetration of societies by governmental authorities and the increase in redistributive policies. The list can easily be extended. History is enormously multifaceted.

Granted, development is not a sensible concept unless used in a historical sense. But if the concept remains closely tied to concrete history, there is no need for it. We already have a more intelligible concept for development *as* history: namely, history. Development must surely stand for something more abstract and "ruleful" (theoretical)—something that is manifested *in* histories (plural).[10]

Why not, then, simply abandon the idea of "political development"? In the first place, the present literature on political development simply does not represent "developmental" inquiry properly. In fact, little but the label itself (plus some other, mostly misused, concepts culled from developmental thinkers) links that literature to genuine developmental thought. The state of the literature, consequently, is irrelevant to assessing the utility of theories of development, properly constructed. (It might be added that the disjunction of the label from the theorizing it represents is ironic because developmental thought occurs at the very origin of modern social science in the nineteenth century and was devised to deal with its core issue: what it is to be "modern.") Second, the core issue that gave rise to developmental thought has hardly been transcended by later history. It remains obtrusive and urgent and it is still very much a puzzle. Finally, the potential of developmental thought for unraveling the puzzle it was meant to solve has hardly begun to be realized. The failure is the result of misunderstanding its intention. Very summarily, this intention was to understand our own societies (and, by extension, others) by finding their location in social time as a critical theoretical dimension.

THE NATURE OF DEVELOPMENTAL THOUGHT

Social Time and the Puzzle of Modernity

Societies exist in, and "move" through, history—and social history differs from other sorts of history. Obviously, then, social theories must somehow come to grips with the nature and significance of "social time." One issue that is thus posed is how to think of the flow of history: whether to treat history annalistically, as a continuous thread, or as passing through distinct phases—as Geertz puts it, "a medium through which certain abstract processes move."[11] A further issue arises if the latter tack is chosen: how to think of history as an abstract medium. For the most part, that question has been dealt with via picturesque metaphors, above all that of organic growth and decay.[12] Developmental thought is preeminent in trying to transcend mere imagery in the treatment of social time,[13] as well as in the extent to which such time is treated as a puzzle and a key to understanding.

The context in which developmental thought appeared had much—perhaps everything—to do with its animus. Developmental theories began, simplistically, early in the nineteenth century and attained their apogee early in the twentieth. Roughly, the period runs from Comte, the first volume of whose *Cours* appeared in 1830, to Durkheim and Weber; this period was, as we know, one of rapid, tumultuous, broad-scale, and above all almost wholly unprecedented changes, in scope and in kind, in the West. The changes need no elaboration. They include the spread of industry; the rapid growth of science and technology; the "disenchantment" of the world, as Weber called it, through rational perceptions and behavior; growing bureaucratization; democratization and its many concomitants (the appearance of political parties, changes in the composition of elites, and so on); nationalism and the emergence of new states; vastly increased social mobility; great cities; transformed networks of transport and communications; revolutions; reaction; and much else. Such extraordinary changes, especially while still novel, were bound to pose profound puzzles. They were also bound to unhinge established ideas about the nature of societies' movement through time. And they were, at the least, likely to make the proper understanding of historical process appear fundamental to all worthwhile social understanding. The belief in the critical significance of social time, and of the location of particular societies in it, emerges most categorically in Durkheim's sociology. For Durkheim, all was time-bound and, therefore, culture-bound: not just "social facts," but even the epic issues of moral philosophy (because moral imperatives are senseless out of their historical context) and those of validity and truth (because no universal mind exists, only particular cultural *consciences collectives*).[14]

Thus, the core problem of developmental thought was the puzzle of modernity. That puzzle had numerous related facets. Where were Western societies on the continuum of history? How did they get there? What forces had moved them from some long-past primal condition to the present? Where was historical process taking them? These questions differ from the way the problem of modernity is put now. In its earlier version, the issue was Western society: "we" rather than "they"; modernity rather than achieving modernization. Comparisons with premodern societies might, of course, help in finding solutions, but "we" were the problem. It follows that developmental theories could hardly have conceived of modernity in terms of the general condition, or selected facets, of "advanced" societies. Their first task was to diagnose that condition itself, in contrast to other conditions of societies.

In order to come to grips with the problem of modernity, and with the more general problem of passage through social time, the developmental theorists devised a mode of theory as unprecedented as the social conditions that they tried to understand—a change in thought perhaps as momentous as the appearance of Newtonian mechanics and cosmology in the physical sciences. To understand their mode of theorizing, it is particularly necessary to grasp two things at the outset. One is that the developmental theorists tried, in essence, to find patterns in pervasive novelty and seeming flux—to get bearings in a world devoid of all fixity and precedents. The second involves the nature of conceptions of social time available for them to find such patterns—conceptions they rejected as inadequate for their task. Discussion of these earlier conceptions should help to clarify the nature and novelty of developmental thought by contrast; and discussion of perceived shortcomings in the conceptions should clarify the animus of developmental theory—and thus also the traits such theory should possess.[15]

Nondevelopmental Thought

Universal-abstract theory. The strict antithesis of developmental theory is a body of social thought not far removed from it in history, and still its chief competitor. For want of a conventional label, I will call it universal-abstract thought. In such thought, there is no temporal dimension at all, or at least none that matters.

Although societies and polities exist in history, it is possible to theorize about them as if they did not. Many social and political issues are universal. In politics, the manifest universal issues are those of authority and subjection: the origin or basis of governmental authority, its proper domains, the obligations and rights of subjects and princes, the nature of justice, and so on. Since these issues arise wherever a polity exists, it may seem simple logic to seek their solutions independent of contexts, including temporal contexts. Before the nineteenth century, sociopolitical theory was addressed chiefly to such "universal" issues and aimed at such atemporal solutions.[16]

If issues are not tied to contexts, it will seem plausible to seek solutions by methods that also ignore contexts. The systematic method of abstract thinking thus is deduction, and, in fact, the prototypical method of universal-abstract thought was social geometry. One invoked axiomatic truths and deduced theorems (mostly to serve as normative imperatives) from them. Both the axioms and deductions often were odd and hardly involved tight geometric reasoning. Sometimes, to be sure, premises were stated as explicit postulates, as in the opening of the Declaration of Independence. More often, they made apparently empirical assertions, especially about human nature: that human life is "nasty, poor, brutish, and short," or that people have a "natural identity of interests." Or they postulated some alleged primordial sociopolitical event—usually a social and/ or governmental "contract." At best, the links between the postulates and theorems also were quasi-mathematical; but the spirit of universal-abstract theories certainly was geometric.

Geometry, of course, is wholly abstract. It is a tool for imposing logical exactness on understandings of experience. If geometry as such is made into theory, the world that is theorized about will necessarily seem static, timeless, ahistorical, and noncultural. The universal-abstract theories of Hobbes or Locke (among many others) do seem to pertain to a sort of clockwork social universe. Time exists in it; but societies move in time like planets through their orbits.

Such a theoretical world can only be plausible if one's sense of social life is fundamentally one of fixity. Surely this at least partly explains the historical location of sociopolitical geometry. It postdates the upheavals of the Renaissance and the Reformation. It played a major role in the *philosophie* of the *ancien régime*. It was, in short, the characteristic thought of embryonic "modernity" not yet become mysterious and perceived as a sort of permanent, if still youthful, maturity. Therefore, developmental thought should be understood, above all, in counterpoint to universal-abstract social and political theories. To repeat, Durkheim insisted on temporal answers even for the seemingly timeless issues of such theories.

Of course, there existed, alongside universal-abstract thought (indeed, long preceding it), modes of social thinking in which time does play a role, sometimes a considerable one. It would be strange if this were not the case. None of these modes of thought, however, could be suited to the goals of developmental theory—though one came close in time and traits and may be considered its flawed precursor.

Social time in classical and Christian thought.   In Greek and Roman philosophies, as in the early myths that the classic philosophers rationalized,[17] all time is cyclical: the myth of Demeter made into rational philosophy. The cycle manifestly is fundamental to political philosophy in Aristotle ("the same opinions appear among men infinitely often") and underlies history in Polybius. It was perhaps inevitable that early thought about social time should use the imagery of cycles. The obvious reason is that the perception of time as a cycle surely is the most immediate experience of our personal time as organisms, and of the organisms all about us, in the recurrence of germination, growth, withering, and rebirth.

The idea of organic growth is not incompatible with developmental thought. Perhaps it even is the prototype of all developmental thinking, as Nisbet argues.[18] Growth and development have always been inseparable ideas. But this does not apply to the notion of organic cycles. The idea of cycles, after all, is close to being atemporal: it involves infinite repetition— changeless change. The idea may be a useful deus ex machina for historical explanation: things happen, as they often do in Polybius, because the time is ripe for them; or they do not happen because their season is not yet. But the notion obviously will not do if the *explanandum* is considered unprecedented. In fact, when the Greeks and Romans thought of the emergence of their own civilization, they used a quite different imagery: that of a gradual trajectory, so to speak—from an age of childish ignorance and contentment to philosophic wisdom and serenity.[19] The inconsistency can be explained by the fact that the classical philosophers, quite unlike the developmentalists, knew their historic place: despite imperfections and corruption, they considered themselves to be at the end of "advancement"—certainly not on a novel journey to an unknown destination.[20]

The conception of history as a trajectory, essential in developmental thought, is, of course, the basis of the Christian idea of social time. The Christian trajectory is a pilgrim's progress. This is especially explicit, before Milton, in St. Augustine: "The education of the human race . . . has advanced . . . through certain epochs or, as it were, ages, so that it might gradually rise from earthly to heavenly things."[21] The pilgrim's advance, though, was gloomy, as befit the time of Alaric's sack of Rome; it was an advance through corruption toward apocalypse. Such a vision could hardly speak to thinkers in a hopeful age. But, more important, what makes the Christian idea of history irrelevant to developmental thought is, again, what is most basic in the latter: puzzlement over social time as a variable. The Christian (and especially the Augustinian) thinkers also knew their historic place: at the nadir of time, when an old world had died and a new one had not yet germinated. It is difficult to think of anything less appropriate to the mystifying ferment and burgeoning of the developmental theorists' world.

Progress theory. A considerable, and familiar, body of thought that lies much closer to developmental theory certainly does not share Christian gloom, nor does it envisage the apocalyptic transformation of a dying world: progress theory. The nature of theories of progress (from Fontenelle and Leibnitz, through the greater intricacies of Kant, to the detailed "sketch" of Condorcet, and beyond) surely needs no discussion here. Progress theory is one of the staples of academic political education.[22] What does need discussion, and a fair amount of it, is why progress theories do not measure up to the developmentalists' task and therefore differ from developmental thought.

We must be especially careful to distinguish progress theories from developmental theories because it is common to think of progress theory as an early version of developmental thought. No doubt there are continuities and resemblances. They occur contiguously in time, and the line of division between late progress theory and early developmental thought (like Comte's) is blurred. But, seen whole, progress theory differs from developmental thought in crucial ways—especially in ways that are important for dealing with modernity as a puzzle.

Most significant, neither the future nor the past really were treated as a puzzle in progress theory in the first place; consequently, the present also was considered to be transparent to clear minds. Even if any specific location on the path of history might be hard to fix exactly, the path itself was known. It was, typically, defined by the continuous growth of rational knowledge, not least through the waning of superstition and magic. Such a belief seemed plausible, even obvious, when only the lighter side of modern secular history was in evidence.[23] Although in most progress theories, the future was a vague, poetic vision, the theories at least were of paradise glimpsed, if not yet gained. In any case, paradise was certain.

To be sure, there were, as always, thinkers of skeptical disposition (like Hume and Voltaire) who did not so much dissent as abstain; there were also the gloomy-minded. But it was not until the French Revolution and its aftermath that the simplistic, sunny theory of progress wobbled. In the context of developmental theory, pretty visions of constant progress toward Utopia were as out of place as doom-speaking. The world was growing richer, more knowledgeable, busier, more secure. But much of what was novel also was patently ugly, and novelty coexisted with reaction.

Also important was the belief of progress theorists in a certain fixity in change itself. That is why some progress theorists fit well into the category of abstract-universal thought. Fixity existed especially in "human nature"; history was the social realization of that nature over time. In retrospect, we ourselves can discern a considerable temporal puzzle here. But that the theorists of progress did not do so is evident in their tendency to write what has been called "conjectural history," the prototype of which is the *Discourse on the Origin of Inequality*. It is still more evident in their searches for the essence of their own refined identity in rude or savage peoples. (Adam Ferguson's *Essay on the History of Civil Society* is the outstanding case in point).

Surely there is all the difference in the world between theories that profess to understand the present through the remote past and those in which the nature of the trajectory from past to present to future consists of deeply sensed mysteries. Granted that developmental thinkers, like theorists of progress, made much of rudimentary societies and did so in order to understand themselves and their own times. But developmental theory did not seek the sophisticate in the savage. Rather, like Melville, developmental theorists stressed contrast. Above all, where progress theorists wrote with certainty about the flow of social time, developmental thinkers puzzled and theorized.

Developmental Thought

We can now outline the essential traits of developmental thought (its form), in contrast to earlier treatments of social time.[24] Each trait can be related to some facet of the puzzle of modernity. And, in each case, the point can be substantiated that contemporary work on political development represents developmental thought inadequately.[25]

Inherent change.   The foremost trait of developmental thought is that it proceeds from the premise that change is inherent in society. Thus, social statics and dynamics coincide, and the dichotomy between order and change is false; order, as Comte said, is order-in-change.[26] All other traits of developmental theories follow from the first in some fashion. The sheer scope and obviousness of change in the context in which developmental theories were formulated demanded that change be regarded as inherent, and thus ubiquitous, in social life.

What is most important theoretically about the premise of inherent change is that it involves an explicit choice at the fundamental dividing line between all theories, the primary branch point at which alternative theories occur. I have made this argument extensively elsewhere,[27] so I will be sketchy about it here. In explanation, the matter to be explained can be considered inherent or contingent. If contingent, it occurs because of abnormal (literally aberrant) conditions that happen fortuitously. If inherent, it occurs ineluctably, unless impeded or diverted by chancy conditions. (Thus, our deaths are inherent, our illnesses contingent.) Everything in theory depends on the choice made at this branch point. As a familiar example, I would cite the fatefulness of the change from the Aristotelian conception of motion, which was contingent, to the Galilean, in which motion is considered to inhere in matter. Developmental theory was, potentially, just as revolutionary.

How does the premise of inherency set developmental thought apart from other modes of sociotemporal thinking? First, in early ideas of social time, change was inherent in society only as changeless change, as repetition; or else, necessary change was a "one-shot" apocalyptic transformation. Even in progress theories, the trajectory of social time always came, inherently, to rest—and rest was never far off.

In all thought before developmental theory, then, social motion was Aristotelian. It tended toward a *telos:* a literal end. Also (Thucydides is typical), the events of concrete history tended to be explained largely by manifestly contingent causes: by the particularities of acts, contexts, wise or unwise choices, and the like. Historical philosophy and explanation were bifurcated and inconsistent. In the former, cyclical necessity prevailed; in the latter, accidents. This bifurcation is still evident even (or especially) in Marx as a philosopher of history and interpreter of particular events.

The first task of developmental thought, then, is to formulate a really general theory of social time; the next is to apply it, as explanation, to particular cases at particular points in particular histories. "Really general" means abstract theory regardless of time, place, and circumstance—theory that spans the whole of history, from primal origins to modernity. Clearly, the contemporary literature on political development does not come close to discharging that task. In much of it, even our own development seems to have begun only in the nineteenth century, or not long before.[28]

Dimensional change. It is necessary in developmental theory to construct what Simmel called "abstract grammars" with which to make sense of the immensely complex actual flow of social time and to locate concrete cases in such time.[29] These grammars, in Kantian terms, are forms of history that fit the contents of particular histories. If social change is regarded as inherent, that flow must be along a continuous dimension— although aberrant conditions might slow down movement, or produce apparent rest, on the dimension.

To define such a dimension, developmental theorists had to characterize its poles: the nature of the primal and of the fully advanced conditions of society—the latter not really "final," but a vision of the future that could link with present and past. Only in this way could developmental theorists hope to find their own place in history, in relation to the remote past and the uncertain future. The polar conditions seem simplistic, and indeed they are so, intentionally. Maine, for instance, considered the poles of the continuum of history to be relations based on status and on contract; he explicitly called them formulas—abstract tools for constructing "the law of progress."[30] The polar types of Toennies were community (*Gemeinschaft*) and association (*Gesellschaft*): abstract concepts constructed to correspond to "external" (viz., concrete) collectivities; to describe old and new; and to find underlying themes in familial, economic, political, religious, aesthetic, and scholarly life.[31] Durkheim's orienting concepts referred to polar modes of social solidarity, the mechanical and organic;[32] these concepts, again, were used as highly abstract forms to make sense of concrete cultures, by a theorist preeminently aware of their variability. Weber's poles were traditional and rational systems of action: pure types that were useful for describing and explaining impure (concrete) cases.[33]

In regard to the construction of such continuous dimensions, the contemporary literature on political development again falls dismally short. Writers tend to take positions on modernity (as we saw, simplistically), but not explicitly on premodernity, and least of all on the primal conditions from which development flows. Huntington just tells us that traditional political systems vary.[34] And Lerner, typically, says no more than that traditional systems lack modern traits.[35]

Growth and stages. If social change is dimensional, all cases fall between minimal and maximal poles. Historic flow along a dimension thus involves changes in degree, or quantitative growth. Throughout the corpus of developmental thought, change in scale in fact played a major role. In Toennies, for example, *Gemeinschaft* involved small-scale units (household, kinship, village, neighborhood, town); *Gesellschaft* was associated with large entities (city, nation, cosmopolitan life, markets, industries, scientific fields). In Durkheim, organic solidarity was associated with growth in the sheer "volume" of society and in "moral density": the number and variety of interactions in which people participate. "Lower" societies were spread out sparsely, lacked cities, had few and slow modes of communication and transport; "higher" ones had the opposite traits, and, above all, denser networks of interaction as a result.[36] In Simmel, the quantitative element played a critical role even more explicitly. Virtually the whole of Simmel's thought was based on a distinction between two-person (dyadic) and three-person (triadic) relations. This distinction was, for Simmel, a metaphor for small and large—a basis for showing that even a change merely from a relation of two to three would have enormous consequences.[37]

An essential premise of developmental thought, nevertheless, is that not just change (singular) is inherent in societies, but also changes (plural). The developmental conception of social change is typological.[38] Just as the premise of inherent changes responded to the obtrusiveness of change in the developmentalists' social world, so the positing of qualitative changes accommodated their sense of novelty—of new species being originated. Size and growth do matter, but chiefly as bases of generic changes. Durkheim's distinction between mechanical and organic solidarity clearly was typological; but the long process by which organic solidarity replaces the mechanical type results from quantitative change. At the outset, there is a growth of what Durkheim called "moral density"—of the volume of interactions (and hence of regulative mores). As this occurs, conflicts increase—if only through proximity, like conflicts among animals living off the same parts of a tree. The chief mechanism available for reducing conflicts caused by proximity is a kind of distancing: the division of labor separates people and, as a bonus to harmony, makes them more mutually dependent. In this way, a generically quite different kind of solidarity replaces that of early societies. In the latter, solidarity results from the sameness of their parts; in advanced societies, its source is just the opposite: differentiation.[39]

If social change is both quantitative and typological, an obvious issue arises: how to reconcile the two. The developmentalists' solution (the only solution possible) was to think of the flow of social time as involving stages: critical thresholds at which growth in degree generates changes in kind. Comte posited three such stages: theological, metaphysical, and positive. Spencer considered social change to be more obviously continuous, but also to involve typological change: from homogeneous to heterogeneous societies.[40] Obviously such change is quantitative, but Spencer himself referred to the result as "transformations."

The idea of social stages, essential in developmental thought, sharply distinguishes such thought from progress theories.[41] In theories of progress, change is the growth of some desirable aspect of society (typically, rational knowledge) and a concomitant zero-sum decline in its obverse (superstition or ignorance). Progress theorists thus could, and did, envisage a final resting place for society: in the elimination of its defects. If, on the other hand, the inherency of typological changes is posited, social time must be open-ended. A historical process not conceived in simple monotonic, zero-sum terms can hardly arrive at absolute completion. The resulting theory is gloomier, appropriate to a time of puzzlement about society.

Again, contemporary work on political development has virtually nothing to say about how quantities (and which quantities) flow through political time and become converted into generic transmutations at critical stages. The imagery of developmental thought is much used: for instance, "takeoff." So is terminology that seems typological—above all, the labels "traditional" and "modern." I have already commented on the vacuity of both. If the polar types are vacuous, it follows that "takeoff" and intermediary types (e.g., transitional society) also must be mere imagery. The essential task of developing a theory of political stages—linking changes in degree and kind—remains unfulfilled.

Ruleful, necessary change. One way to orient thought to a world inherently in transmutation, in which all is perceived as time-bound and culture-bound, is to treat all cultures as having "meaning" only in themselves. In that case, understanding consists merely of interpretation. It is no accident that *Kulturwissenschaft* and the method of *Verstehen* came into being when developmental thought also flourished. As universal-abstract thought best represents the perception of underlying social fixity and uniformity, so interpretative sociology—"thick description," or cultural aesthetics—is one major response to the perception of social flux and variability.[42]

Cultural science, however, provides no orientation to the general flow of history and offers no solution to the puzzle of modernity. Changes (and differences) may be inherent in societies, but no account of the process of change is provided. The alternative—and the fundamental difference between social science and cultural interpretation—is to proceed from the premise that societies pass through the stages of social time in a ruleful manner. In that case, modernity—as a stage or passage to a stage—may become comprehensible, in comparison to other cultures, as a particular location on a general and necessary sociotemporal continuum. Also, in this way, comfort can be provided in a still ugly, unfinished world. The tumult of early modernity may be regarded as the onset of a higher stage in which, as in any pure type, all will at last fit coherently. At the same time, the naive optimism of believers in finality can be avoided.

Thus, again, it is a critical task of developmental theory to construct a comprehensive theory of history—one that identifies distinct stages in a continuous flow of social time which links primal to modern society. Such abstract history must, of course, especially describe and explain how changes on the dimension of time have produced whatever is qualitatively distinct about modernity.

As we have seen, though, the puzzle of modernity did not just involve location in historical time. It also involved questions about how we arrived at our temporal location and others at theirs and about where history was taking us and them. A related task of developmental theory, then, was to identify, alongside uniform motion, the uniform forces pushing societies ineluctably along the continuum of history—especially forces inherent in societies. Only thus was it possible to see the necessity of what had occurred since primal times, and only thus can one have a sure sense of direction in looking ahead—orientation to present, past, and future.

All developmental theories posit such an underlying moving force (and special forces at different stages) that pushes societies through time. Specifying such a force—describing historical gravity, so to speak—is, needless to say, a very difficult task. What force could possibly do what was theoretically needed? Obviously, it had to be absolutely fundamental—something "essential" in the very nature of societies and thus always present as a dynamic force, through qualitative changes. The early evolutionists saw the problem, but they tended to circumvent it because they wanted a quick fix to make sense of change. Their circumventions involved truisms— resort to unspecified "properties of our species," as Comte put it[43]—that is, to human nature. But as evolutionary thought itself evolved, the solutions became less vacuous. In Spencer, for instance, the driving force behind social change was the desire for social efficiency, which Spencer equated with complexity of structure. In Durkheim, it was something even more obviously essential: social existence as such—the need for solidarity among the elements of society.

Here, once more, contemporary theorists of political development fail dismally to live up to the form of developmental thought. Not only is their continuum of political time truncated, but the force supposedly driving underdeveloped societies is, generally, little more than an unexplained urge to be more developed. At bottom, this is a truism à la Comte; it involves an assumed intrinsic "property of our species," reinforced by the extrinsic accelerator of cultural diffusion. What is absent, above all, is a theory of the fundamental force, or forces, that brought "us" to our political condition and continues to push us through political time.

Conclusion.   It should be obvious that the mysteries of modernity, as I said above, still are very much with us. For a long time, in contemporary political inquiry, they were shifted to the Third World. But now, again, they arise in reference to ourselves: for example, in the concerns with the nature and future of postindustrial societies, and their governability. Developmental thought was itself developed to deal with these puzzles. Surely, it is uniquely suited to do so; thus, it is sensible to take such thought seriously—that is, to try to construct developmental theory properly. Hence this section, as groundwork for the next.

The quintessential developmental theorist, Durkheim, best summarized the spirit of the developmental mode of thought:

> Every time we explain something human, taken at a given moment in history ... it is necessary to go back to its primitive and simple form, to try to account for the characterization by which it was marked at that time, and then to show how it developed and became complicated little by little, and how it became that which it is at the moment in question.[44]

I propose now to do this, in broad strokes, for the political aspect of human experience.

SKETCH FOR A REVISED THEORY OF POLITICAL DEVELOPMENT

The passage from Durkheim succinctly describes what is needed to renovate the idea of political development. A more detailed agenda of questions to be dealt with follows from the summary of the traits of developmental thought:

1. What conception of continuous growth can plausibly describe the long passage from primal to highly advanced polities?
2. What is the essential nature of polity in its "primitive and simple" form?
3. What forces make the "advancement" of primal polities toward "higher" forms ineluctable (or at least highly probable)?
4. What distinctive stages lie along the trajectory of political time? In what ways do these stages involve both quantitative growth and change in kind?
5. What forces move polities from stage to stage?
6. What do the answers to these questions imply for polities that are at present less developed, and for "advanced," modern polities?

What Conception of Continuous Growth Describes the Passage
from Simple to Highly Advanced Politics?

I have argued that contemporary theories of political development are historically myopic. Even in Georgian England—hardly remote history— the traits now most widely associated with political development were still embryonic. Democratization was certainly not far advanced. The suffrage was severely restricted; leaders (e.g., M.P.s) either were nobles and gentry or their handpicked clients, bound to serve their patrons' interests.[45] In regard to bureaucratization, administrative and judicial roles remained entangled, nationally and locally; recruitment was highly ascriptive; specialization and formalization were elementary.[46] Among the more familiar conceptions of political development, only the "clarification" of societal authority was mature, for the messiness of corporate jurisdictions had certainly been cleared up by the eighteenth century.

How, then, can one characterize a continuum of political time on which the Georgian polity itself belongs to a rather advanced period? Recall that such a continuum must involve quantitative growth and must be a "form" that can contain much variable content. Moreover, the dimension involved must be anchored in time by minimal and maximal poles, one corresponding substantially to rudimentary cases, the other a vision that links perceptions of modernity to its remote and nearer past and, still more important, to an approximated future.

I suggest that the most serviceable way to characterize such a continuum is also the simplest: *what grows in political development is politics as such—* the political domain of society. Through political history, political authority and competition for politically allocated values have continually increased. Using Durkheim's terminology, we might regard this as growth in "political density," perhaps as a special aspect of a growing "moral density." More and more political interactions occur, overall and in place of nonpolitical interactions.

To avoid confusion about what is being argued here, a conceptual distinction must be made. One can think of "the political" as any relations that involve, say, legitimate power, or conflict management, or the regulation of social conduct, and the like. In that case, "politics" may simply exist throughout society and not be located in any clearly defined social domain or institution. Or one can think of "politics" as the functions and activities of such a concrete domain: that of the heads of societies, the princes, chiefs, or kings (for, in its modern sense, politics is associated with government, and government and social headship are synonymous). What I argue is that, through political time, the "princely domain" has constantly grown—increasingly penetrating society. And, in conjunction, political activities and relations in the less concrete sense have also grown. Expropriation by "princes" and expansion of political activity occur in conjunction.

One pole of the dimension of political time thus might be called the *social polity*. In the social polity, as a pure type, there exists a "princely" domain: some institution of headship of society, chieftaincy, firstness. That domain, though, is little differentiated from others, in the sense of having separate organizations and administrative staffs; it is anything but a subsociety—neither a "machine" nor a "system" in itself. Above all, next to nothing is done by princes, at least as we understand political activity: there is almost no active princely management of society. The society is virtually all, and the polity virtually nothing. Relations of power exist; regulations of conduct and of conflicts occur; but they do so throughout society, not in special relation to chieftaincy.

At the other pole is *political society*. In political society as a pure type, "private" relations have been wholly preempted by the "public" domain of the chiefs. The institutions of that domain are highly differentiated and separately organized; governmental officers and staffs constitute a large subsociety. That subsociety is a complex system in itself, while at the same time it permeates social life.

The passage from social polity to political society can be described summarily. The domain of princes, who at the outset do virtually nothing, has great, indeed irresistible, potential for growth: power resources. Over a long period, these power resources are gradually realized. The chiefs of society convert headship into primacy, and primacy into actual control— at first very slowly, then with gathering, ultimately runaway, momentum. The momentum results from the fact that, as power resources are converted, they are not used up, but in fact increase. As this process unfolds, growth in degree corresponds, at specifiable periods, to transmutations of type. In our own modern period, we approach a condition in which the distinction between polity and society has again become blurred—not because the public realm is minimal, but because it has virtually eliminated all privacy. This, though, is not an end, but itself a stage in a continuing process. The political society generates its own dynamics; and we should at least be able to discern the forces likely to move it, even if not yet where it is destined to go.

This conception of political time has been anticipated by other theorists. It parallels Durkheim's view of more general social development. The minimal pole of the continuum is grounded in the anthropologists' notion of "stateless" societies.[47] The conception of political development as expropriation is in Weber: the emergence of the modern state was, for Weber, a process of continuous expropriation by princes of "autonomous and 'private' bearers of executive power," resembling the expropriation by large capitalist enterprises of small, independent economic units.[48] In his publicist essays written shortly after the Russian Revolution, Weber envisaged the further, accelerating, and continuous expropriation by the political domain of economic life, and then also of the more intimate, and the scientific and cultural, spheres—a remarkable prevision. The idea of "total" politics now also is a recurrent theme in works on modern democratic states. Sharkansky, for example, refers to runaway governmental growth "in response to incessant demands for more services" and repeatedly alludes to the erosion of the "margins" of formal government as a consequence.[49] The vision of political society informs especially the critiques of modern governments by perceptive (if also hotheaded) "libertarians": Hayek, Oakeshott, Ellul, Nisbet, and others.[50]

What Is Polity in Its "Rudimentary" Form?

To sustain the thesis that what grows and changes in political development is the political domain per se, one must, first of all, characterize that domain in its "primitive and simple form," from which advancement proceeds. None of the many structural or functional notions that political scientists have used to define the essence of polity seem to make sense for its very early forms.[51] What seems distinctive and universal to the princely realm in its simplest form is that its occupants and practices represent the very fact that society exists. Chiefs, khans, liegelords "embody" society. They are figures through whom societies personify themselves or sometimes (much the same) the ideal order of things imperfectly reflected in social order. They stand for the fact that a common, thus moral, life exists, and they celebrate the common life and make it compelling.

Surely that is fundamental in society, if anything is, because societies are nothing if not collective entities with which members identify—that is, define themselves. Thus, ceremony and symbolism—what Bagehot called the dignified parts of government—are not to be regarded as mere pretty trappings of power; nor are consummatory (expressive) and instrumental polities,[52] or "sacred" and "secular" ones, distinctive types at all developmental stages. At the "simple" stage (thus, perhaps, always), symbolism is the very nature of the princely, not a guise. That is why, to us, the primal political domain seems empty. Primal "symbolic politics" does not stand for "real politics." It stands for society.

The evidence suggesting that primal politics is symbolic is considerable.[53] For instance, in Schapera's study of sub-Saharan tribes the following points emerge:[54] The chiefs, as heads of societies, do not do much at all; they are simply marked out from others (e.g., in costume), exalted (in special rituals), subjects of rejoicing and of eulogies.[55] Tribes are often defined simply by identification with chiefs, not by territoriality or even kinship. Sometimes no abstract tribal name exists, only that of the chief. Often, tribal names are the inherited names of the ancestors of chiefs, and at times chiefs are named by the tribal name. In some cases, any injury done to a member of a tribe is regarded as an injury to the chief (as we talk about crimes against society). In short, the collective and the personal are thoroughly joined in the chief's personage. Much the same comes out in Lucy Mair's studies of primitive governments and African kingdoms.[56] Mair argues, indeed, that the substantive wielding of "power over the conduct of public affairs" generally is not so much the chief's or the court's function as that of lesser figures, for whom kings are mouthpieces.[57] Lowie's work on North American Indian tribes makes a similar point.[58]

More important from the developmental point of view, we find this to be true also in the primitive condition of a prototypical advanced society— English society. (England may be considered as a good concrete approximation of an idealized case of continuous development: something close to an experimentally contrived universe—free of uncontrolled, deceiving contingencies—which any theory of sociopolitical development should fit closely.)

Anglo-Saxon society approaches the extreme of what I have called social polity.[59] If a "public sector" existed in that society, it could only have been that of king, *folkmoot*, and *Witan*. The king was principally a source of social identity, as were all lesser chiefs of the English tribes. His one significant activity was leadership in the common enterprise of making war, and practically no other common enterprise was engaged in. The *folkmoot* originally was not a council, but simply a local muster of warriors. By 900, local moots had pretty much been displaced by the *Witan*, a "national" council of "wise men." But the *Witan*'s essential function simply was to advise the king on the nature of "unchanging custom." Here the primacy of society is especially evident: while the king embodied its consciousness of itself, the *Witan* kept him honest, as the guardian of its mores.

Much the most perceptive study of primal politics as I conceive it is Geertz's magnificent book on the nineteenth-century "theatre-state" in Bali, *Negara*.[60] Geertz alone seems to have grasped fully the critical significance of political ceremony and ritual: of the "poetics" of power as against its "mechanics"—as Bagehot alone discerned that the dignified parts of English government were not mere vestigial histrionics, but essential to its "efficiency." Geertz does temporize between regarding theater as essential in polities as such and considering Bali an exotic alternative to politics as efficient power.[61] But, at least in Bali, "power served pomp, not pomp power."[62]

What Forces Make the Growth of Primal Polity Ineluctable?

Chieftaincy in primal polities is much indulged and rewarded, with awe and with goods. But that does not immunize chiefs (much less their retainers) against the appetite for mundane power; and, perhaps just because the chiefs are symbolic figures—awesome rather than powerful—power struggles are pervasive in primal societies.[63] For the purpose of developmental theory, it is necessary to show next that in such struggles the princely domain has overwhelming resources for subduing rivals and enlarging its effective control over society. What, then, are its power resources?

By itself, the representation of societies is an essential resource for power—perhaps the one seed that is capable of growing into political society. Societies are requisites of personal identity, safety, the satisfaction of material needs. But, though necessary, they are highly intangible. They are complex even when they are rudimentary. Seeing them as networks, or complexes of roles, or fields of interaction, or patterns of exchange— these are major feats even for modern professionals. Even if the task of abstract understanding were less difficult, such understanding would hardly move affections, which surely are needed for identification and legitimacy. So the personal symbols of society derive potential from the fact that they perform the most necessary of societal functions: making society appear "real."

It is true that there are other ways of making societies tangible. Primal societies, in fact, are always personified in their gods, through rites and magic. Thus, priests and magicians are the logical (and actual) main rivals of the chiefs for principal power. But the chiefs themselves are generally presumed to have special links to the supernatural, magical world—for instance, as rainmakers, healers, invokers of prosperity, possessors of sacred objects (fishing spears and the like), and as wielders of curses.[64]

These links to the supernatural not only reinforce secular symbolism (or make it sacred) but also associate chiefliness and "potency," for the magical world is a world of fateful powers. Chiefs are also considered especially potent figures in the material sense of prowess. All societies have collective business of some sort—in primal societies, for instance, moving camp and herds.[65] The function of making decisions about societal business naturally tends to be lodged in the locus of collectiveness. The one universal collective business of rudimentary societies is warfare: in defense against predatory others, for conquest (slaves, tribute, etc.), or, often, simply as a ritual.[66] So chiefs, though they have rivals in heroes,[67] generally are the main loci of potency as prowess. This accounts for the strange *duty* of chiefs in some tribal societies to be in good health, as well as for the use of wars of succession (in which the strongest survive) and for the frequent use of the phallus as a symbol of chieftaincy.

To exist, and to carry out collective enterprises, societies must, of course, be harmonious in some degree. Conflicts must be managed, quarrels mediated, crimes avenged. There is a universal social need for adjudication and, again, a "natural" tendency to associate that necessary function with society's embodiments. The actual management of conflicts and deviance tends, in fact, to be decentralized and dispersed in primal societies—a matter of self-help in feuds, revenge, and exacting reparations. But the chief always has at least some vague special responsibility in regard to justice. For instance, we are told by Traill that a basic function of the Anglo-Saxon kings was to go about the kingdom putting down "evil customs." Traill's catalogue of judicial duties actually is a list of things kings could *not* do; and it seems evident that kings were little more than especially prestigious "oath-helpers."[68] Still, justice and chieftaincy had special, even if largely hortatory, links.

The moral, surely, is evident. The primal princely domain is ages removed from the monopoly of legitimate power. But where could there be greater potential for eventual monopoly than in a domain standing for society itself; for potency, military and magical; and for justice? "Dignity" and "efficiency," granted, are obverse faces of politics—but also interchangeable resources.

What Are the Stages of Political Time?

The fact remains that in primal polities, whatever the chief's potential, one can barely detect an active public core. Our own political world could hardly differ more. At "our" location in political time, as stated, it is difficult to find anything that is clearly private. I am not referring to "totalitarian" polities, or only to those, but (less categorically) to the other typically modern form of polity: popular democracies. (Modern democracies, in historical perspective, simply are the gentler twins of totalitarian rule, mitigated by open competition, free communications, and a sense of rights and liberties—which, compared to earlier times, no longer really divides the public from the private, but is a sense of political decency.)

I have described the extraordinary pervasiveness of political authority in contemporary British society elsewhere and need not dwell much on details.[69] To convey the flavor of the matter, suffice it to say the following: (1) The national government (as in other modern democracies) now directly controls about half of GNP, and indirectly plans, guides, and channels most of the remainder. (2) Parliamentary sessions, once convened only occasionally, fill up the whole available legislative work-year, and even this at the cost of large omissions—uncontrolled "executive legislation" and a severe decline in the role of private members. (3) The Cabinet has virtually disappeared; as I wrote in 1958:

> Cabinet functions have become dispersed to an almost unfathomably complex administrative and deliberative machinery. Decisions once made collectively in the Cabinet are now made by cabinet committees, by individual Ministers, bureaucrats, the Treasury, official committees, party machinery, and even private associations; and, most often, by interaction among all of

these bodies. If power is concentrated anywhere in the British machinery of government it is concentrated not in the Cabinet but in this complex framework of decision-making.[70]

One can argue that what mainly mitigates the darker aspects of fully politicalized society is the very inability to control such a concentration of functions, due to sheer diversity and overload. The gentle myths of liberal rule surely help, but perhaps no more than the fact that monolithic authority itself is too large to manage. Privacy, in political society, is found in the interstices of authority; it is, perhaps, itself mainly a product of the structure of the public realm.

How did this transmutation to something close to "political society" come about? What lies beyond the primal polity's potential for growth? This is an enormous question, and we have not even the beginning of a plausible answer. As such a beginning, I suggest a six-stage process. The process is "logical" in that each stage manifestly is a condition for the next. The stages also make sense in the context of the English polity—our standard case for observing gradual, evolutionary "unfolding" (the literal meaning of *développer*) in politics. For this reason I will use English history—in gross summary—to exemplify the stages.

The politics of primacy. I have already treated the first stage, primal polity, using Anglo-Saxon England to illustrate its nature. The second stage involves what might be called the struggle for, and achievement of, primacy. The forces that push polities to and through that stage (and later stages) will be discussed presently. Here, it must suffice to say that nothing in political development can possibly come before the clarification of a distinct public domain that, in regard to "efficient" functions, is minimally *primus inter pares.* Without this, there is nothing that may grow. One may suppose that the establishment of a realm of substantive primacy—one that involves more than symbolic headship—will not be a tranquil process but will involve stubborn conflicts over domination and autonomy. Aside from chiefs, there are others who have politically convertible resources: religious, economic, and military. But, as we have seen, the chiefs generally have much weightier resources for providing political goods—not least, safety, in a context of continuous struggle among social domains: Hobbes's good, and no doubt the fundamental value.

This general stage fits, in England, the period of *feudal monarchy,* say of the twelfth century. The feudal monarchy certainly was quite different from the Anglo-Saxon, despite the fact, generally agreed, that the Conquest caused no sharp break. The domain of the Angevin and early Plantagenet princes, to be sure, remained mainly on the level of symbol and pomp; its practical authoritative functions were sparse. What is most conspicuous about the period is struggle for "dominion" as such. The histories portray incessant turmoil. But the tumult was not about policy, in our sense. It involved competition about spheres of autonomy and subjection; and the fundamental source of that struggle was a lack of clarification and resolution of the functions of the great and small corporations of society— all authoritative in their own domains and constantly striving to expand or protect them.

Corporate boundaries now, though, mattered for more than symbolic reasons. They mattered because the princely domain had begun to acquire a critical function: material extraction—a condition of all effective action, and thus an obsession in feudal monarchy. The Treasury preceded all other political institutions in development. The classic account of twelfth-century royal "administration" is FitzNeal's *Dialogue on the Exchequer,* the exchequer being its one great administrative creation. It regularized the royal revenues, and the great pacification under Henry II was, at heart, a matter of reestablishing the central revenues in face of embezzlement by the barons. Extraction increased political "density," and the latter changed institutions.

Still, Henry's charter upon his coronation was little more than an assurance of liberties, grants, and customs. Petit-Dutaillis's study of feudal monarchy does tell us that the King's *concilium* attended to "all sorts of business";[71] but, as to particulars, he lists only personal issues (e.g., marriages) and familiar matters of peace, war, loyalty, treason, and the administration of justice.

The last is important, however. Judicial activities now were much enlarged and wholly reorganized—coequal with pomp and war as the core of royal primacy. Indeed, aside from finance and war, the whole royal establishment now looked like a sort of national judiciary. The King's "prime minister" was the chief justiciar; the curia had become a "normal court" for the kingdom, not just an occasional tribunal; the judicial circuits, administering common law, had been established; and central justice had largely expropriated the seignorial jurisdictions, of which only a few islets remained.[72]

The feudal monarchy thus achieved, gradually, a considerable legal and extractive permeation of society, as a material basis for primacy. Contestation persisted for a long time, but in an increasingly muted, one-sided way. The nascent monopoly over extraction, the increasing practical responsibility for the management of conflicts, and the emergence of specialized institutions to handle these functions, realized a potential already present in the primal polity; but, more important, all this added to the growth potential of the prince's domain.

The "prophylactic" polity. Substantive primacy, especially when added to symbolic headship, is both gratifying in itself and a supremely valuable resource for acquiring additional resources. Once it is established, struggles for its possession inevitably occur. One of the fundamental tasks of politics is to institutionalize such struggles in order to defuse them—a basic function, for instance, of competition among political parties. But institutionalization is always gradual—a sort of subtheme of development. Early on, contestation for possession of the domain of primacy must involve—in greater or lesser degree—unregulated, brutal conflicts. Lacking institutionalization (or the transformation of real and deadly conflicts into ritualized competition) damage can be limited only by prevention: prophylaxis.

In the prophylactic polity, the overriding objective of the prince is to detect and disarm usurpation, while that of others is to seize or control principality. To protect principality, it is functional to place it in a tangible physical domain and to draw potential usurpers into that domain. Hence, the identification of primacy with the prince's court. It is there that the game of trying to get and keep primacy and its perquisites is played; politics turns inward.

To a degree, however, prophylactic politics must also reach out into society, further than before. Courtly politics cannot be wholly isolated because the discontents of society might play into the hands of usurpers. Therefore—rather than for altruistic reasons—the princely domain begins to furnish something else that is valuable to society: a degree of controlled social order, as prophylaxis in everyday life against society's *misérables*. The result is both a qualitative change in the nature of politics and the increased penetration of society by its political domain.

In England, *the era of the Tudors* illustrates the stage. The late medieval and Renaissance political struggles in England increasingly had a flavor different from those of feudalism. They were epitomized, and pretty much ended, by Tudor rule, for which "absolutism" is an egregious misnomer. Nothing really was absolute. Rather, the Tudors—especially Elizabeth—successfully coped with conspiracies *within* the realm of princely authority. If anything authoritative was absolute it was courtly absolutism, which transformed lords into mere courtiers. Concomitantly, political competition was courtly competition—scheming within the firm.

Nevertheless, one can discern a threshold in the permeation of society by authoritative policy. Outside of the royal palaces, authoritative regulation was still sparse; but before the Tudors (conflict management and extraction aside), authoritative space, outside its royal core, had been virtually empty. A good many histories refer to an abundance of "proclamations" by the Crown, and subservient parliaments and courts, in Tudor times.[73] Elizabeth's parliaments did indeed pass 429 bills. The figure is often mentioned to impress. Actually, it brings out only the limitations of policy making. Elizabeth's reign lasted forty-five years; nowadays, British legislative output runs to about a hundred bills a year. Much of Elizabethan "legislation" had to do with issues of diplomacy, foreign intrigues, war, and extraction. Some of the regime's authoritative activities, however, involved a novel extension of authority into society: the systematic maintenance of roads and bridges, the licensing of alehouses, controls over wages, the mobility of labor, entry into trades, dealings in commodities, interest rates, and—most familiar—a uniform law to care for the poor.

Growing political density surely is evident, especially since this reaching out into society supplemented unprecedented ceremonial activity (royal equipages and pageantry) and an even greater increase in foreign adventurism, war, and defense. The primacy of feudal monarchy clearly was now being put to use as a generalized resource. Perhaps this was a response to much-increased "social density": the manufacturing revolution in textiles, mining, iron making, and petty trades (perfumery, barbering, etc.)—a response, in general, to a busy society of promoters, speculators, patentees, dramatists, composers, astronomers, astrologers, physicians, surgeons, alchemists, sorcerers, explorers. What Black calls "the chaos of society,"[74] however, did not engender policy as an attempt to impose any sort of rational order. Rather, the point of authoritative "outputs" seems to have been an extension of the defusing of courtly intrigues: the prevention of social discontents and marginality that were potentially threatening to the security and isolation of the courtly domain. The increased permeation of society under Tudor rule aimed, above all, at prophylaxis: controlling vagabonds, dealing with food riots, limiting speculators, usurers, and drunkards. The Poor Law and the relentless pursuit of religious recusants are all of a piece in this effort. A valuable resource was now being hoarded—though not yet much used for additional gain.

The polity of interests.   When principality no longer needs to be preoccupied with usurpation, but has been institutionalized at least in accepted rules of succession, politics can turn outward for reasons other than prophylaxis. The primacy of a social domain above other domains and, even more, the "distancing" of courts from societies, inevitably lead to a conception of princely power and the social order (not "orderliness") as being somehow unrelated. The initial extroversion of the princely domain thus can hardly be concerned with such matters as engineering social harmony or just distribution. In introverted politics, these are matters for natural order or divine ordination. When politics turns outward from the court, then, the purpose initially is not so much to manage society as to exploit primacy as a resource: the gainful use of primacy by privilege. In the polity of interests, competition overshadows majesty. Though it in no sense in-

volves democratization, the arena of politics as competition becomes much
enlarged and structurally altered. It still takes place in the court, but now
also in institutions associated with the court (e.g., parliament) and, to a
degree, in society. Through the "outputs" sought by patrons and their
clients, the polity, as Durkheim would say, markedly "condenses." Royal
administrative and judicial institutions become a rather complex "machinery" government.

In England, such acquisitive exploitation of established primacy—and
through it the much enlarged penetration of society—is the essence of the
Georgian period.[75] One sees the scope of the eighteenth-century British
polity best in the activities of its local officials. The justices of the peace
were broadly charged with collecting and delivering revenues; assuring the
proper practice and flow of trade; looking after the poor, the food supply,
prices, and wages; licensing brewers and drinking houses; supervising gaols;
establishing asylums and confining lunatics; seeing to the lighting of streets,
their paving, policing, and cleaning. All this required at least an embryonic
differentiation of political labor—though bureaucratization had hardly yet
begun. There were now distinct judicial and administrative sessions, distinct highway and licensing councils, as well as individual specialists, like
road surveyors and constables. Late in the century, new statutory authorities, with special duties, appeared: for instance, turnpike trusts, corporations for administering relief to the poor, and, above all, a growing
number and variety of improvement commissions.[76]

This expansion of activities, and of organizations for performing them,
was not intended to manage society. The overriding trait of the Georgian
polity was that it was a marketplace of influence and spoils. The central
level did not really manage society, yet there was extraordinary jockeying
among parliamentarians and, as a result, ministerial instability. According
to Namier, men went into parliament partly out of a sort of "predestina-
tion" (men of "political families"), but even more as clients looking after
patrons' interests: as placemen and as purveyors and receivers of favors
(there was, says Namier, a "universal . . . plaguing of Ministers on behalf
of friends and relations");[77] to advance themselves in the military and
administrative services or reap rewards from service; to obtain contracts,
jobs, subscriptions, loans, and remittances. The Enclosure Acts and what
Beer calls "canal politics" epitomize this extraordinary politics of interests.

The politics of incorporation and of incumbency. When the domain of
politics is used chiefly for acquisitive purposes by privileged groups, other
groups will try to become incorporated into the game as players, rather
than be excluded from it as passive victims. As the stakes grow (that is,
the spoils increase) so, one may suppose, does the appetite for shares.

Certainly the pervasive theme of early modern (nineteenth-century) British politics is democratization. Tilly depicts the process as one in which excluded subjects first become "challengers," and then, through challenge, incorporated "members" of the polity:[78] voters and those eligible to hold office. The transformation of challenge into membership occurs because the challengers have resources of their own that can be effectively mobilized—if only strikes, violence, and the like.

As the polity's membership expands and thus becomes more diverse in interest, the political penetration of society necessarily grows rapidly in scope; when "civic inclusion" is virtually total, so is the politicization of social life—but not just in the sense of universal citizenship. Two other processes occur that rapidly transform social into political space. One is familiar: as new members are incorporated, the volume of political demands grows, and with it, the volume of outputs; with outputs, the network of committees, agencies, departments, boards to define and deliver them; and, with such organizations, their own demands: "withinputs," as David Easton calls them.

Perhaps this chain reaction sufficiently explains the rapid development of political society out of acquisitive politics. I would suggest, though, that a second process supplements the demand-response relation and perhaps is more consequential. It bears at least a vague resemblance to the Tudor preoccupation with political prophylaxis. To put it starkly: political primacy in the modern polity clearly is more than ever worth possessing and keeping in possession; however great the resources of princes before, they were puny compared to the fully realized monopoly over legitimate power. The theater of political struggle, though, is no longer confined to the small stage of the court; it comprises society as such. Thus, the modern counterpart of coping with conspiracy in order to retain control over the princely domain is either mass suppression or the search for mass support (plus the special support of the more powerful, better organized interests). Mass support is elicited, at least in part, by going *beyond* responsiveness: by "redistributive" policies that make large public groups into clients— collective placemen. The unparalleled scale both of repression in authoritarian modern polities and of the political provision of all sorts of goods in welfare states serves the maintenance of incumbency. No doubt welfare policies and other distributions of benefits result from good intentions; but surely, they also provide benefits, in the form of political support, for their providers. At any rate, here is a parsimonious explanation of the substantial consensus on social policy in the contemporary British welfare state. The politics of incorporation leads logically to that of incumbency.

"Political density" during these stages grows rapidly toward its maximal pole. The vastness of the business done by the machine of government requires, as Durkheim realized, more and more internal complexity of structure, in large part just for keeping things sorted and coordinated; it requires the development of a political "system,"[79] which is not at all the same as a machinery of government. Structures of political competition also become highly organized and institutionalized networks of organizations. In gist, the pomp of primal chiefliness virtually disappears within the systems and networks of the polity.[80]

Two important questions should be raised about the abstracted stages to determine whether they indeed constitute a general developmental sequence. First, do the stages occur, *mutatis mutandis,* in other longitudinal political processes, and do they furnish a good typology for the "cross-sectional" classification of polities in the present? If so, we can assert (in the manner of early exponents of the "comparative method"—Ferguson, Comte, Tylor, Morgan)[81] that typological differences among polities are basically developmental: namely, that there is history, not just histories. Second, would a schematic treatment of political functions, goals, and structures by stages indeed show qualitative distinctions in each class, along with the quantitative growth of the political domain? These questions cannot be treated briefly; they are posed here as items on an agenda to follow up this essay.

What Forces Move Polities from Stage to Stage?

In the preceding section, I have tried to show sequential connections between stages of political development: how the earlier stages are preconditions for those that follow, and how these, in turn, are latent in preceding stages. (An important, familiar issue for praxis—too large to be tackled here—is raised by the question whether stages can be skipped, without the occurrence of pathologies and without regression.) This demonstration, though, says nothing about the forces that propel polities from stage to stage. We need at least a summary answer to complete our sketch for a theory of political development.

In developmental theory, one wants, ideally, to identify a general motive force that operates throughout developmental time (akin to physical inertia) and also special forces, generated in each earlier stage, which similarly lead to each later stage.

The general motive force at work in the sequence of stages I have described is surely the drive for the direct and indirect benefits of "efficient" primacy in and over society—the direct benefit of social elevation and indirect perquisites, such as material goods. That drive characterizes most directly the transformation of primal, ceremonial polity. The maintenance of primacy for getting other values follows in the polity of interests and leads to the challenges that incorporate excluded groups in the domain of primacy. The possession of higher positions—primacy in the domain of primacy—animates political motion in the most advanced stage.

Although primacy seeking is the essence of the initial developmental transformation of polities, it is clear that struggles for establishing an "efficient" principal domain are only resolved when an urgent societal need for such resolution arises. In the West, that need arose from the differentiation of society into distinct but overlapping "corporations" in virtually continuous collision. One may surmise, more generally, that an initial locus of efficient primacy will emerge when it is functionally critical to social integration that this occur—that is, when the integrative force of "mechanical solidarity" no longer works. The theatrical chiefs are destined to win struggles to perform the integrative function and to reap its benefits.

If there is such a thing as "pure" power politics, it occurs when struggles for primacy have been resolved. Pure power politics is about possessing primacy, not about establishing it. Once the domain of the prince itself is safe, a different propulsive force emerges; we might call it resource conversion.[82]

The results of converting political into other goods now come to pose a quite different, but again functionally critical problem of integration: not of society but of the political domain itself, for the sake of its effective operation. The need for political integration has two facets. As new groups are incorporated into the polity, the plethora of interests and demands they generate must be coordinated: in Almond's terminology, a need exists to aggregate interests, so that demands may be effectively pressed and responded to. More important, as society is greatly politicized through processes of civic incorporation, the machinery of government grows into a complex system; as a result, efficient management of the system itself must increasingly become a sine qua non of political goals, even exploitative ones. Without efficient political management, social life itself is imperiled, precisely because the polity pervades it; and, without such management, power itself is a chimera. In this way, we can see in political development a diminution, if not a metamorphosis, of pure power politics—and still avoid the "fault" of tendermindedness.

Thus, while struggles for primacy propel politics throughout developmental time, at each stage they take different forms and are reinforced by special forces: forces of greed and, more important, forces generated by collective functional needs. These themes of politics—primacy seeking, power seeking, greed, and integration—are familiar. What are not familiar are the special roles they play at different stages of political development.

The process of political development moved by these forces is monotonic in two senses. I have stressed one—the politicization of society. The long trajectory from social polity to political society can also be considered a modulation from "dignity" to "efficiency" (the most fundamental qualitative social change conceivable), and each stage of the process can be treated as a changing balance between the two. In parallel, polities change structurally from personage to court, to machine, to system.

CONCLUSION

The idea of political development, then, seems to me capable of renovation along the lines sketched. What I have tried to present is a design along proper "developmental" lines. The design is, and must continue to be, far from a completed theoretical structure. But if it proves to have merit, it helps to answer the final question raised above. It has important implications precisely for the issue that a developmental theory should illuminate: the puzzle of our own modernity. I will mention one such implication for a critical problem in modern political life.

We have lately heard much about a crisis of authority in highly advanced societies. The evidence is overwhelming that there is at least a malaise about authority. Strangely, that malaise seems to exist concurrently with the progressive growth of what people supposedly (and no doubt actually) want authority to be: decent, down to earth, participant, lenient, concordant, open to achievement. Might not the solution of this riddle lie in the "disenchantment" of theatrical politics (which moves affections), by rationally effective but too-drab systems? After all, society and polity remain intangible mysteries; the social sciences are devoted to their understanding. They have become all the more mystifying as they have grown in scale, density, and differentiation. At the same time, dignity has waned in relation to efficiency. More and more, our representative figures are capable but plain, managers not princes: Fords, Carters, Wilsons, Heaths; in our families, schools, and workplaces, authority increasingly also has derogated rank. We want this, and it seems good; but can we live with it?

Perhaps that is what Weber saw when he forecast a political "polar night of icy darkness and hardness." Perhaps, too, the tension between the needs for what Weber called matter-of-factness and devotion is the force propelling us into the future of political time.

NOTES FOR CHAPTER 6

1. The salient exploratory works are Emerson, *From Empire to Nation* (Boston: Beacon Press, 1960), and Gabriel Almond and J. S. Coleman, eds., *The Politics of the Developing Areas* (Princeton: Princeton University Press, 1960). Among the pioneers, two others also stand out: K. W. Deutsch, "Social Mobilization and Political Development," *Political Science Review* 55 (1961): 493–514, and Lucian W. Pye, *Politics, Personality, and Nation Building* (New Haven: Yale University Press, 1962).

2. Samuel P. Huntington and Juan I. Domínguez, "Political Development,"

in *Handbook of Political Science,* ed. Fred I. Greenstein and Nelson W. Polsby (Reading, Mass.: Addison-Wesley, 1975), 3: 98–114.

3. The term decay is used in Huntington's sense, as an antonym to order. See Samuel P. Huntington, *Political Order in Changing Societies* (New Haven: Yale University Press, 1968), chap. 1. Earlier, Huntington had used decay as an antonym to development; see "Political Development and Political Decay," *World Politics* 17 (1965): 386–430.

4. Huntington and Domínguez, "Political Development," 3.

5. Ibid.

6. A prototype (ten definitions) is in Lucian W. Pye, *Aspects of Political Development* (Boston: Little, Brown, 1966), 33–45.

7. Gabriel A. Almond and G. Bingham Powell, *Comparative Politics: A Developmental Approach* (Boston: Little, Brown, 1966), 28–29, 190–212; A. F. R. Organski, *The Stages of Political Development* (New York: Knopf, 1965), 7.

8. Max Weber, "Politics as a Vocation," in *From Max Weber: Essays in Sociology,* trans. and ed. H. H. Gerth and C. Wright Mills (New York: Oxford University Press, 1946), 84–86.

9. Robert T. Holt and John E. Turner, *The Political Basis of Economic Development* (Princeton: Van Nostrand, 1966), 57–58.

10. Although Binder surely was right in writing that "it cannot be expected that Western scholars could wholly escape the influences of their own political cultures," there is no evidence at all for his views that this need not "eventuate in a narrow parochialism" or that a "general theory of political development" can "emerge from a specific history." Leonard Binder et al., *Crises and Sequences in Political Development* (Princeton: Princeton University Press, 1971), 67.

11. Clifford Geertz, *Negara: The Theatre-State in Nineteenth-Century Bali* (Princeton: Princeton University Press, 1980), 5.

12. The standard work on this subject—and, surprisingly, the only history of thought centered on conceptions of social time—is Robert A. Nisbet, *Social Change and History: Aspects of the Western Theory of Development* (New York: Oxford University Press, 1969). Nisbet's work treats at considerable length, and splendidly, what I discuss tersely in this section. His book can elucidate anything that seems obtuse here. I have drawn a great deal on his study, as anyone writing about social and political development must. I do differ from Nisbet in some respects, one of which is especially important. Nisbet holds that all Western thought is developmental. Different theoretical accounts of social change in history seem to him to be only variations on a continuing theme, already present in classic myth. I think this argument is forced and impedes understanding of the idea of development. Theories of social development, it seems to me, are more notable for their novelty than for anything they have in common with previous thought.

13. This, *pace* Nisbet, is a fundamental aspect of its novelty.

14. This much misunderstood concept is the foundation of the most profound attack on all moral and epistemological absolutes. Nevertheless, Durkheim is nothing if not a moral philosopher and a believer in verities. The paradox is resolved by Durkheim himself in the preface to his first masterpiece, *The Division of Labor in Society* (New York: Macmillan, 1933).

15. The subject of predevelopmental conceptions of social time, plus critical analysis of them, no doubt deserves a full essay, or—as in Nisbet—a considerable book.

16. I do not mean to say that noncontextual theorizing ceased in the nineteenth century. It has remained with us—during the nineteenth century chiefly in utilitarianism and its derivatives (including modern economics) and, not quite so clearly, in idealist thought.

17. See Mircea Eliade, *Cosmos and History: The Myth of the Eternal Return* (New York: Harper Torchbooks, 1954), chaps. 2 and 3.

18. Nisbet, *Social Change*, chap. 1.

19. The opposition thinking in terms of cycles and trajectories is used in Theodor Gomperz, *Greek Thinkers* (London: John Murray, 1901), 1: 141.

20. I agree here with J. B. Bury, contra Nisbet, that the Greeks had no (philosophic) idea of "progress." See *The Idea of Progress* (New York: Macmillan, 1932), 19.

21. St. Augustine, *The City of God* (New York: Random House, 1950), Book 10, 14.

22. The recognized *summa* on the subject is Bury's *Idea of Progress*.

23. Nisbet, *Social Change*, 105.

24. It should be noted that developmental theories fall into two fairly distinct subtypes. One comprises what we generally identify as social evolutionary theory. Comte, Spencer, and Morgan, among others, are members of the earlier species, not quite liberated from progress theory; note, for instance, Comte's vision of a "final" positive-industrial utopia. Nisbet calls the other subtype "neo-evolutionism" (*Social Change*, 223–239). It includes the thought of Ferdinand Toennies (in *Gemeinschaft und Gesellschaft*), Durkheim, Simmel, and Weber. One might simply call this species mature developmental thought—less simplistic, and with the tendentious faith in progressive betterment of the earlier species removed.

25. For distilling the general traits of developmental thought, Nisbet's treatment of the "premises" of socio-evolutionary theories in *Social Change* is invaluable (166–188). I draw on him—though not on his vocabulary—for reasons not necessary to spell out here.

26. Ibid., 166–167.

27. Harry Eckstein, "Theoretical Approaches to Explaining Collective Political Violence," in *Handbook of Political Conflict*, ed. Ted Gurr (New York: Free Press, 1980), 138–142.

28. Huntington is an exception; he goes back all the way to the Tudors. See his *Political Order*, 122–139.

29. Kurt Wolff, trans. and ed., *The Sociology of Georg Simmel* (Glencoe, Ill.: Free Press, 1950), 22.

30. Sir Henry Sumner Maine, *Ancient Law* (London: Murray, 1861).

31. Ferdinand Toennies, *Community and Society*, trans. Charles P. Loomis (New York: Harper Torchbooks, 1963), 231–232.

32. Durkheim, *Division of Labor*, 70–132.

33. Max Weber, *Economy and Society* (Berkeley: University of California Press, 1972), 1: 24–26, 215–220.

34. Huntington, *Political Order*, 148.

35. Daniel Lerner, *The Passing of Traditional Society* (New York: Free Press, 1958), esp. chap. 2 and pp. 85–89.

36. Durkheim, *Division of Labor*, 275–280.

37. Wolff, *Sociology of Georg Simmel*, 145–169.

38. Nisbet, *Social Change and History*, 162.

39. Durkheim, *Division of Labor*, 256ff.

40. Herbert Spencer, *Essays Scientific, Political, and Speculative* (New York: Appleton, 1891), 60.

41. This is said despite Condorcet. It seems to me that in the *Sketch* the notion of stages is simply a literary convenience.

42. I consider Clifford Geertz to be its outstanding present practitioner. See *The Interpretation of Cultures* (New York: Basic Books, 1973)—especially 3–30 (on "thick description") and 412–453 (on the social meaning of Balinese cockfights).

43. Auguste Comte, *The Positive Philosophy* (London: George Bell, 1896), 2: 229.

44. Emile Durkheim, *The Elementary Forms of the Religious Life* (Glencoe, Ill.: Free Press, 1947), 3.

45. Samuel H. Beer, *British Politics in the Collectivist Age* (New York: Knopf, 1962), 22–31.

46. D. L. Keir, *The Constitutional History of Modern Britain* (London: Adam & Charles Black, 1938), 292–320.

47. See, for instance, Lucy Mair, *Primitive Government* (Harmondsworth, Middlesex: Penguin Books, 1962), part 1—especially the chapter on "minimal government" (61–77).

48. See Gerth and Mills, *From Max Weber*, 82.

49. Ira Sharkansky, *Whither the State?* (Chatham, N.J.: Chatham House, 1979).

50. See, for example, Kenneth S. Templeton, Jr., ed., *The Politicization of Society* (Indianapolis: Liberty Press, 1979).

51. For a catalogue of such notions, see Harry Eckstein, "Authority Patterns: A Structural Basis for Political Inquiry," *American Political Science Review* 67 (1973): 1142.

52. These are Apter's terms; see David E. Apter, *The Politics of Modernization* (Chicago: University of Chicago Press, 1965), 24ff.

53. I do not use the term *symbolic* entirely as does Murray Edelman in *The Symbolic Uses of Politics* (Urbana: University of Illinois Press, 1964). Edelman considers political symbolism to be an aspect of political practices that "condenses" them (and thus evokes emotions) or provides simple "references" to complex facts (his example is accident statistics). At times, Edelman comes close to what I mean by symbolic politics: see, for instance, pp. 16–17. This is not to say that his use of the notion is wrong. It is different—much more diffuse.

54. I. Schapera, *Government and Politics in Tribal Societies* (London: Watts, 1956).

55. Ibid., chap. 4. Varying "powers" are associated with chiefliness (102ff.). I will refer to the most common below. But simply being chiefly is clearly the heart of the matter.

56. Mair, *Primitive Government*; and Lucy Mair, *African Kingdoms* (Oxford: Clarendon Press, 1977).

57. Mair, *Primitive Government*, 63, 69; Mair, *African Kingdoms*, 107–8.

58. R. H. Lowie, "Political Organization among American Aborigines," *Journal of the Royal Anthropological Institute* 78 (1948): 1–17.

59. Dating is difficult here, but a sensible time for looking at the Anglo-Saxon polity surely is circa 900 C.E. A sense of an English society had crystallized then out of the diverse identities of Teutonic tribal invaders and become personified in a single chief, Edward of Wessex. *Beowulf* remains the best primary source for understanding Anglo-Saxon life. See also J. E. A. Jolliffe, *Constitutional History of Medieval England* (Oxford: Oxford University Press, 1967), parts 1 and 2; Dorothy Whitelock, *The Beginning of English Society* (Harmondsworth, Middlesex: Penguin Books, 1952); and Sir Frank Stenton, *Anglo-Saxon England* (Oxford: Oxford University Press, 1943).

60. Geertz, *Negara*.

61. Ibid., 127, 135.

62. Ibid., 13. (Geertz's book appeared some months after I wrote the first draft of this paper for the NSF Conference on Economic and Political Development, Wayzata, Minnesota, October 1980.)

63. For example, ibid., 24.

64. See Mair, *Primitive Government*, 65, 66, 76; Mair, *African Kingdoms*, 39. Geertz, *Negara*, considers the link to the supernatural order the very basis of Negara; see 17–19, 104–5.

65. Schapera, *Government and Politics*, 211ff.

66. Geertz, *Negara*, 24.

67. See, for example, Daniel Biebuyck, *Hero and Chief* (Berkeley: University of California Press, 1978).

68. H. D. Traill, ed., *Social England* (New York: Putnam, 1894), 1: 134.

69. See Samuel H. Beer and Adam Ulam, eds., *Patterns of Government*, 2d ed. (New York: Random House, 1962), chap. 10.

70. Ibid., 235.

71. Ch. Petit-Dutaillis, *The Feudal Monarchy in England and France* (London: Adam & Charles Black, 1948), 128.

72. Ibid., 138.

73. Keir, *Constitutional History of Modern Britain*, 98.

74. J. B. Black, *The Reign of Elizabeth: 1558–1603* (Oxford: Clarendon, 1936), 217.

75. The great work on the Georgian polity is Sir Lewis Namier, *The Structure of Politics at the Accession of George III* (London: Macmillan, 1957); the standard history is J. Steven Watson, *The Reign of George III: 1750–1815* (Oxford: Clarendon, 1960); the best concise political perspective on the period is provided by Samuel H. Beer, *British Politics in the Collectivist Age* (New York: Knopf, 1965).

76. Keir, *Constitutional History of Modern Britain*, 312–316.

77. Namier, *Structure of Politics*, 76.

78. Charles Tilly, *From Mobilization to Revolution* (Reading, Mass.: Addison-Wesley, 1978).

79. I use "system" here in the manner of general and political systems theorists; the latter seem to me pertinent only—anyway chiefly—to modern polities. See, for instance, James G. Miller, "Living Systems: Basic Concepts," *Behavioral Science* 10 (1965): 193–237; David Easton, *A Systems Analysis of Political Life* (New York: Wiley, 1965).

80. The elevation of the leader in totalitarian polities can certainly be regarded as a reaction against the profound sobriety of typical modern political systems. It is, to be sure, more satanic than sacred. And surely the system uses the leader, perhaps more than vice versa.

81. Nisbet, *Social Change and History,* 189–208.

82. In the Lasswell-Kaplan terminology: turning political "base values" into other "scope values." See Harold D. Lasswell and Abraham Kaplan, *Power and Society* (New Haven: Yale University Press, 1950), 83–92.

SEVEN

A Culturalist Theory of Political Change

Author's Note: I stated in chapter 1 that I chose the culturalist perspective as a basis for theorizing for reasons, but not as a closed dogma. One of the reasons—not the only one or even the most important—was that its principal alternative among other perspectives, rational-choice theory, seemed a highly inadequate basis for explaining what I wanted to illuminate for myself: my piece, so to speak, of the German experience. Ironically, the most serious criticism of culturalist theory became that it could not be a basis for explaining political change at all, least of all for very rapid change—Germany after the Second World War was the favored case in point—though other rapid changes in Germany's political history since 1871, including the change from Weimar to the Nazi regime, were always conveniently left out of discussion.

In this essay I deal with the criticism that the culturalist perspective cannot cogently cope with change, by constructing a culturalist theory that covers every possible kind of political change. Readers will note that the theory can be used to explain both the disruptive change in Germany to Nazism and the emergence of an apparently stable political order in the Bonn Federal Republic (especially in connection with chapter 5)—but via general theory, not idiographic interpretation. The explanation may not be valid; much work still must be done before one can make that claim. The point, as stated, is only that it is distinctly possible to construct pertinent explanations of political changes on a culturalist basis.

The chapter also may be read with the sections of chapter 4 that deal with testing theories. It has always seemed to me incumbent on theorists

Originally published in *The American Political Science Review* vol 82 (1988): 789–804. Reprinted by permission. Copyright © 1988 by the American Political Science Association.

to specify predictively, prior to observation, what data should and should not turn up if hypotheses are to be considered falsified or validated. In physical theories that method is generally evident to everyone, but often for technical reasons before the observations required are possible. One valid, logically deduced prediction of an unknown is worth a myriad post hoc explanations, however clever. Consequently, this chapter states both what sort of political changes the culturalist perspective can and cannot accommodate.

The political culture approach to building positive political theories and to political explanation has been with us since about 1960 and has been much described abstractly and much applied to concrete cases. The seminal works are Almond and Coleman's and Almond and Verba's.[1] Applications of the approach are covered comprehensively in a retrospective on the influence of their work by Almond and Verba.[2] Explications of it as a contender for paradigmatic status in political science, so to speak, occur in numerous works.[3] My own use of the concept of culture, which I consider more precise than that of others, is discussed in the Appendix.

Political culture theory may plausibly be considered one of two still viable general approaches to political theory and explanation proposed since the early fifties to replace the long-dominant formal-legalism of the field—the other was political rational-choice theory. Indeed, determining which of the two modes of theorizing and explaining—the "culturalist" or the "rationalist"—is likely to give the better results may be the single most important item now on the agenda of political science.[4]

Whether or not it is advisable to take the culturalist road to theory depends above all on the ability to produce a cogent culturalist theory of political change: a theory consistent with the assumptions (postulates) of the approach and confirmed by experience. Criticisms of culturalist political theories certainly have emphasized the occurrence of certain changes in political structures, attitudes, and behavior and culturalist accounts of their occurrence in order to impugn the approach. Rogowski,[5] for example, has argued that political culturalists have been very offhand in dealing with change—that they have tended to improvise far too much in order to accommodate political changes into their framework. They have done so, he writes, to the point that they no longer have a convincing way to treat political change at all. His argument is directed at culturalist theory in general, but he singles out Almond's work with Powell as especially indicative of the sins that culturalists commit.[6]

This argument—and others to similar effect—strikes me as cogent criticism of how culturalists have in fact dealt with political changes. Furthermore, difficulties accounting for change in general and for certain kinds of change especially seem to me inherent in the assumptions on which the political culture approach is based.

Difficult, however, does not mean impossible or implausible. It is quite possible to deduce from these assumptions a logically cogent account of how political change, and every kind of such change, occurs. My purpose here is to provide such an account, as remedy for the "ad hocery" that Rogowski rightly criticizes.

THE POSTULATES OF CULTURALIST THEORIES
AND THE EXPECTATION OF CONTINUITY

The basic reason why a culturalist account of change is intrinsically difficult to construct (hence, why culturalists have in fact tended to waffle in explaining political change) is simple: the postulates of the approach all lead to the expectation of political continuity; they make political continuity the "normal" state.

The Postulates of Culturalism

To see why this is so we must first make explicit the fundamental assumptions from which culturalist theory proceeds—its "axiomatic" basis, so to speak. These assumptions unfortunately have been left implicit in culturalist writings. It is necessary to make them explicit if one is compellingly to specify what experiences are "normal" in a culturalist world and what conditions culturalist theory can and cannot accommodate.

The touchstone of culturalist theory is the *postulate of oriented action:* actors do not respond directly to "situations" but respond to them through mediating "orientations." All else either elaborates or follows from that postulate. What exactly, then, does the postulate assert?

"Orientations to action" are general dispositions of actors to act in certain ways in sets of situations. Such general dispositions pattern actions. If actors do not have them, or if orientations are ill formed or inconsistent, actions will be erratic: patternless, anomic. The idea of "orientations to action" follows a particular psychological stimulus-response model: not the simple "single-stage" behaviorist model in which nothing "subjective" intervenes between the experience of situations and responses to it (actions) but "mediational" models in which responses to stimuli (actions in situations) are considered results both of the experience of objective situations and actors' subjective processing of experience. "Orientations" do the processing. We may call them, as did Bentley, soul-stuff or mind-stuff. The critical methodological task of studies based on such models is, of course, to penetrate reliably and with validity into the subjective.

Orientations are not "attitudes": the latter are specific, the former general, dispositions. Attitudes themselves derive from and express orientations; though attitudes may, through their patterning, help us to find orientations. If orientations frequently occur in collectivities they may be called "culture themes," as by Mead and Metraux.[7] Pye has distinguished four sets of such "themes" that he considers useful for making cultural comparisons on the societal level: trust-distrust, hierarchy-equality, liberty-coercion, parochial-national identifications. Putnam considers the theme of conflict or its counterpart, harmony, critical for cross-cultural analysis.[8] These themes exemplify how orientations are general dispositions that pattern sets of actions and sets of specific attitudes. It is conventional to regard orientations as having three components: cognitive elements that, so to speak, decode experience (give it meaning); affective elements that invest cognition with feelings that move actors to act; and evaluative elements that provide goals toward which actors are moved to act.[9]

The assumption of oriented actions would be vacuous without the addition of a second postulate, which we might call *the postulate of orientational variability:* orientations vary and are not mere subjective reflections of objective conditions. The significance of this postulate lies particularly in this: if the processing of experiences into actions were uniform—if it were fixed at the biological level or if it always involved "rationalist" cost-benefit calculation—then mediating mind-stuff could simply be left out of theory. In Hempel's terms, we would only need to know "initial conditions" (situations, structures) to explain actions, since we already know the universal covering law needed to complete an *explanandum.* No doubt ingenuity is required in relating conditions to actions via uniform orientations: the rational choice theories we have provide more than enough cases in point. But this does not alter the logic of the argument that without orientational variability we remain in a strictly behaviorist world. Similarly, if actions are merely "superstructural," we manifestly need only to know situations to explain actions. In that case, only the explanation of deviant cases (like false class consciousness) would require the use of mediating variables.

If orientations are not inherent in actors but variable, then something that is variable must form them. And if orientations are not simply subjective reflections of varying objective situations, then the variable conditions through which they are formed must themselves be cultural. Orientations are not acquired in some automatic way; they must be learned. Thus, a *postulate of cultural socialization* must hold if the first and second assumptions hold: orientations are learned through the agency of external "socializers." The repertoire of cognitions, feelings, and schemes of evaluation that process experience into action must be imparted by the socialized carriers of culture. The process can be direct, by "teachers" who are culturally variable actors; or it can occur indirectly simply through the experience of variable cultures.

"Rationalist" theorists do not, of course, reject the notion of political socialization. That would be silly. What divides culturalist and rationalist theorists here involves the issue of late-in-life learning, or resocialization.

In regard to that matter, culturalists proceed from a *postulate of "cumulative" socialization*. This means two things. First, although learning is regarded as continuous throughout life (which is not likely to be questioned) early learning—all prior learning—is regarded as a sort of filter for later learning: early learning conditions later learning and is harder to undo. Second, a tendency is assumed toward making the bits and pieces of cognitive, affective, and evaluative learning form a coherent (consistent, consonant) whole.

The postulate of cumulative learning provides the culturalist account of how two fundamental needs of actors in societies are satisfied: the need for economy of action and the need for predictability in interaction. Life would hardly be bearable, even possible, if one had to think out every action, taking into account all pertinent information and lack of information. Orientational schemata thus save virtually all decision costs. Social life, similarly, would hardly be possible without reliable preknowledge of others' actions and of the effect of one's own actions on those of others. Without such preknowledge social life would tend to be entropic. As Crozier has cogently argued, "uncertainty" of action also begets power—arbitrary power.[10]

Both economy of action and predictability in interaction are diminished to the extent that individual orientations are inconsistent and that early learning may readily be undone. These conditions have effects similar to a lack of orientations to actions and of socially shared orientations altogether. They lead to erratic, incoherent behavior by individuals and in social aggregates: anomie in the former; the absence of anything like a stable *conscience collective* in the latter.

It should be pointed out that the culturalist solution of the problems of economy of action and social predictability is not a unique solution, however plausible it may seem. Thus, in the rationalist perspective, economy of action is provided by "ideologies" or by the sensible delegation of decision-making powers.[11] The fixity required for predictability in social life follows from the very fact that rational choice is considered a fixed disposition. If this is so, one can anticipate the actions of others and adjust one's own behavior to the anticipation. Social predictability may also be achieved through rationally formulated and enforced contractual arrangements or general legal rules. (It should be apparent that the two accounts of economy of action and social predictability provide a good basis for evaluating the relative power of culturalist and rationalist perspectives.)

To summarize: "Cultural" people process experience into action through general cognitive, affective, and evaluative predispositions; the patterns of such predispositions vary from society to society, from social segment to social segment; they do not vary because objective social situations or structures vary but because of culturally determined learning; early learning conditions later learning and learning involves a process of seeking coherence in dispositions. And this is so in order to "economize" in decisions to act and to achieve predictability in social interactions.

The Expectation of Continuity

When the postulates of the political culture approach are made explicit, it should be evident why political culture theorists *should* have difficulties in accounting for political change. The assumptions of culturalist theory manifestly lead to an expectation of continuity, even in cases of changes in the objective contexts of political actions.

The expectation of continuity in aggregate (and individual) orientations follows most plainly from the assumption that orientations are not superstructural reflections of objective structures, but that they themselves invest structures and behavior with cognitive and normative meaning.

Cultural continuity also manifestly follows from the assumption that orientations are formed through processes of socialization. To the extent that socialization is direct (by precept), generational continuity must occur, the socializers being formed, "cultural" people. To the extent that socialization is indirect (by experience), generational continuity still follows; experience with authority occurs first in the family, then in schools, where unformed children encounter formed adults. In either case, what is true of one generation should continue substantially to be true in the next. This applies as much to cultural divisions in a society as to more general culture types and themes—if any exist in the first place. This, incidentally, makes the political culture perspective quite compatible with the finding that political regimes typically are short-lived.[12]

The expectation of continuity in political cultures follows, most obviously, from the assumption of orientational cumulativeness, namely, that earlier learning conditions later learning and that actors tend to seek orientational consonance. The first allows some room for adult socialization and resocialization—but not much. The second makes unlikely the internalization of piecemeal orientational change that might increase dissonance.

But if change in culture patterns and themes are categorically excluded, political culture theory must immediately be thrown out as obvious nonsense: changes happen, including cultural changes. The saving grace of culturalist theory here is that continuity is, so to speak, an ideal-typical expectation—one that holds in an *abstract,* parsimonious cultural world. It is an expectation akin to that of inertia in the Galilean conception of motion. Physical inertia does not rule out changes of direction or rest, acceleration, and deceleration. It does make such phenomena depend on contingent factors that may or may not impinge on objects in motion. Continuity is the inherent (lawful) expectation and so, therefore, is resistance to change of motion: exceptionally great forces are needed to induce great changes in direction or velocity. The notion of continuity as inertia in motivations (the psychological counterpart of physical motion) thus opens the door to culturalist accounts of change.

Through that door, however, the tendency toward improvised, post hoc accounts of political change may enter—may be bound to enter. If one's preferred theoretical approach implies a strong bias toward the continuity of culture or resistance to cultural change, then it is always tempting to extemporize theory-saving "special" conditions, or adjustments in concepts or theory to handle occurrences of change—especially major change. If, say, theoretical difficulties arise from emphasizing early socialization, then why not just relax that emphasis and assign more scope for late socialization or adult resocialization? If the assumption of a tendency toward orientational consonance makes it awkward to explain certain observations, then why not simply posit more toleration for dissonance? Or why not redefine consonance? In that way, however, one is likely to end with the term *continuity* meaning nothing more than "not completely (or instantaneously) changeable"—which drains the term of all reasonable meaning. This is exactly the point of Rogowski's criticism of how culturalists have in fact accounted for political change.

The remedy is to develop an explicit general culturalist theory of change, consistent with culturalist assumptions, in order to prevent ad hoc tinkering with culturalist postulates and their implications. Such a theory should state, prior to explanations of specific changes, the characteristics of change that the political culture approach can logically accommodate and those that do not fit its constraints.

To formulate such a theory, I will consider two broad types of cultural changes: those arising "naturally" from changes in situations and structural conditions and those that result from "artifice"—deliberate attempts to transform political structures and behavior.

SITUATIONAL CHANGE

Pattern-Maintaining Change

Actors must often face novel situations with which their dispositional equipment is ill suited to deal. The world changes or presents us with experiences that are unfamiliar for other reasons (e.g., the penetration of peasant societies by market forces). The unfamiliar is encountered routinely in maturation, as one proceeds from family to school, from lower schools to higher ones, and from schools to participation in adult institutions. At the level of society and polity, novel situations arise from internal "development," however development may be conceived. Novel situations also arise from socially internal discontinuities (economic crises or political disruptions, like those caused by governmental instability or collapse, or from changes brought about by protest movements), or from externally imposed changes. Immigration brings actors into unfamiliar situations. So does internal migration and social mobility. The encounter of novel situations will, no doubt, occur much more frequently among individuals than on the macrolevel, but it also occurs in groups and societies.

Novel situations may be short-lived results of ephemeral upheavals. In that case no cultural adjustments are needed, nor are they likely to occur. What, however, should one expect if such situations persist?

If cultures exhibit inertia, then it should be expected that changes in culture patterns and themes will occur so as to maintain optimally such patterns and themes; that is to say, changes in culture are perfectly consistent with culturalist postulates if they occur as adaptations to altered structures and situations and if the function of change is to keep culture patterns in existence and consonant. "Pattern maintenance" (Parsons's concept) can take that form just as well as strict cultural continuity.

The French have a half-facetious adage for this sort of pattern maintenance: the more things change, the more they remain the same. The saying no doubt fits (used to fit?) France. The pragmatic masters at pattern-maintaining change, however, have been the British. Tory concessions to British working-class voters and interests are the usual case in point. Their function—sometimes "latent" but in the case of Disraeli's Tory democracy quite explicit—was to maintain Tory hegemony in the face of considerable sociopolitical change through the maintenance of as much as possible of what the Young England Circle considered the feudalistic virtues: the disposition to defer to one's betters and action by the betters on behalf of the lower orders. The point applies to reforms of the suffrage and also to the less well-known role of the Tories in the evolution of the British welfare state, which Tory governments not only have kept virtually intact but also much of which they pioneered.

An alternative to pattern-maintaining change is to subject unfamiliar experience to procrustean interpretation in order to obviate cognitive or normative change. "Perceptual distortion" has turned up frequently in experiments on how individual cognitive dissonance is handled. We know at least a little about the same way of dealing with the unfamiliar on the political macrolevel. To give just one example: party political elections in Northern Nigeria were initially regarded as a version of long-familiar elections to chieftaincy, in which the "candidates" were a small number of ascriptively defined eligibles.[13] The extent to which perceptual distortion can be adaptive to unfamiliar experience no doubt is highly limited. However, where institutions like elections to chieftaincy exist in traditional cultures, the adaptation of dispositions to other kinds of elections should be easier than in other cases.

Change Toward Flexibility

Highly modern societies have traits that make it especially likely that actors and aggregates of actors will frequently confront novel situations. Social mobility, vertical and horizontal, is the most obvious cause. Because any changes in dispositions are costly (dysfunctional) in the culturalist perspective, one should expect, as a correlate to the expectation of pattern-maintaining cultural change, that the more modern societies are, the more the elements of their cultures will be general, thus flexible. No doubt there are considerable limits upon how general and flexible orientations can be and still perform their functions of making experience meaningful, actions economical, and interactions predictable. In more modern societies one should not expect culture to change as readily as situations and structures. Situational and structural change tend to occur with great frequency and rapidity in modern societies, and the assumption of orientational inertia postulates resistance to frequent, swift reorientation. Rather one should expect that the rigidity of cultural prescription will relax, so that culture can accommodate much social fluidity.

The tendency toward cultural flexibility can itself be regarded as a way to maintain cultural patterns and themes. As societies become more changeable, the elements of culture increasingly become "forms" that can subsume a variety of "contents." It is probably no coincidence that some sociologists early in the twentieth century (especially Simmel)[14] adapted the Kantian distinction between form and content to social analysis. Durkheim argued much the same point directly. In early societies, he wrote, "the collective environment is essentially concrete . . . [and] the states of conscience then have the same character." ("Culture" is not a bad translation of his notion of a *conscience collective*.) As societies develop, the "common conscience" is obliged to rise above diversity and "consequently to become more abstract. . . . General ideas necessarily appear and become dominant."[15]

I want to make three other points pertinent to the expectation that cultural abstractness and flexibility will grow with social development. First, the disposition to act "rationally" introduces just the kind of general and flexible culture trait that inherent social fluidity requires. (Durkheim already associated rational attitudes and behavior with the abstractness of thought necessary in highly developed societies.)[16] The rationalization of modern life—which Weber considered to be its governing trait—thus may be an accommodation to structural conditions rather than, contra Weber, their underlying cause.

Second, the obviously difficult problem of finding a proper trade-off between two warring imperatives in modern societies, that of cultural flexibility and that of cultural fixity, is bound to be a practical difficulty, not just a theoretical one. Reconciling fixity with flexibility, abstractness, and formality may be a crucial element in what has widely been perceived as growing malaise in highly modern societies. Anomie will follow not only from lack of internal guides to action but from guidelines too general and loose to serve in the relentless particularity of experience. Highly modern society thus may be intrinsically acultural and, for that reason, transitory or susceptible to surrogates for culture—including cults and dogmas.

The expectation of cultural flexibility, finally, should apply to *all* highly modern societies. It thus pertains to polities initially based on rigid dogma (like communist societies) that have successfully pursued modernization. In such societies, the first expectation, that of cultural inertia, should hold. Old culture should resist new dogma. The expectation of pattern-maintaining change (or perceptual distortion) should hold as well. So one should expect also that as culture changes in such societies, it will change toward greater flexibility—and therefore to reinterpretations of dogma that make it increasingly pliable.

Cultural Discontinuity

Contextual changes can be so considerable or rapid or both that neither pattern-maintaining changes nor changes that gradually relax cultural rigidity to deal with social fluidity are possible. Rapid industrialization is the case in point usually cited. Changes resulting from war or from the formation of new polities also generally involve upheavals in social contexts. Such upheavals may result as well from economic traumas like the great inflation of 1923 in Germany (which led to far greater social disruption than the Great Depression—or possibly even the Black Death). And traumatic change sometimes strikes special segments of society rather than the whole.

We must deal, therefore, with social discontinuity, as well as "normal" change. Culturalists have tended either to avoid the matter or, worse, to treat cases of social trauma simply as "deviant cases" in which the theoretical constraints of their perspective are off—not least, the expectation of cultural inertia.

Obviously, traumatic social discontinuity will have cultural consequences different from contextual stability or less rapid, less pervasive change. Even in such cases, however, we may not simply improvise. If the assumptions of culturalists are correct, then traumatic social discontinuity should have logically expectable consequences, no less than other change.

The one consequence of social trauma absolutely precluded by culturalist assumptions is rapid reorientation. Social upheaval may overcome cultural inertia, but if so, actors should be plunged into a collective infancy in which cognitions that make experience intelligible and normative dispositions (affect, evaluative schemes) must be learned again, and learned cumulatively. No culturalist may expect, for instance, a democratic political culture to form, in a few short years, in a society like Germany after World War II, or "national" orientations to form rapidly in postcolonial tribal societies. Instead, changes in political cultures that occur in response to social discontinuity should initially exhibit considerable formlessness. For *formlessness* one may substitute other terms, like Durkheim's *anomie* or Merton's *deinstitutionalization*. The essence of the matter is that culture loses coherent structure. It becomes highly entropic.

The idea that rapid, large-scale contextual changes are personally disorienting and culturally disruptive is hardly new. Lipset argued a generation ago that rapid economic development is associated with political extremism ("anomic protest movements" like anarchism and syndicalism),[17] despite the fact that high levels of such development are related to political stability. Huntington later made much the same point,[18] and Olson has probably developed it most cogently.[19]

To say that formlessness under conditions of socioeconomic discontinuity should be "considerable" is not mere hedging. Cultural entropy can never be complete. If it were, no patterned action or interactions would be possible at all. In any case, social discontinuity never is total—intimate social units, like the family, survive the greatest upheavals (may, indeed, be strengthened by them, as refuges of predictable order); so too do structures that are supposedly merely instrumental—for example, bureaucracies. As well, if learning is cumulative, older people should exhibit a good deal of orientational inertia even when traumatic socioeconomic change occurs. We may surely suppose that the more ingrained orientations are and the more they are consonant systems, the less susceptible they are to "disorientation"—the more mechanisms like perceptive distortion will be used to invest experience with accustomed meaning.

Governmental authority will, of course, survive cultural discontinuity. In fact, it is likely to become more powerful to the extent that internalized dispositions cannot govern actions and interactions. How then do people act politically if political culture is highly formless?

We can get useful clues to answers from the growing literature on an analogous experience: how children adapt to novel situations that they enter in highly discontinuous ways: going to school, for instance, or going from one to another type or level of schooling. Much of the literature on this subject, like studies by Wakeford and Woods,[20] has been informed by Merton's path-breaking study of the bases of deviant behavior, which dealt in general terms with behavior under more or less "anomic" conditions.[21]

Under conditions of cultural discontinuity, conformity with authority is still likely to occur, but it will tend to have certain characteristics. In Merton's terminology, it will tend to be *ritualistic* or else *self-serving* (opportunistic and of dubious morality, as general culture defines morality). Ritual conformity is compliance without commitment. One does what the rules or rulers prescribe, not for any discernible reason but (quoting from a lower-class British pupil interviewed by Woods) "because I behave meself . . . I just do what I'm told . . . [I] ain't got much choice." Conformity of this sort may be supposed to occur frequently in cases in which the former political cultures and subcultures prescribed high compliance ("subject cultures," as Almond and Verba called them). Self-serving, opportunistic conformity bends norms and rules for private advantage—including that of getting ahead in the competition for political power. Charles Dickens observed a lot of that sort of behavior in his travels in America as he reports them in his *American Notes*. Thus, in regard to a very successful businessman, " 'He is a public nuisance, is he not?' 'Yes sir.' . . . 'And he is utterly dishonest, debased, and profligate?' 'Yes, sir.' 'In the name of wonder, then, what is his merit?' 'Well, sir, he is a smart man.' "[22] I mention Dickens because one should especially expect "smart" conformity in immigrant societies or immigrant segments of society, where (as in schools) discontinuity occurs through movement into an unfamiliar but intact culture. Perhaps one should expect it even more in cultures greatly unsettled by upheaval. Thus, Burke presciently remarked (in 1790) that when cultural constraints are off, "the worst rise to the top."[23]

More commonly than conformity, one should expect what Merton called *retreatism* under conditions of cultural discontinuity. Retreatism involves withdrawing from the "alien" larger society into the smaller, more familiar worlds of family, neighborhood, village, and the like. In Almond and Verba's scheme of concepts, it should show up as increased "parochialism." In the small worlds of schools, retreatism tends to involve self-imposed isolation—for instance, into remote places and daydreams or what Woods calls removal activities—"unserious pursuits which are sufficiently engrossing . . . [to make participants] oblivious for the time being of [their] actual situation"—or both.

Rebellion against, and intransigent resistance to, authority are also likely responses to the experience of cultural decay. A voluminous literature links social, economic, and political discontinuities to political violence—from Marx to Moore and Skocpol. Rebellion and intransigence, however, are always likely to be costly and call for much energy; retreatist behavior into parochial worlds or ritualistic conformity are thus more likely, especially where governing power—if not authority—is strong.

What should follow over time from contextual and cultural discontinuity? If economy of action and predictability indeed are imperatives in individual and collective life, one should expect new culture patterns and themes to emerge. But if dispositions are formed by cumulative learning, they should emerge only slowly (over generations) and, in the transitional period, at great costs resulting from raw power, withdrawal, and (because of withdrawal) forced mobilization and rebelliousness against it. Thus, the process of reformation of political cultures should be prolonged and socially costly. This is all the more likely to be the case if parochial units remain intact refuges from discontinuities in society, economy, or polity.

The expectation is logical also if older people, as is likely, cling to long-fixed dispositions even in the face of strong forces that might unsettle inertia. We might thus posit as a general expectation that in the process of cultural reformation considerable age-related differences should occur. In fact, age, in cases of pronounced discontinuity, might even be expected to be a major basis for subcultural differentiation. If indeed this were found to be so, the cultural perspective on theory would be enormously strengthened over alternatives. Empirical work pertinent to the expectation, however, is lacking; and as culturalists have built adult learning increasingly into their approach in order to accommodate ill-fitting facts, the incentive to inquire into age-related cultural differences, in both established and transitional contexts, has regrettably declined.

I want to make another point about the reformation of dispositions and culture patterns, more briefly. As the young should be more susceptible to reorientation than the old, so one should expect to find in social macrostructures particular segments that have traits especially conducive or susceptible to reorientation. By "conducive traits" I mean structural or dispositional traits readily accommodated to new culture patterns or, indeed, anticipations of them. In Western traditional societies, for instance, there always existed a large island of achievement in a sea of ascription—the celibate clergy, which hardly could be ascriptively recruited. The clergy, in fact, played a considerable role in the emergence of modern political institutions—despite their stake in the distribution of traditional privileges. Similarly, socially "marginal" groups—groups that occupy the fluid interstices of established cultures—should be highly susceptible to reorientation, thus "vanguards" in the reorienting of unsettled societies. There is a good deal of literature making the case that this is indeed so.[24]

POLITICAL TRANSFORMATION

By *transformation* I mean the use of political power and artifice to engineer radically changed social and political structures, thus culture patterns and themes: to set society and polity on new courses toward unprecedented objectives. Transformation, typically, is the objective of modern revolutions. It can also be the objective of military conquerors and of nation builders or other modernizers. Revolutions, however, provide the most unambiguous and dramatic cases. I will therefore confine my remarks to them—though what is said about them should also apply to transformation attempted in other ways.

Hannah Arendt undoubtedly was right in arguing that attempts at revolutionary transformation are distinctively modern[25]—that revolutions as we think of them (not mere rebellious attacks on authorities or their actions) begin with the French and American revolutions. As long as political and social structures were considered divinely ordained, or natural, or simply the ways of a folk, the idea of their deliberate transformation hardly could occur. "History" then could only be endless repetition or an intrinsic progress toward a preordained end. Societies and polities could no more be transformed than the heavenly bodies set upon new orbits. One of the decisive traits of modern societies then is the belief that a "new beginning"—a felicitous and not redundant expression—could be made in political and social life.

Initially, making a new beginning did not seem to call for much artifice—no more, perhaps, than a proper constitution. Achieving liberty or equality throughout society simply called for setting polities and societies on their inherently right course—right, given human nature. For reasons not necessary to sketch in the age of the "God that failed," really making revolution—not seizing power but the accomplishment of transformation—came increasingly to be seen as a task, and a difficult task, for political artificers. Unfortunately, systematic studies of that process are few, although the exceptions often have been notable: for instance, Massell's study of Soviet attempts to bring Soviet Central Asia into modernity,[26] and Kelley and Klein's study of the effects on inequality of the Bolivian Revolution of 1951.[27] Inquirers into revolution still are hooked on the issue of their etiology.

Since revolutions are themselves major discontinuities and since they generally occur in periods of social or political upheavals, not least governmental breakdown,[28] the expectations listed in the preceding section should apply to transformation. But I want to state here some expectations that follow from the culturalist perspective especially for processes of revolutionary transformation. Intrinsic interest and contemporary relevance aside, these processes seem to me especially critical for evaluating cultur-alist theories and their bases. After all, transformative processes involve not only adjustment to necessity but also the deliberate engineering of great change, and they are typically backed by great power and control.

As a first expectation we may posit that revolutionary transformation is strictly impossible in the short run. Revolutions certainly bring upheaval. They may also be expected to bring about movement in the direction of their professed goals by readily accomplished actions—instituting wide suf-frage, kicking out the landlords and redistributing land, ending feudal privileges and obligations, and the like. But if discontinuity begets "form-lessness" of culture, then revolutionaries can hardly do much to reorient people in the short run (say, in a generation or so). Reorientation is, of course, the less likely the more intact is the prerevolutionary culture: the more it provides parochial refuges from transformative power or insti-tutional centers of resistance to it. But even if revolution only reflects discontinuity instead of engendering it, the expectation stated still should hold.

If the conventional norms and practices of political life are disrupted by revolution, what can be put in their place? We may posit the answer that revolutionary transformation will initially be attempted by despotic or legalistic means. What, after all, could "order" societies and polities in place of conventional, internalized culture? Only brute power, or else the use of external legal prescriptions as a surrogate for internal orientational guides to behavior. "Revolutionary legalism" was in fact a device used early after the Bolshevik seizure of power, and it overlapped a good deal (even before Stalin) with attempts to "storm" society (especially its more backward parts) with head-on "administrative assault." Neither, according to Massell, accomplished much toward the realization of transformation; responses to it, he writes, included "avoidance," "selective participation," "evasion," "limited retribution," and "massive backlash."

"Legalism," it might be noted here, is likely to be a general response to massive cultural disruption, whether revolutionary or situational or both. Indeed, it can become, in highly unusual cases, a persistent surrogate for normative culture—indeed, a culture form. I have argued this else-where,[29] defining "legalist" cultures as cultures in which legal rules are widely known, such rules are widely used (instead of justice or prudence) to justify political standpoints or decisions, legal actions are the normal mode of dealing with conflicts and disputes, and therefore laws deal in highly detailed—if possible, comprehensive—ways with social interaction and tend to be punctiliously adhered to. Durkheim argued the even more general, related proposition that in the course of development civil law (which regulates social interactions) constantly grows, while criminal, or restitutive, law declines.[30] His argument makes sense if indeed development loosens normative cultural prescription, as I argued, and lessens cultural similitude, as Durkheim argues.

The case I used to make this argument is contemporary West Germany. That, we should note, also is the case Rogowski mainly relies on to argue that reorientation *can* occur rapidly—the crucial point in his critique of culturalist theory.[31] Rogowski seems to me to miss the real import of "deviant cases"—that through their very abnormal characteristics they can be used to shed light upon the factors that condition typical cases.

What of the long-run prospects of revolutionary transformation? I suggest the expectation that the long-run effects of attempted revolutionary transformation will diverge considerably from revolutionary intentions and resemble more the prerevolutionary condition of society. The expectation is not that little change in "content" will occur: in who holds power, gets privilege, and so on. No inevitable Thermidorean Reaction is posited. The argument is somewhat less categorical: reconstructed culture patterns and themes will diverge widely from revolutionary visions and will tend to diverge from them in the direction of the patterns of the old society and regime. The degree to which the expectation holds obviously depends on the extent to which the old culture was already in disarray.

Several points made earlier lead to this expectation. Culture must still be learned on a comprehensive scale, as in all societies; and although revolutionary teaching can no doubt play a considerable role in shaping the young, it can hardly replace socialization in small parochial units. Nor are teachers or role models likely to be, extensively, the sort of marginal individuals who are steeped in revolutionary dogma as a surrogate for convention—or people for whom the revolutionary vision has much meaning at all. Sheer cultural inertia will also play a role in the process of revolutionary decay; so will the tendency toward turning change into pattern maintenance—perhaps by a progressive transformation of revolutionary visions into mere revolutionary rhetoric; so—to the extent that the new rulers succeed in modernizing—will the tendency of modern cultures to be general, abstract, and (especially pertinent here) flexible; so will "retreatist" and "ritualist" responses to discontinuity; and so will the tendency of opportunistic conformists to get ahead, by scheming or approval, in unfamiliar contexts.

In fact, it may well be the case that the short-run effects of attempted transformation are greater than the longer-run effects. More can be done in upheaval than when life again acquires fixity. Kelley and Klein have argued precisely this point, on the basis of generalizing the case of the Bolivian Revolution of 1951.[32]

Whether all this also entails the expectation that in the longer run incremental change will accomplish more than attempts at radical transformation we can perhaps leave an open question here. But note that the rulers of the Soviet Union came increasingly to view the achievement of cultural change as a matter for what they called "systematic social engineering" for—as Massell describes it—"a pragmatic commitment to relatively patient and systematic social action, wherein at least as much time and effort would be devoted to the building of bridges to traditional society . . . as to actual and direct confrontation with the traditional system."

CONCLUSION

It may well be the case that the political culture approach has been used to explain political changes in the sort of ad hoc and post hoc manner that saves—and thus weakens—theories rather than testing and strengthening them. Culturalists hardly have a monopoly on such theoretical legerdemain—certainly not when compared to rational choice theorists—when discomfiting facts confront them. But I have tried to show here that culturalists must have a strong propensity toward improvised theory saving when dealing with political change, since their assumptions lead, necessarily, to an expectation of cultural continuity—at any rate in a "pure" (abstract, ideal-typical) cultural world, where all matters falling under "ceteris paribus" are in fact "equal."

Nevertheless, it should be evident that a cogent, potentially powerful theory of political change can be derived from culturalist premises. The theory sketched here specifies that changes in dispositions, in response to contextual changes, should be pattern-maintaining changes or—if the contextual changes involve modernization—changes toward normative generality and flexibility; that in response to abrupt social discontinuities cultural dispositions should, for a considerable period, be "formless"— incoherent in individuals and fragmented in aggregates; that in such cases retreating into intact parochial structures occurs, while conformity should become ritualistic or opportunistic; that revolutionary artifice cannot accomplish cultural transformation in the short run; that such transformation will be attempted by despotic power or (mainly hopeful) legal prescriptions; and that, in the longer run, attempts at revolutionary transformation will tend to be regressive or at least have quite unintended outcomes. Note, however, that nothing here rules out engineered change, so to speak—attempted structural reforms of politics. In the modern world, political tinkering, on small or grand scales, is endemic. The theory simply states what should result from such tinkering.

The problem of testing the theory against experience obviously remains, as do problems of operationalizing concepts for that purpose. But theory comes first.

If the power of a culturalist account of political change is to be compared with that of different approaches to political theory and explanation, then general accounts of change, derived from noncultural postulates and similar to that presented here, are needed. Political-culture theories, admittedly, have not heretofore met the challenge of developing a general theory of change; but neither have other types of theories.

APPENDIX: *CULTURE*

The term *culture,* unfortunately, has no precise, settled technical meaning in the social sciences, despite its centrality in them. The variable and ambiguous use of key concepts generates unprofitable arguments that are merely definitional. Hence I append a note that places my use of the term, as sketched in the first section, in its conceptual context.

My use of the term *culture* tries to make explicit, at the axiomatic level, what is implicit (occasionally almost explicit) in the works of Almond and his various collaborators. Their use of the concept seems to be based squarely on Talcott Parsons's "action frame of reference." Parsons first worked out that "frame of reference" as a way of synthesizing four apparently diverse, all highly influential, early modern social scientists: Mar-

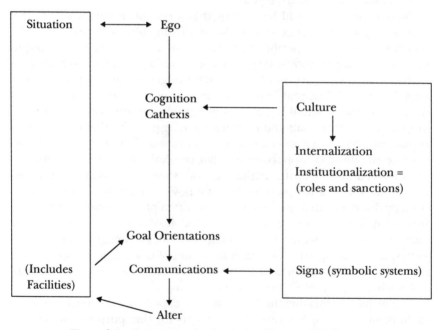

Figure 7-1. Interaction in the Action Frame of Reference

shall, Pareto, Durkheim, and Weber.[33] He and collaborators developed action theory in a large series of works, the most useful of which probably is the multiauthored book, *Toward a General Theory of Action.*[34]

The action frame of reference is based, at the microlevel, on Parsons's notion of an interaction, societies being complexes of interactions (some earlier sociologists called them acts of "sociation"). The notion is depicted on Figure 7–1. In brief translation, (1) ego (an actor) is in a "situation"—an objective context; (2) ego cognitively decodes that context and invests it with feeling (cathexis)—thus the context comes to have meaning for the actor; (3) the manner of investing situations with meaning is acquired through socialization, which consists mainly of early learning—this imparts the modes of understanding and valuing prevalent in societies or sub-societies or both, and in aggregate, these may be called a society's "culture"; (4) socialization leads to the internalization of cognitive and affective meanings (viz., the cultural becomes personal) and their institutionalization (the definition of expected behavior in social roles and of sanctions in case of deviation from expected behavior) makes smooth and regular patterns of interaction possible; (5) cognitions and affective responses to them define goals and ways to pursue them; (6) cognitions, feelings, and goals are communicated to alter (another actor) through the use of "signs" (symbolic expressions of culture that make ego's actions intelligible to alter)—but actions also depend on objective facilities that are part of any actor's situation and that independently affect the choice of goals; (7) alter responds, changing the situation in some respect, so that the process resumes.

Note especially that the action frame of reference emphasizes neither subjective nor objective factors but rather how the two are linked in interactions. Culturalists focus on the matters in the box on the right, but they should also bring that on the left into interpretation and theories. This I have tried to do throughout this essay, emphasizing how culture conditions change in varying contexts of objective change.

Alternatives to the notion of culture I use come chiefly from cultural anthropology. I use the plural intentionally because the meanings of culture vary a great deal in that field. One can probably subsume these meanings under four categories: (1) Culture is coterminous with society: it is the whole complex of the ways of a "folk," of human thought and action among particular people. Park comes close to that view.[35] (2) Culture is social life in its subjective aspects: the knowledge, beliefs, morals, laws, customs, habits of a society. One finds this meaning (and these illustrative words) in the seminal work of Tyler and, later, Benedict and Kluckhohn.[36] (3) Culture is what differentiates societies from one another, for the purpose of idiographic description but also for theorizing through comparisons and contrasts (agreements and differences). I take the seminal work here to be Malinowski's.[37] (4) Culture is the distinctive, variable set of ways in which societies normatively regulate social behavior.[38]

The fourth set of meanings comes closest to that used here. My use of the concept of culture here seems to be justified by usage in political science and, more important, by its suitability to testing theories through the catholic deduction of unknowns once its postulates are explicitly stated. Anyway, my version of the concept is that about which theoretical conflicts have thus far occurred in political inquiry.

NOTES FOR CHAPTER 7

1. G. A. Almond and J. S. Coleman, *The Politics of the Developing Areas*, (Princeton: Princeton University Press, 1960); G. A. Almond and S. Verba, *The Civic Culture* (Boston: Little, Brown, 1963).

2. G. A. Almond and S. Verba, eds., *The Civic Culture Revisited* (Princeton: Princeton University Press, 1979).

3. For example, J. Bill and R. L. Hardgrave, *Comparative Politics: The Quest for Theory* (Columbus: Merrill, 1973), and R. E. Dawson and K. Prewitt, *Political Socialization* (Boston: Little, Brown, 1969).

4. H. Eckstein, *Support for Regimes* (Princeton: Center of International Studies Research Monograph 44, 1979).

5. R. Rogowski, *Rational Legitimacy* (Princeton: Princeton University Press, 1974).

6. G. A. Almond and G. B. Powell, *Comparative Politics: A Developmental Approach* (Boston: Little, Brown, 1966).

7. M. Mead and R. Metraux, *Themes from French Culture* (Stanford: Stanford University Press, 1954).

8. R. B. Putnam, *The Beliefs of Politicians* (New Haven: Yale University Press, 1973).

9. L. W. Pye and S. Verba, *Political Culture and Political Development* (Princeton: Princeton University Press, 1965).

10. M. Crozier, *The Bureaucratic Phenomenon* (Chicago: University of Chicago Press, 1964).

11. A. Downs, *An Economic Theory of Democracy* (New York: Harper & Row, 1957).

12. T. R. Gurr, "Persistence and Change in Political Systems," *American Political Science Review* 68 (1974): 1482–1504.

13. C. S. Whitaker, *The Politics of Tradition: Continuity and Change in Northern Nigeria 1946–1966* (Princeton: Princeton University Press, 1970).

14. G. Simmel, *The Sociology of Georg Simmel*, trans. K. Wolff (Glencoe, Ill.: Free Press, 1950).

15. E. Durkheim, *The Division of Labor in Society* (Glencoe, Ill.: Free Press, 1960), 287–291.

16. Ibid.

17. S. M. Lipset, *Political Man* (Garden City: Doubleday, 1960).

18. S. P. Huntington, *Political Order in Changing Societies* (Cambridge, Mass.: Harvard University Press, 1968).

19. M. Olson, Jr., "Rapid Growth as a Destabilizing Force," *Journal of Economic History* 23 (1963): 529–552.

20. J. Wakeford, *The Cloistered Elite* (London: MacMillan, 1969); P. Woods, *The Divided School* (London: Routledge and Kegan Paul, 1979).

21. R. K. Merton, *Social Theory and Social Structure* (Glencoe, Ill.: Free Press, 1949).

22. C. Dickens, *American Notes & Pictures from Italy* (London: Oxford, 1957).

23. E. Burke, *Reflections on the French Revolution* (London: Methuen, 1923).

24. M. Rejai and K. Phillips, *Leaders of Revolutions* (Beverly Hills: Sage, 1979); E. R. Wolf, *Peasant Wars in the Twentieth Century* (London: Faber & Faber, 1973).

25. H. Arendt, *On Revolution* (New York: Viking, 1963).

26. G. Massell, *The Surrogate Proletariat* (Princeton: Princeton University Press, 1974).

27. J. Kelley and H. S. Klein, *Revolution and the Rebirth of Inequality* (Berkeley: University of California Press, 1981).

28. L. P. Edwards, *The Natural History of Revolutions* (Chicago: University of Chicago Press, 1927); and C. Brinton, *The Anatomy of Revolution* (New York: Vintage, 1965).

29. H. Eckstein, "On the 'Science' of the State," *Daedalus* 104 (1979): 1–20.

30. Durkheim, *Division of Labor.*

31. Rogowski, *Rational Legitimacy.*

32. Kelley and Klein, *Revolution.*

33. T. Parsons, *The Structure of Social Action* (New York: McGraw-Hill, 1937).

34. T. Parsons and E. A. Shils, eds., *Toward a General Theory of Action* (Cambridge: Harvard University Press, 1951).

35. R. E. Park, "Introduction" in E. V. Stonequist, *The Marginal Man* (New York: Scribner's, 1937).

36. E. B. Tyler, *Primitive Culture* (London: John Murray, 1871); R. Benedict, *Patterns of Culture* (New York: Houghton Mifflin, 1934); C. Kluckhohn, *Culture and Behavior* (New York: Free Press, 1962).

37. B. Malinowski, *A Scientific Theory of Culture* (New York: Oxford University Press, 1944).

38. W. H. Goodenough, *Description and Comparison in Cultural Anthropology* (Chicago: Aldine, 1968); W. G. Sumner, *Folkways* (Boston: Ginn, 1906).

EIGHT

"Observing" Political Culture

Author's Note: This essay was completed just before this book was prepared and is published here for the first time. Because it deals with the second main criticism of "culturalist" theory, I have adjoined it to the chapter outlining a culturalist theory of political change. However, it deals with a major methodological issue and thus also belongs in the earlier section on "Political Science."

INTRODUCTION

The political-culture approach to theory and explanation has, in just one generation, passed from undoubted domination of macropolitical studies, to doubt or rejection, to what appears to be an early renaissance—even if in more or less modified forms.[1]

Doubts about the approach no doubt arose from its too-quick popularity, its rapidly acquired faddishness.[2] More important, they arose for two much more serious reasons: the apparent inability of culturalists to account for political change without cheating; and the fact that culturalists made fundamental something subjective, hence not immediately observable, which they variously called orientations to action, predispositions, or (dubiously) attitudes. In essence, they made central to the construction of "positive" political theory, akin to theories in the natural sciences, what had long been considered the principal barrier to doing so by the German *Geistes-* or *Kulturwissenschaftler* (cultural scientists, as conceived by Dilthey, Windelband, and Rickert) who influenced Max Weber's conception of *verstehende Soziologie.* This barrier was the meaning, or understanding, of experiences and actions to actors (cognitive, affective, evaluative, as usually broken down), governed by "rules" that are always culturally defined,[3] thus probably unique, and acquired by learning within cultures.[4]

One reaction to this emphasis on subjectivity (on highly variable "life-worlds," as Husserl called them) was a sort of crusading antipositivism: the reduction of social science to the mere "interpretation" of cases. The rejection of social science on the ground of its subjectivity was pushed under more or less fancy labels: hermeneutics, phenomenology, semiotics, ethnomethodology, or "thick description."[5] In able hands, like Geertz's, studies in this vein produced fascinating information and striking insights, but at extreme costs in reliability and validity (in their technical senses), not to mention parsimony and predictive power. Compared to earlier reactions to the philosophers of cultural science, especially Weber's, the later reactions argued, in effect, for throwing out both baby and bath water.

A second reaction also was extreme. In gist, it amounted to solving the problem by circumventing it. For the most part, this was done by rational-choice theorists, who assumed a universal disposition toward "efficient" action in cost-benefit terms. Culturally learned preferences would, at some point, have to be poured into utility functions, but not necessarily and certainly not initially.[6] To a lesser extent, and less clearly, the difficulty also was evaded by the various forms of "structuralism," drawn from the diverse sources of Lévi-Strauss, Piaget, and, of course, structural linguistics. We might note, however, that structuralism, rather strangely, has been symbiotically related to the "phenomenological" reaction.[7]

Now a substantial return to culturalist theory seems to be in process. But this is not due to the fact that culturalists have solved the decisive problems that caused earlier doubts about their approach. The renaissance of culturalist theory appears, in most cases, to be more a reaction against the earlier reactions. The revival of the approach occurred, in part, because "phenomenology," for all intents and purposes, abandoned positive theory, and also because clever formalistic exercises upon rational-choice assumptions are still a far cry from validity (and have been empirically impugned—e.g., in coalition-theory) as well as being based on dubious, or highly time-bound and, of all things, culture-bound assumptions. To justify the renaissance of culturalism, more is needed than the shortcomings of other modes of analysis. The problems that made culturalism doubtful must be plausibly solved, if we are not to go through this cycle of rejection and counterrejection all over again.

In an earlier essay I tried to deal with the issue of political change within the culturalist framework (see chapter 7). Here, I want to confront the second issue: how to deal with "meaning" for purposes of "positive theory."[8]

THE SUBJECTIVITY PROBLEM

In the work that started political-culture theory, Almond and Verba, after granting that *culture* is a word overburdened with meanings in social study, define it succinctly as "psychological orientation toward social objects . . . the political system as internalized in the cognitions, feelings, and evaluations of its population,"[9] instilled by socialization. Despite the large variety of meanings attached to the concept, before and since, "psychological" (that is, subjective) orientation has always been central in the idea of culture. To be sure, terminologies differ. For instance, Geertz writes about instilled "programs" that govern behavior, as against behavior per se,[10] and Barnes identifies culture with "shared assumptions about how the world works and should work."[11] Kaase used terms like *Einstellungen* (attitudes) and *Prädispositionen* as central to culture, as against *Verhalten* (behavior) or *Handeln* (acting).[12]

Recent revised versions of political-culture theory retain the centrality of the subjective. The latest of these versions is "grid-group" culture theory, first developed in the work of Mary Douglas and in Douglas and Wildavsky on risk,[13] and fully developed in a forthcoming work by a team headed by Wildavsky.[14] "Grid-group" cultural theory à la Douglas and Wildavsky essentially does two things. It posits, first, a small number (five) of general clusters of "preferences" for ways of political life, to reduce (make "parsimonious") the vast variety of particular cultural traits and themes; Almond and Verba also did this, differently, in their work of 1963. Second, it proposes a theory of political viability: polities can survive if, and only if, social preferences and social relations are congruent. The preferences (viz., "ways of looking at the world") manifestly are general normative dispositions and thus subjective. It seems plausible to hold that the perception of congruence between preferences and actual relations also will largely be culturally defined, by cognitive dispositions—like those that led French revolutionary crowds to rally to the king, as the (perceived) people's guardian.

Political-culture theories, then, in all forms, focus inquiry on subjective matter. Anything subjective can, at best, only be indirectly observed in the phenomena we experience. This raises questions. Can subjective dispositions be observed at all? (Reichel,[15] for example, has severe doubts about this; he holds that the decisive problem in political-culture research is "uncertainty": that is, problems of determining just what empirical observations are to be considered as manifestations of political culture.) If dispositions are to be considered observable, then how? And how rigorously can they be observed: how reliably and validly, in the technical methodological senses of these terms?

We may be tempted to dismiss these problems too easily, in the manner of Hartz on the role of "ideas" as data in political research.[16] Very briefly, Hartz argues that positivist study is study of the "existential" (what exists); ideas exist; ergo, political ideas are as appropriate a subject for positivist study as any other: *quod erat demonstrandum*. This is simplistic. Hartz happened to be concerned with ideas that are the observable artifacts produced by political philosophers—with what the old-style behaviorist, Bentley,[17] called "writing-activities." These undoubtedly "exist" and are directly observable, even if often hard to decipher correctly. But the matter is not so simple when one deals with silent and implicit orientations, dispositions, perceptions, especially on the macrolevel; they are not to be found in libraries or bookstores. There may be strongly suggestive evidence that orientations to action do "exist"; Hyman's seminal work on political socialization,[18] among many others, provides heaps of it. But a version of Lord Hewart's dictum about justice applies here: facts, for positive study and theory, must not only exist; they must be seen to exist; they must be observable facts. The issue is not put correctly by Hartz. It is not whether ideas are facts, but whether they are observable and rigorously so.

In regard to cultural dispositions, the old behaviorists had a point not to be ignored. They held that one can observe only objective behavior and objects, and that ideas, attitudes, dispositions are, in Bentley's pungent words, nothing but "mind-stuff," "soul-stuff," or "spooks" imputed to behavior. Note that this was never meant to say that people have no subjective dispositions. It meant that if inquiry focused on the dispositions it must inevitably be infirm (*unbestimmt*, in Reichel's word), especially, to a considerable extent, arbitrary and intuitive. Not the least difficulty discerned was that subjective *explanations* would tend to be truistic and, in the philosophical sense, trivial (mere words, saying nothing). The danger of triviality in political-culture studies is in fact serious. It exists chiefly in the tendency of culturalists to state observed patterns of behavior in a cultural language and then to claim that doing so somehow explains the patterns. It has, for instance, been observed that some countries have multiparty systems. Why? A typical political-culture explanation is that the countries have fragmented political cultures. What is the evidence for this? Often, in large part, that they have multiparty systems. In the same vein, some countries experience frequent political violence, supposedly because they have "cultures of violence," for which the chief evidence is that they experience frequent political violence. The fallacy in this sort of "explanation" is evident. Political-culture theories tend to be circular: statements in which an *explanandum* (something to be explained) is identical with a proposed *explanans* (an explanation). Otherwise put, political-culture explanations have tended to be translations into a special language, and no more.

The subjectivity problem that afflicts political-culture studies thus involves two issues: (1) Either political culture simply is a pattern of political behavior in a society or subsociety—in which case, why talk about political culture in the first place? Or (2) political culture is something else: the dispositions that underlie the activities and generally pattern them. In the latter case, back to square one: how can one observe the general dispositions with reasonable assurance of validity?

POLITICAL CULTURE AND SURVEY RESEARCH

The standard solution of the subjectivity problem in political-culture research has been to use a special technique that supposedly taps orientations directly: survey research into political attitudes. The leading macrolevel example is by Almond and Verba,[19] whose study of democratic cultures was largely based on an interview schedule of 131 items, many subdivided into numerous subitems: the schedule occupies twenty-three large pages of an appendix to *The Civic Culture*. Putnam's excellent book on the "beliefs" of politicians in Britain and Italy is another case in point, using both a large number of closed questions and the coding of replies to open-ended ones.[20] A plethora of other examples could be given. The most intriguing, perhaps, is a sort of canned, standardized questionnaire proposed by Berg-Schlosser for determining the political cultures of any and all societies (which, if it made sense, would, of course, be very useful for comparative study).[21]

The idea that underlies the survey-research solution of the subjectivity problem is familiar. One uses artfully devised questionnaires and interview schedules to obtain data considered to reveal unmistakably and directly people's general political orientations or more specific attitudes. Such research is considered particularly appropriate if one deals with large aggregates of respondents, so that psychological testing or even more arduous techniques for getting at perceptual maps are not feasible.

Much is said for the usefulness of survey research in numerous studies.[22] As a solution to the subjectivity problem in political-culture research, however, the technique poses substantial difficulties, two of which, I think, are insuperable. I deal with most of them only briefly here because the matter is much discussed in the cookbook literature on social science methodology.

First, there is a practical difficulty: survey research is extremely costly. The resources required for it are unlikely to be available to most researchers. One should not dismiss this difficulty because it is only "practical," because the social sciences are, and are likely to remain, the poor relations of research funding. Sometimes it prevents research altogether; often it forces researchers to make do with what can be done, not what they ought to do.

A second difficulty, practical but less readily soluble, involves access to respondents. Not all polities are open to survey research (especially by Americans), some by law (as in the case of Burma), more often because of obstacles by officials unable to distinguish between research and intelligence work, inquiry and snooping. In some cases, also, potential respondents are too fearful and suspicious to be good subjects for surveys.

A third difficulty, about which much has been written, is intrinsic in survey-research technique: there are nearly always doubts about the trustworthiness of responses to even the best designed survey instruments. Converse has discussed one especially serious reason for this,[23] the expression of "nonattitudes": attitudes about matters regarding which subjects lack the knowledge to have attitudes in the first place. There are many others. Respondents, if suspicious, may give intentionally misleading responses. Or they may give answers they consider expected of them (a special kind of "nonattitude"); this is especially prevalent among school children who confuse questionnaires with tests. Or responses may vary with contextual factors; for example, there is the well-known phenomenon of deceptively high levels of political knowledge just before general elections. The wording of questions may contaminate responses, as may the presence or demeanor of researchers. And so on. Survey researchers have been ingenious at guarding against the difficulty posed by misleading responses but, of course, imperfectly so. The basic problem is not that distortions may occur, but that it is hard (indeed impossible) to know whether, and to what extent, they have occurred—unless one already knows what surveys are conducted to find out.

The absolutely insuperable difficulty posed by the survey-research solution is logical (and epistemological); that is what makes it insuperable. Responses to survey instruments still are "behavior" that only supposedly represents orientations. They undoubtedly provide more data than mere "raw observation" and conceivably more revealing data. But there is no getting around the fact that they are, in Bentleyan terms, "speaking-activities" or "writing-activities," not the subjective thing itself.

There is an ineluctable "epistemic gap" (as Northrop called it)[24] between objective behavior and subjective dispositions. Certainly, survey research cannot bridge it; logically no observational technique can.

These arguments may seem glum, but they at least allow us to state the decisive problems in observing political culture. There are two. First, how can culturalists get more reliable, more trustworthy data than by survey research? Second, how can the apparently unbridgeable "epistemic gap" between behavior and orientations be narrowed, even if not eliminated, so that its existence makes little difference to theory?

A PROPOSED SOLUTION OF THE SUBJECTIVITY PROBLEM

Obtaining Data

If any single technique for getting data about a subject is likely to be flawed, it seems plain ordinary sense always to use a variety of such techniques. The results can then supplement one another; up to a point, they might cancel out errors that arise from each technique used singly; they provide checks on one another; and if they produce overlapping findings, one may be especially confident that something correct has been found. Campbell has called this procedure the use of multitrait-multimethod matrices.[25] The method is analogous to geological "triangulation": measuring heights not otherwise measurable, or distances not readily traversable, by the use of a series of imperfect measures (of triangles from points on a baseline). That method is, in fact, sometimes used in preference to direct measuring, even where that is possible, because of its exactness.

In trying to get at culture, a considerable variety of different measures is, at least potentially, available for the similar purpose of observing the apparently unobservable. One of them, for all its imperfection, is survey research. There are many others. A large number of textbooks have been written about them. Without being comprehensive, I will discuss a few.

One method designed to get at the inherently unobservable is content analysis, a once widely used and quite sophisticated technique that seems now, unaccountably, to have lapsed into disfavor and even unfamiliarity in many cases. Its purpose was the quantitative analysis of communications, using explicit defined categories to capture their content; the use of the categories was binding in analysis to prevent the arbitrary selection of materials that might merely strike inquirers as intuitively "interesting"; and the measurement of the categories was carried out by appropriate, rigorous procedures. Newspaper editorials and speeches were the sort of materials studied, in all cases to find the "meanings" (mostly values) they conveyed. For instance, Lasswell, Leites, and their associates devised a "symbol analysis" that was used during the Second World War by several branches of the U.S. government to analyze the contents of newspapers, noting the frequency of the symbols they used and whether positive or negative meaning was attached to them.[26] White similarly studied the prewar speeches of Hitler and Roosevelt, classifying every value statement (5,326 of them) under predefined categories.[27] A good overview of the content-analysis technique, although it emphasizes attitudes in international relations, is provided by North et al.[28]

Content analysis, of course, has many flaws of its own, including problems regarding the predefined variables used in carrying it out, problems in measuring them accurately, and problems of the "significance" of findings because it is only too easy to get hooked on counting as such. Not least, it poses sampling problems; for instance, it seems heavily biased toward elite communications, such as speeches by conspicuous political leaders. However, its use, as stated, is recommended here only as a flawed way of deciphering meanings, among other such ways. And content analysis has undoubted advantages over survey research in getting at cultural meanings. One is that it is designed to get at implicit meanings of which subjects themselves might not be aware. Of course, details and nuances that idiographers usually catch get lost in the mechanical use of preselected variables and methods of measurement, but all techniques of generalizing, even about a particular society, pay that price—and the generalizers know it and consider it worthwhile.

A method that political science culturalists seem somehow to have missed, yet that seems tailor-made for deciphering meanings, is Osgood's "semantic differential" technique; its nature and rationale is discussed comprehensively in Osgood, Suci, and Tannenbaum's *The Measurement of Meaning*,[29] and the technique is applied, almost entirely by Osgood and his collaborators themselves, in a long-sustained series of works that covers some three decades.[30] The technique is a type of projective technique. It is used to elicit responses to stimuli—in this case, cards that present words which are genuine opposites, like honest and dishonest, not short and tall—in regard to some object (a picture, for example) that may potentially reveal meanings with a minimum of deception by respondents (as in the case of nonattitudes) and contamination by the presence of observers.

Again, I refer to the semantic differential technique only as part of the arsenal of techniques available to get at meanings. However, that method seems to me to be especially notable because it has in fact produced enlightening findings; for instance, to cite just one, Israelis react more intensely to words denoting activity than to those that evoke strength, whereas Arab cultures seem to react intensely to cues that involve strength but not those that denote activity.[31] On the face of it, this finding illuminates much experience. (After all, Nasser seemed genuinely surprised that his threats to drive the Israelis into the sea were taken at face value in 1967; he was, after all, only flexing muscles.)

Greenstein and Tarrow have used what they call a semiprojective technique that seems particularly suitable for studying children's dispositions because children are likely to confuse questionnaires and the like with tests, but their technique obviously has wider applicability.[32] In gist, subjects are told the beginning of a story and then asked to continue it; their responses are then subjected to more or less systematic analysis. To illustrate, one story, designed to get at dispositions toward political authority began with this cue: "The [head of state] has to attend an important meeting. He [she] is late, so he [she] drives to the meeting over the speed limit. A policeman stops him [her]." Here is part of how a twelve-year-old French girl continued, after considering that the president, then de Gaulle, might be issued a speeding ticket:

> *Girl:* But they must let it pass, because it is the president. . . . He tells them he is late, that he has to go to a meeting. Perhaps the gendarmes let him go, telling him to go on less rapidly, because he could have an accident. Let's say that he pays attention to their orders, if he is afraid, or perhaps he does not pay attention to them saying to himself: "It is not right that a gendarme should give me orders." And maybe he will tell his chauffeur to *speed up,* or at any rate not to slow down.
>
> *Interviewer:* What do you think? Would he say go slower or go faster?
>
> *Girl:* Perhaps in order to be safe he slows down a little, for he says to himself: "If there is an accident, I will not be there any more to direct the country [*la patrie*]."

Compare how a British working-class girl of the same age continued the story:

> *Girl:* Well, really the police wouldn't really stop the queen driving the car because somebody would be escorting the car to the meeting and they would stop the rest of the cars so she wouldn't really need to be going fast. People have got time to wait for the queen. She wouldn't really be late.
>
> *Interviewer:* Let's suppose for the purpose of this question that the queen was driving by herself in a car and she wanted to go out and get away from other people and the police stopped her for going too fast.
>
> *Girl:* Well, the police might have stopped her, but as soon as they saw it was the queen they wouldn't take her in for speeding or anything like that.
>
> *Interviewer:* What do you suppose the policeman would say?
>
> *Girl:* I think he would be astounded, because really the queen, she doesn't drive the car on her own. And she knows Britain's speed limits, so she wouldn't have gone really fast.

Or take the way an American worker's son elaborated the scenario (not, to me, very reassuringly):

> *Boy:* The policeman was giving him a ticket and everything. And once he saw it was the president he told him he could go and that. And the people that were standing around thought it was unfair and everything. So they started running after the car. They were pulling the bumper and that. They were wrecking it, and they forced the policeman to give him a ticket. He was late for his meeting.
>
> *Interviewer:* Well, why did they think it was unfair that he didn't get a ticket?
>
> *Boy:* Well, because the president is just a person and everything.
>
> *Interviewer:* Well, what did the president think about all of this?
>
> *Boy:* He thought it was all O.K. He thought it was fair that he should get one.

Interviewer: What does the policeman think when he sees that he has stopped the president's car?
Boy: He thinks he'd better let him go or else he'll get mad and that and start telling the chief and he'd fire him or something.

These responses surely tell one a lot, even on just an intuitive basis, and Greenstein and Tarrow do subject them to intensive analysis; but they also use rigorous quantitative techniques on the aggregates of responses.

Not to overlook the obvious, there also is "raw observation" (though we may feel better if we give it a label that sounds more dignified, like "participant observation") to provide clues to cultural meanings. A strange notion seems to be abroad in the social sciences: that such observation does not provide "data." When I used it in my own work, I was accused by a survey researcher of being merely "anecdotal"—not "scientific."[33] Natural scientists, it seems to me, would regard this notion with disdain. Granted that they use vastly complex mechanisms and techniques of observation. They do not use them merely to observe, but to observe more and better: a necessity at a stage of development we hardly have reached. Moreover, raw observation can be carried out thoughtfully, even with considerable rigor (see the literature on participant observation). And it has several advantages over special techniques of observation designed to decipher the subjective. It is not artificial and is therefore unlikely to be either mistaken by subject or contaminated by observers; and, unlike survey research, one can do it almost anywhere.

In general, then, findings obtained by a variety of techniques always are worth more than those obtained by any single mode of observation, where all such modes are inadequate. Genuinely rigorous "triangulation," of course, requires one to know precisely the nature and extent of measurement errors in particular imperfect observations, as surveyors do. We know a little about this in regard to some of our methods; for instance, we know that, in community-power research, asking people questions like, Can you tell me who has political power here? will lead to findings that exaggerate considerably the concentration of power in the community. But we know how modes of inquiry distort observations in too few cases, and, where we know, we know too inexactly. However, the principle of the matter is clear: progress is possible; difficulty is not a good reason for not trying; and although it might be foolish to hope that we can attain the precision of geological triangulation, we can approximate it—but only if we try.

Narrowing the Epistemic Gap

The greater difficulty, the crux of the issue of whether political culture is "observable," is how to make negligible the epistemic gap between behavior and orientations (that is, meanings, dispositions, attitudes, mind-stuff). The solution proposed here is, of course, applicable, mutatis mutandis, in all inquiries that pose the subjectivity problem.

To begin: One must never pretend that subjective orientations have been directly revealed by any technique of observation or by any set of such techniques. There simply is no way around the point that orientations are always imputed to behavior. This, however, is not (yet) a concession to the narrow behaviorists, for the simple reason that imputations may be valid. The issue we have come to can therefore be restated in a form clearly more conducive to solution: How can subjective orientations be validly imputed to behavior? In regard to this, we already have discussed the principal fallacy to be avoided if a plausible answer is to be found. It is the statement of circular explanations: the mere translation of objective observation into a cultural language. Such statements, as I have said, trivialize problems: the explanatory statements simply restate *explananda;* they add nothing to them; and they allow us to deceive ourselves into thinking that we have said something when we have said nothing.

The trivialization of theories by translation and circularity is unavoidable if a particular orientation to action is imputed to any particular activity. We simply cannot say, for instance, that a person participates because he is participant. Political orientations must be regarded as dispositions that underlie, thus organize and pattern, sets of perceptions and activities: the larger and more diverse the sets the better for theory. This is inherent in the very conception of "orientations to action" anyhow. They are, as I wrote in an earlier paper, "general dispositions of actors to act in certain ways in sets of situations. [They] pattern actions. . . . Orientations are not 'attitudes': the latter are specific, the former *general* dispositions. Attitudes themselves derive from and express orientations; though attitudes may, through their patterning, help us find orientations."[34] (For attitudes here one can, of course, substitute actions or behavior.) If, for example, we say that "X is tolerant," we say that X does not object (or, better, is oblivious) to sets of traits of people or of their behavior widely disapproved in a collectivity. The set might include Jews or Catholics, blacks or Asians, illegal immigrants or guest-workers, homosexuals or eccentrics, self-absorbed or stupid people, and the like; it is unlikely to cover all people or behaviors (say, child abusers: everyone draws a line somewhere), but the statement describes a general pattern of matters directly observable, or else it says nothing.

If orientations are so regarded, then statements about them or sets of them (cultures or subcultures) are statements of "regularity": they are lawlike statements or, more simply, theories. They are never descriptions, not even "thick" ones—though I do not mean to deride the clues to cultural theory that acute observation of a particular activity (say, a Balinese cockfight) may provide.

This, by the way, is rather an old view, dating to the origins of contemporary social science, although recent theorists of culture, and others who stress "meaning" in social inquiry, seem unaware of that fact. Weber, the apostle of *verstehende Soziologie,* for example, wrote, in his posthumous magnum opus:

> Every interpretation aims at self-evidence or immediate plausibility. But an interpretation which makes the meaning of a piece of behavior as self-evidently obvious as you like cannot claim *just* on that account to be the causally valid interpretation as well. In itself it is nothing more than a particularly plausible hypothesis.[35]

Weber's point was restated by Morris Ginsburg in 1956:

> It appears to be a basic assumption of *verstehende Soziologie . . .* that what we know within our minds is somehow *more* intelligible than what is outwardly observed. But this is to confuse the familiar with the intelligible. There is no inner sense establishing connexions between inner facts by direct intuition. Such connexions are in fact *empirical generalizations,* of no greater validity than the similar generalizations relating to outward facts.[36]

This has a crucial implication, which Weber also pointed out. If one is to have confidence in the validity of statements about orientations, then they must be treated like any other hypothetical assertion. At the outset, statements about culture may simply be summaries of observations: verbal summaries or the scientific-looking ones we find in regression tables, frequency curves, histograms, smoothed ogives, and so on. Political culturists usually stop at that point—if they get to it. But theory, to be considered valid, must be tested; and statements about cultures, or anything else, cannot be tested by the data from which they were derived in the first place—even if the nature of a frequency distribution, or our intense immersion in a culture as participant observers, may justify the intuitive surmise that tests *will* validate or invalidate, so that they might not be worth the cost of being carried out.

If one cannot test theoretical statements by data used to formulate them, it follows that one must posit, by logically deduced prediction, as yet *unobserved* data that should turn up, given certain "initial (or determining) conditions,"[37] if our assertions about orientations or cultural sets of them are to be considered valid. (Weber mistakenly thought that the validity of imputed meanings can only be determined by psychological tests—which are still a way of getting directly at the subjective.) Such predictive tests, positing unknowns, can be carried out in two ways.

First, one may predict behavior in situations either that have not yet occurred or, if they have, to which the responses are still uncertain. I will give a real-life example (that happened to turn out well) from a work of mine that, as mentioned above, was criticized by an eminent authority for using "anecdotal material."[38]

In my study of Norwegian authority-culture, I argued that Norwegians are consensualists in decision making. More specifically, it appeared that they follow this decision rule: agree widely (unanimously, if possible); if wide agreement is not possible, then appear to be in wide agreement; if that also is not possible, then drop the subject. This is a statement about subjective cognitions—"actions widely agreed upon are likely to be right actions"; about affect—Norwegians "feel" uncomfortable with small majorities; and about evaluation—Norwegians value wide agreement, and processes of forming consensus thereby become their decision processes. Thus, the statement contains all the elements into which Almond and Verba break down orientations.[39]

The statement is a (low-level) theoretical generalization, based on a large and eclectic variety of mostly raw observations, from the behavior of small neighborhood and club committees to transactions of parliamentary business. Admittedly, the generalization was illustrated by what may accurately be described as "anecdotes." In an essay replying to this point, among others,[40] I pleaded guilty to anecdotalism but also pointed out that the generalization was based on much else; that empirical generalizations should be based on the best obtainable data; but that despite their basis, what *really* counted in the end was how such generalizations stood up to appropriate testing by the accurate prediction of unknowns.

As it happened, a "natural" occasion for such prediction had arisen about the time that this debate was going on. In 1965, a general election brought to power what Norwegians called a bourgeois coalition, after thirty years of social-democratic (Labor party) rule. This coalition consisted of a very odd assortment of parties that had in common perhaps only opposition to the Labor party's long dominance. The coalition combined urban, and urbane, business interests with an agrarian party (in a country in which the rural-urban split looms large); nonreligious, if not downright antireligious, parties joined a Christian fundamentalist party; and a small party, chiefly of white-collar intellectual liberals, was added to the odd alignment. The common wisdom in political science is that such coalitions cannot last. They defy the now common rule that coalitions must minimize "preference disagreement," or "policy distance," merely to form.[41] The common wisdom in Norway, academic and general, was the same. However, the common notions ignored the decision rule I have summarized. That rule led to a quite different expectation, stated in my paper of 1967:[42] the coalition would endure by simply avoiding divisive issues (like religion or urban and rural interests likely to clash); it would work smoothly by concentrating on the least divisive issues (such as almost universally desired tax reforms); it would do little or nothing to change the Labor party's welfare-state legislation (Labor still had about 40 percent of the parliamentary seats—hardly a negligible minority); and it would break down if absolutely forced by circumstances to deal with a deeply divisive issue (for example, an issue that involved what Norwegians call "cosmopolitanism": close connections with the continent, divisions about which originated, no doubt, in the long colonial domination of Norway by Denmark). As it happened, all these predictions turned out to be correct. They thus validated—failed to falsify, despite defying both plausible theory and sheer good sense—the cultural generalization. The coalition lasted, although it did little besides tax reform, until the question of joining the EEC came up as an unavoidable issue; it then disintegrated.

The case was, in one way, lucky. Something happened in Norway at just the right time to allow a "natural experiment." That probably is only rarely the case. Usually, one may surmise, similar tests do not yet exist; they must be awaited; and they may simply not turn up, anyway not for a long time—quite as in the natural sciences.

Because that is so, a second way of testing whether cultural "meaning" has been validly deciphered may be desired over the first. One may carry out such tests by predicting responses to stimuli controlled by inquirers—not least, by doing survey research into as-yet-unknown responses by logically predicting the findings that should turn up if one's conceptions about a culture are valid. If in fact one has conceptions of culture, however arrived at—multitrait-multimethod "triangulation" is still best—then it should not be difficult to devise questions or other stimuli to test the conceptions. This is the best use, in my view, to which survey research intended to get at orientations can be put, both epistemologically and practically. Models of political culture can be built in all sorts of ways, less expensive in funds, time, personnel, and so on, than typical survey researches. Questions can be few if carefully devised for testing (especially if not used in attitudinal fishing expeditions), and samples may be small if thoughtfully selected for a carefully defined purpose. Unfortunately, neither survey research nor other modes of inquiry into culture have ever been so used. Their findings have been treated as definitive results, not as steps toward such results. But survey research, and other techniques, *could* be so used, at low cost and with potentially high payoffs.

Perhaps one other step that is desirable, even if not absolutely necessary, still is missing. What, in effect, we have, if all the above is done, is simply a tested hypothesis, essentially like any other. To narrow the epistemic gap between meaning and observation, it would still be useful to establish more firmly that a regularity exists because of subjective orientations rather than other factors. One can do this in at least three related ways: by multivariate analysis intended to establish the relative strengths of direct contextual factors (e.g., SES) as against factors associated with processes of socialization; by comparing the strength of synchronic and diachronic factors in mature subjects (because orientations are supposedly instilled chiefly by experiences early in life and upon my argument are highly resistant to change);[43] and by observations that might, or might not, establish that adult behavior is relatively stable despite changes in its context: something already done, by summarizing much psychological research, in Herbert Hyman's seminal work on political socialization.

CONCLUSION

All this is not meant to say that we can directly observe subjective matter by following the recipe here proposed. The epistemic gap between "inner" and "outward" facts, as stated, cannot be more than narrowed. But surely that is of no great consequence for the normal purposes of everyday academic inquiry: constructing, testing, and using theories.

It is especially worth adding that the solution of the subjectivity problem here proposed is exactly similar to how natural scientists treat unobservables, like time, electricity, or magnetism. No one in the "hard" sciences shies away from such concepts simply because they are not directly observable but experienced only through their effects—and in that sense are "spooky." They are, however, treated as theoretical constructs; their nature is imputed to a large number and variety of observations, using various research procedures; and conceptions of their nature have been subjected to careful tests. By now, they seem "real" in the objective sense; one would no doubt be held for an idiot if one were to contest paying one's electricity bills on the ground that one should not be charged for figmental "mind-stuff." The construct works in all sorts of ways, and so we, and the utility companies, may safely consider it "real," for our, and their, purposes. Indeed, we must—or else dismiss much good theory.

I make this point to emphasize the assertion that nothing about positivist inquiry compels dealing only with direct observables. That Skinnerian view belongs to primitive and naive positivism; its resemblance to what goes on in the hardest sciences is not even coincidental. Nor does cultural meaning condemn us to hermeneutics or any of its relatives. In "observing" culture one must comply with only one imperative, though it is burdensome: one must be highly cautious, ingenious, rigorous, and, above all, skeptical about one's own ideas. But this is imperative in all researches.

NOTES FOR CHAPTER 8

1. See citations in chapter 7, esp. n. 1, 2, 3, 8, and 9; M. Kaase, "Sinn oder Unsinn des Konzepts 'Politische Kultur' für die vergleichende Politikforschung,

oder auch: Der Versuch einen Pudding an die Wand zu nageln," in *Wahlen und Politisches System,* ed. Max Kaase and Hans-Dieter Klingemann (Opladen: West-deutscher Verlag, 1983); R. D. Putnam, *The Beliefs of Politicians* (New Haven: Yale University Press, 1973); R. M. Merelman, *Making Something of Ourselves: On Culture and Politics in the United States* (Berkeley: University of California Press, 1984); M. Thompson and A. Wildavsky, "A Poverty of Distinction," *Policy Sciences* 19 (1986): 163–199; R. Inglehart, "The Renaissance of Political Culture," *American Political Science Review* 82 (1988): 1204–1230; M. Thompson, R. Ellis, and A. Wildavsky, *Cultural Theory: Foundations of Socio-Cultural Viability* (Boulder, Colo.: Westview, 1990).

2. P. Reichel, "Politische Kultur—mehr als ein Schlagwort?" *Politische Viertel jahresschrift* 21 (1980): 382–399.

3. L. Wittgenstein, *Philosophical Investigations* (London: Blackwell, 1953).

4. See also P. Winch, *The Idea of a Social Science* (London: Routledge and Kegan Paul, 1958).

5. H. G. Gadamer, *Philosophical Hermeneutics* (Berkeley: University of California Press, 1976); A. Schutz, *On Phenomenology and Social Relations* (Chicago: University of Chicago Press, 1970); H. Garfinkel, *Studies in Ethnomethodology* (Englewood Cliffs, N.J.: Prentice-Hall, 1967); C. Geertz, *The Interpretation of Cultures* (New York: Basic Books, 1973).

6. J. M. Buchanan and G. Tullock, *The Calculus of Consent* (Ann Arbor: University of Michigan Press, 1962); R. L. Curry, Jr., and L. L. Wade, *A Theory of Political Exchange* (Englewood Cliffs, N.J.: Prentice-Hall, 1968).

7. P. Pettit, *The Concept of Structuralism* (New York: Harper & Row, 1977).

8. I elucidated the nature of such theory in H. Eckstein, "A Comment on Positive Political Theory," *PS* 22 (1989): 77.

9. G. A. Almond and S. Verba, *The Civic Culture* (Princeton: Princeton University Press, 1963).

10. D. Elkins and R. Simeon, "A Cause in Search of Its Effects or What Does Political Culture Explain," *Comparative Politics* 11 (1979): 127–146.

11. S. H. Barnes, "Politics and Culture" (Washington, D.C.: Bureau of Intelligence and Research, U.S. Department of State, 1986).

12. Kaase, "Sinn oder Unsinn."

13. M. Douglas, *Natural Symbols: Explorations in Cosmology* (London: Barrie and Rockliff, 1970); M. Douglas and A. Wildavsky, *Risk and Culture* (Berkeley: University of California Press, 1983).

14. Thompson et al., *Cultural Theory.*

15. Reichel, "Politische Kultur."

16. L. Hartz, "The Problem of Political Ideas," in *Approaches to the Study of Politics,* ed. Roland Young (Evanston, Ill.: Northwestern University Press, 1958).

17. A. F. Bentley, *The Process of Government* (1908; rpt. Cambridge, Mass.: Belknap Press, 1967).

18. H. H. Hyman, *Political Socialization* (Glencoe, Ill.: Free Press, 1959).

19. Almond and Verba, *Civic Culture.*

20. Putnam, *Beliefs of Politicians,* 241–302.

21. D. Berg-Schlosser, *Politische Kultur. Eine neue Dimension politikwissenschaftlicher Analyse* (Munich: Ernst Vogel, 1972).

22. For example, H. Cantril, *Gauging Public Opinion* (Princeton: Princeton University Press, 1944); A. Campbell and G. Katona, "The Sampling Survey: A Technique for Social Science Research," in *Research Methods in the Behavioral Sciences,* ed. Leon Festinger and Daniel Katz (New York: Dryden, 1953); E. R. Babbie, *Survey Research Methods* (Belmont, Calif.: Wadsworth, 1973); and the comprehensive citations in P. E. Converse, "Public Opinion and Voting Behavior," in *Handbook of Political Science,* ed. Fred I. Greenstein and Nelson W. Polsby (Reading, Mass.: Addison-Wesley, 1975), 4: 75–169.

23. P. E. Converse, "Attitudes and Non-attitudes: Continuation of a Dialogue," in *The Quantitative Analysis of Social Problems,* ed. Edward R. Tufte (Reading, Mass.: Addison-Wesley, 1970).

24. F. S. C. Northrop, *The Logic of the Sciences and the Humanities* (New York: Macmillan, 1948).

25. D. T. Campbell, "The Indirect Assessment of Social Attitudes," *Psychological Bulletin* 47 (1950): 15–38; D. T. Campbell and D. W. Fiske, "Convergent and Discriminant Validation by the Multitrait-Multimethod Matrix," *Psychological Bulletin* 56 (1959): 81–105.

26. H. D. Lasswell, N. Leites, and Associates, *Language of Politics* (New York: George W. Stewart, 1949).

27. R. K. White, "Hitler, Roosevelt, and the Nature of War Propaganda," *Journal of Abnormal and Social Psychology* 54 (1949): 81–99.

28. R. Z. North et al., *Content Analysis* (Evanston, Ill.: Northwestern University Press, 1963).

29. C. E. Osgood, G. J. Suci, and P. H. Tannenbaum, *The Measurement of Meaning* (Urbana: University of Illinois Press, 1957).

30. C. E. Osgood, *Lectures on Language and Performance* (New York: Springer-Verlag, 1980).

31. C. E. Osgood, "Semantic Differential Technique in the Comparative Study of Cultures," *American Anthropologist* 66 (1964): part 2, 171–200.

32. F. I. Greenstein and S. Tarrow, *Political Orientation of Children: The Use of a Semi-Projective Technique in Three Nations* (Beverly Hills: Sage Professional Papers in Comparative Politics, No. 01-009, 1970).

33. H. Eckstein, "Norwegian Democracy in Comparative Perspective," *Tidsskrift for sammfunnsforskning* 8 (1967): 305–321.

34. H. Eckstein, "A Culturalist Theory of Political Change," *American Political Science Review* 82 (1988): 789–804. See chapter 7 above.

35. M. Weber, *Wirtschaft und Gesellschaft* (Tübingen: Mohr, 1956). (See also the complete English translation by G. Roth and C. Wittich, *Economy and Society* (New York: Bedminster, 1968). (Note: Weber's italics: P. Winch's translation.)

36. M. Ginsburg, *On the Diversity of Morals* (London: Heinemann, 1956).

37. C. G. Hempel's terminology in *Aspects of Scientific Explanation* (New York: Free Press, 1965), 232; italics added.

38. H. Eckstein, *Division and Cohesion in Democracy* (Princeton: Princeton University Press, 1966).

39. Almond and Verba, *Civic Culture,* 16.

40. Eckstein, "Norwegian Democracy."

41. A. De Swaan, "An Empirical Model of Coalition Formation as an N-person Game of Policy Distance Minimization," in *The Study of Coalition Behavior,* ed. S. Groennings et al. (New York: Holt, Rinehart & Winston, 1970); E. C. Browne, *Coalition Theories: A Logical and Empirical Critique* (Beverly Hills: Sage, Comparative Politics Series, No. 01-043, 1973).

42. Eckstein, "Norwegian Democracy."

43. Eckstein, "Culturalist Theory of Political Change."

NINE

Explaining Collective Political Violence

Author's Note: Aristotle's *Politics* singled out three crucial problems of political theory, after long empirical and taxonomic discussions. Two are macrolevel problems: the causes of "revolutions" and political stability. One is a microlevel problem: civic education, comprising both what we would recognize as pedagogy and socialization.

Aristotle's emphasis on revolutions and their obverse had autobiographical foundations in the upheavals that occurred in Athens of the fourth century B.C.E. Inquiries into revolutions have occurred largely in reaction to immediate experience ever since. Following the headlines has been an affliction of political science, an obstacle to genuine accumulation; and inquiry into revolutions is a particularly good case in point. It has waxed and waned, in modern times, as revolutions themselves have been obtrusive or not. Much was written about the subject after the French Revolution and its aftershocks, after 1848, after the Russian Revolution and Stalin's "revolution from above," and, in my time, after Vietnam and other highly conspicuous insurgencies.

My own inquiries into the subject obviously also stem from elements of autobiography, as stated in chapter 1. Still, I have tried, in this case and others, to transcend immediate and personal experiences by inquiring into revolutions on a general level, recognizing that most significant events of current relevance pose universal problems and that particular events may best be illuminated by general theories. Yet much writing about the subject since the 1960s still seems tied to the headlines. Much of it seems

This article appeared in *Handbook of Political Conflict: Theory and Research,* ed. T. R. Gurr (New York: Free Press, 1980), 135–166. Reprinted by permission. Copyright © 1980 by the Free Press, a division of Macmillan, Inc.

to proceed from the premise that the phenomenon, as it concerns us, began only after the Second World War. And only a few inquirers (for example, Skocpol) have been led from current concerns back to earlier phenomena. (That we need history to understand recent events was the point of an article of mine recently published—coauthored by Raj Desai— "Insurgency: The Transformation of Peasant Rebellion," *World Politics* 42 [July 1990]: 441–465.)

I point this out, in part, to place my own involvement in studies of revolutions into perspective. It began at a luncheon with the associate director of Princeton's Center of International Studies, shortly after I went to that university in 1959. Distinguished work in the center (originally at Yale) had, by that time, been done in international relations and security studies, but the center had for some time also cultivated comparative political studies. Not long after joining it, at lunch in early 1960, the associate director asked me what, in my view, might be a good subject on which a center project might be constructed. I mentioned that revolution might be such a subject. It had a long pedigree in scholarship, but nothing significant of which I was, and am, aware had been done with it since Brinton's *Anatomy of Revolution* in 1938. I pointed out not only the classic nature of the subject but also that we were living in a revolutionary period; the Greek, Malayan, Algerian, and Indo-Chinese insurgencies (and some lesser ones) had already occurred, and the fact that they did not immediately involve the United States seemed to me beside the point. To show why it was beside the point, I argued that in a time of nuclear standoff, revolutionary conflict might reasonably be expected to be used, or at least be attempted to be used, as a surrogate for all-out war—not necessarily that the Great Powers would foment the conflicts, but that they would become involved in them, perhaps dangerously so. This is not hindsight after Vietnam; I made the same point in a publication that appeared in 1962.

The response to the suggestion was that, with the associate director's blessing, I should go forth into the world to try to raise money for the project.

I then began a Grand Tour of funding agencies, governmental and private. At first I was optimistic about obtaining funds; the events mentioned had happened, the arguments for renewed study seemed compelling, and we had started our own involvement, even if still barely perceptible, in Vietnam. But, only a short time before that involvement became vast, no one cared. John Gardner, then at the Carnegie Foundation, did, in the end, seem to see the point; he provided $90,000 for a three-year project. (Two or three years later, millions were being spent on research into insurgency—more correctly, counterinsurgency.)

The project started in 1961. We called it the Internal War Project. This calls for explanation. I had long been uneasy about Brinton's choice of cases in *Anatomy of Revolution,* less because he included the American War of Independence, which bothered many people, than because he included the English Civil War. Oranges and apples should be distinguished—unless, of course, one studies fruit. The worst outcome of inquiry, surely, is discarding a perfectly decent theory because it does not fit a case it should not fit in the first place. More generally, "revolution" seemed to be a term used for a rotten pot of quite dissimilar events: coups, short-lived riots, rebellions to remedy grievances, long drawn-out and intense events to change all of society, anticolonial (and/or pro-Marxist) guerrilla wars, not to mention supposedly major peaceful changes, like the Industrial Revolution. In the project, we were concerned with violent internal conflicts broadly speaking, but, to avoid conceptual confusion, I decided to use the long-established French notion of *guerre intérieure,* simply because it had no conventional meaning in English. "Revolution" could be treated as a subtype of the genus, among others—a subject on which I wrote a long (unpublished) paper to orient research in the project. The tendency now is to label the genus differently: collective political violence. I have no quarrel with that, as long as "revolution" and other types of violent events remain a well-defined species under the genus so that one can theorize at both the more general and more specific levels. Perhaps it should be added that my unease about revolution as the general label was vague but became crystallized by Hannah Arendt's *On Revolution* (1963).

The project's first activity was convening a conference of outstanding scholars to help us get a grip on the subject. The conference was a gathering of glittering All-Stars in social science. For me, its outcome reinforced my conviction that the social sciences, as they then were, had little to offer on the subject. Considerable pressure was put on me to publish the conference papers and to write an introduction to them. I did not really want to do so, although, in view of the stature of the participants, it would have been easy to go into print. Pressure prevailed, and a book appeared (*Internal War: Problems and Approaches* [Westport, Conn.: Greenwood, 1964]). My introduction to the book was painful to write; it is a thinly veiled criticism of the book's contents, in the form of an agenda for required research on internal wars, which covers everything from "pretheoretical" conceptual problems to the issue of the outcomes of such wars: their short-term and long-term effects on societies.

Subsequently, I wrote and published a more specific, orienting paper on the causes of internal wars, for the project ("On the Etiology of Internal Wars," *History and Theory* 4:2 [1965]: 133–163; not included in this book). In retrospect, both the book and article seem to me weak; but the book was used for an extensive period (including at the Army War College), and the article was republished many times. I take this as an indication of the sudden hunger for academic studies of revolutionary violence, no doubt generated by the Vietnam war.

The Internal War Project was woefully underfunded. Still, it produced considerable results. Here is a sample. The project launched the work of perhaps the two most influential contemporary theorists on collective political violence, Ted Robert Gurr and Charles Tilly, whose divergent views are summarized here. Gurr was brought into the project because he had already written a dissertation on the subject, and Tilly was asked to join it because of his excellent book on the Vendée. In addition, the project spawned Paret and Shy's influential book on guerrilla warfare of 1962 (one year after Osanka's dreary compilation of pieces on the subject); Gil AlRoy's monograph on peasant involvement in internal wars; Janos's study of coups; and Victor Wolfenstein's psychoanalytic study of revolutionary personality, the first of its genre. Much, not all, of the voluminous work on collective political violence published in the 1960s and 1970s grew out of work begun in the project, directly or indirectly. I take pleasure in that. I would take more if, as well as directing the project, I had had resources to do research of my own in it.

In this chapter, I try to take stock of where studies of collective political violence had taken us by 1980. The chapter may be read as a jaundiced essay, but it was not intended to be gloomy; research rarely leads to the discovery of the sort of critical juncture of alternatives discussed in the essay. That we cannot yet tell which alternative is likely to be the more fruitful is no disgrace.

Between problems and solutions in "positive" (if readers prefer, "scientific") inquiry there lies a crucial step. If this step is ignored, as is usual, cumulative theory building will almost certainly not occur. Instead, one ends up with an accumulation of alternative, untested, generally ambiguous hypotheses. The step I have in mind involves the most fateful aspect of what, in an earlier essay on political violence, I called "problemation":[1] *the discovery of the most fundamental problem requiring solution if a progressive development of theory about a subject is to occur.* In this essay I try to show what that basic problem is in studying collective political violence.

Large numbers of social scientists have studied political violence since the early 1960s, when the subject, after one of those long hiatuses that characterize its study, was back in vogue. Production of work has been anything but scant: Zimmerman's magisterial review of the literature lists about 2,400 items,[2] most of them published since 1960 (though he includes some stones perhaps better left unturned). It might seem odd, then, that an essay should now be devoted to a discussion—not even, as readers will find at the end, a solution—of a "basic," a "primary" problem. But this is not at all odd. The discovery of primary problems usually culminates much work in positive study: it is a critical and difficult achievement. Before core problems can be defined with precision, there usually is much prior observation, speculation, debate, and, especially, diffuse dissatisfaction, a sense of growing mystery rather than of illumination. One gradually comes to see, through long groping, the basic puzzle that a subject presents: where to begin if a genuine unfolding of theory is to occur. Two decades seem a long time to get to that point, but it usually takes much longer (though afterward progress is swift).

The most basic problem in studying any subject is to choose a fruitful theoretical approach. Usually that choice lies among many candidates, in which case a still more basic problem is to narrow the choice down to viable options. This chapter deals with basic alternative approaches to theories about collective political violence. What then, first of all, is a theoretical approach?

In essence, an approach is, of course, a route or tactic one chooses to follow toward a new or difficult objective. All routes depend primarily on starting points. The starting point in theorizing is always axiomatic in nature, explicitly or implicitly: it involves assumptions deemed fruitful. Any such assumption is an initial commitment that is considered vital if one's goals in inquiry are to be achieved effectively. It is fairly common to call this a "perspective" of inquiry. A perspective is the core of a theoretical approach, which, when fully elaborated, also includes key descriptive concepts, key secondary problems, and the specification of appropriate methods—all matters that depend on the choice of a fundamental perspective and that are more subject to change through feedback from research. A perspective usually takes the form of specifying the basic nature of a subject matter. For instance, physical events are "shaped matter in motion," or markets are "patterns of interaction among rational value-maximizers." Alternatively, a perspective may spotlight a key variable: one facet of a complex subject that is most important to grasp. Since all that constitutes a theoretical approach follows from its axiomatic basis, this essay asks: what are the crucial alternatives among basic perspectives that may be used to elaborate theories about collective political violence, and how can we choose among them?

The discussion cannot be brief, for the subject is enormously consequential, but space dictates that I omit much that ideally should be included. I ignore essentially descriptive case studies, still the main genre in the field, for my interest is in theory. Since my concern is with macrotheory, approaches to the explanation of individual aggression also are not considered here;[3] because of the linkages between micro- and macrotheory, this is more regrettable. The chapter is concerned with process (especially one aspect of it), and so omits ideologies and personality traits of revolutionary leaders.[4] To make its coverage of the literature manageable I deal with contemporary studies, and only a sample of these.

More seriously, I skirt issues of definition (or, better, delimitation), thus ignoring my own early advice to students of the subject.[5] But issues of definition and operationalization have always been too intricate for brevity. Early on, the problem was a lack of considered definitions. Now we suffer from overabundance and too much diversity. In any case, the fate of competing definitions will turn in the end on the promise of opposing theoretical approaches to a tentatively conceptualized subject, rather than on abstract discussion: the issue of the "essential nature" of a subject must ultimately determine its conceptualization.

For my purpose here, I assume that there are no fundamental quarrels with the following definitional notions:

1. collective political violence involves destructive attacks by groups within a political community against its regime, authorities, or policies;[6]
2. revolutions are the extreme cases of collective political violence, in regard to (a) their magnitude (scope, intensity), (b) targets (the political community or "regime"), (c) goals (degree and rapidity of change desired), and (d) the extent to which there is conflict between elites and counterelites.[7]

Most important, I emphasize one theoretical problem, that of "etiology": why does collective political violence, in general or in particular forms, occur, and why does it occur at different levels of magnitude and intensity? That problem has certainly held center stage since about 1960, while the study of other phenomena (the "process" of revolution, issues of prudent action by authorities or rebels, determinants of outcomes, problems of postrevolutionary rule) have waxed and waned. Not least, the issue of etiology is the problem on which theoretical approaches now differ most, especially if we include in it the problem of why political violence takes different forms. And we may surmise that the solution of this problem has important repercussions for all others.[8]

"CONTINGENCY" VERSUS "INHERENCY"

In a very early essay on the etiology of collective political violence—the label then used was "internal war," following French usage in the eighteenth and nineteenth centuries and the language of the Federalist Papers[9]—I discussed a number of options in explaining its causes. Some of the choices to be made were between:

1. "preconditions" or "precipitants"—more remote or more proximate causes
2. "incumbents" or "insurgents"
3. "structural" or "behavioral" (cultural, attitudinal, psychological) factors
4. "specific occurrences" (say, economic depressions) or "general processes" (long-run patterns that may occur in numerous theoretically equivalent forms)
5. "obstacles" to collective political violence or "positive" factors that make for internal-war potential.

The result was a tentative model (not empirically grounded like that in Hibbs) in which internal wars are explained by complex balances of very different and logically heterogeneous factors.

The theme of such complex balances constantly recurs in the literature. Gurr's "simplified" model of the determinants of political violence lists seven factors that may act to enlarge or lessen its magnitude.[10] Another version of his model list three proximate determinants, but also nineteen factors that determine the values of the more general determinants.[11] In Hibbs's causal universe, positive and negative factors run amok. About thirty factors are directly or indirectly linked to coups, collective protests, and internal wars.[12] The occurrence of these events involves the interplay of all the factors, facilitative and obstructive.

Undoubtedly, all concrete events, physical and social, result from the confluence of just such numerous positive and inhibiting factors. The business of positive theory is not to reproduce this complexity of the concrete, because that route takes one back to what makes experience mystifying in the first place. The task of positive theory is to cut through puzzling complexity to illuminating essentials: to find parsimony within intricacy. How can we do this after so much preliminary study on collective political violence?

The way to start, surely, is to find the most basic branch point for choice in theorizing. My thesis here can be put in a sentence: in studying collective political violence, the first and most fateful choice lies between regarding it as "contingent" or "inherent" in political life.

Nature of Contingency and Inherency

At the outset, I propose a broad thesis about basic branch points in building positive theories, regardless of subject. It seems historically true that primary branch points in theoretical inquiry are all alike: all involve a choice between contingency and inherency. Why so I will try to show momentarily. First, we must understand in a general way the nature of the two notions.

Something is *contingent* if its occurrence depends on the presence of unusual (we might say aberrant) conditions that occur accidentally—conditions that involve a large component of chance. An auto accident clearly is contingent in this sense. Drivers may or may not make mistakes; cars may or may not fatefully malfunction. It is with reason then that we call such occurrences "accidents." Note immediately that contingency does not entail indeterminacy. We can specify that if a particular driver does something, an accident will probably occur. We can also determine general conditions that increase or decrease the probability of accidents. Contingencies thus are not random, and "may–may not" events can sometimes be controlled. Such events, though, do raise questions of explanation and theory in a special form: one wants to know what caused an accident where "normally" none was expected to occur. We are not mystified when a driver gets from here to there without malchance. We want to explain when the opposite occurs. Contingency implies unexpected, something out of the ordinary, something not understood without special explanation.

Per contra, something is *inherent* either if it always will happen (e.g., entropy) or if the potentiality for it always exists and actuality can only be obstructed. Just when the inevitable occurs or hindrances are removed is decided by contingencies: chance occurrences that hinder or facilitate. As contingency does not entail randomness or inability to control, so inherency does not imply fully predictable determinacy. The decay of an automobile surely is inherent, even without any accidents. When or how it will fall apart, though, is not fully predictable. But basic questions of explanation differ in cases of inherency: we usually want to know why the inherent did not occur sooner, what obstructed or delayed decay and "termination." In contingencies, then, the puzzle is "why"; in inherency it is "why not?"

There is a certain sense in which one could always say that contingencies are inherent in entities or events and thus score debating points. No car, no accident. If you drive, it is always possible that something untoward will happen. An accident could be considered one of a driver's inherent "repertoire" of possibilities. (My terminology comes from a theory of collective violence.) But that would be as fatuous and misleading as saying that walking into the path of a meteorite is included in my inherent repertoire of living. One could say, just as fatuously, that the final decay of cars generally is contingent, for something circumstantial usually does end them. Everything ends in a circumstance, but obviously it would be disastrous to throw out the second law of thermodynamics on that basis. The reinterpretation of contingency into inherency is verbal flimflam; the two are antithetical.

Nevertheless, the silly statements are of some help here. In the concrete world, contingency and inherency are almost always intertwined and hard to disentangle. What seems manifestly contingent to one observer may seem just as obviously inherent to another. This has been the case with studies of collective political violence. Occurrences, at bottom, must always be regarded as the one or the other. Consequently the issue of contingency versus inherency always arises. Both always occur in a mix hard to disentangle, but they cannot, logically, both be equally basic. Any theory that supposes the contrary, or avoids the issue, must end by making experience illogical, hence unintelligible.

Note three matters before the argument is taken further. First, the distinction between contingency and inherency is often stated in different terminologies. The most common alternative language involves abnormality, irregularity, or aberration versus normality or regularity. In social science, the same distinction has been made as an antimony between "causal" and "purposive" behavior;[13] Hempel's term for the latter is "dispositional."[14] The distinction is between actions caused extrinsically (by contextual factors, and thus contingent) and actions chosen "intrinsically" (upon will, tactics, calculation, or other disposition in actors) from a repertoire of alternatives. Related to the notions of aberration and normality is the concept of "continuity." Thus we have been told that war may be treated as the extreme end of a single political dimension: routine politics continued by other means. War, of course, may also be regarded as lying in a realm separate from regular politics. As stated, these various differences are nominal. Those I employ here are rooted in long philosophic usage.

Second, precisely because contingent and inherent conditions are in most cases mixed in concrete occurrences, the issue usually is not whether something *is* the one or the other, but whether a subject is *better regarded* as basically inherent or contingent. The issue is not, literally, truth but explanatory "fruitfulness": the ability to explain cogently numerous matters through logically related propositions; to allow the subsumption of narrower theories under broader ones; perhaps, above all, to allow the deduction of good, previously unformulated theories. There have, to be sure, been decisive tests of the contingent or inherent nature of certain experiences. Usually, however, they occur long after the experience. (Between Copernicus's brainstorm and Galileo's tests, about sixty years elapsed; between Galileo and Newton, about a century.) In the meantime, one can only choose more or less sensibly—and try to devise projects that allow wiser theoretical choices at the crux.

Third, all kinds of occurrences (of collective violence or anything else) assumed to belong to a general "class" need not be contingent or inherent (see my remarks on this in the conclusion of this chapter). But if answers as to contingency or inherency differ by type of event, it is just about certain that the events do not belong to a single genus. Initially, though, let us assume that occurrences of collective political violence do constitute a broad type, in order not to sacrifice parsimony before we must.

Examples and Consequentiality of the
Contingency-Inherency Distinction

The nature of our primary branch point can be illustrated by analogies to several very disparate fields.

Physical science furnishes the best-known example. At the divide between ancient and modern physics are divergent ways of regarding a critical property of objects: their motion. Nothing physical can be explained without a theory of motion, and thus also of rest. Motion can be regarded in Aristotle's manner: as the result of force exerted by (contingent) external movers, so that objects are "normally" at rest, or tend toward it. The alternative—inobvious, but correct—is that motion inheres in objects, so that rest is a condition resulting from a confluence of contingencies. External movers do affect motion, but they affect only its "accidents" (velocities, paths, rest), not motion in itself. It should be evident—as it was to the Inquisition—that the distinction is fateful in the extreme for physical theory, cosmology, and theology, even though particular motions are usually explained fully only by a combination of intrinsic and extrinsic factors. One thing that makes the distinction fateful, as suggested earlier, is that it poses different primary problems. For Aristotelians, the crucial problem involves the occurrence of motion: hence their labored teleological, to us absurd (but long believed) account of gravity. For Galileo the equivalent puzzle is rest, as itself a kind of motion. It would be nicely convenient to put Aristotelian and Galilean notions together in a single formulation. But since objects cannot be both "inertly" moving and unmoving, the result would be messy and illogical, in contrast to the power and elegance of modern physics.

In the life sciences, there exists an analogous core problem. Death (termination, entropy) is inexorable. But how should one regard illness and other disturbances of "normal" functioning? One possibility is the familiar bacterial explanation and its extensions: diseases result from the invasion of organisms by virulent microorganisms, and disabilities result from diseases, or from accidents, or from the consequences of other external matters (like dominant parents or competitive siblings). Diseases and disabilities are thus contingent—pathological. The alternative is to regard them as particular routine states of the living system: stress on systems is always present; the system defends and usually maintains itself through homeostatic devices, sometimes to avoid disturbance altogether, sometimes to recuperate; thus both illness and health essentially are intrinsic matters of the state of biological systems in interaction with their contexts. As one ages, of course, one becomes more vulnerable to stress, and homeostasis is more difficult to achieve. That does not resolve the fundamental problem: which version of disease and disability, the contingent or the inherent, is the better for all or some pathologies as the base of theory? There is no single, agreed-upon view on this issue.

The current debate in structural linguistics between adherents of "deep-structure" theory and "empiricism" furnishes another example. Its consequentiality lies, of course, in that it raises the fundamental issue of the very nature of speech. In politics, as I have argued elsewhere, the analogous general branch point is between "culturalist" theories that explain political actions basically by (contingent) learned "orientations," and "rational-choice" theories that postulate an inherent tendency to maximize influence. In studies of social stability and integration, which is close to our subject here, there is a basic confrontation between considering the "normal" state of society to be harmonious or conflictual—for instance, between functionalists and systems theorists, on the one hand, and class theorists, on the other.

Two Antithetical Explanation-Sketches
for Collective Political Violence

How would a contingency theory about collective political violence compare with an inherency theory? At this point, we need broad "explanation-sketches" to illustrate the opposing approaches; in the next section I summarize actual theories that should fit one or another of the sketches.

Explanation-sketches consist of an initial spelling out of laws and initial conditions—scientific *explanantia*—to be filled out and made into a full-fledged theory through research "for which the sketch suggests the direction."[15] Explanation-sketches are more than the tentative commitments of theoretical approaches, but much less than final statements of theories.

Contingency theory should conform to the following sketch:

1. The fundamental disposition of individuals (or groups) in politics is toward "peace": the resolution or avoidance of violent conflicts. There would be no governments otherwise (see "contract" theorists). Satisfaction of political values is normally sought through pacific competition (electoral, through interest groups, by petitions, et cetera). Violent conflict is not in the normal "repertoire" of political competition.
2. The disposition toward pacific politics may be blocked and diverted under specifiable and "special" (aberrant) conditions. Given the disposition toward peace, the conditions should not readily occur, least of all in extreme forms of conflict. Collective violence thus involves the blockage of inherent tendencies by peculiar causes.
3. The critical problem in studying collective political violence thus is why it occurs as often as it does.
4. As to "peculiar causes," the pacific disposition may be blocked when

some other, discomfiting human disposition (which governments exist to suppress) is activated. This may be a disposition toward aggression or it may be a disposition toward comparing one's condition in
life with that of others.

5. It follows that choices of collective political violence are highly "affective" rather than coolly calculated.

6. The tendency to act violently in politics may be increased by cultural
patterns—learned modes of action (these are always variable and
"contingent," of course). Violent action may be a learned response;
and to the extent that this is so, pacific dispositions are more readily
diverted.

7. Given the affectivity of collective political violence, two factors
should play a rather minor role in its explanation (though they may
play some role as "mediating" variables that reduce or increase probability). These are coercive balances between incumbents and their
opponents and other factors that facilitate the successful use of violence.

Readers can construct an explanation-sketch for inherency theory by
inverting the contingency-sketch, but it will save effort if an equivalent
framework is constructed explicitly here:

1. The fundamental disposition of individuals (groups) in politics is to
maximize influence, or power, over decisions. This disposition may
flow through numerous channels, of which collective violent action
is one: extreme but "normal."

2. Since there are alternative channels for seeking power, the choice
of violence must be activated, but activation readily occurs—though,
of course, not as readily at the extreme of revolution. Collective
political violence is a normal response to commonplace conditions.

3. The critical problem for inherency theory, given the normality of
violence, is why collective political violence does not occur more
often than it does.

4. The activation of the choice of violent channels is a matter of tactical
considerations (not arousal of virulent affect).

5. Tactical choice involves cost-benefit calculation. Thus, the violent
mode of political competition is chosen if lower-cost channels of
influence seeking are blocked, provided that violent means have a
prospect of success that warrants their use. For extreme cases (revolutions) the ideal combination is blocked alternative channels, including those of lower-level violence; high valuation of goals; and
perception of low capacity by opponents to inflict high costs.

6. Cultural patterns should play only a minor role; and to the extent

that learning plays a role, it should inhibit violence at least as much as promote it, by teaching people that it is a high-cost resource.

7. More objective factors, like coercive balances or facilitating factors, should play a major and primary role in explaining collective political violence.

It should be evident that the two sketches intersect at some points, so that the allure of unparsimonious combination is, as always, considerable. But it should also be evident that what is primary, important, necessary in one case is secondary, minor, chancy in the other. Most important, the sketches lead in quite different directions in research (in logic and, as we will see, in practice): most patently, toward conditions that arouse exceptional types and degrees of affect (especially anger) versus conditions that influence calculations of cost-benefit ratios in choosing modes of political goal-seeking (especially intrinsically high-cost channels). Most fundamental, as in all political theorizing since ancient times, are two antithetical conceptions of political man: as a creature in search of either peace or power.

MAJOR ILLUSTRATIONS FROM STUDIES OF COLLECTIVE POLITICAL VIOLENCE

We proceed to theorists who illustrate the opposed approaches. The theories do not add much to the explanation-sketches. We do not yet have "finished" theories of collective political violence, but we do have "evolving" theories; unfortunately, they are becoming more and more complex and logically messy.

Contingency: The Relative Deprivation (RD) Family of Theories
Contingency theories of collective violence pivot on the notion of systemic breakdown where homeostatic devices normally provide negative entropy. It has been pointed out, correctly, that this implies sharp discontinuities between routine and nonroutine political activity, that the cause of violent action must be discontinuous (rapid, extensive) change in the context of politics and that collective and individual behavioral pathologies should significantly covary, where the former is a "version" of the latter.[16] Almost all such theories are subsumable under the notion of relative-deprivation theory, of which Gurr has been the leading exponent.

"Why men rebel." Gurr's RD model can be summarized thus: (1) collective political violence is a form of aggression; (2) aggression results from anger, which is produced by frustration; (3) the fundamental cause of feeling frustration is an imbalance between what one gets and what one considers one's due: in Gurr's language, "discrepancy between men's value expectations and their value capabilities."[17] Obviously, the propensity to

feel frustrated and its consequences are in a special sense "inherent." However, it is a dormant disposition until aroused by special extrinsic forces strong enough to overcome the tendency toward pacific acquiescence. The greater the scope and intensity of RD, of course, the more likely is violent behavior per se as well as at high "magnitudes."[18]

The above is only a first step. Aggression is not yet rebellion. It must be politicized if it is to appear as collective political violence, and latency must become actuality. Here, mediating (secondary) variables that do not themselves involve the frustration-anger-aggression nexus come into play. They include "normative justifications" for political violence or the lack of them, from Sorelian glorifications of violence to Gandhi's doctrine of nonviolence at the other extreme.[19] Such justifications are themselves, of course, contingent, and unlikely to have consequences without prior frustration.[20] Also included are "utilitarian justifications," which are chiefly tactical considerations: estimations of the rational sense in collective violence. These involve calculations of numerous balances concerning the organizations of regimes and dissidents, their respective resources (actual and potential), and the availability of alternative channels of action. A third mediating variable decides whether politicized aggression surfaces as fully actualized collective violence, and involves something obviously tactical: the balance of coercion between regimes and dissidents.[21] The relation of that balance to magnitude of violent political conflict is curvilinear: strife will be greatest if there is an even balance of coercion. At the extremes, where coercion is highly unequal, regimes collapse virtually without being pushed or dissidents lie low out of fear or are quickly put down. Gurr also has at times invoked still other factors, especially environmental conditions that facilitate strife:[22] transportation networks, geographic traits, demographic characteristics—and, not least, the external support given dissidents.

In a contingency theory, such factors should themselves depend on rather fortuitous circumstances—as they do in Gurr. More important is an implication that must be read into relegating the factors to the inferior status of mere mediating variables. Causal-path analysis aside, the implication is that the role of tactical variables diminishes as the more fundamental factor of frustration grows: desperate, impassioned people will not act coolly or be much governed by tactical calculations, even about coercive balances. This is the only logical way to combine rationalistic with essentially nonrational motivation. Nonrationality also implies that a major role be assigned to culturally variable learning. This too occurs in Gurr's theory, the cultural variable being the extent to which a culture of violence, rooted in the past, exists.[23]

Similar theories.   Gurr's theory belongs to a large family. Tilly traces its ancestry to Emile Durkheim—though Tilly's treatment of Durkheim (whose puzzle, after all, was solidarity in a differentiated society, not conflict) is debatable.[24] More obvious precursors among the great sociologists are Gaetano Mosca and Vilfredo Pareto. Pareto traces the decline of elites to the contingency of insufficient cooptation of dangerous, competent members of the nonelite, those in whom the deep-structural residues of combination (organizational skill) and force (ability and will to use coercion) coalesce. The exclusion of such men produces in them a kind of political RD.[25] Mosca propounded Pareto's theory of elite-circulation earlier, though less elaborately. He also argued that the resort to violence is often a reaction to the estrangement of elites from masses: an elite's adoption of foreign ways—a kind of cultural deprivation. Whether or not such estrangement occurs is, of course, no more intrinsic to elitism than is the exclusion of a dangerous counterelite. In Pareto, especially, the most obviously symptomatic indication of contingency, blockage of a normal process, is central.

Among contemporary writers, the most influential member of the family, next to Gurr, probably is Huntington.[26] As in Pareto, the sense of deprivation in Huntington's theory is political, though less a matter of blocked channels than of their paucity or their insufficient capacity to handle "loads." In skeletal form: Huntington argues that revolutions and lesser forms of collective political violence are artifacts of rapid socioeconomic modernization. Such modernization "mobilizes" people and induces them to enter the arena of political conflict. No harm will be done if political channels can handle their demands and activities in pressing them. But if political development lags, blockage occurs, and aggressive modes of action are generated. Note the incidence of extreme political violence in conditions of socioeconomic development, especially in centralized monarchies, narrow-based military dictatorships, and in new nations.[27]

The notions of overload and adaptation to stress belong to the world of systems theories. Since such theories are essentially concerned with negentropy as a normal state, any theory of collective political violence derived from the systems perspective belongs to the universe of contingency (though entropy is inevitable in the very, very long run). C. Johnson has been perhaps the leading systems theorist of revolution,[28] at any rate if we do not look far beneath his language. The causal chain in Johnson is quite similar to Huntington's, ignoring nominal differences: rapid change leads (sometimes) to system disequilibrium (the overload of mechanisms of homeostasis), which produces individual pathologies as well as collective movements. The sense of deprivation (Johnson actually avoids psychological concepts and speaks of dysfunction) arises, of course, at the point of overload, or blockage. Similarly, Wolf's account of peasant rebellions,[29] though making more of tactical considerations than Huntington

or Johnson, rests on aberration: peasants—not capitalistic "cultivators"—
resist the encroachment of market economies; but when traditional
peasant life cannot be maintained and alternative arrangements are too
ill-developed or restrictive, tensions arise and peasants rebel.[30] Here,
aggression is unleashed by a combination of cultural and economic frustrations.[31]

We can perhaps best divide the members of the family of contingency
theories according to whether their normal model is essentially macrocosmic or microcosmic. In the first case, notions of systems and of their
aberrations under conditions of extrinsically imposed strain are used to
identify pathologies. In the latter case, apart from cultural learning, the
microcondition is more manifestly and explicitly a sense of deprivation,
relative to others or to more abstract conceptions of what is justly due.
Thus Gurr's theory is microcosmic (individual), and Huntington's and
Johnson's, macrocosmic (societal) in emphasis; but they converge at the
explanandum, *collective* political violence.

Inherency: The Collective Action (CA) Family of Theories

Inherency theories of collective political violence at present are less
common than contingency theories. They seem more numerous than
they actually are because of a proliferation of labels for the same thing:
resource-mobilization theory, political process theory, theories of group
dynamics, mobilization theory, strategic interaction models, and political
contention theory. "Collective action theory" is used here because the
postulate of the approach is that violent collective action is not aberrant
but simply one of many alternative channels of group activity; like any
other it is chosen by tactical calculation. Thus it belongs on a continuum
or is part of a repertoire: different, sometimes extreme, but not off the
normal scale.

"From mobilization to revolution." CA theory is chiefly the work of
Charles Tilly and his associates; its *summa* is Tilly's recently published *From
Mobilization to Revolution.*[32] An earlier and more succinct overview appeared in 1975. Again, what I present here is a skeleton of a theory that,
like Gurr's, has grown in complexity to accommodate data and objections,
to the detriment of elegance.

Tilly begins with a simple conception of the polity. Polities have members, who have formal access to the political decision-making process, and
challengers, who do not.[33] All are contenders for power—with members,
of course, enjoying privileges. Members use their resources in a game of
continual jockeying to enhance their power; challengers try, as a condition
to all else, to get into the game. To be allowed to play, there are entrance
fees. The higher the fees, the greater the pressure needed to become

members; and at some point of cost-efficiency, violent action among contenders occurs, with revolution as the most extreme, but still normal, form of such action.

This is the barest précis. Some key points need to be added. Before any collective action (say, a strike, election, demonstration, charivari, riot) can occur, there must be a confluence of shared interests[34]—though Tilly deliberately skirts the issue of how collective interests come to be perceived and pursued, perhaps wisely, given his purpose. The interests must possess organization: a combination of shared categoric traits and a pattern of frequent interaction, or network.[35] Beyond this, organized interests must be mobilized; by this Tilly means the possession and use of resources that may help achieve goals.[36] Even at this point, collective action will not occur unless there is sufficient opportunity for it.[37] This is essentially a matter of power to repress (especially of credible threats) or, more generally, to make collective action costly. The obverse of repression is, of course, facilitation, not in the sense that Gurr usually employs the term, but with emphasis on political toleration of, or help to, the activities of groups in conflict.

There remains the question of what (if not contingent matters like anger or strain) activates violent collective action, particularly in the more extreme form of revolution rather than lower-cost actions. The answer is a process:[38] (1) contenders (insiders or outsiders), organized around some specially motivated core group, make claims incompatible with a polity's survival in its existing form; (2) the claims gain increasing acceptance, usually under conditions of alienation resulting from governmental malfunctioning: failures to meet obligations (provide benefits) or unexpected demands for resources (usually taxes); note here the intrusion of a glaring contingency—but only (as in Galilean motion) as an accelerator or as something that channels activity into a special path; (3) threatened authorities either cannot, or will not, or will not efficiently, block the potential for extreme action by suppression; hence (4) a condition of multiple sovereignty comes to exist. That condition never occurs after a short-run breakdown; it is always the result of a long-run chain of events. Multiple sovereignty involves mutually exclusive claims to legitimate governmental control, accepted by many (on both sides); often it is manifest in the establishment of parallel governments; and a struggle for partners in coalition occurs. Upon the reintegration of sovereignty, the process ends.

Apart from challengers' egregious "claims to resources," mysterious in origin, it seems plain that the crucial force that channels collective actions to violent political actions, once the (obvious) conditions of any such actions exist, is governmental inefficiency, timidity, and weakness. Revolutions thus occur when obstacles to strong pressures are unblocked; they are not, as typical contingency theorists believe, the very result of blockage.

Hence the assertion in our explanation-sketches: for inherency theory, the pivotal problem is what *prevents* extreme conflict from taking place; in contingency theory, the issue is what *causes* it at all.

Relatives of CA theory. Tilly himself locates the ancestry of his theory in John Stuart Mill—with a nod also to Marx and Marxists, for whom inherency takes more the form of ineluctable historical process. Mill and the Utilitarians are aboriginal CA theorists in that they regard all action as based on the rational pursuit of self-interest (pleasure), in contrast to Durkheim's notion of aberrant phases in the unfolding of the division of labor, or Weber's notion of chiliastic traumas in the unfolding of a disenchanted world.

Among contemporary writers, we find versions of CA theory in numerous strategic interaction models of behavior.[39] Such models treat forceful courses of action, such as strikes, not as releases for potent emotions but as moves in games—they involve bargains, coalitions, lying low or pouncing, to maximize one's take. A. O. Hirschman's elegant *Exit, Voice, and Loyalty* resembles Tilly's in that Hirschman accounts for "secession" from a social entity, protests (opposition) of various kinds within such entities, and acquiescence as a "repertoire" of responses to discontent;[40] choice among them is considered a matter essentially of cost calculation. In an unfortunately discursive but fascinating work on violence by American blacks during the sixties, H. L. Nieburg argues at least implicitly in a similar vein.[41] People prefer low-risk methods of resolving conflicts; the discovery of a method that offers a decent chance of success at low risk is a matter of trial and error (strategic interactions, in less plain words). In that process, violence may be used, usually under conditions of rapid social change, new group formations, and high levels of social uncertainty. In-groups and out-groups maneuver toward some new political balance, until a proper new low-risk mode of resolving conflicts is found; if not found, a life-and-death struggle for domination occurs. Violence here is, as in all CA theories, a "move" likely to be made if expected costs do not exceed expected benefits—more accurately, violence is used if it is the best available course of action. For manifest reasons, it often is the only viable choice for systematically disadvantaged groups. Nieburg's work represents a special form of rational choice: the choice of actions occurs not so much by hard calculation as by experience—trial and error among a set of (abstractly) equivalent actions.

EVALUATION

We now come to the crux. How can one make a reasoned choice at the branch point?

Unfortunately, there is no simple, workable way. One might simply reflect on the actual incidence of collective political violence. But that leads nowhere. One reason is logical. One might, superficially, expect something "inherent" to occur more often than something "contingent," but after a bit more thought it is clear that this is not necessarily so: contingencies can frequently occur (like physical rest), and inherent tendencies may not generally be unblocked. (That is why people so often leap, like Aristotle, into obvious, but mistaken, positions. Concrete nature is masterful at deceit.) In actuality, violent actions occur very often; but they do not occur as often as alternatives. Sorokin found, over two millennia, about one year of violent disturbance out of every four.[42] From this it may follow that it does not take much to make violence occur contingently or that it does not take much to block the tendency toward it or make other actions more attractive.

It also goes without saying that studies by the theorists themselves fit whatever tack they choose—though sometimes in an eyebrow-raising way. Gurr, for instance, consistently does get good statistical results. But so does Tilly, when he confronts his models with data (which he does less well than Gurr). This is hardly surprising, since their models must come together at some point of explanation of concrete events, which, as stated, do nearly always have both contingent and inherent causes. At the same time, difficulties of research findings, even if manifest, are often glossed over or interpreted in a dubious way. To my knowledge, Tilly and collaborators have never succeeded in solving a crucial problem early recognized: finding "reliable procedures" for enumerating contenders, measuring mobilization, and specifying the relationship of groups to existing structures of power. Operationally, the theory is in limbo at all crucial points. Gurr, however, has been much criticized for his choice of "indicators" of RD. Deprivation is a "state of mind" that Cantril studies psychologically,[43] but that is inferred in Gurr from objective (economic and political) indices. That begs many questions. One also wonders about: (1) the fact that Gurr and Duvall account for 75 percent of the variance in "civil conflict" across eighty-six countries in the early 1960s with five "causes" and eleven variables, in a simultaneous equation model[44]—which could be worse, but hardly is conclusive; (2) the fact that mediating (secondary) variables in work by Gurr always account for a good deal of the variance in magnitude of civil strife, with social-structural facilitation always a significant variable—a result that CA theorists surely can turn to their own account.

At the very outset, then, we confront ambiguity. We should try to reduce it by inspecting available data bearing logically on one theory or the other. I will do so by discussing a number of selected issues, potentially helpful in choosing at the branch point.

Alternative Channels

If CA theory is the fruitful tack, a clear relationship should show up between the incidence of collective political violence and the availability of alternative channels for making and realizing "claims." We may thus posit that democracies ("open" polities) will rank low on the dependent variable. By extension, political violence should at least decline discernibly in cases of regular electoral competition. But since the less advantaged do not have equal access even in open polities one should find them playing a specially important role in political violence—following the cliché that violence is the resort of the weak: everyone's equal capacity, in Hobbes's state of nature.

The matter of alternative channels would seem immediately vital for anyone who considers all collective actions a set, or repertoire, of equivalent events. However, astonishingly little has been done with the subject by Tilly: some secondary analyses of lower-class actions such as strikes and food riots, and a study of the connection between elections, organized associations, and the occurrence of "demonstrations."[45] We do have more direct evidence—though the subject cries for far more investigation by all inquirers into our subject.

In general, the data run counter to CA theory. Hibbs found virtually no statistical relationship between democratic polities and magnitude of political violence, either of the milder protest variety or with more virulent internal wars.[46] To avoid the possibility that findings were distorted by including "ill-developed" democracies, a relationship was sought between levels of political violence and democratic development, in the manner of Neubauer.[47] Again, no significant relationship emerged with protest, and a weak negative association with internal war was convincingly explained away as spurious. Worse, a positive association turns up between elections and political violence,[48] suggesting, perhaps, that electoral processes activate emotions appropriate also to other outlets. Hibbs also finds that effective exclusion from valued political positions due to ethnic, religious, or linguistic traits usually leads only to mild forms of protest—a finding that also turns up in Gurr.[49]

In the most recent, and most persuasive, study of the subject by Gurr,[50] the results are more complex, but still of scant comfort to CA theorists. One critical finding is that democracies typically had more extensive "civil conflict" (a broad notion that ranges from demonstrations to guerrilla wars) than autocracies. (For simplicity's sake I ignore a third type that Gurr calls "elitist.") Democratic civil conflicts, however, were much less deadly. The first finding clearly impugns CA theory. However, the second provides CA theorists with a measure of comfort, since it must be due to a toleration in democracies of protests that, in repressive regimes, never surface or else are forced to take virulent forms. RD theorists can rejoin that grievances in democracies are generally less serious (most obviously because of lesser political deprivation per se). They can also sensibly hold that the greater deadliness of civil conflicts in autocracies may be a result of the actions of regimes, not dissidents; this depends, obviously, on who is killed and under what circumstances.

Two other relevant points: the old saw that violence is the political means of the impoverished—the basis of the McCone Report about the Los Angeles riots in the mid-1960s—simply does not stand up to close examination.[51] There is also the much documented fact that revolutionary leaders do not much differ socioeconomically from other salient political figures, and that they differ more in regard to social marginality than in regard to resources at their disposal.

It seems evident—logically and empirically—that CA theorists must deflate many quantitative findings about the effects of alternative channels by stressing facilitation. Open polities do not block propensities to act of many, or any, kinds as much as closed polities. So they produce more collective political actions of all sorts. And the more advantaged and powerful have more means for deadly violence, no less than other actions: particularly military elites, who are more likely to act politically in closed polities. Our first test thus is one-sided in statistical results, but not hard to argue away.

Facilitation

It seems necessary then to look hard at the CA theorist's chief route of escape: facilitation—that is, how difficult or how easy pertinent circumstances make it to use collective violence in politics. Here, contingency theorists sometimes seem to turn the tables on themselves. Consider Gurr. In his early (now much modified) report,[52] certain highly contextual factors presumed related to the possibility of violence (e.g., transportation networks, density of population, other geographic characteristics, and "external support of insurgents") account for more variance in magnitude of civil strife than anything else (twice as much as persistent deprivation!). Similarly, such facilitating factors as the distribution of value-stocks, complexity and cohesion of organization, number and scope of values (resources) are likely to decrease strife if regimes are better equipped and to increase it to the extent that dissidents possess them. In Gurr's later work, facilitative matters still seem to have crucial effects on whether dissidence is peaceful or violent.

A picture begins to emerge. Having less costly channels available does seem to affect the choice of violent means: so, score a point for inherency. But the cost of violence does not much reduce deadly conflict in democracies, and still less in autocracies, where presumably it is likely to cost more: so, score a point for the other side. All would seem to depend then on what to regard as fundamental. I know no way to decide that issue yet, since CA theory incorporates facilitation (viz., opportunity), as does RD theory. The most we can say is that violence is more likely if easier to engage in and perceived to be more likely to succeed. Tactics play a role—but perhaps only for people afflicted by high RD. It seems necessary, then, to look at other issues that might break what, so far, appears to be a tie.

The Balance of Coercion

The most manifest "facility" for collective political violence is the ability and willingness of regimes to repress, relative to that of dissidents to destroy. We should, of course, expect the balance of coercion to make a difference both in a contingency-sketch of political violence and in its opposite. For contingency theory, though, the tactical consideration involved is of lesser import: as stated earlier, very angry men are not likely to act coolly, even in the face of what Tilly calls "threat." For CA theories, per contra, little would seem more important. What does the evidence suggest?

To begin with, we are handicapped by a flaw in method: the almost universal tendency to use the coercive capacities of regimes as measures of the coercive balance between authorities and dissidents. One exception is an article by Gurr.[53] Gurr uses measures of loyalty and dissidence by military forces and weighs familiar measures of the coercive potential of regimes against foreign support of dissidents and aspects of dissident groups, such as their size and organization, that may be assumed to have a bearing on coercive capacity. The results Gurr obtains actually seem to offer some, but not much, support to CA theorists. The coercive capacity of dissidents does "enhance the prospects for rebellion," the most extreme category of dissidence, whereas that of authorities reduces it. This is what CA theorists would expect. However, (1) regime coercion has "very little effect" on other forms of protest; (2) a different balance, concerning "institutional support" (support by "dense" and pervasive networks of organizations) consistently explains more; (3) throughout, the combined factor of institutional/coercive balance fares only a little better or worse in regard to different kinds of collective violence than a quite different explanatory variable, "justification," which includes both tactically relevant factors (e.g., success of past strife) and nontactical ones (legitimacy), but the latter yields better results than the former; (4) dissident coerciveness enhances the likelihood of rebellion much more than regime coercion inhibits it; (5) the latter has virtually no effect on lesser forms of strife.

What follows? Perhaps nothing, for operational reasons: Leaving aside questions of data sources and scaling, Gurr's evidence comes from twenty-one Western countries over a mere five-year span (1961–1965). However, the clear and strong result that CA theory would seem to call for manifestly fails to turn up. Also, CA theorists must make much of the capacity to inflict high costs (as pointed out in the explanation-sketch for inherency theory above); one therefore should not find that regime coercion is, as it seems to be, the least weighty explanatory factor in all types of strife. After an initial leaning toward CA theory, one thus is led to a contrary conclusion—though that, again, is offset by Gurr's conclusion that "variations in deprivation are not an important direct determinant of total strife."[54] Deprivation exists in the remote background, waiting to be "converted."

CA theory would be best supported by finding a strongly curvilinear relation between conflict and coercion. If one or another side greatly outweighs the other's capacity for coercion, rebellions should not start or regimes ought quickly to collapse, at low cost. The most intense conflicts ought to occur where coercive capacities are closely matched. Granted difficulties in the available data, the most recent study by Gurr shows only slight curvilinearity. In addition, some other results that are very odd from the standpoint of CA theory turn up: in general, a positive relationship seems to exist between governmental coercion and conflict. This includes the finding that the cumulative application of sanctions increases conflict, even at the extreme of sanctions, and that the use of sanctions has no discernible time-lagged effect on conflict. These findings are contrary to Gurr's earlier position or that of the Feierabends.[55] However, they are strongly supported by Hibbs.[56] And they are more consistent with contingency theory than the earlier position.

The unsatisfactory state of the available evidence does provide an escape hatch to CA theorists, at least for now. The tendency, though, has been for coercive balance to be of less importance as studies have improved. Most damaging, perhaps, has been the tendency of CA theorists themselves to argue away inconvenient findings by making fuzzy what should be especially clear in their theories. The problem is illustrated by Tilly's magnum opus,[57] in which repression is treated with unusual convolution—and by aphorism: for instance, "governments which repress also facilitate." Ultimately, Tilly resorts to a promising line of argument, one that involves historical patterns of repression. The special variable involves abrupt changes in such patterns. Unfortunately, the hypothetical relationship is either to "encourage" or "discourage" types of collective action (again, excepting only the obvious exception: very high levels of successful repression). That is simply not permissible—not, anyway, without a lot of added theory.

On the whole, contingency theory emerges healthier than inherency theory from our third test. But we cannot escape the problem of adequate data. For this reason, CA theorists need not throw in their towel yet. We need far more and better light on the issue. We want it especially from

CA theorists themselves; the matter is critical for theories in which "causation" and "channeling" (or blockage) are the same thing. This is useful to know, but leaves our issue still undecided.

When Men Rebel

I referred above to Tilly's use of the historical pattern of repression as an explanatory factor. His doing so may be subsumed under a more general, widely followed line of assessment: to find out *why* men rebel we may be helped by studying *when* they do so. As we shall see, this involves a set of diverse tests that could also be invoked separately. Each, though, fits a general deduction from our two explanation-sketches:

1. For contingency theory: Collective political violence, or such violence in its more extreme forms, should occur when, as the result of some temporal pattern, the specified contingency, such as RD, is or may be expected to be particularly great.
2. For inherency theory: Collective political violence, or its more extreme forms, should occur when, as a result of a temporal pattern, (a) the costs of violent collective action are expected to be especially low, or (b) nonviolent actions in pursuit of highly valued goals have been shown to be unproductive.

There is much historical precedent for seeking explanations of political violence in the nature of historical moments of such violence. The classic source is Tocqueville. His basic argument in *The Ancient Regime* is familiar:

> Revolution does not always come when things are going from bad to worse. It occurs most often when a nation that has accepted, and indeed has given no sign of even having noticed the most crushing laws, rejects them at the very moment when their load is being lightened. . . . Usually the most dangerous time for a bad government is when it attempts to reform itself.

This argument is the theme for numerous variations. We will consider the most important.

Rapid change. There is a large family of theories that attributes extreme and destructive political behavior to an obviously "contingent" condition: unusually rapid, hence unusually unsettling, socioeconomic conditions. Frustrations are likely to arise under such conditions because of disorientation (anomie) and because of the familiar occurrence of an excessive rise in expectations. At a minimum, the conditions of any contingency theory are more likely to be satisfied when change is rapid (and abrupt) than under more settled circumstances.

Olson's influential article on the consequences of rapid economic growth is prototypical of this view.[58] A political, and otherwise modified, version of Olson's argument is Huntington's mobilization-institutionalization hypothesis. Both arguments are backed by persuasive reasoning, as well as the usual selectively chosen, post hoc illustrations. However, the evidence once again is surprisingly inconclusive; in general, only illustrations are used, and illustrations can be found of almost anything that is not wholly absurd.

Tilly and Johnson both have pointed out that contingency theorists should expect a high correlation, in cases of rapid change, between individual pathology (crime) and the collective variety (political violence). One can see why this should be so, the causes of individual and collective aberration (such as frustration) being presumably the same. But again, though the point seems crucial, evidence is strangely meager, and, for us, confusing. Gurr's work of 1970 cites a study that reports a decline in aggressive crimes (by blacks and against blacks) during periods of civil rights demonstrations.[59] That fact, though, can be interpreted almost any way one chooses—though, superficially, it runs against the expectations of contingency theory. By way of compensation, Tilly et al. do find a correlation of the two,[60] but they emphasize that it is low. Perhaps, though, this is the correct expectation—anyway for them—since CA theorists regard different responses to similar conditions as alternatives in a repertoire of actions. If so, individual and group violence should be associated, but not very closely, for some people will choose the one response and others its alternative. Obviously, we need here both better data and better reasoning.

In any case, an impressive number of studies suggests that there is no simple, direct relationship between rates of socioeconomic change and political violence. The relationship, again, seems unusually ambiguous. Tanter and Midlarsky found a negative relationship between economic growth and, as they use the term, "revolutions" in Latin America, but a positive relationship in the Middle East and Asia.[61] Bwy confirms the Latin American result but argues that a different relationship among the variables holds for less developed countries.[62] Flanagan and Fogelman find a negative relationship;[63] Alker and Russett find the same.[64] On the other hand, the Feierabends and Nesvold report a high association between rate of modernization and "instability."[65] Hibbs finds different relations between rapid change and different types of political violence.[66] And so it goes, in a very extensive set of works.

With enough ingenuity, one might perhaps trace this extreme confusion to different uses of concepts and measures. But if the relationship between the variables was very strong, mere differences in preferred indicators ought not to produce such wildly divergent findings.

Adaptation to change. The virulent potential effects of most stresses may, of course, be offset by the proper adaptation of "systems." If socioeconomic change is similar, differences in "adaptation" to it should be matched by differences in its consequences, including collective political violence. An example is the apparent relation (to be sure, small) between historical bourgeois radicalism and the relative lack of opportunities to become ennobled—[67]a nice example of Pareto's hypothesis.

More to the point here is Barrington Moore's thesis that political outcomes (in Moore's case, the nature of regimes, but, by implication, also political processes more generally) depend chiefly on the adaptation of the traditional landed upper classes to "bourgeoisification"—economic modernization, as most of us think of it.[68] That famous thesis fits, post hoc, eight widely assorted cases. But it has run into trouble when extended to other cases (or when examined more closely): by Tilton (Sweden) and Rokkan (the smaller countries in general); note also the critique by Skocpol.[69] Moore's thesis can also be logically subsumed under either contingency theory, if change is emphasized, or inherency theory, if his argument is interpreted as hinging on choices of coalitions. Note, too, that despite the long vogue of "systems" theories in political science, operationally rigorous work on stress due to change, and adaptations to such stress, is virtually nonexistent.

Structural imbalance. As implied earlier, Huntington's thesis rests on the notion of a "balance" of structures rather than on rapid mobilizing as such. This, in a sense, combines the variables of change and adaptation to change. Huntington's theory, of course, places the most inflammatory point in polities where the divergence between mobilization and institutionalization is greatest. As the space between the two narrows, collective political violence should decline. Like Moore, Huntington illustrates his argument. The evidence of other studies, however, runs strongly against him.

Schneider and Schneider accept Huntington's basic argument on the basis of a cross-national study,[70] but their evidence leads them to reject the corollary that "mobilization" should be slow if it is to be balanced by "institutional" adaptations; this is damaging evidence, for one can easily show that the corollary is inherent in the postulate. Sanders concocts a resounding empirical refutation and also presents a strong critique of Huntington's conceptualization (which, of course, weakens the empirical refutation).[71] Other important empirical rebuttals may be found in Yough and Sigelman, and Duvall and Welfling.[72] Huntington himself distinguishes among Western and Eastern types of polities, to which his thesis (presumably) applies differently, and adds some very ill-fitting variables that confuse the nontactical character of his theory: for instance, the effects of foreign wars and interventions.[73]

Unfortunately, again, there seem to be no other theories of structural "imbalance" that have sufficient empirical support to allow a more definite verdict about this mode of theorizing; nor are other possibilities worked out as fully as is Huntington's theory (really, itself an explanation-sketch).

The J-curve.   One major hope remains: that we can infer the conditions of collective political violence from some less simply wrought theory of change—some theory that finds the point of explosion at a particular point, or range, on a curve of change. The leading exposition of such a view is Davies's J-curve theory.[74]

The theory is that revolution is likely when periods of prolonged improvement, the historical pattern most likely to raise expectations, are interrupted by abrupt reversals; then frustrations due to unrequited expectations become intolerable. The J-curve theory, needless to say, involves contingency in its most pristine form, especially considering that it has never been diluted with logically confusing factors suggesting tactical choice—all honor to Davies for theoretical courage. What is the state of the evidence regarding the theory?

The supporting evidence should be very strong, for all contingency theory implies that the condition described by Davies frustrates and angers very deeply. In Davies's original formulation four cases were invoked— once again, as illustrations. Later, four other cases were added.[75] In an impressive independent check, Grofman and Muller provide a clear measure of support by using data on individuals.[76] But they also find strong evidence for a "relative gratification" theory of conflict behavior (drop-rise, or V-curve, theory). Still, their study manifestly remains within the realm of contingency theory and rests on reasoning analogous to, though not wholly the same as, that of Gurr and Davies.

The chief problem with J-curve theory is the abundance of countercases. Consider, for example, the many countries in which the Great Depression of the 1930s did not increase political violence. Surely, the effects of sudden depression, following the orgiastic recovery of the 1920s, were crucial—and no more in Germany than in all the countercases. Moreover, Tilly provides, of all things, a tactical interpretation of the meaning of the J-curve patterns of change.[77] Unfortunately, it seems labored: members should "break commitments where least dangerous." This begs crucial questions: What commitments, and to whom? Moreover, the interpretation accepts the importance of contingent frustration and simply counsels increased coercion in the right place.

Group dynamics.   The question of when men rebel obviously has led, again, to puzzlement, if viewed from the standpoint of contingency theory. Does inherency theory, then, fare better with the question of timing? For RD theorists and their kin, the flashpoint of collective political violence should occur at a point of social process when rage or despair are most acute—when expectations and capabilities are most distant. For CA theorists, in contrast, violent action, being relatively high in cost in most circumstances, should generally be chosen after lower-cost channels are perceived as ineffectual, provided only that the balance of coercion does not manifestly rule out successful violence.

A tactical scenario that makes the resort to violence especially likely can readily be constructed. A group of contenders makes political claims cheaply: say, by petition. No response is made by authorities. Pressure is stepped up, perhaps through a stoppage of work; but still no response. A more dangerous organized demonstration is used next. The authorities remain intransigent and call out some squads of police to indicate determination. A more intense demonstration occurs; perhaps now some undisciplined elements or provocateurs throw rocks or do some looting. The authorities call on police and militia; heads are broken. At this point it will be clear that only violent collective action has any prospect of success at all. And, given some chance of success and intensity of claims, the high-cost method will be used. The moral is that negative sanctions precede collective political violence. On this point, CA theorists have differed from RD theorists almost from the beginning, for manifest reasons.

Tilly's argument along the lines just sketched is predated by the report of the National Advisory Commission on Civil Disorders. The report held that intervention by the police "almost invariably" preceded larger-scale violence—though, of course, the police might simply be acting in learned anticipation of what might occur anyway. A more convincing finding occurs in Hibbs:[78] milder forms of aggression do generally escalate if regimes use coercion; in fact, that is the strongest of all factors leading to "internal war" in Hibbs's eclectic model. Hibbs, though, can hardly be conclusive on the point at issue here. For one thing, it is not peaceful action that is converted by force, but aggressive action into more aggressive action: the optional channels *start* with violent behavior. In addition, Hibbs's data are cross-sectional; they do not follow the same conflicts over time. And, again, there is empirical support also for the other side. Tilly and partners themselves have presented contrary evidence:[79] repression, they argue, works—though, needless to say, they use the point to support the tactical-choice argument. This is a fine example of how one may read the same evidence in contrary ways if one starts from antithetical bases—hence the bases of theory matter a great deal. Repression is used and violent action stops; a routine channel is blocked, or aberrant anger is suppressed. The evidence fits both conclusions equally—and we remain ambiguously suspended between antitheses.

War.   A different argument for inherency involves the removal or weakening of coercive blockages, rather than gradual escalation as a forceful response to repression. A tendency may be present and emerge when resistance to it weakens, or actions may occur to overcome resistance when otherwise behavior would be more moderate.

When is coercion, as an obstacle to turbulent political action, likely to be unusually low? The most obvious answer is that the coercive potential of regimes will be exceptionally low when military forces have disintegrated, leaving the field free to less potent groups. This condition is likely after defeat in war, at least if occupation forces do not step in to help incumbent authorities.

Examples of revolutions after lost wars abound: France in 1871; Russia in 1905 and 1917; Turkey in 1918; China after World War II. Unfortunately, countercases can be invoked just as readily: Japan or Italy after the last great war, for instance. Perhaps these cases only show that losing a war is not a sufficient condition for revolution; but then, neither is it a necessary condition, or even a "normal" occurrence (e.g., France, 1789; Mexico, 1910; Cuba, 1959; etc.). Anyway, the argument surely is more pertinent to the outcome of revolutionary conflicts than to their inception. This is Hammond's point about communist take-overs and, more broadly, that of D. E. H. Russell's study of twenty-eight "mass rebellions" since 1906.[80] Consider also Trotsky's familiar argument that the armed forces usually reflect popular conditions. If so, they would always facilitate violent action, if there is sufficient popular disposition to use it.

Learning: The "Culture of Violence"

Contingency theories belong, in social analysis, to the same family as culturalist theories—theories based on learned orientations to action. Inherency theories are related to rationalist theories—based on the notion that actions are chosen by calculations of cost-efficiency.

There is much writing about the role of learning and culture in relation to political violence. Bandura is the leading exponent of the view that using violence individually is learned, and he makes a good case.[81] On the macrolevel, though, we should expect ambiguous findings about the relation of present to past violence. The use of violent action might, logically, become a learned response, but it might also teach people that its costs tend to be disproportionately large, even if successful. The problem here (as with violence by authorities: repression) is that any curve, or none, can support the cultural interpretation. Much, in other words, is made in the literature of "cultures" of violence, but nothing definitive for the debate between contingency and inherency theories is likely to emerge from studies linking past to present violence.

This point fits findings. At best, a moderate relationship tends to turn up, as in Gurr's work.[82] Still, Gurr later strongly argues the "culture-of-violence" hypothesis on "varied evidence and arguments"—which, as I read them, support equally well utilitarian explanations of violence.[83] Another recurrent theme in studies of the culture of violence, as we should expect, is that "it depends." For instance, statistical relations seem to vary, for some reason, with geographic areas. In Africa, past rebellions are associated with reduced "turmoil";[84] but Latin America is different, and Western Europe different again. Welfling (with Duvall) squares the circle on the basis of type of collective violence: turmoil, it is argued, feeds on itself whereas "elitist" kinds of violence reduce the likelihood of later violence. But they do not do so through learning; rather, the cause seems to be the tactical factor of suppression.[85] Hibbs also reports quite contrary findings for "protest" and "internal war";[86] in his study, conflict akin to the "elitist" type in Welfling seems to be increased by the existence of a "culture" of violence.

As I argued, this contrariness can be accommodated to the premises of contingency theory. But to accommodate the evidence, we will have to specify when violence teaches violence or the imperative of peace. This will be difficult, at best. At present, the evidence may be regarded as typical of the too often ambiguous findings in the literature.

CONCLUSION

We began with an explication of a recurrent antithesis at the basic branch points of theorizing about any subject. We went on to a version of that branch point especially tailored to explaining collective political violence. We found that theories in the field do divide along the lines indicated. And we reviewed many empirical studies that bear on expectations deduced from the postulates of the antithetical approaches. No clear result emerged. Granted, conditions such as inequalities, unsatisfied demands, discrimination, and societal cleavages are related consistently to degrees of conflict. What remains mysterious, in the end, is the basic nature of the link between causes and effects—not least, therefore, understanding why similar conditions so often have dissimilar results.

The findings do not point strongly toward the superior fertility of a particular species of theorizing. "Fertility" in this connection is, first, the capacity of an approach to provide consistently superior explanations of many aspects of an independent variable—explanations that are themselves logically consistent or entailed by a higher-order theory. Second, fertility is the ability of such higher-order theory deductively to yield new, and good, lower-order theoretical relations. On the whole, contingency theory probably has fared better than inherency theory. That may only be a by-product of its more frequent use or it may result from a lesser empirical bent among inherency theorists. More important, we consistently found ambiguities in data bearing on the contingency perspective, no less than its antithesis—problems of interpreting correctly their implications—and often findings that were offset or made doubtful by other findings. Also, relationships that should have been clear and strong frequently were opaque and weak.

Something, then, must be amiss—at least if the premise of this essay concerning basic theoretical choice in studying collective violence is correct. I will conclude with some speculations on what the problem might be.

Surely, the difficulty is not any lack of studies or data. We are inundated with both, and the data cover a vast range of variables, history, geography, and types of polities.

Somewhat more likely (though I doubt it) is that we arrived at a confusing result because the empirical studies cited were an inadequate sample. They certainly do not exhaust the literature and are a mix of methodologically good, bad, and indifferent studies. This implies a challenge to specialists in the field: before embarking on new empirical studies, identify the high-quality works in both approaches and analyze their procedures and results from the perspectives sketched here.

Another strong possibility is that confusion has emerged because of a taxonomic error. We have treated cases of collective political violence as a single class—as Tilly treats a still much larger universe: all collective actions. Even if this is typologically plausible, doing so may be theoretically confusing: as suggested early in this essay, certain kinds of political violence might better be treated as "contingent," others as "inherent." We did frequently find such results in the literature, especially between lesser and greater types of strife. For reasons of parsimony, we ought perhaps to resist using this possibility, but evidence might compel resorting to it. In any case, here is another challenge for analysis.

A third likely difficulty—one common in the social sciences, and one that may well condemn to futility exercises like those just suggested—is method: an overdose of induction. One doubts that underlying determinants can ever be mechanically teased out of the complexity of highly disparate events, no matter how sophisticated the quantitative methods used. A related problem is deliberate eclecticism. Choosing eclecticism at the outset guarantees confusion in the end and thus seems self-defeating—even perverse.

Although we have not found a hero, we have surely found villains: prehedged models and models ground out mechanically from motley data. The resulting "modeled" world appears about as complex (and thus mystifying) as the concrete world it models. In Hibbs,[87] we find no illuminating simplification: we find only a complex world of variables, vertiginous with arrows and proportions. The artfulness of nature wins out over that of theory because, contra Bacon, nature is not "put to the test." One should not be too censorious about this, since Hibbs's deliberate aim is eclecticism. Gurr's model—more surprisingly, because based on an elegantly parsimonious theory—is not much less complex. Is not the reason fear of potential disconfirmation, even at the cost of mixing up a highly plausible line of analysis with its antithesis?

The result always is a realized intention: a model that "fits" the data. But if such a model is irrefutable in principle, it will fit only without really illuminating experience. That, I suggest, is inadvertently the case in Gurr's work, however tenacious and ingenious the work has been. Try to refute the following, which is essential RD theory, à la Gurr:

1. no political violence can occur without politicized discontent (satisfied people do not rebel);
2. no discontent will exist unless somebody feels deprived;
3. politicization involves both normative and utilitarian (tactical) considerations;
4. even so, little or nothing will happen when facilitative and coercive resources available to dissidents and authorities are distributed one-sidedly.

Admittedly, this is a great simplification. But it surely shows, by omitting nonessentials, how RD theory has been insulated against tactical accounts of collective political violence by incorporating them.

Tilly, too, has increasingly complicated his theoretical model, as well as swallowed up inconvenient data by reinterpretations. A still greater difficulty that emerges in his work, and also disarms invalidation, is a kind of clever triviality (in the philosophic sense). Something *seems* to be said to explain a mystifying set of events. But except for labels (members, challengers, etc.) we know it already and so remain mystified. No substantial violent action will occur unless:

1. some group wants something it does not have;
2. a fair number of people agree that their claim is justified;
3. the group is not successfully suppressed to begin with;
4. the group controls some suitable resources (and wants to control more).

And who does not know that extreme rebels lay claim to nothing less than sovereign authority, against the claims of incumbent authorities? I do not mean to be sardonic. The point of the argument is that the "interesting" issues (those that really need explaining) always are a step removed from those Tilly faces: why do "outgroups" actually (not latently) come to want "in," where before they acquiesced? Under what conditions do people come to perceive the illegitimacy of a pattern of governmental authority, rather than continue to acquiesce?

A conclusion seems to emerge. The literature, even if differently surveyed, will probably be inconclusive for us because a well-defined choice among theoretical approaches has not been faced at all by the many scholars of collective political violence. Perhaps this is owing to failure to recognize that such a choice exists. If so, this essay, though it has no "result," should help. More immediate reasons are the understandable desire to be "right," which, in a messy world, is easier to achieve with messy theory than with parsimonious theory. If not tautological, our explanations of collective political violence thus far have been too close to descriptions: too close, that is, to being depictions of the concrete, in the jargon of either contingency or inherency theory. On that basis, explanation hardly can fail; but it also cannot succeed in getting to, or even near, essentials. The remedy is to regard theory as what it is: a tool of explanation, not something that models all facets of the concrete. We want deliberate one-sidedness that may fall in clean, competitive tests, not deliberate, or face-saving, eclecticism. If the choice of a theoretical approach is a choice among conceptions of the essential nature of a set of phenomena, studies that circumnavigate that issue can only defeat us—unless I totally misunderstand the powers of multivariate methods.

We *can* choose between the two most basic models of the political individual: peace-seeking versus power-seeking. But in my view we cannot do it effectively by incorporating both in our initial models. If we do that, results pointing to both assuredly will turn up; both are at work—in physical motion, language, or the malfunctioning of organisms. Nor can we do it by largely arbitrary commitments. Political theorists have always dealt with basic branch points in one way or the other. Thus they have come to no resolution at the foundations of theory; rather, they simply have divided "members" and "challengers" into disciplinary factions, always for suspect reasons—the worst of which is not facing up thoughtfully, with open minds, to the problem of primary theoretical choice.

One way to do so would be to work along a given line to see how far it leads. All considered, I would at present choose contingency theory in the RD version—but in a much more simplified form than Gurr and his associates have used, recognizing that the goal is to construct good "theory," which is an abstract tool of understanding, not to reconstruct concrete reality in all its nuances and complexities. Once the essentials are known, the nagging complexities will (on past scientific evidence) fall into place more persuasively.

NOTES FOR CHAPTER 9

1. H. Eckstein, ed., *Internal War: Problem and Approaches* (New York: Free Press, 1963), 23ff.
2. E. Zimmerman, *Political Violence, Crises, and Revolutions* (Cambridge, Mass.: Schenkman, 1980).
3. For example, E. Fromm, *The Anatomy of Human Destructiveness* (New York: Holt, 1973); K. Lorenz, *On Aggression* (New York: Harcourt, 1966); A. Montagu, *Man and Aggression* (London: Oxford, 1973); R. E. Moyer, *The Physiology of Hostility* (Chicago: Markham, 1971).
4. V. Wolfenstein, *Revolutionary Personality: Lenin, Trotsky, Gandhi* (Princeton: Princeton University Press, 1967).
5. Eckstein, *Internal War*, 8–16.
6. T. R. Gurr, *Why Men Rebel* (Princeton: Princeton University Press, 1970), 3–4.
7. No doubt this leaves loose ends. For instance, should political "violence" really be distinguished from nonviolent actions? What about violent coercion by authorities? How does one measure "extreme" collective political violence? I leave the ends loose here. They should be confronted when required.
8. Research methods are often confused with approaches to theory, on the assumption that good theory may be *discovered* directly by induction. I consider this view mistaken. I therefore ignore "theory" (not findings) arrived at by what Hibbs calls "eclectic model specification." My essay is written precisely to cut through eclecticism, while Hibbs makes intrinsic avoidance of theoretical commitments a virtue. D. A. Hibbs, *Mass Political Violence* (New York: Wiley, 1973).
9. H. Eckstein, "On the Etiology of Internal Wars," *History and Theory* 4 (1965): 133.
10. Gurr, *Why Men Rebel*, 320.
11. Ibid., 332.
12. Hibbs, *Mass Political Violence*, 181.
13. J. S. Coleman, *The Mathematics of Collective Choice* (Chicago: Aldine, 1973), 1–5; C. Tilly, *From Mobilization to Revolution* (Reading, Mass.: Addison-Wesley, 1978), 6.
14. C. G. Hempel, *Aspects of Scientific Explanation* (New York: Free Press, 1965), 457ff.
15. The terms come from Hempel, ibid., 238.
16. Tilly, *From Mobilization to Revolution*, 23–24.
17. Gurr, *Why Men Rebel*, 24; also Gurr, "A Causal Model of Civil Strife," *American Political Science Review* 62 (1968): 1104–1124.
18. Gurr, *Why Men Rebel*, 320.
19. Ibid., 193.
20. Ibid., 197–210.
21. Ibid., 232ff.
22. Gurr, "A Causal Model," 1106.
23. Gurr, *Why Men Rebel*, 231.
24. Tilly, *From Mobilization to Revolution*, 16–18.
25. Pareto could readily incorporate Tocqueville's account of how expectations

rise and boil over into his theory of the circulation of elites. And Tilly should have traced Gurr's forerunners to Tocqueville.

26. S. P. Huntington, *Political Order in Changing Societies* (New Haven: Yale University Press, 1968).

27. Ibid., 275.

28. C. Johnson, *Revolutionary Change* (Boston: Little, Brown, 1966).

29. E. Wolf, *Peasant Wars in the Twentieth Century* (New York: Harper & Row, 1969).

30. Ibid., xiv–xv.

31. Other important members of the family (omitted because of space) are J. Galtung, "A Structural Theory of Aggression," *Journal of Peace Research* 1 (1964): 95–119; D. C. Schwartz, "Political Alienation: The Psychology of Revolution's First Stage," in *Anger, Violence, and Politics*, ed. I. K. Feierabend, R. L. Feierabend, and T. R. Gurr (Englewood Cliffs, N. J.: Prentice-Hall, 1972).

32. Tilly, *From Mobilization to Revolution.*

33. Tilly, *From Mobilization to Revolution*, 53.

34. Ibid., 59–62.

35. Ibid., 62–69.

36. Ibid., 69–84.

37. Ibid., chap. 4.

38. Ibid., 201ff.

39. For references, see ibid., 29–35.

40. A. O. Hirschman, *Exit, Voice, and Loyalty* (Cambridge: Harvard University Press, 1970).

41. H. L. Nieburg, *Political Violence: The Behavioral Process* (New York: St. Martin's, 1969).

42. P. A. Sorokin, *Social and Cultural Dynamics* (1937; rpt. New York: Bedminster, 1962), 3: 409–475.

43. H. Cantril, *The Politics of Despair* (New York: Basic Books, 1958).

44. T. R. Gurr and R. Duvall, "Civil Conflict in the 1960s: A Reciprocal Theoretical System with Parameter Estimates," *Comparative Political Studies* 6 (1973): 135–170.

45. Tilly, *Why Men Rebel*, 15ff., 185–187, 167–171.

46. Hibbs, *Mass Political Violence*, 118–121.

47. D. Neubauer, "Some Conditions of Democracy," *American Political Science Review* 61 (1967): 1002–9.

48. Hibbs, *Mass Political Violence*, table 7.1; also D. Snyder and C. A. Tilly, "Hardship and Collective Violence in France, 1830 to 1960," *American Sociological Review* 37 (1972): 520–532.

49. T. R. Gurr, *New Error-Compensated Measures for Comparing Nations* (Princeton: Center of International Studies, Research Monograph 25, 1966).

50. H. D. Graham and T. R. Gurr, eds., *Violence in America: Historical and Comparative Perspectives*, rev. ed. (Beverly Hills: Sage, 1979).

51. R. M. Fogelson, *Violence as Protest* (Garden City, N.Y.: Doubleday, 1971), 30; and N. S. Caplan and J. M. Paige, "A Study of Ghetto Rioters," *Scientific American* 219 (1968): 15–21.

52. Gurr, "A Causal Model," 1121.

53. T. R. Gurr, "Sources of Rebellion in Western Societies," *Annals of the American Academy of Political and Social Science* 391 (1970): 128–144.

54. Ibid., 142.

55. Gurr, *Why Men Rebel,* 251; I. R. Feierabend and R. L. Feierabend, "The Relationship of Systemic Frustration, Political Coercion, and Political Stability," in *Anger, Violence, and Politics,* ed. Feierabend et al., 429.

56. Hibbs, *Mass Political Violence,* 86–87.

57. Tilly, *From Mobilization to Revolution,* 106–115.

58. M. Olson, "Rapid Growth as a Destabilizing Force," *Journal of Economic History* 23 (1963): 529–552.

59. Gurr, *Why Men Rebel,* 310, n. 92.

60. C. Tilly, A. Levett, A. Q. Lodhi, and F. Munger, "How Policing Affected the Visibility of Crime in Nineteenth-century Europe and America," Center for Research on Social Organization, University of Michigan, Working Paper 115.

61. R. Tanter and M. Midlarsky, "A Theory of Revolution," *Journal of Conflict Resolution* 11 (1967): 264–280.

62. D. B. Bwy, "Political Instability in Latin America," *Latin American Research Review* 3 (1968): 17–66.

63. W. H. Flanagan and E. Fogelman, "Patterns of Political Violence in Comparative Historical Perspective," *Comparative Politics* 3 (1970): 1–20.

64. H. R. Alker and B. M. Russett, "The Analysis of Trends and Patterns," in *World Handbook of Political and Social Indicators,* ed. Russett et al. (New Haven: Yale University Press, 1964).

65. In Graham and Gurr, *Violence in America.*

66. Hibbs, *Mass Political Violence.*

67. G. Shapiro and P. Dawson, "Social Mobility and Political Radicalism," in *The Dimensions of Quantitative Research in History,* ed. W. D. Aydelotte, A. G. Bogue, and R. W. Fogel (Princeton: Princeton University Press, 1972).

68. B. Moore, Jr., *Social Origins of Dictatorship and Democracy: Lord and Peasant in the Makings of the Modern World* (Boston: Beacon, 1966), 429ff.

69. T. Skocpol, *Social Revolutions* (Cambridge: Cambridge University Press, 1979).

70. P. R. Schneider and A. L. Schneider, "Social Mobilization, Political Institutions, and Political Violence: A Cross-national Study," *Comparative Political Studies* 4 (1971): 69–90.

71. D. Sanders, *An Empirical Investigation of Huntington's Gap Hypothesis,* M.A. thesis, University of Essex, 1973.

72. S. N. Yough and L. Sigelman, "Mobilization, Institutionalization, Development, and Instability," *Comparative Political Studies* 9 (1976): 223–232.

73. Huntington, *Political Order in Changing Societies,* 273–308.

74. J. C. Davies, "Toward a Theory of Revolution," *American Sociological Review* 27 (1962): 5–19.

75. J. C. Davies, "The J-curve and Declining Satisfaction as a Cause of Some Great Revolutions and a Contained Rebellion," in *Violence in America,* ed. Graham and Gurr.

76. B. N. Grofman and E. N. Muller, "The Strange Case of Relative Gratification and Potential for Political Violence: The V-curve Hypothesis," *American Political Science Review* 67 (1973): 514–539.

77. Tilly, *From Mobilization to Revolution,* 207.

78. Hibbs, *Mass Political Violence,* 181.

79. C. Tilly, ed., *The Formation of National States in Western Europe* (Princeton: Princeton University Press, 1975), 78, 285.

80. T. T. Hammond, ed., *The Anatomy of Communist Takeovers* (New Haven: Yale University Press, 1975); D. E. H. Russell, *Rebellion, Revolution, and Armed Force* (New York: Academic Press, 1974), 640–641.

81. A. Bandura, *Aggression: A Social Learning Analysis* (Englewood Cliffs, N.J.: Prentice-Hall, 1973).

82. Gurr, "A Causal Mode of Civil Strife," 1121.

83. Gurr, *Why Men Rebel,* 170, 176–177.

84. M. B. Welfling, "Models, Measurement, and Sources of Conflict: Civil Conflict in Black Africa," *American Political Science Review* 69 (1975): 887.

85. R. Duvall and M. B. Welfling, "Determinants of Political Institutionalization in Black Africa," *Comparative Political Studies* 5 (1973): 692.

86. Hibbs, *Mass Political Violence,* 159, 163.

87. Ibid., 181.

PART V

Civic Inclusion

TEN

Civic Inclusion and Its Discontents

Author's Note: In chapter 5 I argued that political development may be regarded as a process that passes through well-defined stages, from "social polity" to "political society." That does not rule out concomitant developmental tendencies, such as Durkheim's view of development as a constantly more complex division of labor or Weber's view of it as the growing disenchantment (rationalization) and bureaucratization of societies, among others. One process may be primary, the others secondary effects of the primary tendency. Or the processes may simply coincide. That issue, at present, is open—chiefly because it has not even been raised.

In any event, I have long been persuaded by Tocqueville's view of social development as involving a "providential" process of growing "equality in the condition of men": not growing material equality but equality in regard to inclusion in, or exclusion from, full "membership" (Tilly's label) in decision making in social institutions or in access to institutions that can make such membership effective. (I present my view more elaborately in the essay that follows.)

Tocqueville's argument was stated explicitly in the preface to *Democracy in America,* and it came with many somber premonitions and surmises about the likely effects of equalization, mostly in the work's less widely read second volume, published five years after the first, in 1840. His premonitions had the ring of plausibility, sometimes recognition, for me, partly because of personal experience of "mass society," partly because of the sympathetic reading of writings about it that I mention in chapter 1—the feeling that the "irrationalists" could not be dismissed only because they

Reprinted by permission of *Daedalus,* Journal of the American Academy of Arts and Sciences; "Values, Resources, and Politics in America's Schools," *Daedalus* 113 (1984): 107–146.

argued what we would rather not have heard. These tendencies, however, did not coalesce until 1981 when I began teaching seminars about workplace authority and authority in educational institutions.

The purpose of the seminars also, initially, was distinct from my interest in "civic inclusion." Their intention was simply to inquire into nongovernmental authority, as a neglected and, to me, important subject—a follow-up to congruence-theory (see chapter 5) and the work to which it gave rise. It was not long, however, before it became evident that discontents with political inclusion, dating to the generation after it became common in Western countries (a point elaborated in a long monograph I wrote in 1984), were closely paralleled with discontents with workplace and educational inclusion. Despite allowances for the intrinsic differences among the three realms, the disillusions seemed eerily similar. That led me to suspect that the source of the discontents should be sought in the nature of the newly included—in aspects of life among the disadvantaged. Because the discontents seemed remarkably similar across cultures, it also seemed likely to me that the unexpected effects of inclusion came from the very conditions of being socially disadvantaged—that is, from the fact of living in relative poverty and with the experience of failure and foreclosed opportunities.

The result was this essay: a first attempt at spelling this view out systematically. The explanatory section of the essay is entirely "social": I emphasize in it the "authority-culture" of the poor.

At the time the essay was written and published, I also sought a supplementary psychological explanation, the subject of the second essay of this section. The fact that it appears here in the form of criticism of rational-choice theory in politics is fortuitous. I was asked to write a paper on political rational-choice theory for a conference marking the thirtieth anniversary of Anthony Downs's *An Economic Theory of Democracy*. It seemed to me that the psychological argument I had been developing for purposes of my concern with civic inclusion also had fundamental relevance to the evaluation of the rational-choice perspective—hence the form of the essay. Readers, however, should treat it mainly as a supplement to this chapter.

I want to add two points to try to prevent misunderstandings that, to my distress, have actually occurred. First, nothing said in either essay is meant to be derogatory to disadvantaged people. On the contrary, I have long tried to put myself empathetically into their shoes—not easy for an advantaged academic—and I regard their behavior as wholly "sensible" in their condition and as adaptive to facts that cannot be wished away. It follows that, if we wish to change the behavior described here, we should change the conditions that give rise to them. Although I have been told that the essays come from "reactionary" attitudes, presumably because they portray ugly things, I consider their implications to be highly radical—

more radical than most radicals probably like, and perhaps too radical to be feasible.

Second, although the essays are written as if we could dichotomize the poor and the affluent, that is done only for the sake of argument. I realize that the distinction is a continuum. Although there may be a threshold between affluence and poverty at which qualitative differences in behavior occur, it seems just as, or more, likely that, as we pass along the continuum, behavior typical of poverty and frustration diminishes and behavior typical of affluence and achievement increases. But that is a matter for inquiries not yet made.

The subject of this essay is what, for want of a conventional term, I call "civic inclusion": in essence, the processes by which segments of society previously excluded from membership (in Charles Tilly's sense) in political and socioeconomic institutions are incorporated into these institutions as "citizens." The *problem* of the chapter arises from what we might call the discontents of the "civic society"—the highly inclusive society. There are dramatic discrepancies between what was expected to follow from civic inclusion and what has in fact happened. My proposed *explanation* of these discrepancies rests on the notion that there exists an authority-culture of the lower classes of society—the beneficiaries of civic inclusion—that has been only poorly understood by the higher-class proponents of inclusion. The lower-class culture is not pretty, particularly when seen from the perspective of certain common liberal values. However, this does not imply acceptance of the idea that a distinctive, self-perpetuating culture of poverty exists (as argued, for instance, by E. Franklin Frazier, Nathan Glazer, Daniel Patrick Moynihan, and perhaps also Oscar Lewis, the giant of the literature on the "culture of poverty"), and especially not that the lower classes deal with authority in reprehensible ways. Rather, I consider lower-class authority to be a positive and adaptive response to the defining trait of poverty: being compelled to live with and manage high scarcity. The authority-culture of the poor is all the more resistant to change because of this.

Civic inclusion has two distinct but not separable meanings. First, it refers to the changing of "subjects" into "citizens." Ordinarily, different members of society have different degrees and kinds of access to its loci of authority, influence, and participation—that is, to the structures and processes of governance. In regard to this, Tilly makes a distinction between people who are "members" and those who are "challengers" in the structures that govern social institutions,[1] and although it is a great oversimplification to put it in these terms (there are many degrees of "membership"), thinking of people as included in and excluded from decision-making structures will do here. Certainly, a major threshold is crossed when excluded groups receive formal entitlements to inclusion, such as (in polities) the vote and right to hold office or (in businesses) the right to participate in management. Second, civic inclusion refers to the gaining of access to institutions that provide capacities and resources, chiefly educational institutions, by groups formerly denied such access.

Since early modern times, there has occurred in developed societies a seemingly ineluctable tendency toward civic inclusion in these two senses, in both the larger and smaller institutions of societies. The process started in politics, through extension of the suffrage and reforms of recruitment to administrative positions; it continued in the provision of access to education—first to elementary schooling, then to secondary education, and then to higher education; now it goes on in workplaces through the spread of mechanisms for participation in their governance.

Something like a genuine developmental process seems to be involved.[2] Tocqueville discovered it long ago, in America, where he found "a fundamental equality" (not least in the lack of "fixed distinctions" in regard to powers and privileges). He soon came to see in equalization a common thread in all of history, only most evident in the most "advanced" society. The process was an "invariable tendency of events," "a providential fact," "the habitual course of nature," "the past and future of history." "In perusing the pages of our history," he wrote, "we shall scarcely meet with a single great event, in the lapse of seven hundred years, which has not turned to the advantage of equality."[3]

Tocqueville thought that America's "fundamental equality" accounted for every distinctive aspect of American life. By extension, one can think of processes of civic inclusion as critical sources of institutional changes in all modern societies. Certain ways in which inclusion engenders change in institutions are highly obvious: for example, through its effects on the size and complexity of structures and on what Durkheim called "social density." Others are less obvious, such as its effects on the heterogeneity of the membership of organizations or the need for the newly included to adapt to old institutions and of the institutions to be adapted to new members. When decision structures become greatly enlarged and more complex; when members of diverse social subcultures come to constitute a common "membership" in such structures; when people not yet adapted to the structures, or to one another, must work together, as a single citizenry—then a highly consequential, probably dramatic dynamic process is inevitably set in motion.

That process filled Tocqueville with a "kind of religious dread." No one, he wrote, could say where the process would lead, since "all terms of comparison are wanting." Nothing less than a new "science of equality" was needed to cope sensibly with the process. Such a science—a set of pertinent theories—did not exist, "even in embryo." One simply tends not to think when "launched in the middle of [a] rapid stream."[4]

We may know more than Tocqueville did about the extent and effects of equalization, but we nevertheless still lack a fundamental theoretical understanding of the process. My purpose here is to make a substantial beginning toward such understanding.

EXPECTATIONS AND DISILLUSIONS

The process of civic inclusion has always begun with blithe expectations— which have invariably been disappointed. The response has always been more inclusion or else cynicism and reaction. In this section of the paper, I want to illustrate this cruel course principally in regard to political and educational inclusion, with briefer remarks about workplace inclusion. In the following section, I identify recurring themes in the literature on disillusion and provide an "explanation-sketch" to account for these themes.

The watershed period of general political inclusion occurred around 1865–1875. In America, the Fourteenth Amendment, which guaranteed to all the privileges and immunities of citizens, was adopted in 1868; in Britain, the Reform Act of 1867 gave workingmen, including a sizable proportion of unskilled laborers, the preponderance of the vote; in France, the Organic Law of 1875 instituted manhood suffrage. Comparable events occurred in other Western countries.[5]

These events were the culmination of prolonged agitation for reform, which was based generally on expectations like those of the British "philosophic radicals." Schumpeter's characterization of the "classical theory of democracy" is a caricature of these ideas, but an accurate one.[6]

Bentham's fundamental prescription for sound representative government was universal manhood suffrage. Only general participation could— and would—lead to policies in the general interest; anything else, like doctrines of natural rights or social contracts ("nonsense upon stilts"), only camouflaged the exploitative corruption of the legal oligarchy—corruption that has since been documented copiously.[7] To universal manhood suffrage were added annual parliaments and vote by secret ballot as guarantees against both the possibility that representatives elected by the general public might still pursue their own special interests and to prevent electoral corruption. The utilitarians' political scripture, James Mill's article on representative government in the supplement to the *Encyclopedia Britannica* of 1825, reiterates the point. The "security of unselfish interest," wrote Mill, could only be attained through an "identity of interest" between public and polity, brought about by full political inclusion. And it *would* be thus attained, for it was impossible for a community to know its good and yet to act against it: the community would know its good "by instinct," plus some education to inculcate civic character. John Stuart Mill emphasized more strongly the need for education in forming such character, but also held that popular participation would itself provide it.[8]

Political inclusion, in short, was expected to end the rule of "sinister interests" (J. S. Mill's phrase) and to begin an era of genuinely public-spirited rule. Even more revealing than what was explicitly expected are matters not even thought about by the advocates of political inclusion: that the existence of a very numerous, much more heterogeneous citizenry might compel structural changes in government and politics; that far from welcoming inclusion, many citizens would exclude themselves through political apathy; that the mass citizenry, which would need leadership chiefly for tutelage for a limited period, might in fact lower the intellectual level of politics; and that the laboring classes might be only weakly attached to liberal values and might even be attracted to despotism.

Even on the other side, among those who sought to protect privileged interests, well-considered dissent from the radicals' arguments was barely heard. Dissent came later, after about a generation of inclusive polities,[9] and when it did come, in reaction to earlier, inflated visions, it came mainly in the form of great—sometimes sad, sometimes bitter—disillusions.

The majority, of course, clung to the illusion, as they always do, but the political writings of the giants of the period 1890–1920 lean toward the opposite extreme. Some of the writers involved remained gentle, if disenchanted, democrats—like the Fabian Graham Wallas, who wondered, in 1908, whether representative government as such might not "prove to be a mistake."[10] Others ranged to the wild extreme of Gustave Le Bon, whose astonishingly influential study *The Crowd*—an attempt explicitly to understand the behavior of the popular classes as they entered into political life—reads like class prejudice raised to the level of racial hatred.[11] S. E. Finer, with reason, attributes the growing doubts about the happy visions of the nineteenth century to the decay of "the liberal-democratic synthesis"—the reactions against positive science, against "rationalist" assumptions, indeed against the possibility of any fixed knowledge at all.[12]

What ideas about the effects of political inclusion ran through the literature of discontent? First, and perhaps most conspicuous, the idea that political inclusion does not really equalize but only restratifies political life was progressively elaborated. The period from 1890 to 1920 (from Mosca's *Elementi* and Michels's *Political Parties,* to Weber's "Politics as a Vocation") saw the discovery of "ruling elites" in democratized societies and, not least and most emphatically, within the political organizations of the newly included themselves—the "least-likely cases" for "oligarchy."[13] Mosca and others discerned in this a sort of steady state of rule by minorities over majorities. But the new ruling elites were novel groupings, not to be confused with the old patrician "political class." Unlike the latter, they were neither precisely defined nor explicitly legitimated as a privileged political class. They rested on a plebeian basis and were recruited in undefined, murky ways. Often, they "circulated" into and joined old elites. Ironically, they were empowered by the very legitimating myths that their existence contradicted. Something unprecedented and wholly unexpected clearly was being generated by political inclusion. J. L. Talmon has referred to its extreme as "totalitarian democracy,"[14] and he locates the origins of that phenomenon in the most "inclusive" political theories of all, those stemming from Rousseau.

Second, a phenomenon now so taken for granted that we reflect little on its consequences was discovered, that of self-exclusion from participatory "membership."[15] The idea that formal entitlements and actual use of them might not much correspond was only fuzzy and embryonic during the period. Moderate writers like Wallas or Bodley were scandalized by the apathy they discerned in democratized polities. Wallas guessed that fewer than 10 percent of British males were really active in politics; even those who vote, he wrote, "shrink with an instinctive dread" from more taxing political participation.[16] Bodley, in regard to France, extended that "dread" even to voting, which, he said, many avoid "for unalloyed recreation."[17] It is, of course, Michels who holds the patent on the discovery of the institutional effects of self-exclusion. The result of broad political inclusion, according to Michels, was not simply new ruling minorities, but "gratitude" for domination, the emergence of leaders as revered cultfigures, the critical rule—as the sources of power in mass politics—of energy and forcefulness (not, as it had once been, birth or cultivation), and of control over media that may inform but that also may manipulate "public opinion" and glorify leaders.[18]

Third, from the late nineteenth century on, numerous writers (e.g., Tarde, Sighele, Burckhardt, and, most notably, Le Bon) argued that the general public was not a "public" at all, but, in effect, a "crowd." The implication was that political inclusion would reduce the intellectual level of politics and thus radically alter the structures and modes of political deliberation—for the worse.

Crowd psychology was developed in contrast to a psychology associated with the advocacy of political inclusion. Wallas called it the psychology of "enlightened self-interest"; we refer to its postulates as "rationalist," both in regard to methods (deliberation, discussion) and ends: the perception of identity between one's own benefits and those of the community. Given the bewilderment that followed experience with political inclusion, attempts were bound to be made to revise or discard the psychological baggage attached to its advocacy by developing a "social psychology." The only available model seemed hopelessly unrealistic. This was Tocqueville's conception of the American public association, on which J. S. Mill based his vision of the members of the inclusive polity: people who enlarge one another's feelings and develop their minds through reciprocal influence; people interlinked and "civilized" by the newspapers; people cultivated by political discussion that makes them conscious that they are particles in "a great community."[19] The countermodel, developed as more realistic, was derived from the behavior of "crowds," chiefly revolutionary crowds. These, after all, furnished the only conspicuous historical examples of "popular" behavior on which a drastically different social psychology might be based—one that might achieve its major end, that of accounting for the vast differences between what had been expected of broad political inclusion and what had actually resulted.

In general, the new "psychology of the popular mind," as might be expected from its prototype, depicted a mass very far from civilized, one, in fact, verging on the barbaric. The crowd displayed "socially induced stupidity," "mediocre wits," high receptivity to fraud, hero worship, admiration for criminals (Le Bon), suggestibility, incapacity for serious discussion, submissiveness, self-prostration before "celebrity" (Michels, citing Tarde and Sighele), soullessness, intellectual proletarianization (Weber), and so on.[20]

A fourth idea that runs through the literature of discontent is that the political organizations of the newly included, far from being organs of political education and advancing public interests, are in effect little more than "gangs"—that is, mechanisms for despoliation, not least of the newly included themselves. Writers on democratic politics between 1890 and 1920 discovered the political machine as an intrinsic feature of the nonexclusive polity. Its prototype was to be found, as was Tocqueville's conception of popular associations, in American cities.

The "machine" can be regarded as the institutional counterpart of the social-psychological idea of the crowd.[21] Its internal structure was (is) extremely hierarchical: monocratic at the top, with those below the boss strictly disciplined, virtually in a paramilitary manner. The machine's purpose was not even really political; it pursued offices for "commercial" reasons. Weber thought of the bosses as political condottieri, "capitalist adventurers" operating in a political market, and he argued that their existence was an inevitable consequence of having included in the polity people with no choice but to live "off" politics, not "for" it. He referred to the bosses also as a species of tax farmers,[22] while James Bryce compared them to stockbrokers and dry goods traders, and, less amiably, called them street vultures.[23] Their chief means for realizing their objectives were spoils, bribes, favors, electoral corruption, intimidation, and, if necessary, violence. Between them and their lieutenants and followers a sort of feudal relationship existed, as it did in the aboriginal robber bands: protection, favors, and "intermediation" with the world of jobs and power were exchanged for loyal support in the pursuit of great political profits.

Popular leadership, then, a generation after the watershed period of political inclusion, was perceived as a cynical hoax. The fraud was made possible by public apathy, the crowd's submissiveness, its blindness to its own larger interests, and, not least, by petty but pressing material needs and the necessity to link the new citizens with what were to them remote political authorities.

The disillusions with broad political incorporation tended for a long time (and to some extent still) to be dismissed by many scholars as the work of cranks, bigots, and misanthropes. No doubt this is true in some cases. But almost a century later, after much more intensive and rigorous political inquiry, the discontents of the earlier period have only deepened or undergone marginal revisions. By now, the early discontents have come to be expressed in a set of large subfields of positive political theory—studies of political participation, of national and community power structures, of public opinion and political behavior, and of party structures and processes.[24]

Some of the more influential scholars in these subfields, despite the now prevalent tone of placid acceptance, in fact express even more profound disillusions than the earlier writers. For instance, C. Wright Mills's conception of the contemporary power-elite is of something far more shadowy and harder to crack than was Mosca's or Michels's. Mills regarded it, somberly, as an elite united not by land, or status, or instruction, or even property, but by sheer organizational power as such.[25] The most influential countermodel, Dahl's, offers only "dispersed inequalities," scattered by narrow interests and attention, as an alternative.[26]

So it goes also in other elaborations of the earlier literature. The voluminous, now widely comparative studies of political participation have arrived laboriously at precise numerical confirmation of what Wallas had already said in an informed offhand guess. "Crowd theory" has become the theory of "mass society" of writers like Schumpeter, Ortega, Mannheim, Lederer, Arendt, Kornhauser, and, perhaps bleakest of all, Mills. And the notion of "mass society" differs little from that of the "crowd" even in mood; its principal function, after all, was to help us understand the occurrence of totalitarian horrors.[27] No doubt the predatory adventure-capitalism of the political machines has been toned down. But we have become far more sophisticated, if less shocked, than earlier writers (like Bryce) about political corruption and crime; and we tend to analyze political wheeling and dealing as the practice of rational prudence—the art of democratic princes. In fact, just as early adventure-capitalism (as Weber argued) evolved into rational, sober, "modern" capitalism, so, in the later literature, Bryce's street-vultures have become Schumpeter's chilly entrepreneurial "dealers in votes" and the rational maximizers of political benefits of Downs and Riker, virtually unencumbered by "economically" inconvenient values and convictions in the competition for political power.[28] The idea of politics as a marketplace has evolved from contempt into analytical orthodoxy. And instead of a politics of public interests, much of the contemporary literature on democratic politics has been summarized as depicting a "politics of private desires."[29]

Educational Inclusion

Since democracy and education always have been linked, it was natural that remedies for the flaws of political inclusion should be sought above all in education, by its expansion to the new citizens and in pedagogic reforms.[30]

In England, already in the eighteenth century, small groups of "enlightened" businessmen and professionals formed societies (like the Lunar Society and the Manchester Literary and Philosophical Society) to promote popular schooling in order to counteract patrician domination and corruption.[31] Bentham advocated popular education as a complement to the universal franchise; London University, in fact, was founded in response to his treatise *Chrestomathia*. James Mill, following Helvétius, held that education alone produces differences in people:

> If you take men who bring into the world with them the original constituents of their nature . . . [that is, if you leave out imbeciles], you may regard the whole of this great mass of mankind as equally susceptible of mental excellence. . . . The power of education embraces . . . the highest state, not only of actual, but of possible perfection.[32]

For democracy, he argued further, a general education that "modifies the mind" and affects "the train of feelings" was needed—in short, education that breeds civic character.

The history of educational inclusion, viewed in broad perspective, thus parallels that of political inclusion. Looked at more closely, however, educational inclusion seems more a remedial response to the flaws of political inclusion, or a supplement to it, so that the expectations associated with it could be achieved.

In Britain, at the time of the Reform Act of 1867, it was realized that "we must educate our [new] masters"; but, though numerous commissions studied education and recommended marginal incorporative reforms, a national system of free, compulsory primary education was not established until the Bryce Commission of 1895 had reported, and Parliament responded in Balfour's Act of 1902. The Bryce Commission also was the first to assert a general right to secondary education, although Balfour's

Act only empowered local governments to provide such education if they wished. Only in 1944, in Butler's Education Act, was a system of universal, free secondary education established.

In the United States, the progress of public, or "common," schooling has been less simple because of decentralization. Its broad outline, however, is much the same. An intense agitation for public schooling, concerning especially the link between education and effective democratic citizenship, occurred during the latter half of the nineteenth century,[33] the period of educational reformers like Henry Barnard, John Pierce, and, above all, Horace Mann. The schools that Mann wanted were to be "common schools," not in the sense of the German *Volksschulen* (schools for common people), but schools common to all: open to all, uniform for rich and poor alike, admitting children regardless of creed or class. "In the warm associations of childhood, Mann saw the opportunity to kindle a spirit of amity and respect which the conflicts of adult life could never destroy. In social harmony he located the primary goal of popular education."[34]

The key to such "civic" schooling lay, Mann believed, in popular control of education. In effect, he projected the creed of political inclusion upon education: lay control per se would continuously define and inculcate in children the "public philosophy." By 1860, the majority of states provided primary schools, and about 50 percent of children received some formal education.[35] A few states were also beginning to provide secondary education and public universities. By the 1890s, free, public primary education was nearly universal, and public education beyond that level was spreading rapidly. The expansion and democratization of higher education continued with increasing momentum until by 1970 about three out of four children finished high school (in 1929, three out of four did not), and 40 percent of the college-age population was enrolled in institutions of higher learning (compared with 14 percent in 1939).[36] These institutions, moreover, had substantially achieved the "impossible" objective of performing both elite functions (transmitting high culture) and popular functions (preparing for vocations and for public service)—something that even the radicals of the eighteenth and nineteenth centuries had scarcely envisioned.[37]

Late in the nineteenth century—and ever since—educational inclusion in America proceeded along two paths in the attempt to realize the aims of "common" schooling. One involved dealing with discrimination in access to schooling, which culminated in 1954 in *Brown* v. *Board of Education.* The other, just as important, concerned reform of the curriculum for the sake of effective citizenship. The seminal figure in the agitation for curricular change was William Torrey Harris; the towering genius was John Dewey. Harris subscribed, to an extraordinary degree, to the old creed that education could and would make good democratic citizens and ful-

CIVIC INCLUSION

filled human beings. "Common schools increased opportunity; they taught morality and citizenship; they encouraged a talented leadership."[38] To do this, however, the schools' course of study, Harris argued, must be changed fundamentally, from conventional rote-learning of dreary, deadening subjects to learning that would cultivate both self-discipline and "self-active" individuals. How to cultivate such individuals through schooling was the central subject of Dewey's *Democracy and Education*. The essential message of Dewey's work was that education proper to democracy must not just provide schooling as such, even on a nondiscriminatory basis, but must end an even more pernicious kind of educational division, that between broadly human study, which forms complete persons, and instruction only for "utilitarian" ends, for making a livelihood, for which "mechanical efficiency in reading, writing, spelling, figuring, together with attainment of a certain amount of muscular dexterity suffice." Such conditions "infect the education called liberal with illiberality." Education in democracies, first and foremost, must be "relevant to the problems of living together" and must "develop social insight and interest."[39]

The great expectations that moved the process of educational inclusion, then, were exactly those associated with political inclusion. The fundamental assumption on which these expectations rested was, in Sir William Jones's phrase, "that all men are born equal, with an equal capacity for improvement." Even if individual and public interests did not naturally coincide (as Locke thought, and William T. Harris emphatically did not), a proper civic education would produce, in all social strata, a populace of harmonious, public-spirited citizens and able leaders. It would, in addition, promote social mobility and lessen nonpolitical inequalities.

As in the case of political inclusion, what was not contemplated is even more revealing than what was expected. No one thought, for example, that the children of the newly included might, in certain ways, exclude themselves from the benefits of education; nor that the changed demographic character of educational institutions might perforce change their structures and processes in undesired ways; nor that mass education might lower the intellectual level of schooling.

The original pervasive optimism has in recent years been deflated severely. The panacea has come to be seen more and more as itself a problem that has, if anything, reinforced the failures of political inclusion.

The first notes of disillusion were, in fact, sounded already in the 1890s, most strongly in Joseph Rice's muckraking articles about public education in *The Forum*,[40] which were based not on hopeful thinking, but on close study of actualities—extensive fieldwork, as we would now call it. Rice depicted a deadly boring and shallow system of education, conducted by incompetent teachers whose main instructional tools were singsong drills, rote repetition, and meaningless verbiage. The principal cause of this, he argued, was the use of schools as objects of despoliation by the political machines—the corrupt hiring of untrained teachers for the usual political benefits. Public apathy made this state of affairs possible in the first place. In gist, Rice found that a flaw of political inclusion itself (machine politics) poisoned the remedy. Readers were scandalized by Rice's articles, but more by the nasty, hard-to-swallow things he wrote than by the conditions he portrayed.

In recent years, skepticism about the value of schooling for democratic socialization has grown—at any rate, the value of schooling as it is in fact provided. A considerable literature on the subject has accumulated since the early 1970s that includes the standard text on political socialization by Dawson, Prewitt, and Dawson, as well as studies by Jennings, Ehman, Niemi, Mercer, Shaver, and others.[41] For good measure, the new literature also is skeptical about the value of schooling for achievement in general— that is, for social mobility and equalization.

The standard explanation of the failure of schooling to fulfill its expected democratizing function is the theory of the "hidden curriculum," which says, in essence, that schools by and large pay much lip service to democratic values and, indeed, teach these values in "social science" (civics) courses, but negate what they preach in virtually all they do. They practice hierarchy, not democracy; teachers control the curriculum, and administrators control behavior outside the classroom; students are not treated as equals, but are placed in individuous ability groupings. And instead of self-discipline, practiced by "self-active" individuals, there is constant surveillance; instead of social harmony (living "together"), egoistic competition for grades and status occurs; instead of self-development through broad educational experiences, there is stultifying standardization.[42] Exceptions exist, not in schools catering to the newly included— those presumably most in need of democratic socialization—but in middle-class schools.[43]

In a recent article, Richard Merelman both amends and reinforces the theory of the hidden curriculum, the latter by providing a rationale for why the curriculum exists. The rationale is based largely on one of the best intensive studies of the consequences of educational inclusion—*Classrooms and Corridors*,[44] Mary Metz's study of the effects of racial desegregation on two junior high schools in Berkeley, California. Metz makes much of the fact that schools do not just perform external functions—that is, they do not simply educate. They are organizations and, like all such, must satisfy internal requisites. Above all, they must maintain internal order; hence the juxtaposition of "classrooms" and "corridors" in the title and the organization of Metz's study. Obviously, without internal order, no sort of education can effectively be provided, nor can education occur if the special ability of teachers to impart knowledge is denied. The critical

democratic values of popular sovereignty and equality in authority, Merelman argues, are clearly inconsistent with these inescapable requisites.
Schools can adapt to the values only by teaching "civics" poorly (and social
science teachers *are* particularly poor), by phony grading of undemanding
studies, and by treating controversial values as fixed facts, which prevents
training in the formation of democratic agreement by debate.[45]

The argument that the value of order is an obstacle to democratic
socialization in schools clearly has merit. Schools deal with children who
hardly are capable of fully governing and teaching themselves. Because
pupils must adapt to the schools' internal order from backgrounds that
are different in structure, internalized norms cannot fully be relied upon
to do the work of external direction. This is true even of schools like the
British public schools, elite schools that are almost total institutions, that
practice a highly developed form of student governance, and most of whose
student members enter after highly congruent experience in preparatory
schools. In the literature on the British public schools, as in much of the
recent literature on other schools, the issues of adaptation and maladap-
tation are of critical importance.[46]

The crucial thesis of Metz's study, however, is not that the need for
internal order is *always* at odds with democratic values. Rather, much more
poignantly, and much more to the point here, it is that effects of educational inclusion have greatly exacerbated the problem of maintaining order
in schools. In so doing, inclusion has made more tenuous any sort of
education, but most of all, the sort of broad, reflective "developmental"
education that, it had long been argued, alone could produce effective
democratic citizens.

In the first place, Metz found that desegregation brought into schools
students whose attitudes toward authority in classrooms and to their educational processes were notably different from those of middle-class white
students. Lower-track students (almost entirely black) were on the surface
unquestioningly submissive, accepting "what they should learn, how they
should learn it, or how they should behave" as "inevitable," but without
embracing the norms and rules of the school. They did not question the
school's character, but they also "remained alien and separate within it."
Hence, they both accepted authority (or, better, established power) and
tried "in the first instance . . . to fool the teacher." They did not experience
the school as a place they could affect in any way or as "an instrument to
meet their own experienced needs." The most that was hoped for was "an
absence of active pain"; the ideal was "boisterous play and little work."
Their passive, self-exclusive attitudes contrasted sharply with those of students in the higher tracks—mostly white and middle class (with a sprinkling
of blacks). The latter questioned teachers much more and tended to con-

sider themselves the teachers' "junior partners" in decision making. This was true most of all of students from upper-middle-class families.[47]

Second, in this way, educational inclusion largely destroyed the schools Metz studied as homogeneous "moral orders," orders in which the members largely agree on organizational goals (in the old middle-class schools, mainly the goal of education for achievement), on the means needed to achieve the goals, and on the authority relations proper to these means. The mere presence of submissive, unmotivated lower-class students was not the only source of this difficulty; even more important was the increased social heterogeneity of the schools' members—which, obviously, is always the result of incorporative processes.

Metz thinks of the definition of classroom relationships as a process of mutual adjustment in which pupils' and teachers' dispositions and perceptions interact as challenge and response: on one side, teachers are "tested," either intellectually or by teasing or disorderly conduct; on the other, teachers respond by "arranging" classrooms, by offering exchanges (grades), by persuasion or manipulation.[48] This view is widely shared by other contemporary "educationists" and corresponds to Crozier's conception of operative bureaucratic structures as shaped by complex group dynamics. Children are perceived as active contestants in the definition of classroom situations; the order of the classroom constantly is "worked out."

It should be evident that the more heterogeneous in background and attitudes pupils are, the more difficult the process of working out moral orders becomes. Where moral order in classrooms is highly tenuous, two kinds of teacher styles, Metz argues, tend to take over: one is proto-authority (para-authority?), which aims only at maintaining obedience, keeping pupils busy and out of trouble; the other is nondirective guidance, which, in gist, means copping out—abdicating the teachers' responsibilities and leaving pupils to work out their own "development." One style will hardly shape democratic character; the other will not shape anything at all.[49]

Schools use a simple practice to reduce the problems stemming from heterogeneity: they place pupils in different tracks—in Metz's schools, four of them. Something like the kind of schooling that the old pedagogic philosophers considered appropriate to effective citizenship, as well as achievement in the broader sense, goes on in the upper tracks. Metz calls this developmental teaching, which occurs along with the older, less participatory kind of pedagogy, incorporative teaching, which Harris and Dewey also valued.[50] But the lower the track, the less this is the case. A kind of aimlessness takes over at the bottom: authoritarian dominance or uncaring near-anarchy. Since the order of the tracks largely follows that of social stratification, we may infer that inclusive schooling, however egalitarian in appearance, only maintains inequality. At most, it seems to provide an outside chance to a few specially gifted and motivated lower-class children to be coopted into the milieus of the higher social classes.

The themes of discontent with political inclusion thus are echoed in Metz's study of educational inclusion. One is self-exclusion; a second, the maintenance, perhaps even reinforcement, of inequalities (elitism) in the guise of apparent equalization. Merelman misses Metz's explanation of these unexpected flaws of educational inclusion—that is, that they result essentially from heterogeneity in schools. This is apparent in the remedies he proposes: to improve the quality of teachers of social science; to set minimum levels of classroom performance (for genuine equality in grading); not to obscure the distinction between facts and values, so that public discussion of the latter can occur in schools.[51] Merelman's culprits—as in the past, when illusions were intact—are the teachers and the curriculum, not the pupils. And again, as before, only some marginal adjustments in the teachers and curriculum will, he thinks, remedy the shortcomings of the incorporative process in education. Metz's analysis plumbs much greater depths.

The difficulties that Metz describes are recurrent themes in the growing literature about what goes on in the newly inclusive schools. That literature is particularly rich in Britain, no doubt because education has long been perceived as fundamental to British social and political structure.[52] I will summarize the chief points that emerge in the literature, without going into the rich, ethnographic details that scholars have used to support them.

First, a large proportion of lower-class pupils in secondary schools seem to be concerned mainly with somehow getting through them, painlessly if possible and without much exertion. Schools are "gaols," "stalags," places to be endured before beginning work—*real* life. Pupils who conform do so, in large part, because they see no alternative and are considered "creeps" who "suck up" to teachers by most of their fellows. Many adapt by "retreating," "working the system," "making out," "getting by." Some do their own "preparing for life"—like the girls observed by Peter Woods, who "spend their day doing each other's hair," in preparation for work as hairdressers. Some spend their time in classes ignoring the lessons, daydreaming, gossiping. A major technique used to "get through" is "having a laugh": infusing hostile alien surroundings with fun and zest—"mucking about," playing pranks. This antischool (self-exclusive) culture, writes Woods (about an English secondary modern school), is "influenced by locally derived working-class values"; that is, the lower-class pupils' parents do not dissuade such aimlessness, but, if anything, encourage it.[53]

Second, just as most lower-class pupils seem most concerned with somehow getting through, so apparently are their teachers. The hidden curriculum, as discerned by Woods, really is "a hidden pedagogy of survival." The resources that teachers use to survive range (echoing Metz) from being blindly authoritarian ("teaching them right," "breaking their wills," "keeping them down") mindless drills, to convenient exchanges ("you play ball with me, and I'll play ball with you"—i.e., I'll be undemanding, playful, entertaining), to teaching simply as ritual or passing time doing pointless things.[54] In essence, pupils who disdain education deal, to a great extent, with teachers who do not provide it—a mutual adaptation that works, but hardly as proponents of educational inclusion expected.

Third, teachers deal with the need to demonstrate pedagogic success by blatant abuses of the system of "tracks" or "streams." They steer pupils likely to do well (mostly middle-class pupils) into the tracks that aim at higher education. Students of lower-class background tend to be firmly guided into lower, often dead-end tracks, and perfunctory instruction often keeps them in those tracks, headed only for manual or domestic labor. Teachers discourage lower-class pupils who aim high ("pretenders") and encourage those who aim lower than they should ("underbidders"), sometimes over the pupils' active protests. The overall result, of course, is the maintenance of old patterns of stratification; indeed, it is the legitimation of largely ascriptive differences by a mockery of achievement.[55]

Fourth, much of the literature on the new inclusive schools shows that the types of pupils recently included behave according to sets of "rules" perceived as deviant, even delinquent, by those in authority. No other subject of study has provided more ammunition for the "labeling" theory of deviance.[56] In general, the rules that lower-class pupils act by tend to give the appearance of irrationality, provocation, impulsiveness, insolence, even proneness to violence and its counterpart, submissiveness to demonstrated strength. They thus evoke the descriptions of the crowd as a model alternative to rational publics. Perhaps the most vivid depiction of these rules, and of the behavior to which they lead, is provided by Herbert Foster, who spent many years teaching in American ghetto schools and training others to do so. The rules Foster describes, in exquisite detail and with unusual honesty (since he obviously dislikes what he describes), he considers evolved "from the urban black male's culture and life style as it is played out in the ghetto's streets and street corners."[57] Their object, above all, is to test the teacher's mettle, especially his physical courage and acceptance of physicality (contests of strength, sexuality) as a condition of legitimacy. The ruleful contests include: *ribbin'*—taunting, denigrating, making fun of people, from their clothing to parts of their bodies; *shuckin' and jivin'*—mock subservience, double talk; *woofin'*—vicious verbal attacks, acting crazy; *the dozens*—insult games intended to make tempers snap; and outright *physical provocation.* Very few teachers win these contests for the right to receive compliance. Beginning optimistically, the majority proceed, via "rejection," to the exaction of fearful, blind discipline in doing petty busywork. At best, they achieve grudging submission. Only about 2 to 3 percent, writes Foster, succeed in establishing genuine pedagogic legitimacy—and thus can really educate.

The discrepancies between these findings and the expectations of Bentham, Mill, Mann, Harris, and Dewey hardly could be larger. The discontents with educational inclusion are still embryonic. But one may guess that they will be even greater than those with political inclusion—if only because education still is regarded as the critical source of effective democratic citizenship.

Workplace Inclusion

Education, of course, may involve either schooling or learning by experience. Recently, the creed that education will form effective democratic citizens has begun to emphasize the latter, particularly in the workplace—which is, after all, along with the family, the institution in which most adults' lives are to the greatest degree immersed. By participating in the direction of the workplace, Carole Pateman has argued, workers will acquire in microcosmic contexts the sense that they can be effective and confidence in their ability to influence decisions. This in turn will lead to actual participation—first, at low, immediately salient levels (shop-floor conditions); then in "management" and the still larger, still more remote context of the polity.[58] In short, workplace inclusion now is supposed to accomplish the task of educational inclusion: forming self-active citizens.

Given the already copious literature on the subject, workplace inclusion warrants more extensive treatment in my argument than space allows.[59] It is sufficient to say here, however, that discontents with workplace inclusion are common. Workers tend, much more than expected, to exclude themselves from the opportunities offered them to participate—less from participation in decisions about their own work, more from higher management decisions, in fact, from any decision beyond the work team. Correlates to a sense that one's actions might affect decisions are low. If shop-floor participation leads to anything, it is to the "active" use of leisure time.[60] Much of the impetus for schemes of worker participation in management, or QWL (quality of work life), seems to come from above, from enlightened graduates of schools of management or from managers who would rather avoid high labor turnover and dissatisfaction.[61] It has also been found that self-governance at the workplace or employee ownership appeals mostly to workers who already hold bourgeois values, that employee ownership seems to accentuate petty acquisitiveness, and that workers as owners generally reproduce old hierarchic structures.[62]

The evidence appears to point overwhelmingly to two conclusions: most workers prefer autonomy to power (two points to Crozier); and all the piety and wit of workplace reformers have not been able to dent the inertia of the existing structure of authority. Of course, unlike political inclusion, which is now a matter of history, we do not know yet what sort of organizational behavior a widely functioning industrial democracy might produce.

THE AUTHORITY-CULTURE OF THE POOR:
AN EXPLANATION-SKETCH

Workplace inclusion reinforces the need to give a reasonable account of two discontents with the results of political and educational inclusion: self-exclusion and the maintenance of stratification and hierarchy. In addition, we need to explain the apparent irrationality, even latent and overt violence (physicality), of mass behavior under conditions of inclusion (rather than as frustrated, or rational, responses to exclusion). And a "science of equality" should provide an account of the tendency of lower-class organizations to spawn institutions in which authority is an odd compound, on the one hand, of dominance and submissiveness and, on the other, of feudalistic mutualities between plebeian lords (bosses) and their followers.

A Proposed Explanation: Rationale and Summary

For all the usual reasons, single-factor explanations will not suffice. To avoid cumbersome theory, however, we should initially attempt to single out some factor likely to be critically important for explaining the gap between expectations from, and consequences of, civic inclusion. I want to suggest that the "authority-culture of poverty"—patterns of authority typical of the institutions of lower-class life—is that factor. Such patterns seem crucial for three reasons.

First, since civic inclusion has to do with the reduction of asymmetries of power, influence, and authority in social organizations, it is important to examine general attitudes toward such asymmetries and behavior regarding them. Second, the fundamental sources of disillusion with the effects of political incorporation have always been the attitudes and behavior of the newly included. Priority, therefore, should be given to examining authority relations experienced in their social milieus; and we may posit that authority in institutions in which the lives of the lower social strata are most immersed need particularly close scrutiny. Finally, though societies no doubt have cultures that cut across class lines, we may also posit that objective conditions of life shared by social strata underlie subcultural differences, as determinants or constraints. For the lower, less-advantaged strata, the most obviously shared objective condition is great scarcity. Thus, it seems reasonable to posit that there exist everywhere essentially similar authority-cultures of poverty—a core of common atti-

tudes toward processes of governance and relations of authority associated
with low incomes, little instruction, and menial work.

My governing hypothesis, then, is that *the effects of civic inclusion are
largely explicable by the culture of authority of the lower strata, and by differences
between lower-class culture and that of the higher strata.* At the very outset, I
want to make clear that the authority relations typical of lower-class life
are not somehow irrational (as may seem to those who have never experienced poverty), but that they are adapted to the ineluctable facts of
material hardship. I support my hypothesis by discussing three institutions
that pretty much cover the social life of the poor: the family, the institutions
of "street society," and lower-class jobs. No more is needed, for a correlate
of high material scarcity is a highly constricted social life in rudimentary
social networks.[63]

Lower-Class Families

All the unanticipated consequences of civic inclusion that I outlined above
can be traced to traits of family life typical among the poor. The poorer
the families, the more this holds; but I am dealing here with the ordinary
poor, not merely with the extreme poverty of destitute people.

With regard to *self-exclusion:* The authority exercised in lower-class families is utterly unlikely to breed participatory dispositions in family members, nor are family relations among the poor likely to produce the sense
that one can be effective in influencing the powers that govern life. What
they are likely to produce are passivity and lack of enterprise, ignorance,
an inability to make reasoned choices, and a tendency to evade difficult
situations.

Josephine Klein's synthesis of works on British subcultures[64]—based on
many sociological case studies, popular works, social novels, and much
else—depicts unrelentingly authoritarian, nonparticipatory dominance.
Lower-class families generally are headed by monocratic fathers, though
they are actually governed more by mothers. Fathers live mostly at work
and with their pals in pubs; when home, they require peace and indulgence
more than power, but can turn despotic, often at unpredictable moments.
Regulation of the family tends to be exceedingly detailed and comprehensive; the intent seems to be to establish routines for just about all the
children's activities. The routines, however, are frequently disrupted by
peremptory orders, and punishments are quick to be invoked to enforce
orders, either routine or impulsive. Husbands rarely "discuss" rules of
conduct with their wives, but rather make specific demands on them. If
"discussion" occurs at all, it generally takes the form of quarrels—struggles
for domination or autonomy. One finds, in effect, no decision-making
processes at all in lower-class families, and hence, no participation in any
sensible meaning.

Regarding the submissive acceptance of *ruling elites:* If the most formative experiences of life are pervaded by the distinction between superiors and inferiors; if superiors are menacing, thus to be appeased; if they are deeply needed for nurture and protection in the very precarious world that poor children confront; then surely we should expect what Michels found—that authority figures tend to be both venerated and perceived as separated from subordinates—figures of some different, higher order. To those who live in such a world, there is no association between compliance and legitimacy. Compliance tends to be mere submission, the acceptance of dominance as a given.

As to *mass behavior:* I want especially to stress here an aspect of authority in lower-class family life that also helps explain self-exclusion and submissiveness to power; it is perhaps the most important facet of authority in lower-class families—the arbitrary nature of authority. Arbitrariness makes life unpredictable, and thus frightening. It breeds anxiety and a sense of helplessness. Good and awful things happen without apparent rhyme or reason, where all seems aimed, above all, at peace for the moment: orders, punishments, and also indulgences (like suddenly smothering babies with love, stuffing the kids with food). An atmosphere of unpredictable kicks and kisses is bound to breed not just passivity and submission but, when reaction is aroused, irritable distrust, unpredictable aggression, riotous impulse, a reactive pattern of ruleless (thus seemingly irrational) submission, and hitting back. In addition, how could discussion occur among people whose dominant mode of making decisions is quarreling, who are suspicious, easily slighted, easily aroused to aggression, and relatively free of internalized standards of propriety?

Even the operation of *organizations as gangs* can be traced, to an extent, to family patterns among the poor (though it has more to do with life "on the street"). Organized despoliation can be attributed to the relative lack of strongly internalized moral restraints toward others among the poor—which includes people to whom one is close. One takes what one can, suffers as one must, and is grateful for indulgences received—surely the essence of the attitudes that maintained political machines. Despoliation seems normal within the very circle of lower-class family life. Klein points out that husbands in the English lower-classes generally try to cheat wives out of what they need to do the tasks demanded of them—even steal from them. Children, of course, also try to sneak material things: if, for instance, food is available, it is gobbled up beyond need. In these ways, the internal "market" of the lower-class family is a sort of microcosm of premodern, nonrational, ruleless capitalism.

All this may sound bigoted—like Le Bon on the crowd. Like much of the extensive literature on the culture of poverty, the conventional account of authority relations in poor milieus in fact tends to be invidious. It turns chiefly on the lack of education and "sophistication."[65] A more compelling explanation of the authority relations I have sketched is that family authority in poor families is of necessity determined by high material constraints and, to a large extent, adapted to that fact.[66]

Scarcity compels people to live in ways that inevitably entail authoritarian relationships and their consequences for personality development. Where affluence is greater, objective constraints on possible modes of behavior are looser; more liberal authority relations at least are possible. This argument also implies that cultural differences among the lower and higher classes in the same society may well be greater than differences among members of the same class in different societies. If so, it follows, then, that inclusion in a system of relationships constructed by affluent people may create greater problems of adaptation, a more acute sense of disorientation, than even so dramatic a change as immigration.

Higher-class writers who discuss the poor (like the philosophic radicals) often seem astonishingly insensitive to the simplest facts of life in the lower strata. The simplest fact of all, of course, is financial stringency and what goes with it. Where everyone has a room of his or her own, access to good, adequate modern plumbing, to telephones, to personal TV sets and hi-fi's, and a full refrigerator, it is no triumph of sophistication to be liberal in the family. Where food is scarce, where people rub elbows all the time, where someone must have the last word over who gets to use the TV or record player—in other words, even in families a good deal above destitution—permissiveness simply is not possible; domestic routines and strict discipline are imperative. Because of that, sanctions must quickly be invoked when orders are breached. Since, moreover, the particular scarcities that need managing are highly unpredictable, the concrete command is more to the point than general norms that allow family members room for interpretation. Demanding and commanding, of course, also express aggressions that follow from frustrations, thus again from stringency; if life is poor, it can hardly fail to be brutish. The combination of stringency and strictness necessarily breeds dependence—an intensely felt need for protection—and a craving for indulgence.

If directives must be peremptory and unpredictable, if they must be backed by summary punishments, if, as a result, general norms are under-developed, then it follows that perceptions of legitimacy or illegitimacy also must be weak or wanting. Authority must shade off into power, pure and simple. The tendency for the two to coincide is reinforced by another unavoidable fact of lower-class life: since constant discipline is necessary, and since mothers are busy with all sorts of chores and often, necessarily, out of the home, much authority devolves on children over children; sometimes children nine or ten years old manage others. In young children of *any* class, restraints are inclined to be low and the moral sense little developed, but these effects tend to be much accentuated by poverty.

Further, how could that sine qua non of liberal authority, decision by discussion, make sense in conditions of stringency and deep insecurity? The better-off have options, and thus discussion occurs naturally. Among the poor, however, we are bound to find the attitude that talking is useless—simply because it usually is.

In these ways, and others, virtually all facets of authority relations in lower-class families can be deduced from the functional imperatives of living in poverty.

Street Society[67]

Sometimes I wonder why I even bothered to go to school. Practically everything I know I learned on the corner. . . . The street is where young bloods get their education.

—H. RAP BROWN
Die Nigger Die

Peer groups are important in all social strata, particularly for youths; they are far more important, however, in the lower strata than in any other. If homes are crowded, regimented, and depressed, those who can will gravitate toward the outside. As the home is something to be escaped, so too are schools for most lower-class youths, since schools do not provide a context with which these young people can identify. In lower-class schools, as we saw, the atmosphere also is oppressive. Teachers seem like alien figures, and the disappointed hopes of adult family members and acquaintances inhibit ambition. Most lower-class youths tend inevitably to become "street boys,"[68] and life on the street—with peers, but emulating adult (male) street society—is as important in molding attitudes, behavior, and personality as life in the family, perhaps more so. Street society includes not only street-corner life in the literal sense, but also the life that occurs in many kinds of sociable institutions—barber shops, drugstores, poolrooms, bowling alleys, arcades, clubrooms, cafeterias, taverns—always within very narrowly bounded "urban villages." The neighborhood streets and gathering places are the relevant worlds of the urban poor, and they often extend only for a few blocks. The rest is alien territory.

Life on the street best explains two facets of the syndrome of authority in lower-class contexts: elitism (and its counterpart, submission) and the tendency to generate gangs (literally or figuratively) as the typical form of organizations. Self-exclusion and aspects of mass behavior also are reinforced by the institutions of the street.

The mean streets provide rich materials for anthropological study, but unfortunately, good studies of them are few, and it is therefore difficult to make these points tellingly. In addition, most of what literature there is on street society deals with the life of the most lowly and is mainly concerned with its more sensational aspects: criminality and other social pathologies or—better—behavior perceived as pathological by middle-class observers.

Nevertheless, what we do have can be considered useful if two premises hold, as I think they do. First, the more grisly, more publicized aspects of life in lower-class neighborhoods are an integral part of routine existence. "If a racketeer commits murder," writes William F. Whyte, "that is news. If he proceeds quietly with the daily routines of his business, that is not news. If the politician is indicted for accepting graft, that is news. If he goes about doing the usual favors for his constituents, that is not news."[69] If the kind of life experienced in the lower social strata is the unavoidable consequence of living with high scarcity and in the confines of constricted social networks, then it must follow that the life of the *most* lowly is only an intensified version of that lived by the less so. And this seems to be true. For instance, we associate gangs with vice and mayhem, and not entirely without reason: a great deal of life on the street is rough and aggressive, as it must be. But gangs vary from being vicious to those that lead a rather innocent club life, and a ruleful one—though the rules, as Foster puts it, "are not middle-class nor Marquis of Queensberry."[70]

Governance in street gangs and their equivalents (clubs, cliques, rat-packs) is exactly what the more disenchanted ruling-elite theorists would expect—dramatically so. Since such gangs are especially salient for the young (who, after all, do not yet work, or work much, at jobs or in school), their socialization outside the family also leads not only to dependence on leaders, but to "veneration" of them. Mills tells us that the power-elite rules by default, but if the masses were tuned in to them, it is doubtful that they would find anything either unfamiliar or illegitimate.

Authority in street gangs of all kinds is uniformly monocratic and rigidly hierarchical.

> The leader is the focal point for the organization of his group. In his absence . . . there is not common activity or general conversation. When the leader appears the situation changes strikingly. The small groups form into one large group. The conversation becomes general, and unified action frequently follows. . . . The members do not feel that the gang is really gathered until the leader appears . . . and when he is present they expect him to make their decisions.[71]

Frederick Thrasher's study of more than a thousand gangs in Chicago found such monocracy without exception.[72] The leaders do often use lieutenants, and indeed, "each member of the . . . gang has his own position in the gang structure."[73] A result, as in all monocracies, is the not infrequent overthrow of a leader by a lieutenant who sets up a gang of his own.

On what basis does such leadership rest, and on what basis may it be challenged? In a nutshell, it rests on what Foster calls physicality and what Thrasher calls gameness—personal prowess, plus some closely related traits, like foxiness (in Machiavelli's sense), excellence in verbal meanness (insults and ridicule), or indeed any kind of competitive excellence (for instance, in bowling). Authority and power—for that matter, brute force—are synonymous in lower-class gangs.[74] The gangs are warrior societies.

Force and its near relatives legitimate because in lower-class life they are highly functional, not irrational pathologies. This is so simply because lower-class street life is not far removed from the "state of nature," like it or not. The lower-class child's life, writes Keller, "is violent, hostile, aggressive, anxious and unstable. . . . He learns to fight for everything; he learns that might does indeed make right."[75] Claude Brown in *Manchild in the Promised Land* writes about Harlem:

> Fighting was the thing that people concentrated on. In our childhood we all had to make our reputations in the neighborhood. Then we'd spend the rest of our lives living up to them. . . . The little bosses in the neighborhood whom the adults respected were little boys who didn't let anybody mess with them. . . . If I had stayed in Harlem all my life, I might never have known that there was anything else in life other than sex, religion, and violence.[76]

How else—if not by prayer or aggression—can the poor achieve what others get in gentler ways? Foster calls violence "the lower-class problem-solving technique." Where other resources are very limited, that is hardly astonishing. And *who* is there to attack, in the small urban villages, but others like oneself?

Under such conditions, strength must be an overriding value; it provides protection in a physically menacing world. Authority in street gangs, then, rests on the same basis as lordship in early Western feudalism, for exactly the same reason. Whether one's locality is overrun by predatory Norsemen, Magyars, and Huns, or by Short Tails, Swamp Angels, and Buckoos, the ability to provide elementary physical security is bound to legitimate domination. Nonviolence, in such cases, is not "natural"; self-defense is. The gang leader, like the early feudal lord, also tends to act in loco parentis, protectively and with strict discipline.

We begin to see here why lower-class organizations tend to have what I called a quasi-feudal character—including the mutualities of support and protection that are the essence of political machines. There is in gangs a strong sense of mutual obligations: services are done for services rendered, favors for favors, among the "men" and between leaders and followers, in accordance with rigid, though tacit, codes.[77] Loyalty counts with game-ness and stealth as a source of status on the street.

Moreover, strength, stealth, excellence in physical competitions, and primal loyalties that solidify groups as mutual-protection societies are bound to be major sources of self-esteem and esteem by others in the societies of the poor. From what else can status be derived? Clearly, not from occupations; perhaps—a rank or two removed from great economic stringency—from religiosity; almost universally from the ability to beat the system—which, if you are in it, can only be through successful hustling. "Because of the lack of successful middle-class adult models to emulate, . . . the black child's model for emulation becomes the hustler, the pimp, the murphy man, the preacher, the athlete (only recently)."[78] The life of hustling, needless to say, often is—must be—highly "sophisticated," but, of course, the sophistication of the streets is not that of the alumni associations. The hustler-hero certainly would not last long in the boardroom (or would he?), but neither (and more surely) would the board member do well on the street.

So far, I have emphasized the links between street life and elitism, but also touched on its links to "nonrational" behavior, to legitimacy, and to the predatory nature of many lower-class organizations. The link to the last of these traits needs some further discussion, since the inadequacies of the organizations of the lower classes as educative, mobilizing structures are critical to the discontent associated with inclusion.

There is a direct relation between the organizations of the street and the political organizations of the poor: the gangs and clubs of the streets long were the cells of political machines, and many of the top and secondary leaders of the machines were recruited straight from the street organizations. Religion, hustling, and politics have always and everywhere been close allies among the poor; all are vehicles for getting on in poor society, sometimes for getting out of it. Robert E. Park and his collaborators have already described the interconnections between street gangs and political machines in their seminal study *The City*. Thrasher, in 1926, documented the point at length.[79] Foster traces the virtual amalgamation of gangs and political machines precisely to the early age of political inclusion in the United States:

> Gangs started out as petty thieves who also fought for their neighborhoods for the fun of fighting. Gradually, however, some of them became very much involved as . . . tools of politicians. In the early days before the Civil War, the composition and objectives of the gangs began to change. In the 1830s district and ward leaders began to purchase saloons, dance houses, and the greengrocery speakeasies in which the gangs congregated, while taking houses of prostitution and gambling under their protective wings. Hence we had the beginning of the amalgamation of the underworld of the gangs with the politicians.[80]

This amalgamation of gangs and machines makes the operation of the machines comprehensible, as it does their astonishing acceptability to the lower strata. What possible concern could members of these strata have had for any "general interest," of the sort about which bookish liberals had written? How could such a concept as the "common interest" have been grasped where the natural leaders, the more gifted and more "sophisticated," had principally to mediate between the neighborhood and the big shots? The machines made sense—functional sense. They were predatory, as life in the lower strata was, and had to be. They worked through the familiar currency of clientelism: favors for favors. They were run monocratically by bosses, with paramilitary discipline. The bosses, quite naturally for political entrepreneurs, tried to amass support cheaply. They did so by giving small "pay" to people who worked for them and by charging fees for favors (getting jobs, fixing cases, and the like), through bagmen and other graft collectors. The chief point was to achieve, as much as possible, a comfortable independence from the machine itself. In return, the machine was expected to get things for the community—and getting things for the neighborhoods was not looked on as somehow shady but as a matter of fundamental rights. The essentially feudal idea of mutual obligations bound members of the political machines to the bosses, and the machines to their political clients. And much of this—spoils, patronage, fixing things for support, getting things for the constituency—remains an essential part of the practical morality of inclusive democracy.

By far the best description of all this is Whyte's—for Boston in the early 1940s, a century after the initial weddings of machines and gangs. Whyte, in fact, entitled the entire general discussion of *Street Corner Society* (after presenting case studies of two gangs, Doc's and Chick's) "Racketeers and Politicians." He also provides a splendid account of how recruitment from gangs into political organizations occurs. For the gang leader, like Doc or Chick in Boston, what was there to do when the gangs disintegrated as the boys married and settled into jobs? They had brains and status, and they were accustomed to leadership. Were they to take on menial work? Obviously not. But what else was there, except politics? So Doc and Chick, quite naturally, switched from running gangs to political activity—the one, from unsuccessful candidacy for office into the oblivion "in the back of Stefan's dimly lighted barbershop"; the other, to the attorney general's staff, by way of his own small organization to distribute handbills, canvass, and speak at meetings.[81]

Lower-Class Work

It goes without saying that the conventional organization of lower-class (unskilled, semiskilled) workplaces only reinforces the tendencies I have described; hence the contemporary preoccupations with the "humanization" of the workplace, with QWL arrangements, and with workers' participation in management. A less simple issue involves the effects that the intrinsic nature of lower-class work has on personality traits and, through them, on dispositions with regard to politics—an issue that has, in fact, been studied a fair amount.[82]

The leading contemporary research, both clinical and statistical, on the subject is that of Melvin Kohn and his associates.[83] The essence of Kohn's argument can be put thus: lower-class jobs predominantly inhibit "self-direction." They are closely supervised and, in other ways, highly disciplined. The basic cause of this is their very nature, especially their extreme simplicity. Complex, nonroutine work requires decisions among options; simple work verges on robotics. There are some exceptions. Some blue-collar jobs do require special skills or, for special reasons, cannot be supervised closely—most of all the jobs of expert dirty workers, like miners and truck drivers; for that reason, such jobs are much prized, despite the arduous, often dangerous work involved. (In fact, danger and arduousness in work generally are treated as badges of honor in the working class.) By and large, however, lower-class jobs are hardly likely to induce participation or make people capable of performing well in decision structures. In simple, menial jobs, the only thing likely to be learned is that one submits or tyrannizes.

In addition, simple, menial work has important psychological consequences that are bound to affect the authority-culture of the lower strata. Such work, for instance, contributes significantly to how morality is conceived. To menial workers, acting "morally" tends only to mean strict adherence to dictates, as against basing behavior on internalized norms or standards consciously devised by oneself. The relationship of this to domination and submission, as well as to "mass" and exploitative behavior, is obvious. Menial work tends to breed, according to Kohn's findings, a sort of blind authoritarian conservatism of the Archie Bunker type; for example: "The most important thing to teach children is absolute obedience to their parents"; "Children shouldn't be confused by reading books"; "Questioning the old ways just causes trouble."[84] Such attitudes can readily be traced to settings in which dictates and dull routines predominate.

Kohn's implicit prescription for remedying the flaws of inclusion is to change work itself, not its organization—especially to "complicate" it, free it of simple, option-free routines—to make of it artisanship in industrial clothes. How and whether this is possible remains to be seen. As things are, lower-class work tends to engender what is surely the ultimate self-exclusion: the dissociation of the self from its activities—alienation. Pateman's visions of the educative value of participation in the direction of the workplace will surely be dashed most of all by that dissociation.

The literature on lower-class work uniformly points to such dissociation: dissatisfaction with jobs, lack of commitment to them, and lack of identification with the workplace. Among the young, this is reflected especially in a tendency to drift from job to job, looking for something rarely (or never) found. By the age of twenty-five, the working-class youths studied by Lillian Rubin had worked, on the average, almost eight years, and half had held from six to ten jobs.[85] As it becomes necessary to settle down, and as hope for something better evaporates, such extreme mobility declines (though layoffs and temporary work still make for a good deal of movement from job to job). Yet, even when settled, the lower-class worker tends to resign and numb himself to his work, to treat the job as something to be got through, much as he "got through" school. This might be considered a definition of menial work, or "labor," in Arendt's sense: work that demeans, that offers no psychic rewards.

The work of most lower-class men thus only reinforces all that follows from constraints in domestic life and their consequences for authority. It does so directly, and also indirectly, by bringing into the home men who need indulgence because they are fatigued and distressed, who oppress because they have been oppressed, who discourage enterprise in children because they have had to learn to numb themselves as a condition of survival.

As for the work of the chief executives—the women—the domestic tasks of lower-class housewives are so deadening and demanding that the women often seek relief in outside drudgery, in "low-status, low-paying, dead-end work made up of dull, routine tasks; work that often is considered too menial for men": being a cleaning-woman, seamstress, waitress, cashier, school-crossing guard, and the like. Worse, women generally seem to *prefer* work that involves service, submission, and suppression of the intellect. And they tend, generally, to enjoy doing such work "because it gets . . . [them] away from home."[86]

I have noted that the descriptions of the effects of civic inclusion in an earlier part of this essay are highly simplified and that the explanation in the section on the authority-culture of the poor is an "explanation-sketch," to be filled in by a great deal of further research. For once, the point is not to disarm criticism with modesty; it is, rather, that if we really want to take civic inclusion seriously—as a value or as a fundamental fact of social life, or both—we must undertake further research on a proper scale and treat the explanation sketched as plausible enough to attempt proper testing.

Pertinent research can proceed along a great many lines, only a few of which I want to outline here.[87] We need, for instance, to do good comparative research on authority relations among ethnically different groups such as Irish, blacks, Chicanos, Italians, Asians. Such research can provide a tough test of what I have argued, because, as stated, my thesis has an inescapable corollary: if high material constraint severely limits options in social behavior and attitudes, then, despite ethnic differences, authority relations among the poor should be much the same—all the more so if such attitudes and behavior are adaptive imperatives in stressful conditions. It would similarly be useful to compare the organizations of the poor historically, by region, cross-nationally, and in rural and urban settings. In America comparisons might also be made between Northern political machines and Southern populist movements. We need many more pertinent studies of inclusive schools (and universities), not least in countries other than the United States and Britain—in countries, for instance, where poverty and affluence involve lesser differentials. It would obviously be useful to study the governance of trade unions, past and present, more widely and from the standpoint of my thesis, and to compare such governance by the type of work performed by the membership. The list could be much expanded.

Assuming for now that the explanation I have proposed holds up, what implications follow? Two above all. First, civic inclusion does change social institutions, but it often changes only their "content," not their "form" (e.g., not elitism but the composition of elites). Still more intriguing, it generates neofeudal relations in advanced societies. And not least, it changes the meaning of dispositions to act (thus action-systems) that we consider identical; for instance, "rationality" shifts from public discussion to define common interests, to entrepreneurial value-maximization, to functional adaptation to exigent conditions. The second major implication, which has much relevance for policy, is that our conventional conception of the relation between inclusion and equalization is the wrong way round. Inclusion does not much make groups equal; rather, substantial equalization of the conditions of life seems to be the prerequisite for inclusion to work as intended. Schools, for instance, do not appear to be effective routes out of the ghettos and barrios; rather, improving the lot of ghetto people seems necessary to make them want to use schools for achievement.

Finally, I want to stress that the value-bias of this paper intentionally is that of Schumpeter's *Capitalism, Socialism, and Democracy*. Like many other scholars of his generation and origins, Schumpeter tried to face up to the facts of malfunctioning democracies, the rise of Nazism, the "dream that failed." To do so, he said unwelcome things about what democracy can and cannot be. He said them for, so to speak, prophylactic reasons, so that a valuable, however imperfect, kind of polity would not be destroyed by false illusions. Critics of his work charged—and stung—him with the allegation of "defeatism" (and worse). Schumpeter replied:

Facts in themselves and inferences from them can never be defeatist. . . .
The report that a given ship is sinking is not defeatist. Only the spirit in
which this report is received can be defeatist: the crew can sit down and
drink, but it can also rush to the pumps. If the men merely deny the report,
though it be carefully substantiated, then they are escapists. . . . Frank presentation of ominous facts was never more necessary than it is today because
we seem to have developed escapism into a system of thought.[88]

If we really want to construct a "science of equality," we need, more than
anything, to act upon that querulous and wise caution.

NOTES FOR CHAPTER 10

1. Charles Tilly, *From Mobilization to Revolution* (Reading, Mass.: Addison-
Wesley, 1978), 52.
2. I spelled out what I mean by "development" in "The Idea of Political
Development: From Dignity to Efficiency," *World Politics* 34 (1982): 451–486.
3. Alexis de Tocqueville, *Democracy in America* (London: Oxford University
Press, 1947), 3–18.
4. Ibid., 18.
5. What follows is a severe condensation of an earlier essay, "Civic Inclusion:
The Political Aspect," *Working Papers on Authority Relations*, no. 3, February 1983,
Program in Authority Studies, University of California, Irvine.
6. Joseph A. Schumpeter, *Capitalism, Socialism, and Democracy* (London: Allen
and Unwin, 1943), 250–251.
7. See especially Samuel H. Beer, *British Politics in the Collectivist Age* (New
York: Knopf, 1965), 22–32, and the sources cited there.
8. For an excellent overview of utilitarian thought, see William L. Davidson,
Political Thought in England: The Utilitarians from Bentham to J. S. Mill (London:
Butterworth, 1915). J. S. Mill's views on the educative effects of citizenship are
well summarized in Carole Pateman, *Participation and Democratic Theory* (Cambridge:
Cambridge University Press, 1970), 28–35.
9. This bears out Bagehot's argument that the effects of large political changes
could be seen clearly only a generation after their occurrence. Bagehot did have
considerable reservations about what others expected from the Reform Act of
1867, but deflating nonsense was part of his style—and his doubts were based more
on the shortcomings of the old oligarchy than the new citizens. See his preface to
The English Constitution, 2d ed. (London: Oxford University Press, 1978), 259–312.
10. Graham Wallas, *Human Nature in Politics* (London: Constable and Company,
1908), 199–200.
11. Gustave Le Bon, *The Crowd: A Study of the Popular Mind* (New York: Viking,
1960).
12. S. E. Finer, "Introduction" to Vilfredo Pareto, *Sociological Writings* (London: Pall Mall Press, 1966), 5–8.
13. For summaries of the early literature on ruling elites, see T. B. Bottomore,

Elites and Society (London: Watts, 1964); Renzo Sereno, *The Rulers* (New York: Praeger, 1962); and James Burnham, *The Machiavellians* (London: Putnam, 1943).

14. J. L. Talmon, *The Origins of Totalitarian Democracy* (New York: Praeger, 1960).

15. An exception is the work on political participation of Sidney Verba, Norman H. Nie, and Jae-On Kim; see their *Participation and Political Equality* (Cambridge: Cambridge University Press, 1978).

16. Wallas, *Human Nature in Politics*, 231–233.

17. J. E. C. Bodley, *France*, rev. ed. (London: Macmillan, 1899), 25, 34.

18. Robert Michels, *Political Parties* (Glencoe, Ill.: Free Press, 1949), esp. 54–65.

19. See Tocqueville, *Democracy in America*, chap. 25, and J. S. Mill, *Utilitarianism, Liberty, and Representative Government* (London: J. S. Dent and Sons, 1910), 278–288.

20. Le Bon, *The Crowd*; Robert Michels, *Political Parties*, 28, 69–74; Max Weber, "Politics as a Vocation," in *Max Weber: Essays in Sociology* (New York: Oxford University Press, 1946), 101–115.

21. The seminal depiction of the nature and ends of political machines is in James Bryce, *The American Commonwealth* (London: Macmillan, 1891), vol. 2. For a good bibliography of the now vast literature on political machines, see Thomas M. Guterbuck, *Machine Politics in Transition* (Chicago: University of Chicago Press, 1980), 307–314.

22. Weber, *Essays in Sociology*, 86.

23. Bryce, *The American Commonwealth*, 105.

24. Bibliographies of more than a hundred major works have become common in overviews of the subject of participation. See, for instance, Lester W. Millbrath, "Political Participation," in *The Handbook of Political Behavior*, ed. Samuel L. Long (New York: Plenum Press, 1981), 4: chap. 4. This is typical; the modern literature on the other subjects in fact is larger.

25. C. Wright Mills, *The Power Elite* (New York: Oxford University Press, 1956), passim.

26. Robert A. Dahl, *Who Governs?* (New Haven: Yale University Press, 1961).

27. The standard synthesis of the theory is William Kornhauser's *The Politics of Mass Society* (Glencoe, Ill.: Free Press, 1959). Kornhauser's work also began to shape the concept of mass society for systematic political sociology, as against angry polemics or fuzzy "philosophy."

28. Schumpeter, *Capitalism, Socialism, and Democracy*, 285; I refer to Anthony Downs's *Economic Theory of Democracy* (New York: Harper & Row, 1956), and William Riker's *The Theory of Political Coalitions* (New Haven: Yale University Press, 1962).

29. See Michael Laver, *The Politics of Private Desires* (Harmondsworth: Penguin Books, 1981)—an excellent summary of the modern theory of "rational choice" in politics.

30. Educational inclusion—its nature, the processes involved, the expectations associated with it, and the discontents associated with the expectations—is a very large subject. We have literature about it since the 1960s, when stock began widely to be taken of the results of advanced inclusion in educational institutions.

Here, I only make points especially pertinent to the theoretical issue of the paper.

31. See *Education and Democracy*, ed. A. E. Dyson and Julian Lovelock (London: Routledge & Kegan Paul, 1975), pp. 9–10. Dyson and Lovelock's book presents a splendid combination of writings and speeches, popular and philosophical, on the relations between education and democracy, from 1791 to 1916—from Tom Paine to John Dewey.

32. James Mill, "Education," in *The Encyclopedia Britannica*, 1825 [my insertion].

33. A good summary of that agitation is in Lawrence A. Cremin, *The Transformation of the School* (New York: Vintage Books, 1964), chap. 3.

34. Ibid., 10.

35. Ibid., 13.

36. Charles E. Silberman, *Crisis in the Classroom: The Remaking of American Education* (New York: Vintage Books, 1970), 15, 17.

37. Martin Trow, "Reflections on the Transition from Mass to Universal Higher Education," *Daedalus* 99 (1970): 232–239.

38. Cremin, *The Transformation of the School*, 16.

39. See extract in Dyson and Lovelock, *Education and Democracy*, 279–281.

40. Joseph Mayer Rice, *The Public-School System of the United States* (New York, 1893; articles from *The Forum* 18–19 republished in book form).

41. A useful synthesis of pertinent studies is in Richard M. Merelman, "Democratic Politics and the Culture of American Education," *American Political Science Review* 74 (1980): 319–332.

42. Ibid., 320. See also Philip Jackson, *Life in Classrooms* (Chicago: University of Chicago Press, 1968), and *Power and Ideology in Education*, ed. J. Karabel and A. H. Halsey (New York: Oxford University Press, 1977).

43. See, for instance, Philip Cusick, *Inside High School* (New York: Holt, Rinehart, and Winston, 1973).

44. Mary Haywood Metz, *Classrooms and Corridors: The Crisis of Authority in Desegregated Secondary Schools* (Berkeley: University of California Press, 1978).

45. Merelman, "Democratic Politics," 326–329.

46. See, for instance, John Wakeford, *The Cloistered Elite* (New York: Praeger, 1969), 128–159.

47. Metz, *Classrooms and Corridors*, 71, 81, 82–83, 73–80.

48. Ibid., chaps. 3–6.

49. Ibid., 61–62.

50. For Metz's characterization of these styles, see ibid., 35–39.

51. Merelman, "Democratic Politics," 326–330.

52. See, for instance, the excellent readings in *Family, Class, and Education*, ed. Maurice Craft (London: Longman, 1970); D. H. Hargreaves, *Social Relations in a Secondary School* (London: Macmillan, 1967), and (with others) *Deviance in Classrooms* (London: Routledge & Kegan Paul, 1975); and, especially apropos to my subject, Peter Woods, *The Divided School* (London: Routledge & Kegan Paul, 1979).

53. The above is a distillation of three sections in Woods, *The Divided School*, 38–51 (on parental influence over pupils), 63–83, and 102–120 (on pupils' ad-

aptation to the schools). Woods's findings are derived from a case study in a particular culture, but his findings typify those of comparable studies.

54. Ibid., 140–169.

55. Ibid., 25–62.

56. See Howard S. Becker, *Outsiders: Studies in the Sociology of Deviance* (New York: Free Press, 1963), and Hargreaves, *Deviance in Classrooms.*

57. Herbert L. Foster, *Ribbin', Jivin', and Playin' the Dozens* (Cambridge, Mass.: Ballinger, 1974), 25.

58. Pateman, *Participation and Democratic Theory,* esp. chap. 3. Pateman correctly cites the Guild Socialists, especially G. D. H. Cole, as the aboriginal sources of her argument.

59. For useful syntheses and references, see *Towards Industrial Democracy: Europe, Japan, and the United States,* ed. Benjamin C. Roberts (Montclair, N.J.: Allanheld, Osmun, 1979); Daniel Zwerdling, *Workplace Democracy* (New York: Harper & Row, 1980); R. Edwards, *Contested Terrain: The Transformation of the Workplace in the Twentieth Century* (New York: Basic Books, 1979); and John F. Witte, *Democracy, Authority, and Alienation in Work* (Chicago: University of Chicago Press, 1982).

60. For evidence, see an article that claims to *support* Pateman: J. Maxwell Elden, "Political Efficacy at Work," *American Political Science Review* 75 (1981): 43–58, esp. the summary tables on 50, 55.

61. See, for example, Witte, *Democracy, Authority, and Alienation in Work,* 13–15.

62. See, for instance, Edward S. Greenberg, "Industrial Self-management and Political Attitudes," *American Political Science Review* 75 (1981): 29–42.

63. Numerous British sociologists have found that for the unskilled (Stacey's term is "roughs") only the family and street society provide significant social networks beyond the job. A rung higher ("ordinary" people), the church also matters. Among the skilled ("respectable" people), so do trade unions. See Josephine Klein, *Samples from English Cultures* (London: Routledge & Kegan Paul, 1965), 53ff. See also Mary Paneth, *Branch Street* (London: Routledge & Kegan Paul, 1944); M. Kerr, *The People of Ship Street* (London: Routledge & Kegan Paul, 1958); and N. Dennis et al., *Coal Is Our Life* (London: Eyre and Spottiswoode, 1956).

64. Klein, *Samples from English Cultures.*

65. See, for example, Lipset's summary of the literature on "working-class authoritarianism." Seymour Martin Lipset, *Political Man* (New York: Doubleday, 1960), 120. For a summary and critique of the literature on the culture of poverty, see Charles A. Valentine, *Culture and Poverty* (Chicago: University of Chicago Press, 1968).

66. If I read Valentine (n. 65) correctly, it is precisely this fact of structural determinism and adaptation that he misses in works on the culture of poverty; see 130–144.

67. The expression comes from the most influential book on street society, William F. Whyte, *Street Corner Society* (Chicago: University of Chicago Press, 1943), xviii.

68. Ibid.

69. Ibid., xvi.

70. Foster, *Ribbin', Jivin', and Playin' the Dozens,* 25.

71. Whyte, *Street Corner Society*, 258.

72. Frederic Thrasher, *The Gang: A Study of 1,313 Gangs in Chicago* (Chicago: University of Chicago Press, 1926).

73. Whyte, *Street Corner Society*, 262.

74. Ibid., 1; Thrasher, *The Gang*, 51, 106, 239; Foster, *Ribbin', Jivin', and Playin' the Dozens*, 102.

75. Cited in Foster, *Ribbin', Jivin', and Playin' the Dozens*, 104.

76. Claude Brown, *Manchild in the Promised Land* (New York: Macmillan, 1965).

77. Whyte, *Street Corner Society*, 256.

78. Foster, *Ribbin', Jivin', and Playin' the Dozens*, 78.

79. Thrasher, *The Gang*, 313–336.

80. Foster, *Ribbin', Jivin', and Playin' the Dozens*, 78.

81. Whyte, *Street Corner Society*, 35–41, 86–93.

82. A good select bibliography on the subject may be found in Carmi Schooler and Melvin Kohn, "Occupational Experience and Psychological Functioning," *American Sociological Review* 38 (1973): 97–118. Along with that article, the following are particularly valuable: Melvin Kohn, *Class and Conformity* (Chicago: University of Chicago Press, 1989); Kohn, "Job Conditions and Personality," *American Journal of Sociology* 87 (1982): 1257–1286; Lillian Rubin, *Worlds of Pain* (New York: Basic Books, 1976), 155–185; Robert Blauner, *Alienation and Freedom* (Chicago: University of Chicago Press, 1964); F. Zweig, *Men in Pits* (London: Gollancz, 1948); Klein, *Samples from English Cultures;* and Dennis et al., *Coal Is Our Life.*

83. Kohn, *Class and Conformity.*

84. Schooler and Kohn, "Occupational Experience," 101.

85. Rubin, *Worlds of Pain*, 155.

86. Ibid., 166.

87. A more comprehensive list of such researches has been worked out by members of the Program in Authority Studies, University of California, Irvine. It is available in "An Agenda for Research on Civic Inclusion and the Authority-Culture of Poverty," May 1983.

88. Schumpeter, *Capitalism, Socialism, and Democracy*, xi.

ELEVEN

Rationality and Frustration

I tried in 1908 to make two points clear. My first point was the danger . . . especially for the working of democracy . . . of the "intellectualist" assumption, that every human action is the result of an intellectual process, by which a man first thinks of some end he desires, and then calculates the means by which that end can be attained.

There is no longer [after World War I and subsequent political events] much danger that we shall assume that man always and automatically thinks of ends and calculates means.

The vast majority of mankind have had enough to do to keep themselves alive. . . . An effective choice has only been given to a tiny class of hereditary property owners or a few organizers of other men's labors.

GRAHAM WALLAS,
Human Nature in Politics (1920)

ARGUMENT OF THE ESSAY: AN OVERVIEW

Rational-choice theories in political science have been criticized and modified entirely for the way they specify the process of attaining goals. A more fundamental criticism of the rational-choice approach to theory and explanation is to question whether political, and other social, behavior is oriented to achieving goals in the first place. That is what I want to do here.

I argue that the applicability of the rational-choice framework, although intended as a basis of highly general theory, is in fact exceedingly limited by time and culture; it is even substantially subculture-bound in societies where it might serve relatively well. This applies both to its pristine (Simon calls it "Olympian") version and modified versions intended to achieve decent fit with observations. The reason for these damaging limitations is that behavior comes in two fundamentally distinct varieties: Maier calls them "motivated" and "frustrated" behavior and considers the latter, persuasively, to be "behavior without goals."[1] I suspect that much, perhaps

Published in *The Economic Approach to Politics*, ed. Kristen Monroe (New York: Scott-Foresman and Row-Collins, 1990). Reprinted by permission. Copyright © 1990 by the Scott-Foresman Publishing Company.

even most, behavior—broadly considered in time, societies, and subsocieties—is of the frustrated kind.

Moreover, I argue here that action instigated by frustration may be regarded as "sensible," although it takes certain forms we usually consider the height of irrationality. It is sensible because it is well-adapted to exigent circumstances that press upon many people, at most times and in most places. By "well-adapted" I mean that the behavior performs well certain ineluctable functional imperatives of existence in societies, without the occurrence of destructive personal stress. These imperatives, in fact, explain how frustration instigates distinctive modes of behavior.

Because frustration-instigated behavior can be considered functionally sensible, rational-choice theories might be tempted to annex it to their framework by applying the term "rational" to it. After all, it makes "sense"; one's goal in behavior might sometimes be not to pursue goals at all. Such stretching of the framework is inadmissible: it would involve verbal legerdemain that maintains the framework while draining it of its most important postulate: behavior is in some way calculated to achieve goals efficiently.

RATIONAL CHOICE AND GOALS

It is hardly possible to imagine rational choices (perhaps "choices" of any kind) that are not intended to achieve goals, or indeed ordered sets of goals. I want to document this point from the political literature about rational choice before discussing the alternate (to us, probably, prima facie) implausible view.

In Downs's seminal work applying economic modes of analysis to democratic theory, rational action is generically defined as action "reasonably directed toward the attainment of conscious *goals.*"[2] Reasonable is equated with "efficient," which in turn refers to using the least possible input of scarce resources to obtain valued outputs. Downs's summary of his whole perspective of inquiry states: "By *rational* action, we mean action which is efficiently designed to achieve the consciously selected political or economic ends of the actor."[3] Note Downs's use of the word *conscious.* Presumably he used it (in my view, rightly) to avoid equating rationality with *any* effective actions, like actions that satisfy impulsive or reflexive urges or otherwise adjust unthinkingly to situations that press upon people.

Economics, of course, deals exclusively with highly goal-oriented behavior: its political personae thus are utility-maximizing voters and politicians. The economic view of politicians was anticipated by Schumpeter, in his major work about politics.[4] However, Schumpeter confines the economic analogy to leaders (political entrepreneurs) who, to paraphrase him, deal in votes exactly as businessmen deal in oil; the mass of voters he treats as hyper-irrational, in the manner of the crowd psychologists.[5]

A second source of political rational-choice theory is the theory of games. Unlike mere play, games are probably the most unambiguously goal-oriented of all activities. Games theory has had a particularly strong influence on another strand of political rational-choice theory: the theory of political coalitions first devised by Riker. That theory is solely concerned with winning and payoffs and equated with such analogues as "parlor games, markets, elections, and warfare," all matters in which action is directed at highly specific goals. Riker tries to disarm doubts about working with assumptions drawn from such seemingly far-fetched analogues mainly by equating the position of politicians with that of fiduciary agents who are morally obligated to act in the maximum interests of their principals.[6]

Michael Laver's excellent work on political rational-actor theories brings out the same view, a generation's work after Downs.[7] Rational-actor models, he points out, must assume (1) that actors pursue goals weighted in cardinal-utility orders and (2) that, in choosing among alternative courses of action, actors also calculate the risks and probable costs of attaining them. The cardinally ordered goals are the first, most fundamental desideratum; consideration of risks or benefits are senseless without them.

In a long series of works that become increasingly focused between 1947 and 1985, Herbert Simon has developed a powerful critique and revision of the postulates of economic theories, especially as applied to administration and politics. Simon moves far along the right track, but still falls short of the most crucial revision needed.

Simon's critique is inductivist: that is, he wants to develop a theoretical model more likely to fit observations than does a "pure" economic model (which proceeds from the postulate of "objective rationality") by being empirically grounded from the outset, chiefly in cognitive psychology. Some theorists will probably disagree with this view for epistemological reasons concerning the nature and uses of theory. But it will be hard for anyone to disagree with Simon's point that if successful predictions derived from a model depend chiefly on the "auxiliary assumptions" introduced into it,[8] often ad hoc and to deal with specific observations, then the model is ripe for basic revision.[9] Simon gives a rather crushing recital of such auxiliary assumptions used in economics itself, and, even more, in politics. To cite only one passage:

> [These] examples teach us the same lesson: the actors in the political drama do appear to behave in a rational manner—they have reasons for what they do, and a clever researcher can usually obtain data that give good clues as to what their reasons are. But this is very different from claiming that we can predict the behavior . . . by application of the objective rationality prin-

ciple. Such prediction is impossible because ... behavior depends ... on [actors'] representation of the world in which they live, what they attend to in that world, and what beliefs they have about its nature. The obvious corollary is that rationalism can carry us only a little way in political analysis.[10]

Simon's modification of the pure, rational-choice model is the notion of "bounded rationality." Such rationality takes into account subjective factors, especially varying levels of knowledge, differences in abilities to compute, completeness or degrees of lack of it in defining alternatives for action, how much the attention is focused on political issues (a function of the emotions, because they assign degrees of urgency), variable spans of attention, and "education" (following Riker, the artistic, or creative, element in politics that generates alternatives for action in the first place).

Throughout the corpus of Simon's work, what results is the notion of satisficing in place of maximizing or optimizing. Satisficing is pursuing some satisfactory outcome of action—not necessarily the most satisfactory, but one that lies within a range of acceptable attainments. Clearly, this is still well within the world of goal-oriented actions. In fact, Simon explicitly writes that, aside from madness, "almost all human behavior consists of sequences of goal-oriented actions."[11] True, goals à la Simon are more broadly defined, and good outcomes have taken the place of best or best possible outcomes. Nevertheless, satisficing remains goal oriented, however much the idea of "efficient" outcomes is loosened and enlarged. Simon's boundedly rational actor still inhabits a world of costs and benefits, punishments and rewards.

In his Madison address of 1985, however, Simon opens the door to something I wish to explore more because it can transcend his revision and lead us to a more fundamental level. The "subjectively rational" actor, Simon argues, not only has internal limitations but adapts behavior to "external situations." Under specifiable conditions, such adaptive behavior has traits that seem to me to preclude considering it rational in any terminology, bounded or unbounded, simply because the most fundamental, indeed logically indispensable, criterion of rational action, goal seeking per se, is either absent or present only in a tortured, metaphorical way. This point applies with special force to groups that no doubt are less numerous in the modern West than in earlier Western or other societies. But I suspect that it applies, in varying degrees, to most people, period.

FRUSTRATION-INSTIGATED BEHAVIOR

To a greater or lesser extent, in all modern societies one subculture cuts across other social divisions: the subculture of the poor. One can dispute who the poor are and how large a proportion of any society they include. Here, I do not mean to refer only to the miserable. Degrees of material scarcity lie along curves, though it is undeniably difficult to specify a threshold where "affluence" ends and "poverty" begins (even if the Department of Labor tells us that about one-quarter of Americans live below the "poverty line"). But it is not difficult to identify groups "who have enough to do to keep themselves alive" without going to the Bowery.

The point I want to make is this: the behavior of the poor, even in highly developed, "achieving" societies, conforms more with the generalization that actions are taken to avoid pain, not to attain pleasure, that is, to cope with pain, or minimize it, or to minimize its very perception. Another way to put this guards at the start against the argument that avoiding pain is simply the reverse of attaining pleasure—part of the rational calculus—rather than being qualitatively different. Behavior by the poorer segments of societies is more like what Norman Maier called frustration-instigated behavior than what he called motivation-instigated behavior.[12] In his study of Southern Appalachians, Richard Ball evocatively called such behavior *analgesic*;[13] the word is apt because analgesia literally is a condition of insensibility to pain.

Such behavior should be regarded as not being oriented toward attaining goals at all: what better way to be insensible to failures and resultant frustrations? It is comparable to what Merton and other writers on social adaptation call "retreatist" behavior:[14] withdrawing into apathy or into small, sheltered worlds of self-limited activity. It also appears to have other traits hardly consistent with being motivated to attain goals efficiently, which I will discuss presently.

FRUSTRATED BEHAVIOR IN EXPERIMENTAL SETTINGS

Maier's work on frustrated behavior is part of psychological learning research and theory. The orthodoxy of that field was, and remains, the reward-punishment perspective, a kind of cost-benefit perspective, even though conditioning is emphasized over calculation. Maier's theroretical aim was to show that behavior, and thus its causes, is two-faceted (motivated or frustrated) rather than being all of one piece—an apparent loss of parsimony, unless one introduces explanatory power into the equation by which parsimony is measured. Maier's point was precisely that the reward-punishment perspective *over*simplified and thus actually ended in avoidable, unparsimonious complications, as well as in notions dubious for therapy.

Yates points out that Maier's work on frustration was unusual in its persistence over a long time span (more than twenty years), the sheer quantity of experimental work done, and in Maier's attempt to work out fully the implications of his findings and theory.[15] Yates also emphasizes its importance as an alternative to the somewhat frayed orthodoxy in learning theory—its almost Copernican nature—and, predictably, his profession's extraordinary imperviousness to the work, on the ground of "prejudice and a priori convictions,"[16] resulting in little follow-up: not exactly unusual in the human sciences.

In the preface to his book's paperback edition Maier himself remarks rather gently on this "initial opposition." He attributes it to a simple misunderstanding: namely, that people took him to say that frustrated *people* have no goals in the first place—which, of course, would make it difficult to explain why they are frustrated. Instead, Maier tells us that he refers to behavior neither influenced nor controlled by goals, or behavior that may in fact lead away from initial goals (like stilling hunger). In his theory, such behavior, to be sure, results from prolonged and systematic frustration in goal-oriented action. However, frustrated people are not a personality type, although susceptibility to the general condition of frustration seems to vary, and it seems possible to go from the frustrated state back to an earlier motivated state, even if not quickly or without appropriate guidance and exertion. Frustrated behavior has "situational" roots, but, once established, it is unusually hard to undo. Under specified conditions, it involves a passage from a general type of behavior to quite another.

Maier came to his distinction between motivated and frustrated behavior through a long series of experiments with rats. His experimental observations, and their interpretations, can only be selectively summarized here. Maier used the Lashley jumping apparatus in his experiments: a platform facing two apertures (cards), marked with different, easily distinguishable symbols: a white circle on a black background and a black circle on a white background. The animal is placed on the platform and induced to jump at one of the symbols. If it chooses the correct symbol, it lands on a feeding platform; if not, it bumps its nose and falls into a net. If food is consistently placed behind a symbol, a consistent preference for the symbol is rather quickly developed, regardless of its position (though rats, for some reason, tend to be position oriented). If, after symbol learning, the food is always placed to the left or right, and the symbol shifted about, the rats readily develop a preference for the correct position. This is typical "goal-motivated" behavior. We are in a world familiar to us, where correct choices lead to benefits and where wrong choices are costly.

What happens if now the location of the food is made random, by symbol and position, that is, unpredictable? What happens is exactly what "rationalists" would expect: after some trial and error, the animals sensibly refuse to jump at all; one might say that random rewards reduce costs to zero.

But what if the rats are forced to jump—for instance, by electric shocks or blasts of noxious air? (Real life, after all, may force human beings to

act when doing nothing may be their preference.) The animals now confront an "insoluble problem." Creating such problems for his subjects, in
contrast with soluble situations, is the crux of Maier's experiment: one is
bound to be frustrated when faced by insoluble problems regarding an
inherent need (food). Essentially, then, behavior becomes stereotyped:
some animals invariably jump at a symbol, others at a position. Moreover,
once stereotypical behavior sets in, it persists regardless of whether all
jumps are punished or rewards and punishment are equally divided. Most
striking is the fact that the stereotyped behavior persists even when food
is placed behind an open aperture. The animals are aware of the location
of the food and sniff it, but they then jump in the stereotyped manner
anyway. Furthermore, once the subject's behavior has become stereotyped,
it seems difficult, and in most cases impossible, to return to the initial
world of patterned rewards and punishment. A small proportion of rats
did in fact manage the return (viz., to variable behavior), but only after a
number of trial jumps vastly larger than before and most readily if they
were "guided." (Devices like metrazol injections to induce convulsions
were considered to be "guidance"!)

Frustrated behavior, then, is *fixated* behavior. It is invariably repeated
action and highly resistant to change even if the fixated response is directly
shown to be ineffective. Punishment, Maier found, in fact generally
strengthened fixation. And punishment here refers to rather extreme
things, like induced convulsions or being subjected to strong blasts of
stinking air. It should be evident that the frustrated subject no longer
inhabits a world of choice at all. Fixated behavior is an end-in-itself, insensible to punishment (costs) and rewards (benefits). Maier found, moreover, that such behavior is highly specific, even more so than "habits."
Thus it also lies outside any world of limited choice—outside any analogue
of satisficing.

Nevertheless, in an odd, hard-to-grasp way, fixation seemed functional
to the subject. The fixated rats seemed to be less tense, to respond more
readily, and to be less susceptible to convulsive seizures, than the rats that
were able to reenter the world of choice or the small minority that did
not become fixated through prolonged frustration. I surmise that the rats
preferred a *patterned* world, regardless of what it is, punishing or otherwise,
once they come to perceive that rewards and punishments are arbitrary.
They avoid the ideal-typical situation of the slave; and they find more peace
in invariable pattern than in choice, to the extent that the outcomes of
choice are unpredictable.

Maier is quite aware of the links long found between frustration and
responses other than fixation, especially *aggression;* he treats that relation
at length, with reference particularly to the magisterial work of Dollard
et al.[17]

Aggression as a response to frustration had generally been regarded as goal oriented. That may, of course, be so in certain cases. But aggressive behavior also often has characteristics that suggest it might be behavior without a goal—part of a syndrome, or family, of such actions, of which fixated action also is a part. For instance, Maier notes that: (1) Aggression seems often to follow frustration even if it is known to be futile. (2) Often it is not directed at the source of frustration, but at innocent bystanders (the "bystander" effect is as well documented as "scapegoating"). To quote Maier (drawing on Dollard et al.):

> Economic frustration leads to violence in the home, strained relationships among friends, crimes against society, lynching, and rioting. As a result problems are not solved and goals are not achieved. But always the innocent bystander is a convenient object. . . . After the response occurs it is rationalized and justified, but such reasons or justifications are not to be confused with causes or goals. Brutal parents justify abuse of their children by contending that the children are being trained, but the cause of the abusive behavior is their own frustration.

What is attained, no doubt, is some emotional relief.[18] One could say that this is a goal, but only by stretching the idea of goals so that they cannot fail to encompass any and all consequences of action; in other words, by being truistic. (3) Finally, and perhaps most telling, even when aggression itself is frustrated it tends to continue; yet, in the reward-punishment perspective, it should decline or be avoided altogether.

Thus, aggression, unless directly aimed at the source of frustration, may be considered of a piece with fixation, an alternative goal-less response to frustration. If this is so, one would like to know when one or another option is chosen to cope with frustration, but that is not an important issue here. (Maier does speculate that actors in "free" situations tend to use aggression but become fixated if circumstances are constrained.) Maier also points out that different goal-less responses to frustration often are combined.

The syndrome of such responses includes two other modes of behavior. It includes *regression:* returning to childhood patterns of behavior, like dependency, bed-wetting, tattletale behavior, whining, excessive crying, and nonconstructive play. Such behavior also had generally been treated as "motivated": it was assumed to be a resort to an earlier "rewarding" response when adult behavior was unsatisfying. However, Maier points out that regression often is merely childish: there frequently is no evidence whatever of a return to anything learned at an earlier stage. He also points out that regressive behavior often ceases abruptly when it relieves frustration: for instance, by "having a good cry." The final set of responses— the responses that most clearly have no goals—involves *resignation:* undiluted apathy toward one's condition. Resigned behavior has been particularly well described in Allport, Bruner, and Jandorf's study of refugees persecuted by the Nazis and in Eisenberg and Lazarsfeld's study of the effects of unemployment.[19] These effects included "extreme limitation of all needs; *no plans*; no definite relation to the future; either *no hopes at all or hopes which are not taken seriously.*"[20] Resignation, which occurred also in some of the experimental rats, clearly is end-of-the-line behavior, the result of especially severe or prolonged frustration on some personalities.

Although Maier might not agree, none of these patterns of behavior seems to me "senseless" in the situations in which they occur; that is, in organisms generally frustrated by having to cope with "insoluble problems," especially over prolonged periods of time. As stated earlier, fixated behavior at least is patterned; it is not anomic. Regressive dependency, the main regressive response, seems to me almost "smart": "If I don't have a decent chance of making a correct choice, you make it for me." Aggression, even if it achieves no goal, lets off steam; also, aggressive actors at least may enjoy the momentary and dubious pleasures of vengefulness. And resignation surely is not nonsensical where anything done is likely to be wrongly done.

Frustrated behavior is not likely to be *immediately* recognizable as "sensible" action. It has no analogue in human behavior likely to be intuitively meaningful to successful achievers, including successful academic achievers, or to people blessed by rewards that come even if wrong choices or no choices are made. If a pattern has not been directly experienced, then, Max Weber has told us, we can only construct it as a conceptually pure type, a crutch to our own understanding: a "concept" to expand limits of empathy and, through empathy, understanding, in the positivist sense.

I want to add three points, briefly.

First, I part company from Maier on one major point. I consider frustrated behavior to be adaptive; he considered it maladaptive. The difference is only semantic. Maier, like all others in his field, regards only behavior that is successful in its outcomes as adaptive and links success to goal-attainment. I follow Merton's use of the concept, which has had much influence in sociology.[21] Merton defines adaptation functionally, as coping with situations one cannot alter without suffering avoidable pain or other damage. For that reason, criminal behavior, retreating from society, submissiveness, and explicitly "curbing motivation for sustained endeavor" are, or may be, highly adaptive:[22] functional or situationally logical. Upon that view, frustrated behavior certainly is adaptive in exigent situations. That may explain why, in most cases, it is hard, or even impossible, to change.

Second, I should, doubtless, address the familiar argument that animals are not people. Experiments like Maier's are heuristic for understanding human behavior. Rats have always served the heuristic purpose well. So has another population—college students. Studies of such students show sufficiently that Maier's theories readily translate to human subjects. For example, Watson studied 230 college students: one group came from highly strict, "regimented" homes; the other group had been given "leeway and respect" at home.[23] Of the first group, 81 percent displayed aggression (e.g., rude answers), regression (like weeping spells), fixation (e.g., cherishing past hurts), or resignation (suicidal tendencies). About half of the frustrated students came from "economically deprived" homes, as against very few in the other group—this at a time when poor students were rather rare in colleges. Frustrated parents seem to produce frustrated children. Maier's large bibliography reports numerous such corroborative experimental studies with human subjects.

Finally, frustrated behavior is not mere risk-aversion, a phenomenon familiar to economic theory. True, frustrated behavior *is* averse to risks. Yet one aspect of it, aggression that is bound to fail, involves acting beyond all consideration of risks. It is not really possible to divorce risk from goals. Recall that Laver calculates risks as an inherent part of "rational," goal-seeking choice. One could also regard it as so high a degree of risk-aversion that the difference in degree becomes a difference in kind, at least for theory.

FRUSTRATED BEHAVIOR IN A SOCIAL SETTING

Because we are *social* scientists, we should go on now to the frustrated condition's analogues and responses in social settings.

One such analogue resembles the experimental situation engineered by Maier in an almost uncanny way. Like experiments, which accentuate conditions, it is an extreme case of persistent frustration in American society: the southern Appalachians. Arnold Toynbee traces their experience of failure and frustration back even beyond their migration to America, to Ulster and Scotland:

> The Scottish pioneers who migrated to Ulster begat Scotch-Irish descendants who reimmigrated in the eighteenth century from Ulster to North America, and these survive today in the fastnesses of the Appalachian mountains. Obviously, this American challenge has been more formidable than the Irish challenge. Has the increased challenge evoked an increased response? If we compare the Ulstermen and the Appalachians of today, two centuries after they parted company, we shall find that the answer is in the negative. The modern Appalachian has not only not improved on the Ulstermen; he has failed to hold his ground and has gone downhill in the most disconcerting fashion. In fact, the Appalachian "mountain people" today are no better than barbarians. They have relapsed into illiteracy and witchcraft. They suffer from poverty, squalor, and ill health. They are the American counterparts of the latter-day white barbarians of the Old World Rifis, Albanians, Kurds,

Pathans, and Hairy Ainus; but, whereas these latter are belated survivals of an ancient barbarism, the Appalachians present the melancholy spectacle of a people who have acquired civilization and then lost it.[24]

Strong stuff, and no doubt too strong. But the southern Appalachians *have* experienced a history of relentless failure and defeat, by physical and social conditions, and Toynbee captures the consequences for them. Harry Caudill, in *Night Comes to the Cumberlands*, writes:

> Coal has always cursed the land in which it lies. When men begin to wrest it from the earth it leaves a legacy of foul streams, hideous slag and polluted air. It peoples this transformed land with blind and crippled men and with widows and orphans. . . .
> But the tragedy of the Kentucky mountains transcends the tragedy of coal. It is compounded of Indian wars, civil war, and internecine feuds, of layered hatreds and of violent death. To its sad blend, history has added the curse of coal as a crown of sorrow.[25]

Caudill adds that a million Appalachians now live in squalor, ignorance, and ill health worse than that in much of mainland Asia. Thomas Ford's edited book on the region tells much the same tale of ill fortune and failure, as does Jack Weller's powerful *Yesterday's People*.[26] They all add up to a picture of people who must regard much of life as an "insoluble problem."

Richard Ball has argued that a general analgesic pattern of behavior has been the result. His notion of analgesic behavior is a useful ideal-typical construct for behavior that, in its most fundamental sense, is not motivated toward attaining goals at all—yet functionally sensible. He finds "sense" in responses to situations, not just in procedures to attain goals, ruefully pointing out that only ritualistic lip service is paid to W. I. Thomas's early emphasis on "the definition of the situation."

The developmental condition that produces an analgesic culture, Ball writes, is "the daily experience of inexorable pressure, insoluble problems, and overwhelming frustrations." This, he continues, is "the life situation of the poor generally," but it is encountered in particularly intense form among Appalachian mountaineers.

Just as the life-situation of the mountaineers resembles the laboratory-situation of Maier's rats, so do their responses resemble those of the rats. Fixated behavior occurs in the extent to which the Appalachians cling stubbornly to old social ways, to a degree that seems perverse to outside observers and often clearly against their own "rational self-interest" (as an outside observer might see it). In a social sense regression is also a common pattern, displayed in various ways: intellectually, through hard biblical fundamentalism and pervasive superstition; psychologically, through "chronic dependency," especially dependence on kin structures as ultimate guarantors of minimal needs; economically, by preferring low, but reliable, welfare payments to less reliable opportunities for getting on, even when the opportunities are available and promising; also, by impulsively squandering welfare checks and other quick and short-lived gratifications—a general trait of childishness. Regression occurs, in its most blatant form, when those who somehow manage to migrate to cities and may in fact have lived quite decently, return home "at the slightest misfortune" to a worse, but familiar, life. Aggression takes, among other forms, that of mutually destructive feuding. And there exists pervasive fatalistic resignation, rationalized by fundamentalist religion.

The standard "political" study of the Appalachians (in this case, coal miners and their occupational authority structures) is Gaventa's *Power and Powerlessness*.[27] Gaventa's description of Appalachian political behavior fits nicely with Ball's analysis of the case and the ethnographies of Weller and Caudill. Its themes are apathy and resignation, less and less resistance to abominable work conditions even when perceived as abhorrent, submissiveness, and sometimes outbreaks of aggression against domination.

Ball points out that the Appalachians proved strangely recalcitrant and exasperating subjects for "social planners" who came to them, well-intentioned, from quite different situations, to improve their lives.[28] To the outside planners, he found, the mountaineers seemed plainly irrational, as well as deviant. In another situation that might have been so. In the past and present situation of the mountaineers, however, one can certainly argue the opposite. At a minimum, their ways have avoided tension and breakdown in a world quite correctly perceived to be hostile and unpredictable. Their nonrational belief-systems explain that world. Their behavior avoids taking chances on the experience of painful outcomes that are, as they see it, likely to occur; they are, in that way, "realistic." There is surely something worse than particular failure: general breakdown.

FRUSTRATED BEHAVIOR AND THE POOR

In discussing the experiences of "social planners," Ball points out that the Appalachians are not at all an isolated case. Similar apparently irrational resistance to well-meant outside intervention appears to have occurred in a quite heterogeneous set of groups: blacks, the elderly, and a variety of other poor people. The recurrent thread that runs through this apparent variety is continuous failure, frustration, and adjustment to their perceived apparent ineluctability.

Here I should refer to the familiar, now wide-ranging, literature on the so-called "culture of poverty," a notion that was originated in the 1950s by Oscar Lewis in his work on Mexican families and American slums and elaborated by other scholars such as E. Franklin Frazier, who anticipated Lewis in work on black families in the 1930s, Daniel Moynihan and Nathan Glazer's work on blacks, Puerto Ricans, Jews, Italians, and Irish in New York City, and David Matza. These studies suggest that much characterizing Appalachia seems to have wide application. Among poor people, sociologists have perceived, above all, negation of the view of action as a "subjectively anticipated sequence of behaviors towards a goal . . . altruistic or directed to self-gain." Action seems "impulsive," driven by blind psychological forces rather than by deliberate calculation. The culture of poverty, as well, involves apathy, self-imposed social isolation, tendencies to immediate gratification, unpredictability of either gentle or aggressive behavior, high conformity, suspicion, and fatalism. This is elaborated in a comprehensive way in Charles A. Valentine's *Culture and Poverty*.[29]

Valentine's work criticizes the literature about the culture, or subculture, of poverty, and his criticisms seem to me sound. He does not criticize, however, the patterns of behavior described in the literature. First, he criticizes the literature's pejorative nature: in the case of Frazier, for instance, his "direct logical leap from social statistics" (about such things as family desertion, illegitimacy, immoral sex "deviant in terms of middle-class norms") to "a model of disorder and instability." Second, he criticizes the view that the culture of poverty is perpetuated by socialization—which no doubt is so, but which it is taken to imply that a sort of self-imposed misery would be quite unnecessary if the poor simply followed the sound American middle-class values of energy, ambition, and doing what is required to get on. Former radicals turned neoconservative have been especially likely to take that line, and small wonder, for the poor seem in fact not to want to help themselves when they can and seem recalcitrant and plainly deviant, to the exasperation of social meliorists trying to improve their lot.

Valentine criticizes Frazier particularly for ignoring the possibility that the apparently "disordered" life of the poor, in this case blacks, might have its "own order and functions." Later, he develops theoretical alternatives to explanations of behavior of the poor by "primitive" cognitive structure, lack of ambition, ingrained laziness, and the like; and almost all the alternatives, he argues, describe life situations and functionally make the case that the described behavior patterns are adaptive to the situations.

Low-income urban districts have describable social structures that include . . . some elements that are *specialized adaptations to conditions of socioeconomic disadvantage or marginality.*

The domestic group may frequently be unconventional in form and process, but both households and kinship are organized in ways that are *adaptive to externally imposed conditions.*

The general contours of individual cognitive and affective orientations to the world are predominantly *realistic and adaptive.*[30]

Here Valentine lists, as realistic and adaptive, such patterns as dependency, infrequent orientation to the future, resignation and fatalism, and tolerance for behavior others regard as pathological.

FRUSTRATION IN OTHER GROUPS

By now, the beginning of a literature about the adaptations of the disadvantaged in a variety of contexts exists. These writings show that the concept of frustrated behavior has wide applicability, and they support the view that its source is adaptation to ineluctable situations. Two examples should suffice.

First, Hyman Rodman published in 1971 a splendid account of family life in the lower-class of Trinidad.[31] (His account, incidentally, was not originally guided by works on the culture of poverty but became the innocent focus of a severe attack on that literature.) Rodman argued that lower-class Trinidadians share the common cultural ideals of marriage and the nuclear family, but that these ideals lack, for them, strong normative control over behavior. The ideals are "stretched" to include alternative marital and familial forms, and some of the stretching is considerable. It includes "promiscuous" sexual relationships, "illegal" marital unions, "illegitimate" children, "deserting" by husbands and fathers, and "abandoned" children—exactly the patterns that led Frazier to conclude that life among many American blacks was plainly disordered. Rodman puts quotation marks around the pejorative adjectives because he does not regard the behavior described by them as *problems* of the lower class but the opposite: "*solutions* [my emphasis] of the lower class to problems that they face in the social, economic, and perhaps legal and political spheres of life." The "solutions" go so far that words like promiscuity, illegitimacy, or desertion are not part of the lower-class vocabulary in Trinidad, while less negatively loaded words like "friending" or "outside children" do play a role in it.

Rodman was not aware of Maier's work, so that he does not discuss frustration-instigated behavior directly. He does show that deviant behavior (deviant even from the norms of the actor, and, in that sense, fixated) may be "situationally logical"; and some specific behavior patterns he describes (e.g., deserting wives and children or promiscuity as a way of life) are not hard to fit into the concept of frustrated behavior.

Second, in a recent article on "civic inclusion" (chapter 10 of this book), I made the point that the apparently nonrational, self-defeating behavior of lower-class pupils in American and British schools comes from an authority-culture that is highly adaptive to the defining characteristic of poverty: high scarcity. The argument needed to make that point is rather complex. Suffice it to say here that apathy toward formally offered opportunities (just "getting through" the day, the term, etc.), submissiveness to authoritarian domination, the testing of teachers for what Herbert Foster has called their "physicality" (including their willingness to use violence) as well as fitting well into the concept of frustrated behavior, seemed sensible in the milieux from which the pupils came and to which they were headed. In fact, they seemed close to deducible from the objective, exigent conditions, if only we proceed from the postulate that people adapt to situations and manage to think ourselves into the pupils' environments.[32]

Take "physicality." In a setting of pervasive physical insecurity, for instance, on the mean streets and in the schools themselves, physicality promises at least a possibility of safety. Just as the capacity for fighting was a basis of acceptable domination during the age of early feudalism, so it legitimates teachers to fearful pupils and makes education possible. But, Foster tells us, only a small percentage of "gentle" middle-class teachers ever understands that. Thus they themselves change their good intentions to what is, for them, better adapted (but educationally useless) behavior.

FRUSTRATION-INSTIGATED BEHAVIOR AS ADAPTIVE BEHAVIOR

Maier was criticized by other psychologists for not showing the nature of the link between the experience of frustration and frustrated behavior as a theoretically distinctive response to it.[33] This seems to me justified. The difficulty arises, in my view, from a point made earlier: Maier's view that frustrated behavior is maladaptive. I would argue that when the most fundamental functional imperatives of existence in societies are considered frustration-instigated behavior seems just the opposite.

Certain compelling functional imperatives do govern our lives, at a deep level; that is why the imperative to adapt to situations exists in the first place. These fundamental imperatives do not include engaging in and winning competitions that involve "rational choice," like economic or political "market" competitions. Such competitions may be exciting, and winning them no doubt is pleasant. But the competitions are better regarded as luxuries one can afford only when the elementary imperatives of life have been satisfied and when life-situations thus provide substantial "degrees of freedom." Up to that point "struggle" occurs, but that is something different.

What are the elementary imperatives for adaptation? The most fundamental, no doubt, is that emphasized by Hobbes: survival. The imperative to survive should not be understood only as sheer physical survival. Often, in social situations, survival refers to somehow "getting through" ordeals, without injurious stress—like getting to the end of an onerous and monotonous workday. For instance, in the case of the lower-class pupils discussed in my 1984 article, surviving often simply meant getting through boring days devoted to trivial, apparently pointless tasks; and it meant getting through school as such without painful exertions, in order to start working life—"real" life. Peter Woods, in a study of a British secondary modern school, found that the behavior of teachers frequently also amounted, at bottom, to what he calls "survival-strategies"—surviving tension and threats created by pupils. And none of the behavior—neither the teachers' nor the pupils'—was discernibly goal oriented, if that means aiming at instruction and educational achievement.[34]

A second imperative of existence surely is *low entropy:* a predictable life, not a life seemingly governed by random or arbitrary forces. (Even rats seem to need that.) That low entropy is a fundamental need for people comes out particularly well in R. W. Southern's discussion of the medieval "idea of freedom" in *The Making of the Middle Ages.* For the medieval mind, Southern states, to be free meant neither the absence of constraints ("freedom from") nor having opportunities and resources to realize goals ("freedom to"). It meant not being subject to arbitrary will. In other words, before the condition of being free could be equated with choosing and with realizing chosen goals, freedom was equated simply with predictable existence. And this should not surprise. Without predictability, choosing means to act anomically. Anomie as an intolerable, often life-destroying, burden on individuals has been discussed in studies as diverse as Durkheim's *Suicide* and DeGrazia's *Political Community.* It is worst when it is not a special individual but a general social state. Stephen Coleman's excellent (and much neglected) *Measurement and Analysis of Political Systems* demonstrated, with great precision, that much political behavior which we view differently is best regarded as entropy-reducing behavior, including elections and revolutions.

A third imperative is the reduction of the *precariousness* of life. By this I mean not knowing, with reasonable probability, what one's condition in life will be in any future, near or far—especially, of course, near. "Unpredictability" and "precariousness" are not the same. The first refers to interactions, particularly interactions with authorities and powers. By precariousness I mean *material* uncertainty. The possibility of sudden unemployment, with little or no alternative support, is an obvious example of high precariousness. A more destructive source of it (because it affects all, like a natural disaster) is high inflation. As we know from concrete cases like Israel, people adapt behavior even to egregious inflation; they *must* do so; but the condition defines the adaptation. One such adaptation to precariousness we know from history: the acceptance of authoritative control. Rogowski has constructed an admirable rational-choice theory of legitimacy, in which he makes good use of contract theories. We would do well to look at actual charters and "constitutions" that granted powers "contractually" to great princes. The reasons for the grants (in the West, at any rate) generally were to assure "the security of persons" and to guarantee "the reliability of the currency" (which goes beyond survival, to precariousness even with survival).[35]

What is the link to frustrated behavior? Consider once more the Appalachians. It should be evident that the Appalachian mountaineers are oriented toward all these imperatives: survival (even if at an abject level), entropy-reduction (even if through apparently irrational fixations or regressive beliefs and practices), and reducing precariousness (even if by chronic dependency and fleeing from opportunity because of minor mishaps).

CONCLUSION

Frustrated behavior—behavior without goals—is widespread because it has very deep roots in the basic, inescapable imperatives of human existence. Unless we take this fact into account we will continue procrustean, and certainly not parsimonious, stretching of cost-benefit conceptions to account for phenomena to which they are irrelevant. On the practical side, we will also continue attempts to meliorate conditions that undoubtedly call for improvement, but we will do it in all the wrong ways, doing harm or nothing while trying to do good.

Psychologists like Maier invariably theorized for the sake of therapy. They often failed because *they* were fixated, as it were, on inadequate theoretical perspectives. This charge, I hold, also applies to rational-choice theories of politics—for all their ingenuity and elegance. Their key failure comes from Downs's initial assumption as axiomatic truth: action always is directed "toward the attainment of conscious goals." It is not.

NOTES FOR CHAPTER 11

1. N. Maier, *Frustration: The Study of Behavior Without a Goal* (Ann Arbor: University of Michigan Press, 1949).

2. A. Downs, *An Economic Theory of Democracy* (New York: Harper & Row, 1957), 4; italics added.

3. Ibid., 20.

4. J. A. Schumpeter, *Capitalism, Socialism, and Democracy* (London: Allen and Unwin, 1943).

5. Ibid., 262–263, 285.

6. W. H. Riker, *The Theory of Political Coalitions* (New Haven: Yale University Press, 1962), 23, 24–28.

7. M. Laver, *The Politics of Private Desires* (Harmondsworth, Middlesex: Penguin Books, 1981), 21–38.

8. H. A. Simon, "Human Nature in Politics: The Dialogue of Psychology with Political Science," *American Political Science Review* 79 (1985): 293–304.

9. Ibid., 296–302.

10. Ibid., 300.

11. Ibid., 297.

12. Maier, *Frustration.*

13. R. A. Ball, "A Poverty Case: The Analgesic Subculture of the Southern Appalachians," *American Sociological Review* 33 (1968): 885–895.

14. R. K. Merton, *Social Theory and Social Structure* (Glencoe, Ill.: Free Press, 1949).

15. A. J. Yates, *Frustration and Conflict* (New York: Wiley, 1962).

16. Ibid., 2.

17. J. Dollard et al., *Frustration and Aggression* (New Haven: Yale University Press, 1939).

18. Maier himself makes this point; see *Frustration,* 105–7; see also D. W. Baruch, "Therapeutic Procedures as Part of the Educational Process," *Journal of Consultative Psychology* 4 (1940): 165–172.

19. G. W. Allport, J. S. Bruner, and E. M. Jandorf, "Personality under Personal Catastrophe," *Character and Personality* 4 (1941): 1–22; P. Eisenberg and P. F. Lazarsfeld, "The Psychological Effects of Unemployment," *Psychological Bulletin* 35 (1938): 358–390.

20. Quoted in Maier, *Frustration,* chap. 3; italics added.

21. Merton, *Social Theory and Social Structure,* chap. 4.

22. Ibid., 139.

23. G. Watson, "Lax versus Strict Home Training," *Journal of Social Psychology* 5 (1934): 102–5.

24. A. Toynbee, *A Study of History* (New York: Oxford University Press, 1946).

25. H. M. Caudill, *Night Comes to the Cumberlands* (Boston: Little, Brown, 1962).

26. J. E. Weller, *Yesterday's People* (Lexington: University of Kentucky Press, 1965).

27. J. Gaventa, *Power and Powerlessness: Quiescence and Rebellion in an Appalachian Valley* (Urbana: University of Illinois Press, 1980).

28. Ball, "A Poverty Case."

29. C. A. Valentine, *Culture and Poverty* (Chicago: University of Chicago Press, 1968).

30. Ibid., 131–134; italics added.

31. H. Rodman, *Lower-Class Families: The Culture of Poverty in Negro Trinidad* (London: Oxford University Press, 1971).

32. H. Eckstein, "Civic Inclusion and Its Discontents," *Daedalus* 113 (1984): 107–146.

33. Yates, *Frustration and Conflict,* 30ff.

34. H. Foster, *Ribbin', Jivin', and Playin' the Dozens* (Cambridge, Mass.: Ballinger, 1974).

35. R. Rogowski, *Rational Legitimacy* (Princeton: Princeton University Press, 1974).

INDEX

Alker, H., 328, 339n, 395n
Allport, G. W., 385
Almond, G. A., 62, 63, 104, 105, 136, 144, 149, 175n, 179, 226n, 232, 258, 258n, 260n, 266, 276, 284n, 288, 290, 298, 301n, 302n
Alroy, G. 307
Anomie, 201–207, 274, 327
Apter, D. E., 62, 63, 105, 175n, 186, 225n, 262n
Arendt, H., 220, 285n, 306, 351, 371
Aristotle, 76, 77, 79, 87, 146, 154, 155, 236, 239, 304, 313; and comparative politics, 60
Aron, R., 23, 39, 42, 56n, 57n, 212
Augustine, Saint, 237, 261n
Authority-culture of the poor: in families 362–365; in relation to frustrated behavior, 391–392; in relation to material scarcity, 363–365; in street society, 365–369; in work, 369–371
Authority patterns: balanced disparities in, 207–212; congruence of, defined, 188–192; in Great Britain, 192–197; universality of, 186–188; in Weimar Germany, 197–201
—congruence theory of, 186–207; and anomie, 201–207; and role segregation, 203–205; and strain, 202–207

Aydelotte, W. D., 399

Babbie, E. R., 302n
Bacon, F., 154, 335
Bagehot, W., 59, 60, 115n, 145, 146, 210, 247, 248, 373n
Balfour, A., 44
Ball, R. A., 382, 388, 389, 395
Bandura, A., 332, 340n
Banks, A. S., 123, 173n
Barnard, H., 353
Barnes, S. H., 288, 301n
Baruch, D. W., 395n
Behavioralism, 37, 50, 52, 102
Becker, H. S., 175n, 176n, 376n
Beer, S. H., 104, 225n, 262n, 263n, 373n
Bellak, L., 124, 172
Benedict, R., 283
Bentham, J., 347, 352, 360
Bentley, A. F., 80, 88, 97, 267, 289, 291, 301n
Biebuyck, D., 263n
Bill, J. A., 114n, 284n
Binder, L., 260n
Black, J.B., 254, 263n
Blauner, R., 377n
Bluntschli, T., 80, 85
Bodin, J., 69
Bodley, J. E. C., 145, 349, 374n
Bogue, A. G., 339n
Bossuet, J., 70
Bottomore, T. B., 373n

My thanks to William Koetzle, who did most of the work needed to prepare this index. H.E.

Bracher, K. D., 225n
Brahe, T., 114n
Brinton, C., 285n, 305, 306
Brown, B. C., 122, 173n
Brown, C., 367, 377n
Brown, H. R., 365
Browne, E. C., 303n
Bruner, J. S., 385, 395n
Bryce, J. (Lord), 89–95, 100, 101, 145, 224, 350–352, 374n
Brzezinski, Z., 111
Buchanan, J. M., 174n, 301n
Burckhardt, J., 220, 349
Burke, E., 276, 285n
Burnham, J., 374n
Bury, J. B., 261n
Bwy, D. B., 328, 339n

Campbell, A., 292, 302n
Campbell, D. T., 302n
Cantril, H., 302n, 332, 338n
Carter, G., 111
Carter, J., 259
Case studies: advantages of, 160–172; defense of, 163–172; nature of, 120–125; value of, versus comparative study, 131–136
—types of, 133–134, 136–173; configurative-idiographic, 136–138; crucial, 152–172; disciplined-configurative, 138–143; heuristic, 143–147; pedagogic, 144; plausibility probes, 147–152
Catlin, G. E. G., 64, 87, 182, 224n
Caudill, H. M., 388, 389, 395n
Cavendish, Lord, 155
Chassan, L., 124, 172
Cicero, 24, 60
Cobban, A., 100, 101
Cole, G. D. H., 111, 208
Coleman, J. S., 62, 175, 225n, 226n, 259n, 266, 284, 337, 338
Coleman, Stephen, 393
Collective political violence: collective action theory of, 319–321; definition of, 309; J-curve theory of, 330; relative deprivation theory of, 316–319
—contingency theories of, 310–315; evaluation of, 327–332; examples of, 313–314; explanation-sketch for, 314–315
—inherency theories of, 310–316; evaluation of, 327–332; examples of,

314–315; explanation-sketch for, 315–316
Comparative politics: and Bryce, J., 84–94; and Friedrich, C. J., 94–98; post-World War II development of, 98–109; present state of, 60–65, 110–114; and Wilson, W., 79–80
—origins of, 65–77; in Machiavelli, 66–67; in Montesquieu, 68–70
Comte, A., 41, 42, 46, 70, 233, 237, 239, 241, 243, 257, 262n
Condorcet, M. J. A. N. (Marquis de), 70, 81, 237, 262, 276, 292–293, 302n
Configurative studies. *See* Case studies
Congruence, theory of, 150–151, 159–160, 165–166; and economic development, 216–220; and mass society, 220–222; origins, 179–181; and religion, 213–216
Cooper, Duff, 196
Costello, C. C., 124, 173n, 175n
Craft, M., 375n
Cremin, L. A., 375n
Crick, B., 209, 226n
Crozier, M., 269, 284n, 357, 360
Cultural theory: postulates of, 267–271; and revolution, 278–281; and survey research, 290–291
—subjectivity problem in, 288–290; solution of, 292–300
Culture: conceptions of, 282–284; of poverty, 288–290
Curry, R. L. Jr., 174n, 301n
Cusick, P., 375n
Cycles, historical and organic, 236

Dahl, R. A., 62, 175n, 182, 224n, 351, 374n; and democracy, 148–149
D'Annunzio, G., 36, 186
Darwin, C., 82
Davidson, P. O., 124, 173n, 175n
Davidson, W. L., 373n
Davies, J. L., 339n
Dawson, P., 339n
Dawson, R. E., 284n, 355
De Grazia, 393
De Jouvenel, B., 182, 225n
Democracy, 70, 100, 205–207; Bryce on, 90–94; congruence theory of, 186–207; Dahl on, 148–149; and economic development, 201; economic development theory of, 216–220; and educational inclusion, 352–360;

Friedrich on, 97–98; mass society, theory of, 220–222; and political inclusion, 347–352; religious theory of, 213–216; and Weimar German authority patterns, 199–200; and workplace inclusion, 360

Dennis, N., 376n

Desai, R., 305

Descartes, R., 69

Deutsch, K. W., 216, 225n, 226n

Deutsch, W., 259n

Development, political: concept of, 231–233; in England, 251–256; forces of, 248–250; and nature of the polity, 247–248; origins of, 245–247; and political density, 256–257; and political evolutionism, 243; and power politics, 258; and progress theory, 242; sketch for a theory of, 244–259; stages of, 250–257; and universal-abstract theory, 236

Development, social, Tocqueville on, 346–347

Developmental thought: nondevelopmental thought in contrast to, 235–238
—traits of, 238–244; dimensional change, 240; growth and stages, 240–242; inherent change, 239–240; ruleful, necessary change, 242–244

Dewey, J., 353, 354, 357, 360

Dicey, A. V., 115n

Dickens, C., 276, 285n

Dilthey, W., 286

Disraeli, B., 272

Dollard, J., 384, 385, 395n

Diminguez, J. I., 230, 259n, 260n

Dore, R., 118

Douglas, M., 288, 301n

Downs, A., 174n, 284n, 344, 352, 374n, 379, 394

Durkheim, E., 27, 40, 57n, 104, 220, 233, 234, 236, 240–241, 243–246, 255, 256, 260n, 261n, 262n, 278, 279–280, 283, 284n, 285n, 317, 321, 343, 346, 393

Duvall, R., 322, 329, 333, 338, 340n

Duverger, M., 111

Dyson, A. E., 375n

Easton, D., 63, 64, 129, 174, 263n

Edelman, M., 262n

Edinger, L. J., 225n

Educational inclusion: disillusions with, 354–359; expectations of, 352–354; and maintenance of school order, 356–358

Edwards, R., 285n, 376n

Einstein, A., 155, 157, 266

Eisenberg, P., 395n

Elden, M., 376n

Eliade, M., 261n

Elkins, D., 301n

Ellis, R., 301n

Ellul, J., 46, 57n, 247

Emerson, R., 259n

England: balanced disparities in, 208–209; cultural change in, 272; example of congruent authority patterns, 188–189; example of a social polity, 248; political development of, 251–256; socialization into authority patterns, 206
—authority patterns in, 192–197; adult organizations, 194; business organizations, 194–195; pressure groups, 192–194; school and family life, 196–197
—summary history of, 251–255; Anglo-Saxon period, 299; feudal monarchy, 251–252; Georgian period, 255; Tudor period, 253–254

Feierabend, I. K. and I. R., 326, 328, 338, 339n

Ferguson, A., 69, 238, 257

Festinger, L., 302n

Finch, H. A., 56n, 57n, 58n

Finer, H., 173n

Finer, S. E., 348, 373n

Fiske, D. W., 302n

Flanagan, W. H., 339n

Fogel, R. W., 339n

Fogelman, E., 328n, 339n

Fogelson, R. M., 338n

Fontenelle, J., 237

Ford, T., 388

Formal theory, 125–126

Foster, H. L., 360, 366–368, 376n, 377n, 392, 395n

Fraser, J. G. (Sir), 82

Frazier, E. F., 345, 390, 391

Freeman, F. A., 115n

Freud, S., 47

Friedman, R., 174

Friedrich, C. J., 89, 94–98, 101, 111, 225n

Fromm, E., 337n

Frustration-instigated behavior, 381–394; and adaptation, 386, 392–394; and

aggression, 385; in experiments, 382–
  387; and fixation, 384–385; and the
  poor, 389–391; and regression, 385–
  386; in social settings, 387–392

Gadamer, H. G., 301n
Galileo, 154, 239, 270, 312
Galtung, J., 338
Garfinkel, H., 301n
Gaventa, J., 389, 395n
Geertz, C., 233, 248, 260n, 262n, 263n,
  287, 288, 301n
George, A., 118
Germany, authority patterns in, 189–199
Gerth, H. H., 22, 56n, 57n, 58n, 260,
  262n
Gide, A., 212
Ginsberg, M., 297, 302n
Glaser, B. G., 175n
Glazer, N., 345, 390
Gomperz, T., 261n
Goodenough, W. H., 285n
Graham, H. D., 338n, 339n
Greenstein, F. I., 162, 260n, 293, 295,
  302n, 376n
Greer, T. H., 86
Grofman, B. N., 330, 340n
Gurr, T. R., 117, 159, 175n, 176n, 181,
  284n, 307, 310, 316, 317–319, 322–
  328, 332, 335, 336, 337n, 338n, 340n
Guterbuck, T. M., 374n

Halevy, E., 145, 375n
Hammond, T. T., 332, 340n
Hardgrave, R. L., 284
Hargraves, D. H., 375n
Hargreaves, L., 114n
Harris, W. T., 353, 354, 357, 366
Hartz, L., 289, 301n
Hayek, F. A., 247
Heckscher, G., 61, 111
Hegel, G. W. F., 70, 71, 81
Hempel, C. G., 125, 139, 174n, 175n, 268,
  302n, 312, 337n
Herman, C., 198
Hibbs, D. A., 117, 310, 323, 326, 328,
  331, 333, 334, 335, 337n, 338n, 339n,
  340n
Hirschman, A. O., 321, 338
Historicism, 70–77, 80–83, 94; and
  Montesquieu, 69; reactions against,
  72–77

Hobbs, T., 236, 251, 323, 392
Holt, R. R., 125, 138, 173n, 174n, 175n
Holt, R. T., 260n
Hume, D., 69, 238
Huntington, S. P., 230, 231, 240, 259n,
  260n, 261n, 262n, 275, 285n, 318,
  328, 329, 338n, 339n
Hurwitz, L., 176n
Husserl, E., 287
Hyman, H., 289, 300, 301n

Ingelhart, R., 301n
Inkeles, A., 206, 225n
Internal war project, 305–307

Jackson, P., 375n
Jandorf, E. M., 385, 395n
Janos, A., 307
Jaspers, K., 23, 56n
J-curve theory of revolution, 330
Jenks, E., 81
Jennings, I. (Sir), 225n
Jennings, K., 209, 335
Johnson, C., 318, 319, 338
Jolliffe, J. E. A., 263n
Jones, W. (Sir), 354

Kaase, M., 288, 300n, 301n
Kant, I., 46, 138, 237, 240
Kaplan, A., 264n
Karabel, J., 375n
Katona, G., 302n
Katz, D., 302n
Kaufmann, H., 175n
Keir, D. L., 262n, 263n
Keller, S., 367
Kelley, J., 278, 285, 291
Kemeny, J. G., 125, 173n
Kerr, M., 376n
Kim, J.-O., 373n
Klein, H. S., 278, 280, 285n
Klein, J., 362, 363, 376n
Klingemann, H. D., 301n
Kluckhohn, C., 283
Knies, K., 25
Kohn, M., 370, 376n, 377n
Kornhauser, W., 179, 212, 220–221, 226,
  351, 374n
Kracauer, S., 198

Lanson, G., 68

Laski, H., 87, 205
Lasswell, H., 63, 64, 87, 187, 205, 264n, 292, 302n
Laver, M., 364n, 380, 394n
Lazarsfeld, P. F., 386, 395n
Le Bon, G., 220, 349–350, 363, 373n, 374n
Lederer, E., 220, 351
Legalism, 279–280
Leibnitz, K., 237
Leites, N., 292, 302n
Lerner, D., 240, 262n
Levett, A., 339n
Levi-Strauss, C., 287
Levy, M. J., 105, 186, 225n
Lewis, O., 345, 389
Lippmann, W., 88
Lipset, S. M., 63, 175n, 179, 212, 216–219, 224n, 225n, 275, 284n, 376n
Locke, J., 85, 87, 236, 354
Lodhi, A. Q., 339n
Long, S. L., 374n
Lorenz, K., 337n
Lovelock, J., 375n
Lowi, T. H., 175n
Lowie, R. H., 248, 263n
Luria, Z., 122, 173n

McClelland, M., 159, 176n, 181
McCone report, 324
Machiavelli, N., 60, 67–69, 91, 115n, 146, 366
MacIver, R. M., 83
McKenzie, R. T., 188, 225n
MacLeod, W. C., 82
Macridis, R. C., 111, 122, 173n
Maier, N., 382–388, 391, 394n, 395n
Maine, H. S., (Sir), 81, 82, 240, 261n
Mair, L., 248, 262n, 263n
Malinowski, B., 117, 158, 175n, 284, 285n
Mann, H., 353
Mannheim, K., 220, 351
March, J. G., 64
Marshall, A., 282
Marx, K., 59, 60, 70, 82, 88, 107, 205, 239, 277, 321
Mass society. *See* Stable democracy
Massell, G., 278, 281, 285n
Mayer, J. P., 56n
Mead, M., 269, 284n
Meinecke, F., 69

Melville, H., 238
Merelman, R. M., 301n, 355–356, 358, 375
Merriam, C., 180, 182, 224n
Merton, R. K., 116n, 173n, 276, 285n, 382, 386, 395n
Metraux, R., 268, 284n
Metz, M. H., 355–359, 375n
Michels, R., 23, 56n, 85, 86, 88, 93, 98, 117, 158, 198, 199, 205, 225n, 348, 349, 350, 351, 363, 374n
Middle-range theory, 42, 71, 81, 94, 95, 97–98, 101, 104, 109
Midlarsky, M., 328, 338n, 339n
Mill, J., 347, 352, 374n, 380
Mill, J. S., 59–60, 85, 95, 156, 182, 321, 348, 350, 373n, 374n, 375n
Miller, J. G., 263n
Mills, C. W., 23, 56n, 57n, 58n, 260n, 262n, 351, 366, 374n
Montagu, A., 337n
Montesquieu, C. L. de, 60, 66–70, 71, 79, 94, 104, 115n
Moore, B. Jr., 277, 329, 339n
Morrison, H., 209
Mosca, G., 28, 60, 85, 86, 88, 98, 101, 141, 146, 211, 318, 348, 351
Moyer, R. E., 337n
Moynihan, D. P., 345, 390
Muller, E. N., 330, 340n
Multi-trait, multi-method matrix, 292–293
Munger, F., 339n

Namier, L. (Sir), 255, 263n
Natural Law, 66
Natural rights, 78, 90
Naumann, F., 25, 34
Nesvold, B., 328
Neubauer, D., 323, 338n
Neumann, S., 75, 111, 225n
Newman, J. R., 176n
Nie, N., 373n
Nieburg, H. L., 321, 338
Niemi, R., 355
Nietzsche, F., 29
Nisbet, R. A., 236, 247, 260n, 261n, 262n, 264n
North, R.Z., 292, 302n
Northrop, F. S. C., 153, 291, 302n
Norway, and cultural theory, 298–299

Oakeshott, M., 247

Olson, M., 275, 285n, 327, 328, 339
Organski, K., 232
Ortega y Gassett, J., 220, 351
Osanka, K., 307
Osgood, C. E., 122, 173n, 293, 302n

Paige, J. M., 338n
Paneth, M., 376n
Paret, P., 307
Pareto, V., 85, 86, 88, 92, 93, 98, 101, 104, 114n, 141, 146, 211, 283, 318, 329, 337n
Park, R. E., 283, 285n, 368
Parsons, T., 56n, 104, 109, 116n, 186, 225n, 272, 282, 283, 285n
Pateman, C., 373n, 376n, 376n
Perry, W. J., 83
Petit-Dutaillis, C., 252, 263n
Pettit, P., 301n
Phillips, K., 285n
Piaget, J., 287
Pierce, J., 353
Platt, J. R., 131, 165, 174n
Plausibility probes. *See* Case studies
Political development: and non-western systems, 101; and political evolutionism, 81–84; theories of, 80–84; Weber, M. on, 23–24, 42
Political evolutionism, 80–84; and democracy, 80; legacy of, 83–84; and political development 81–82, 243; and some change, 107; theories of, 81–83
Political inclusion, 347–352; expectations of, 347–348
—disillusions with, 348–352; crowd psychology, 349–350; elitism, 348–349; political machines, 350–351; self-exclusion, 349
Political socialization, 75, 102, 104
Political sociology, 85–88, 101
Political systems: classification of, 61–62; conceptions of, 65–70; elements of, 62–63
Polsby, N. W., 260n, 302n
Polybius, 60, 236
Popper, K., 80, 125, 174n
Positivism, in reaction to historicism, 71, 73
Potter, A., 225n
Poverty. *See* Authority-culture of the poor
Powell, G. B., 232, 260, 266, 284n

Prewitt, K., 284n, 355
Progress theory, 237–238; and political development, 242
Protestant ethic, 130
Przeworski, A., 174n
Putnam, R. B., 268, 284n, 290, 301n
Pye, L. W., 20, 175n, 259n, 260n, 268, 284n

Ranney, A., 111
Rational choice theory, goals in, 379–381
Redlich, F., 115n
Reichel, P., 288, 289, 301n
Rejai, M., 285n
Relative deprivation theories. *See* Collective political violence
Revolution: and cultural theory, 278–281; definition of, 309. *See also* Collective political violence
Rice, J. M., 354, 375n
Richardson, J. M., 125, 173n
Rickert, H., 286
Riker, W. H., 174n, 352, 374n, 380, 381, 394n
Riley, W. H., 173n
Roberts, B. C., 175n, 376n
Rodman, H., 391, 395n
Rogowski, R., 176n, 266n, 267, 271, 280, 284n, 285n, 393, 395n
Rokkan, S., 175n, 329
Roscher, W., 76, 77, 78
Roth, G., 302n
Rousseau, J.-J., 82, 349n
Rovere, R., 211
Rubin, L., 371, 372n, 377n
Russett, B. M., 328, 339n
Russell, D. E. H., 332

Sait, E. M., 83, 116n
Sanders, D., 329, 339n
Schapera, I., 247, 262n, 263n
Schmoller, G. von, 47
Schneider, A. L., 329, 339n
Schneider, P. R., 329, 339n
Schooler, C., 377n
Schumpeter, J. A., 93, 347, 351, 352, 372, 373n, 374n, 377n, 379, 394n
Schwartz, D. C., 338
Scientism, 45–48, 53
Seely, J. (Sir), 82
Semantic differential, 293

Semi-projective technique, 293
Sereno, R., 374n
Shapiro, G., 339n
Sharkansky, I., 262n
Shils, E. A., 56n–58n, 62, 104, 285n
Shy, J., 307n
Sigelman, L., 329, 339n
Sighele, S., 349, 350
Silberman, C. E., 375n
Sillitoe, A., 196
Simeon, R., 301n
Simmel, G., 36, 240–241, 261n, 273, 284n
Simon, H. A., 380, 381, 394n
Singer, C., 176
Skinner, B. F., 300
Skocpol, T., 277, 305, 329, 339n
Smellie, K. B., 209
Smith, A., 69
Smith, G. E., 83
Snyder, D., 338n
Social time: in Christian thought, 237; in
    Greek and Roman thought, 236–237
Sorel, G., 317
Sorokin, P. A., 322, 338
Southern, R. W., 393
Spencer, H., 241–243, 262n
Spiro, H. J., 224n, 225n
Stable democracy: definition, 183–185; and
    economic development, 216–220; and
    mass society theory, 220–222; and
    religion, 213–216
Stanton, F. (Sir), 263n
State: Locke, J., on, 876; monistic theory
    of, 87; origins of, 81–84; and political
    evolutionism, 83–84; Renaissance
    conception of, 66
Steding, C., 56n
Strain, social, 202–207
Strauss, A. L., 175n
Strauss, L., 44, 55n, 57n
Street Society. *See* Authority patterns
Subjectivity, of the concept of culture, 288
Suci, G. J., 293, 302n
Survey research, 290–292
Swaan, A. de, 303n

Tacitus, 60
Taine, H., 140, 141
Talleyrand, M., 183
Talmon, J. L., 349, 374n
Tannenbaum, P. H., 293, 302n

Tanter, R., 328, 339n
Tarde, G., 349, 350
Tarrow, S., 162, 176n, 293, 295, 302n
Templeton, K. S., 262n
Teune, H., 174n
Textor, R. B., 123, 173n
Theoretical approaches, nature of, 308
Theory: building of, 130–131; grounded,
    153; nature of, 125–126; traits of good,
    126–130
Thomas, W. J., 388
Thompson, M., 301n
Thrasher, F., 366, 368, 377n
Thucydides, 239
Tilly, C., 263n, 307, 317, 319, 322, 325,
    328, 330, 331, 334, 335, 337n–340n,
    343, 345, 373n
Tocqueville, A. de, 28, 59, 60, 94, 115n,
    145, 146, 179, 327, 337n, 343, 350,
    373n, 374n; on social development,
    346–347
Toennis, F., 261n; and dimensional change,
    240; and quantitative growth, 241
Tolstoy, L., 40
Toynbee, A., 387, 388, 395n
Traill, H. D., 250, 263n
Troeltsch, E., 23, 25, 56n
Trotsky, L., 332
Trow, M. A., 225n, 375n
Tufte, E. A., 302n
Tullock, G., 174n, 301n
Turner, J. E., 260n
Tyler, E. B., 283, 285n

Ulam, A., 263n
Universal-abstract theory, 235–236

Valentine, C. A., 376n, 390, 395n
Verba, S., 136, 137, 139, 140, 143, 149,
    174n, 175n, 176n, 266, 276, 284n,
    288, 290, 298, 301n, 302n, 374n

Wade, L. L., 174n, 301n
Wakeford, J., 276, 285n, 375n
Wallas, G., 88, 348, 349, 351, 373n, 374n,
    378
Watson, G., 387, 395
Watson, J., 263n
Weber, Marianne, 55n, 56n, 58n
Weber, Max, 61, 75, 85, 98, 101, 104,
    130, 146, 199, 224, 256, 260n, 261n,
    273, 283, 286, 302n, 321, 348, 350,

351, 374, 386; contemporary relevance of, 50–54; ethical pluralism of, 47; on development, 232, 233, 234, 240, 246, 247; on meaning, 45; on the nature of politics, 31–36; on politicians, 34–37; on science, 22–27, 37–54; on scientism, 45–48; social context of, 27–31; on tension between politics and science, 22–27, 37–54

Welfling, M. B., 329, 333, 340n
Weller, J. E., 388, 389, 395n
Whitaker, C. S., 284n
White, R. K., 302n
Whitelock, D., 263n
Whyte, W. F., 117, 158, 176n, 366, 369, 376n, 377n
Wildavsky, A., 288, 301n
Willey, J. R., 176
Wilmott, P. 196, 225n
Wilson, W., 76, 78–80, 89, 90, 259; and comparative politics, 79–80

Winch, P., 301n
Windelband, W., 136, 174n, 286
Witte, J., 376n
Wittgenstein, L., 301n
Wittich, C., 302n
Wolf, E., 318, 338
Wolfenstein, V., 307, 337n
Wolff, K., 261n, 262n
Woods, P., 276, 359, 375n, 393
Woolsey, T., 77, 78, 79, 89, 90; and natural rights, 78

Yates, A. J., 382, 395n
Yough, S. N., 329, 339n
Young, M., 196, 225n
Young, O. N., 114n
Young, P., 301n

Zimmerman, E., 307, 337n
Zweig, F., 377n
Zwerdling,, D., 376n

Compositor: Impressions
Text: 10/12 Baskerville
Display: Baskerville
Printer: Edwards Bros.
Binder: Edwards Bros.